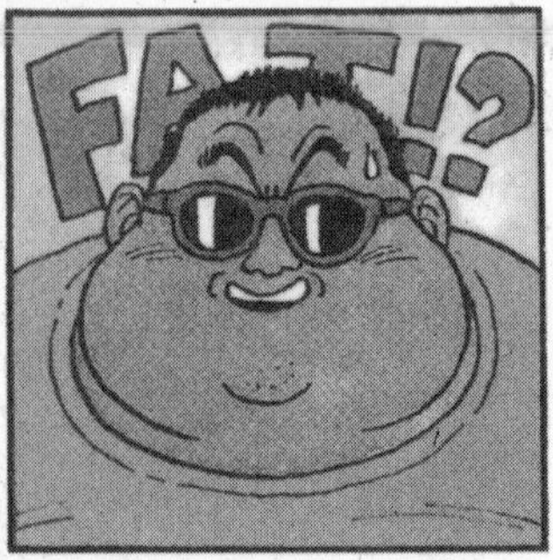
FAT!?

鳥山 明

Recently, whenever I run into someone who hasn't seen me in awhile, they always say the same thing: "You've gained weight!" And it's true, I've gained weight! I'm 174 cm (5'8") tall and I weigh 195 pounds. I don't *look* that heavy…my arms and legs and chest are the same size as when I was thinner, so I just look pitiful! I think I should probably get some exercise or I'll really look like the picture above. Also, I need to go on a diet. Agggh! I ate too much again!

–Akira Toriyama, 1992

Widely known all over the world for his playful, innovative storytelling and humorous, distinctive art style, **Dragon Ball** creator Akira Toriyama is also known in his native Japan for the wildly popular **Dr. Slump**, his previous manga series about the adventures of a mad scientist and his android "daughter." His hit series **Dragon Ball** ran from 1984 to 1995 in Shueisha's **Weekly Shonen Jump** magazine. He is also known for his design work on video games such as **Dragon Warrior**, **Chrono Trigger** and **Tobal No. 1**. His recent manga works include **Cowa!**, **Kajika**, **Sand Land**, **Neko Majin**, and a children's book, **Toccio the Angel**. He lives with his family in Japan.

DRAGON BALL Z VOL. 16
The SHONEN JUMP Graphic Novel Edition

This graphic novel is number 32 in a series of 42.
This graphic novel contains material that was originally published in
English in **SHONEN JUMP** #15-18.

STORY AND ART BY
AKIRA TORIYAMA

English Adaptation/Gerard Jones
Translation/Lillian Olsen
Touch-Up Art & Lettering/Wayne Truman
Cover & Graphics Design/Sean Lee
Senior Editor/Jason Thompson
Managing Editor/Frances E. Wall
Editorial Director/Elizabeth Kawasaki
VP & Editor in Chief/Yumi Hoashi
Sr. Director of Acquisitions/Rika Inouye
Sr. VP of Marketing/Liza Coppola
Exec. VP of Sales & Marketing/John Easum
Publisher/Hyoe Narita

Published by VIZ Media, LLC
P.O. Box 77010 • San Francisco, CA 94107

The SHONEN JUMP Graphic Novel Edition
10 9 8 7 6 5 4 3 2
First printing, June 2004
Second printing, April 2006

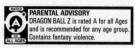

PARENTAL ADVISORY
DRAGON BALL Z is rated A for all Ages
and is recommended for any age group.
Contains fantasy violence.

THE WORLD'S
MOST POPULAR MANGA

www.viz.com

www.shonenjump.com

SHONEN JUMP MANGA

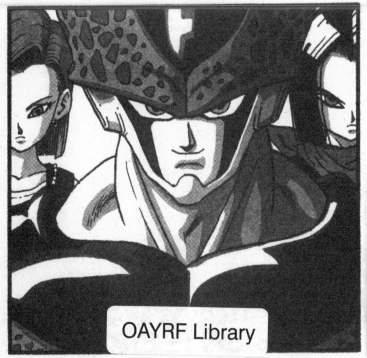

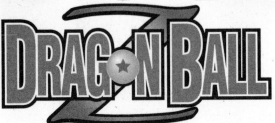

DRAGON BALL Z

Vol. 16

DB: 32 of 42

STORY AND ART BY
AKIRA TORIYAMA

THE MAIN CHARACTERS

Bulma

Goku's oldest friend, Bulma is a scientific genius. She met Goku while on a quest for the seven magical Dragon Balls which, when gathered together, can grant any wish.

Son Goku

The greatest martial artist on Earth, he is one of the last of the Saiyans, an almost extinct alien race. Like Trunks and Vegeta, he can power-up by transforming into a "Super Saiyan." He also has the power to teleport.

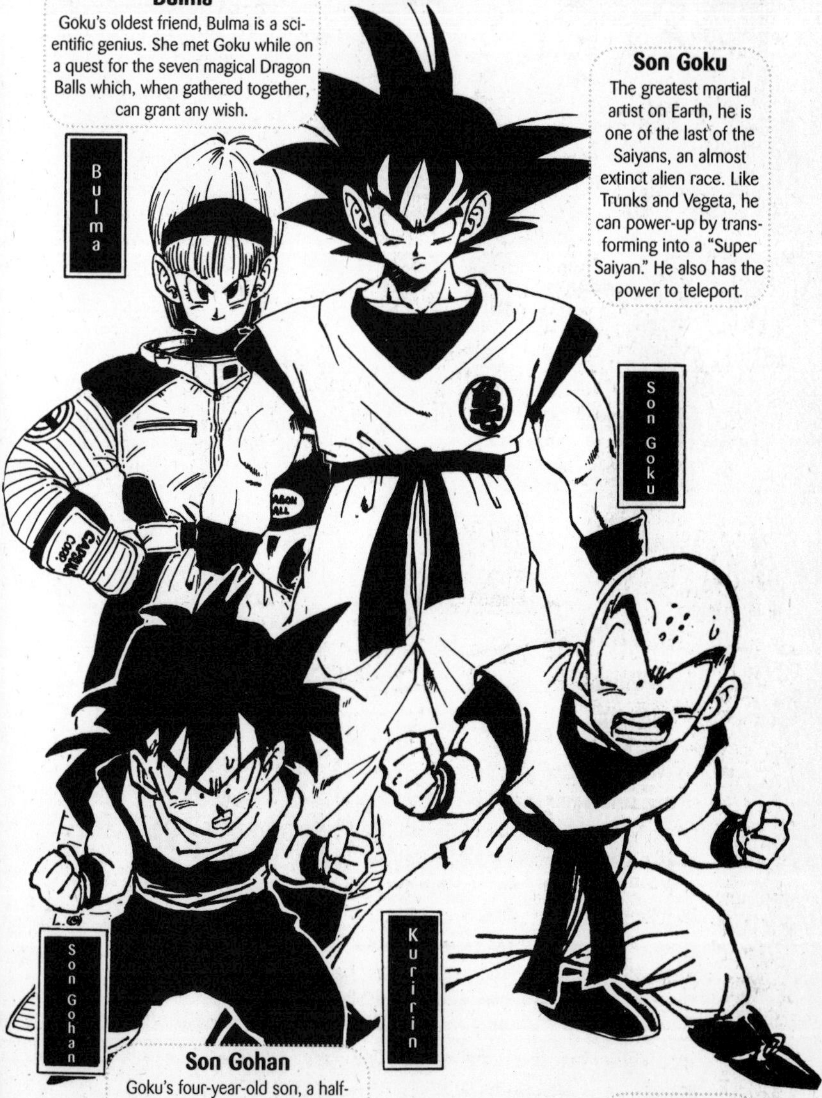
Bulma
Son Goku
Son Gohan
Kuririn

Son Gohan

Goku's four-year-old son, a half-human, half-Saiyan with hidden reserves of strength. He was trained by Goku's former enemy Piccolo.

Kuririn

Goku's former martial arts schoolmate.

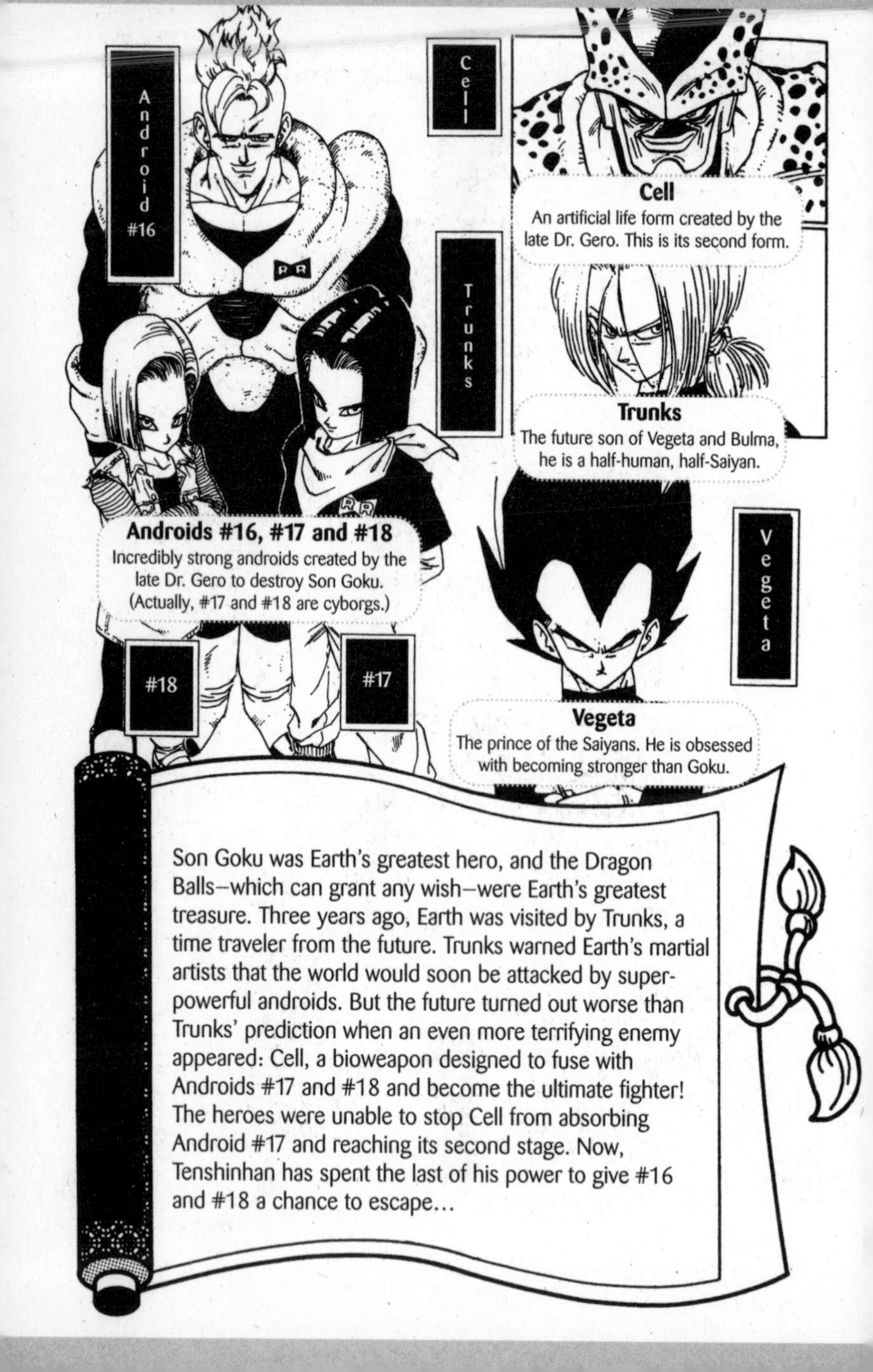
Cell
Cell
An artificial life form created by the late Dr. Gero. This is its second form.
Trunks
Trunks
The future son of Vegeta and Bulma, he is a half-human, half-Saiyan.
Vegeta
Vegeta
The prince of the Saiyans. He is obsessed with becoming stronger than Goku.
Android #16
Androids #16, #17 and #18
Incredibly strong androids created by the late Dr. Gero to destroy Son Goku. (Actually, #17 and #18 are cyborgs.)
#17
#18

Son Goku was Earth's greatest hero, and the Dragon Balls—which can grant any wish—were Earth's greatest treasure. Three years ago, Earth was visited by Trunks, a time traveler from the future. Trunks warned Earth's martial artists that the world would soon be attacked by super-powerful androids. But the future turned out worse than Trunks' prediction when an even more terrifying enemy appeared: Cell, a bioweapon designed to fuse with Androids #17 and #18 and become the ultimate fighter! The heroes were unable to stop Cell from absorbing Android #17 and reaching its second stage. Now, Tenshinhan has spent the last of his power to give #16 and #18 a chance to escape...

DRAGON BALL Z 16

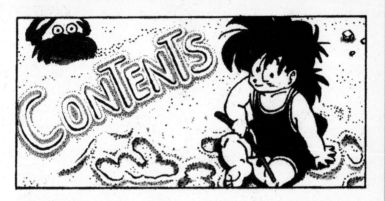

CONTENTS

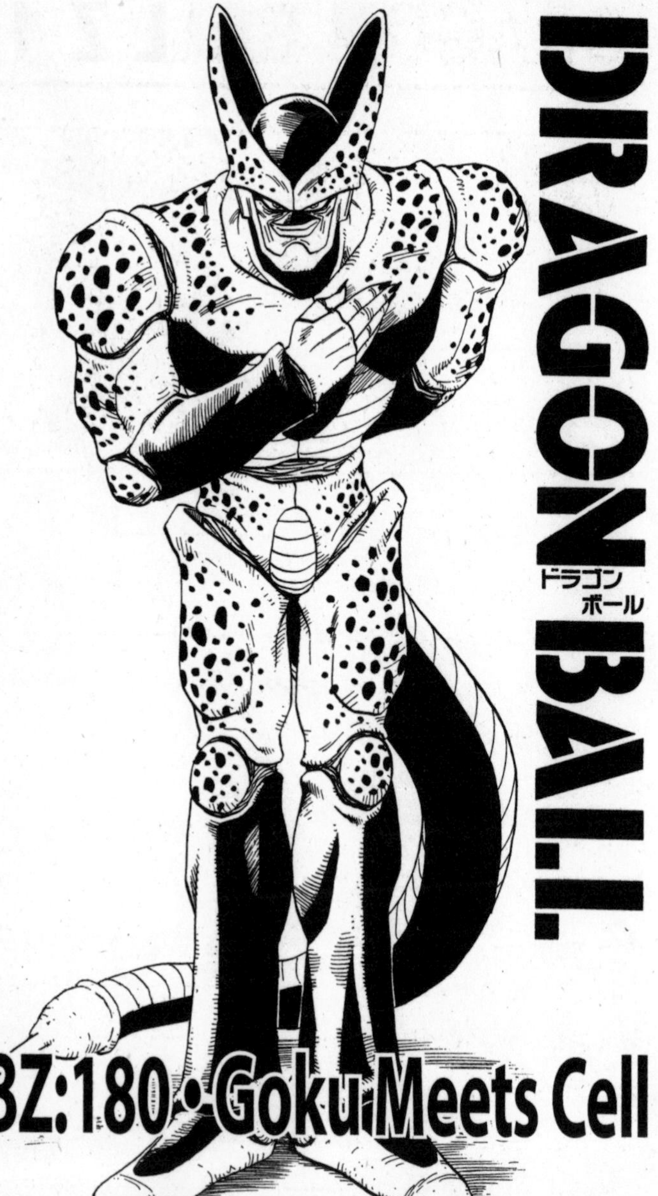
DRAGON BALL
ドラゴン
ボール

DBZ:180 • Goku Meets Cell

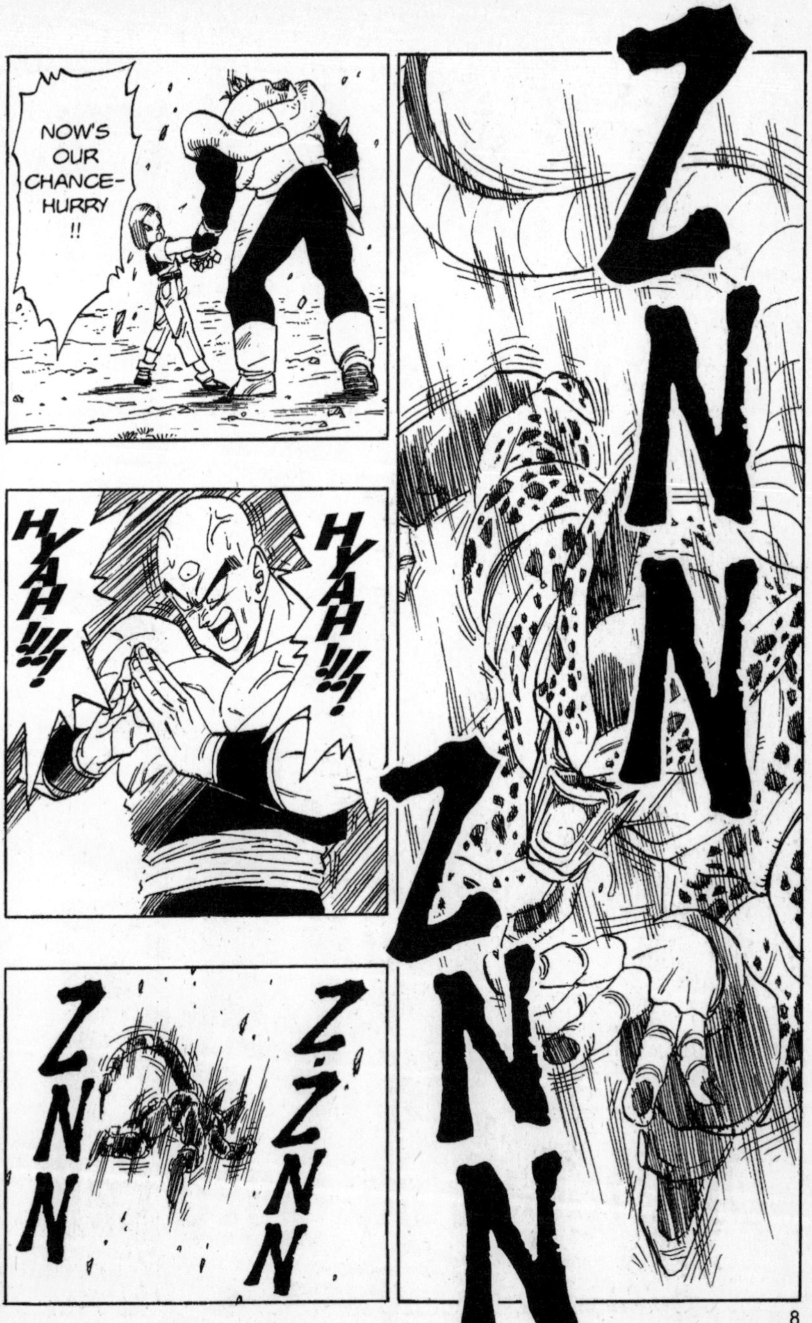

ZNNN
ZNNN
NOW'S OUR CHANCE-HURRY!!
HYAH!!!!
HYAH!!!!
Z-ZNN
ZNN

READ THIS WAY

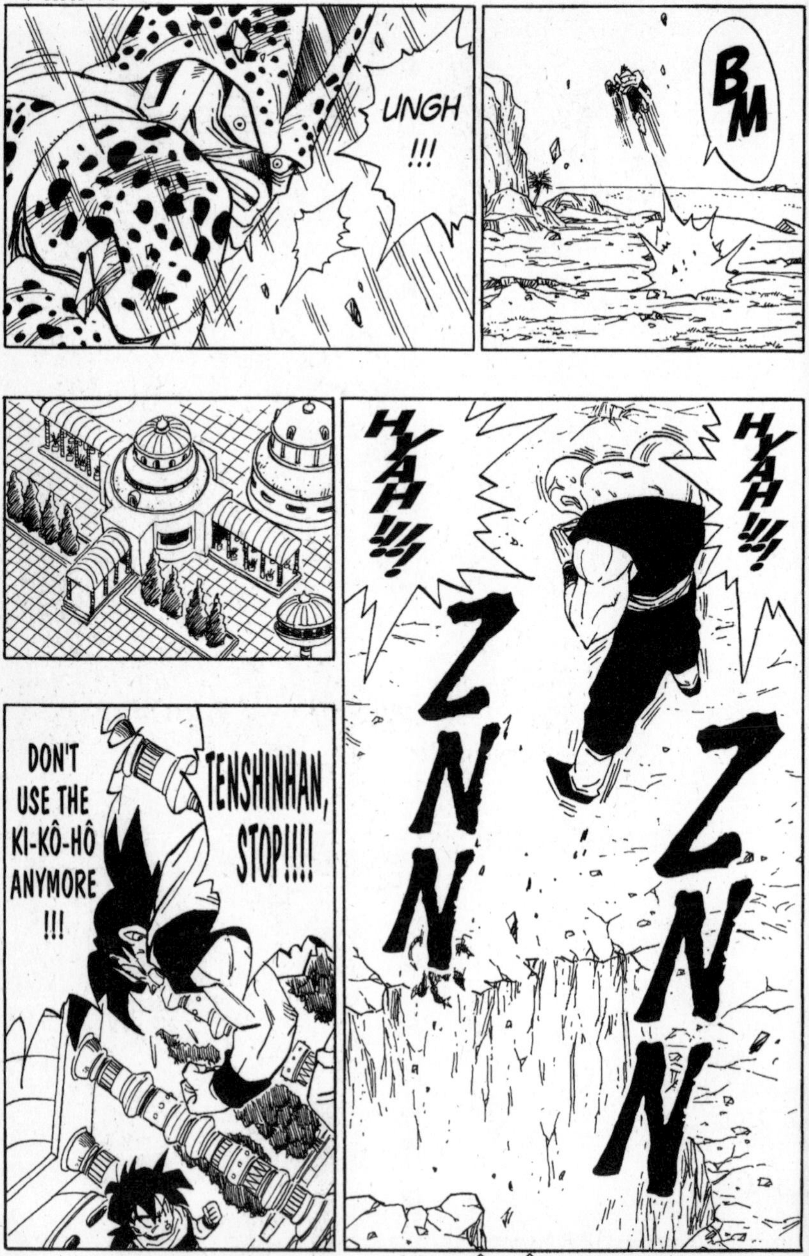
BM
UNGH !!!
HYAH!!!
HYAH!!!
ZNN
ZNNN
TENSHINHAN, STOP!!!!
DON'T USE THE KI-KÔ-HÔ ANYMORE !!!

* "KI-KÔ-HÔ" = ENERGY CANNON

READ THIS WAY

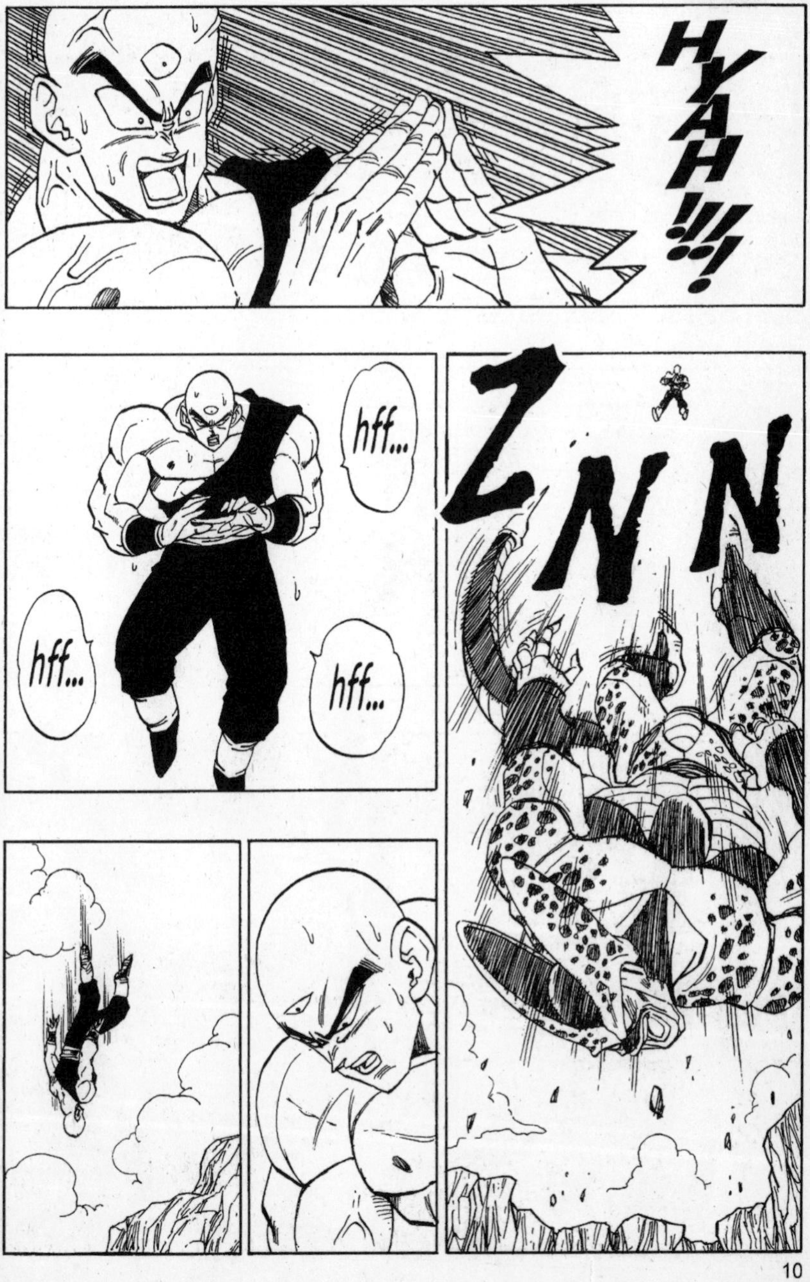

HYAH!!!!
ZNN
hff...
hff...
hff...

READ THIS WAY

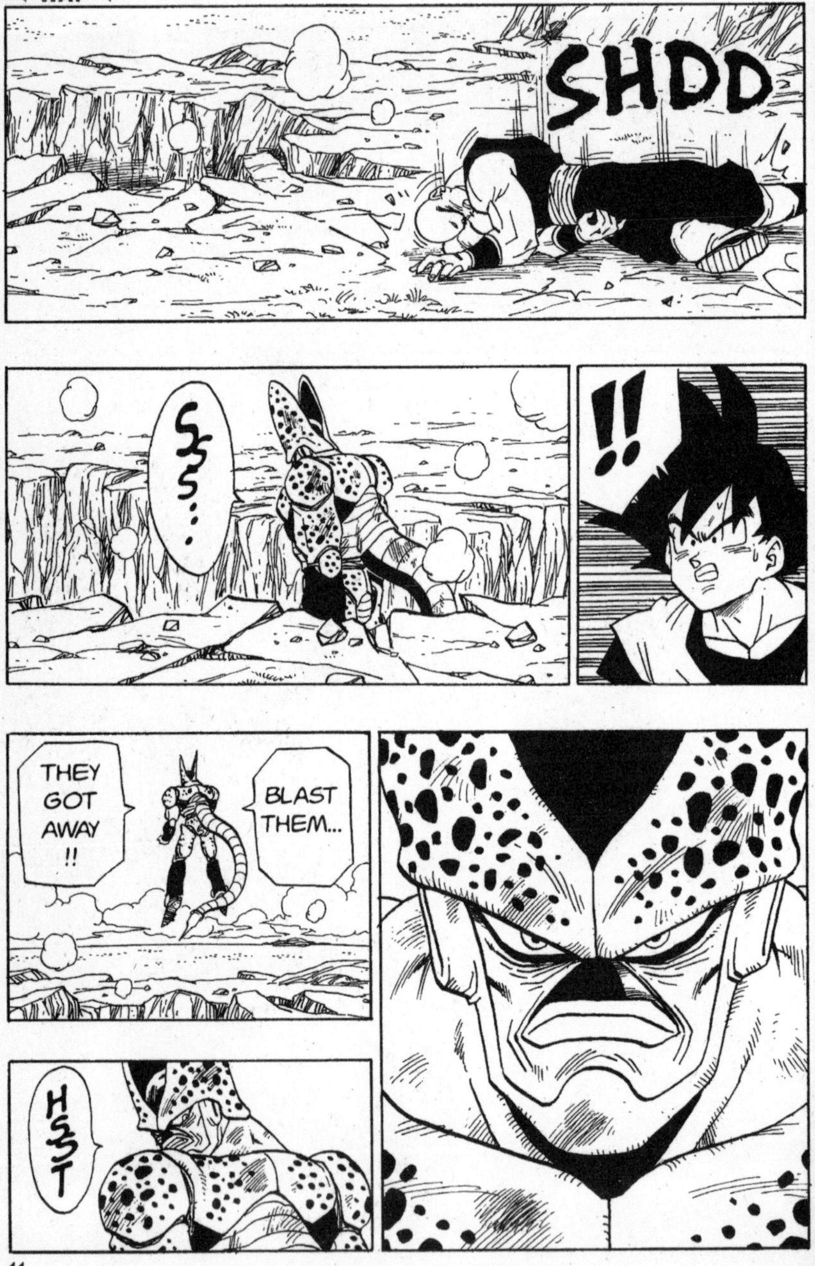
SHDD
!!
SSS...
BLAST THEM...
THEY GOT AWAY !!
HSST

READ THIS WAY

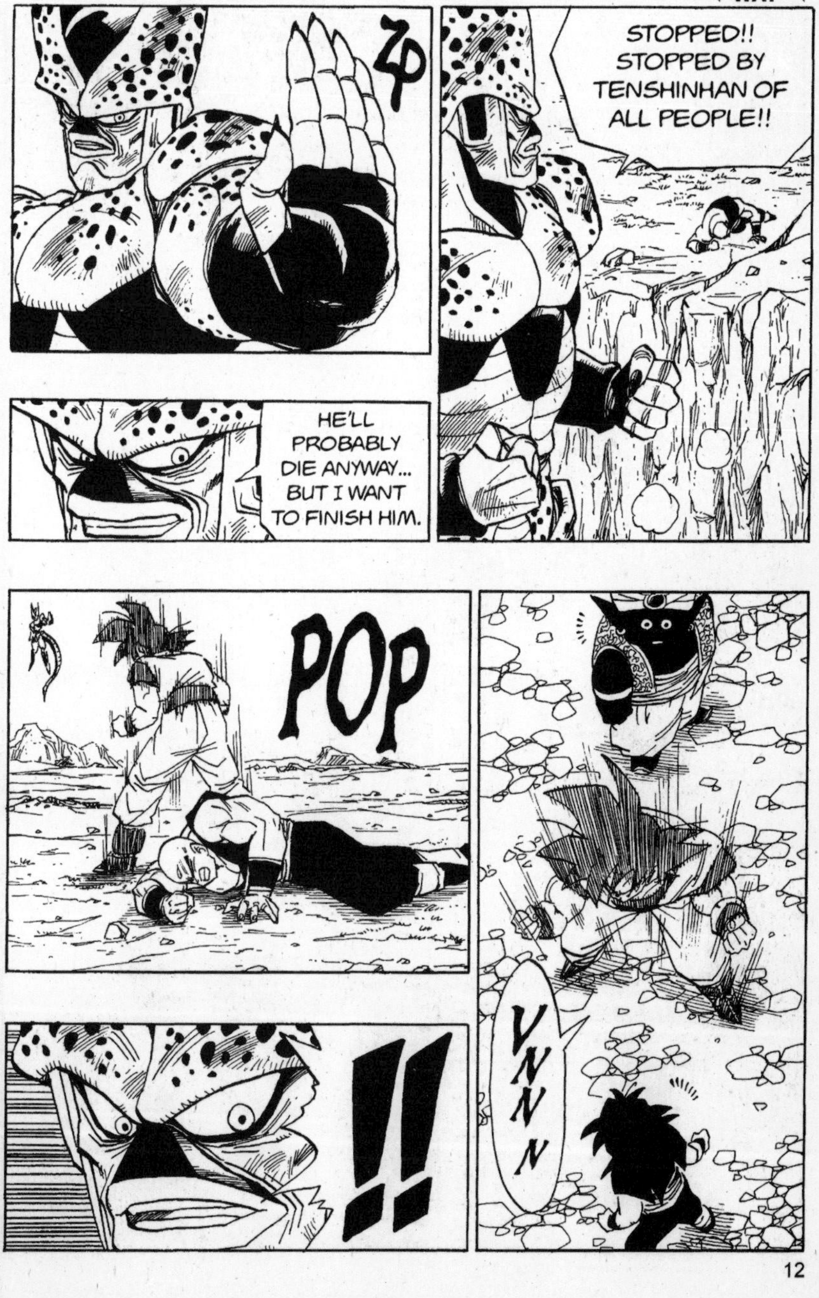

STOPPED!! STOPPED BY TENSHINHAN OF ALL PEOPLE!!
ZP
HE'LL PROBABLY DIE ANYWAY... BUT I WANT TO FINISH HIM.
VNNN
POP
!!

READ THIS WAY

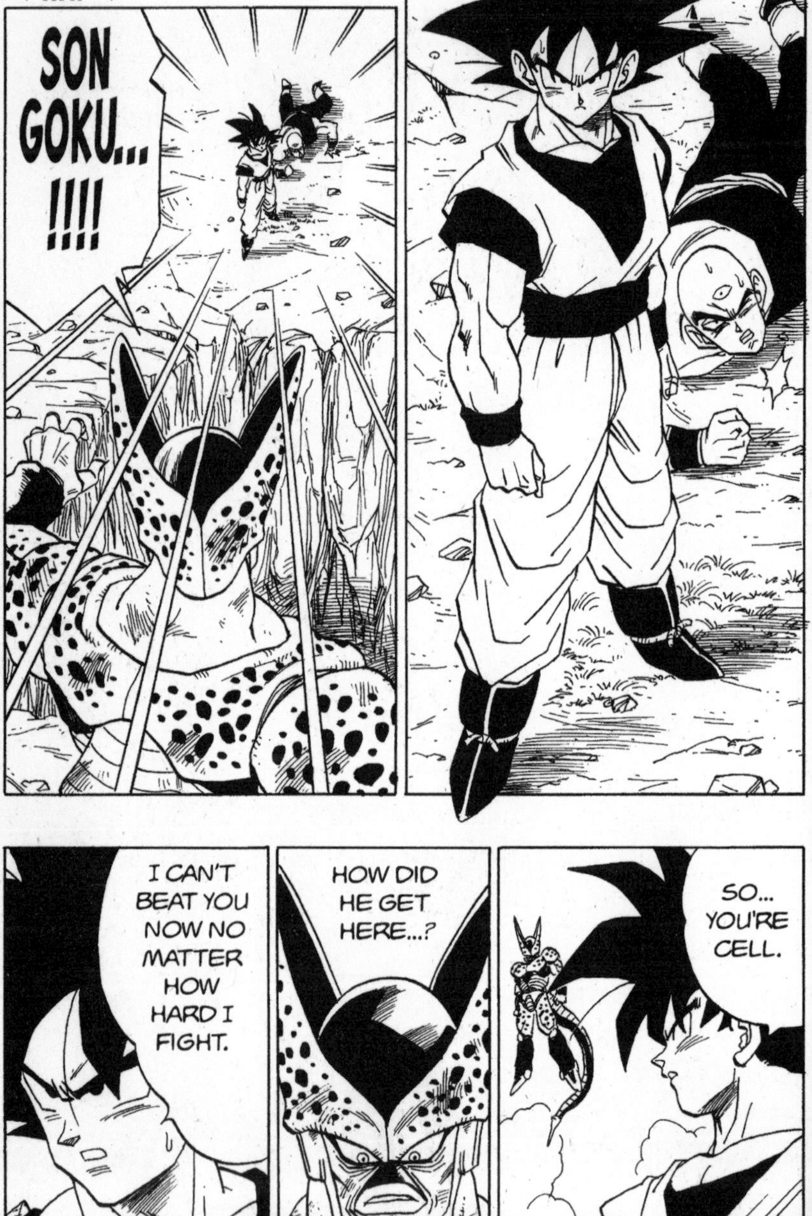
SON GOKU...!!!!
SO... YOU'RE CELL.
HOW DID HE GET HERE...?
I CAN'T BEAT YOU NOW NO MATTER HOW HARD I FIGHT.

READ THIS WAY

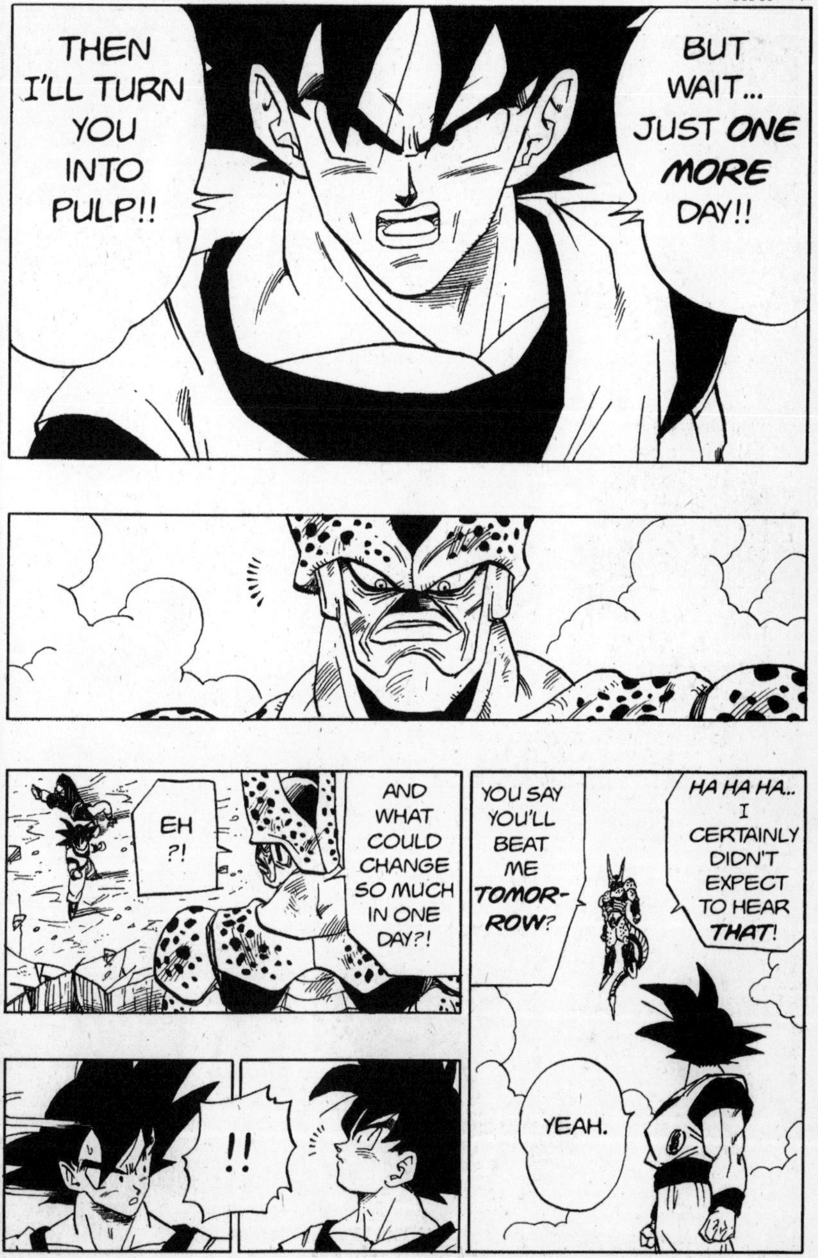

BUT WAIT... JUST **ONE MORE** DAY!!
THEN I'LL TURN YOU INTO PULP!!
HA HA HA.. I CERTAINLY DIDN'T EXPECT TO HEAR *THAT*!
YOU SAY YOU'LL BEAT ME ***TOMORROW***?
YEAH.
AND WHAT COULD CHANGE SO MUCH IN ONE DAY?!
EH?!
!!

READ THIS WAY

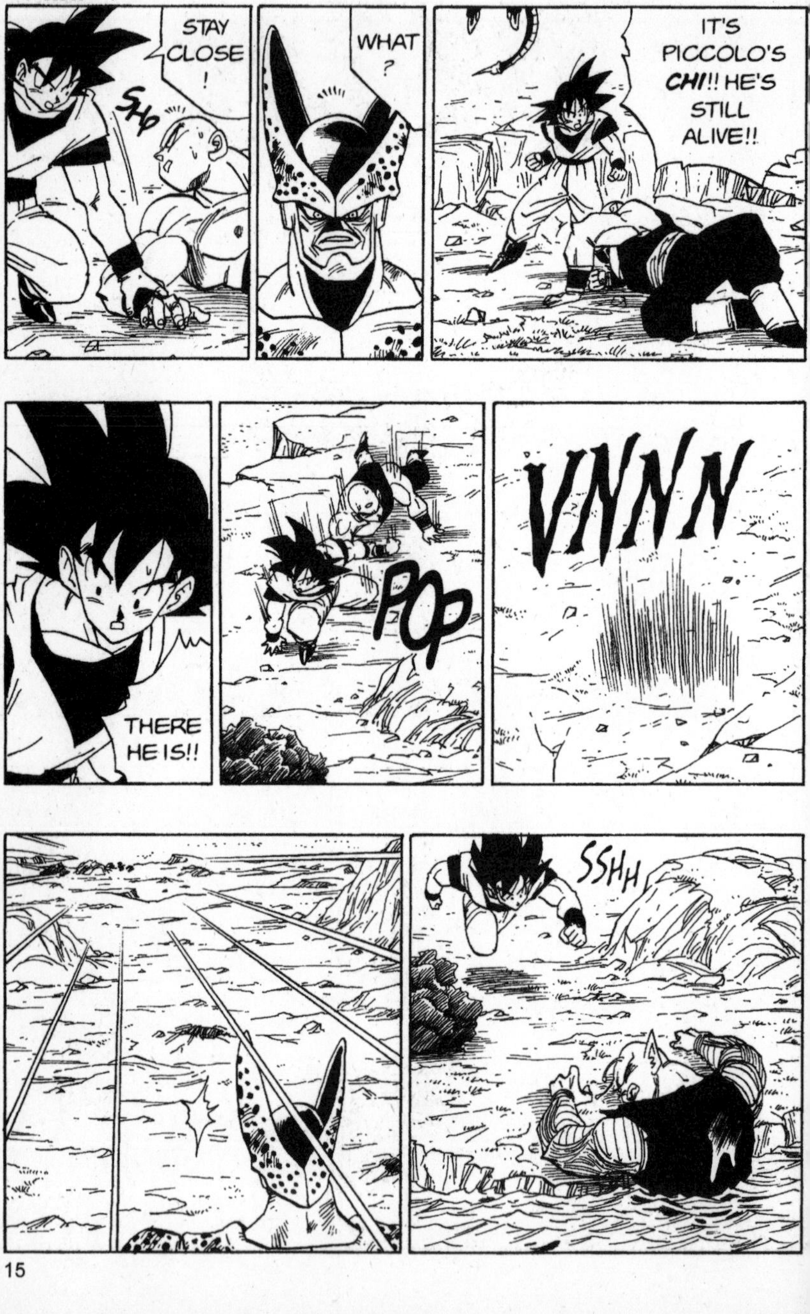
IT'S PICCOLO'S CHI!! HE'S STILL ALIVE!!
WHAT ?
STAY CLOSE !
SHP
VNNN
POP
THERE HE IS!!
SSHH

READ THIS WAY

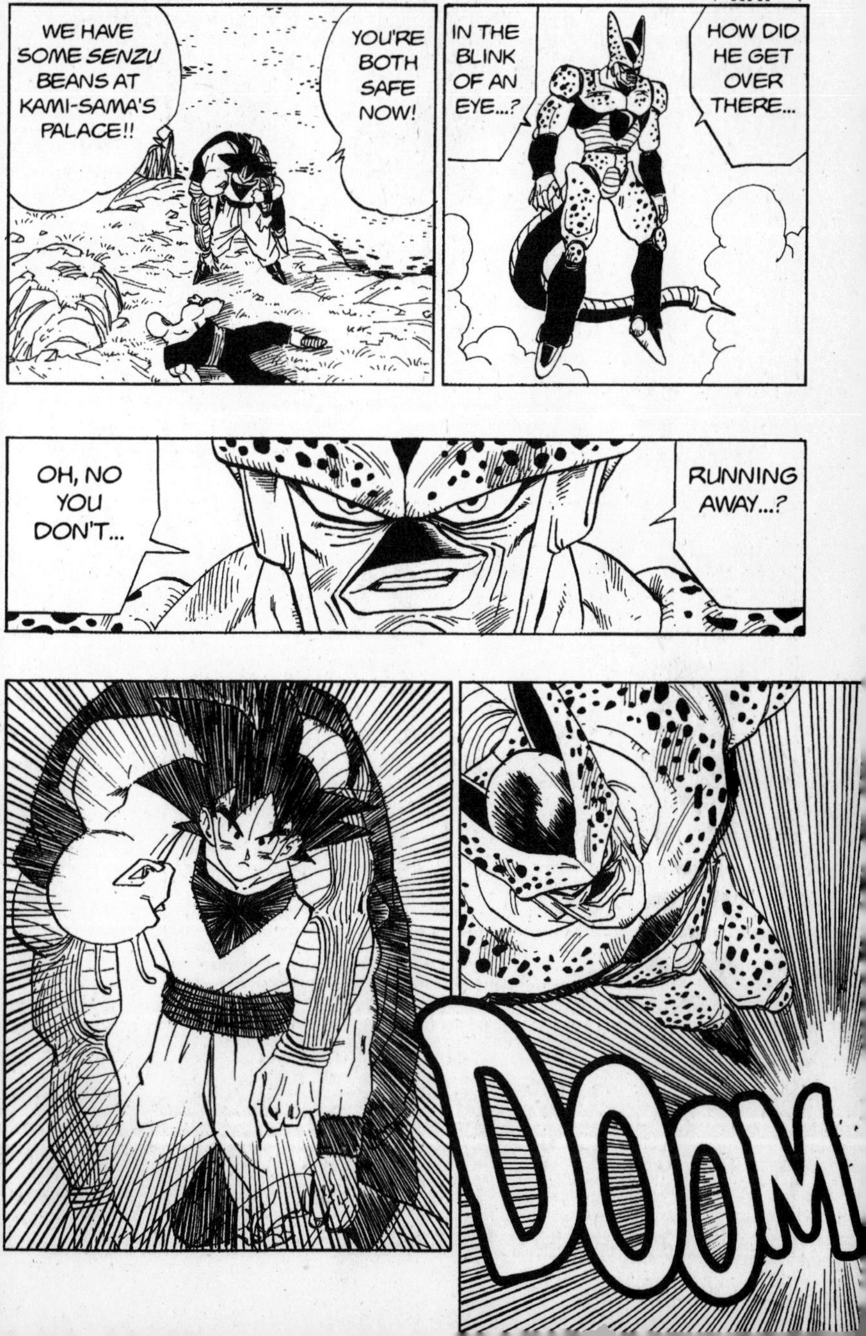
HOW DID HE GET OVER THERE...
IN THE BLINK OF AN EYE...?
YOU'RE BOTH SAFE NOW!
WE HAVE SOME *SENZU* BEANS AT KAMI-SAMA'S PALACE!!
RUNNING AWAY...?
OH, NO YOU DON'T...
DOOM

READ THIS WAY

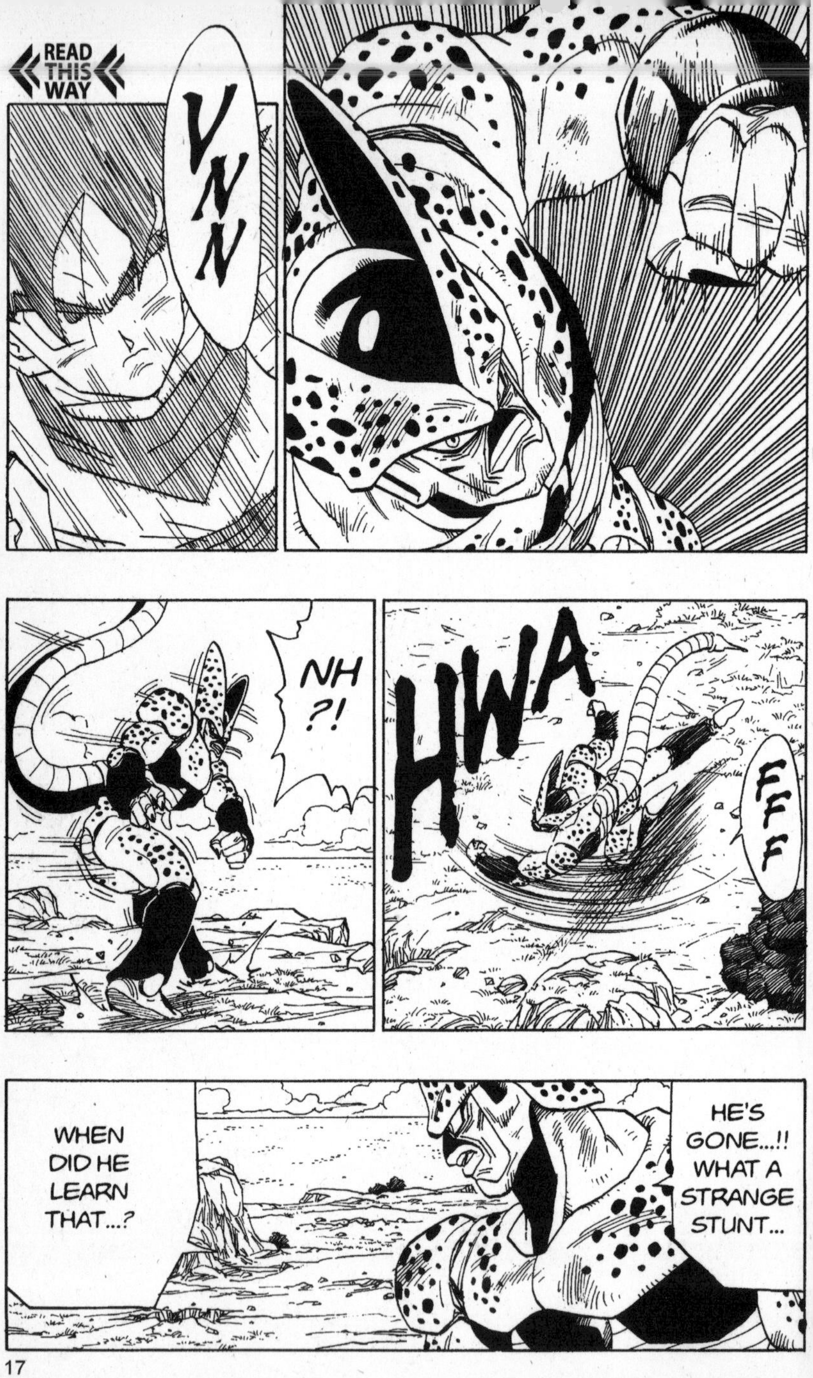
VNN
HWA
FFF
NH ?!
HE'S GONE...!! WHAT A STRANGE STUNT...
WHEN DID HE LEARN THAT...?

READ THIS WAY

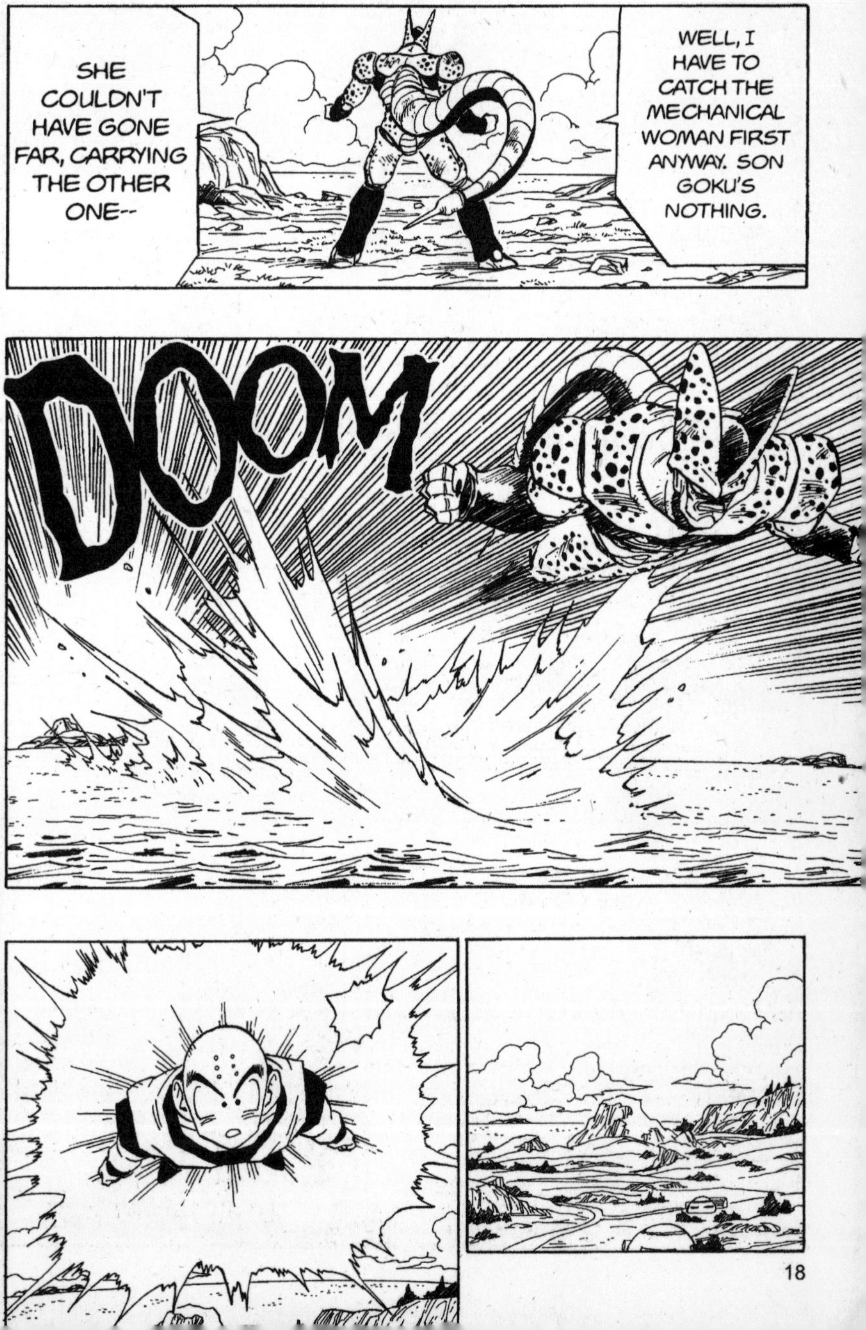

WELL, I HAVE TO CATCH THE MECHANICAL WOMAN FIRST ANYWAY. SON GOKU'S NOTHING.
SHE COULDN'T HAVE GONE FAR, CARRYING THE OTHER ONE--
DOOM

READ THIS WAY

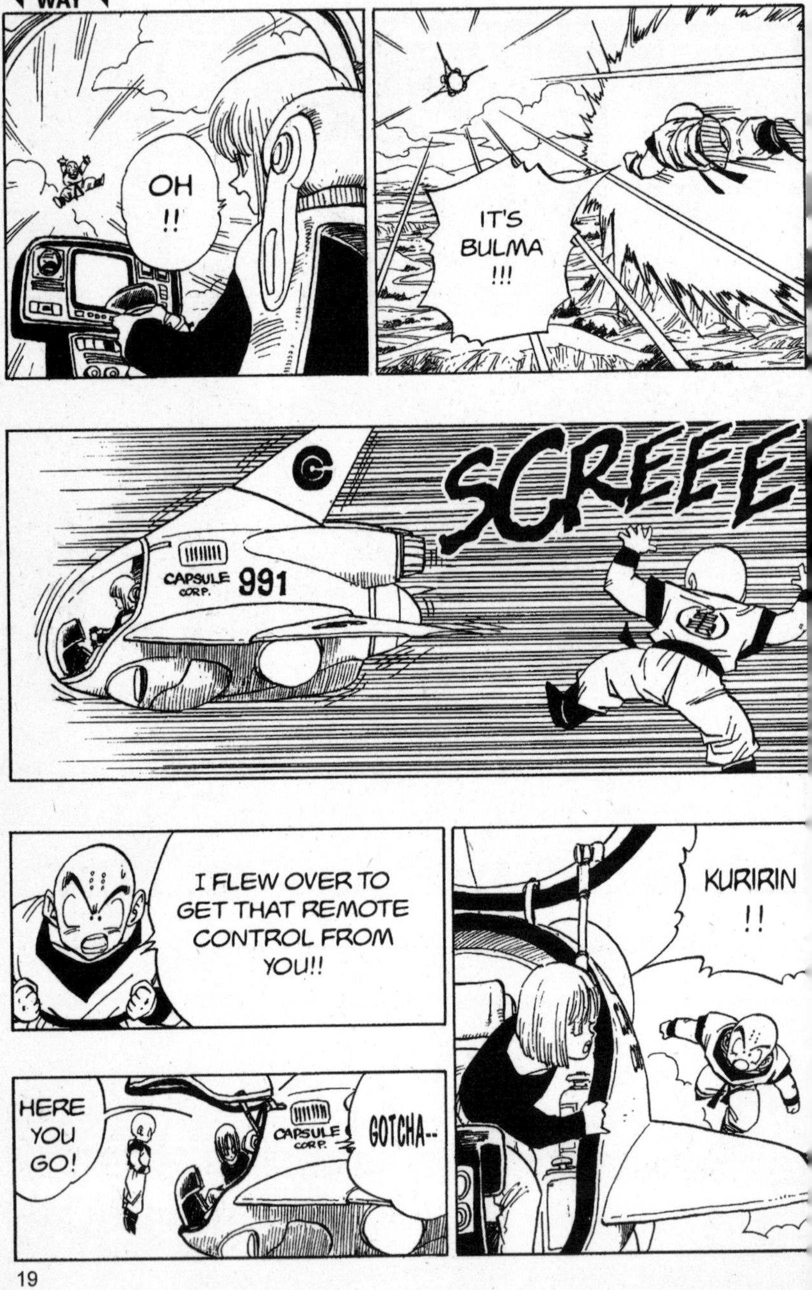

IT'S BULMA !!!
OH !!
SCREEE
CAPSULE CORP. 991
KURIRIN !!
I FLEW OVER TO GET THAT REMOTE CONTROL FROM YOU!!
GOTCHA--
CAPSULE CORP.
HERE YOU GO!

READ THIS WAY

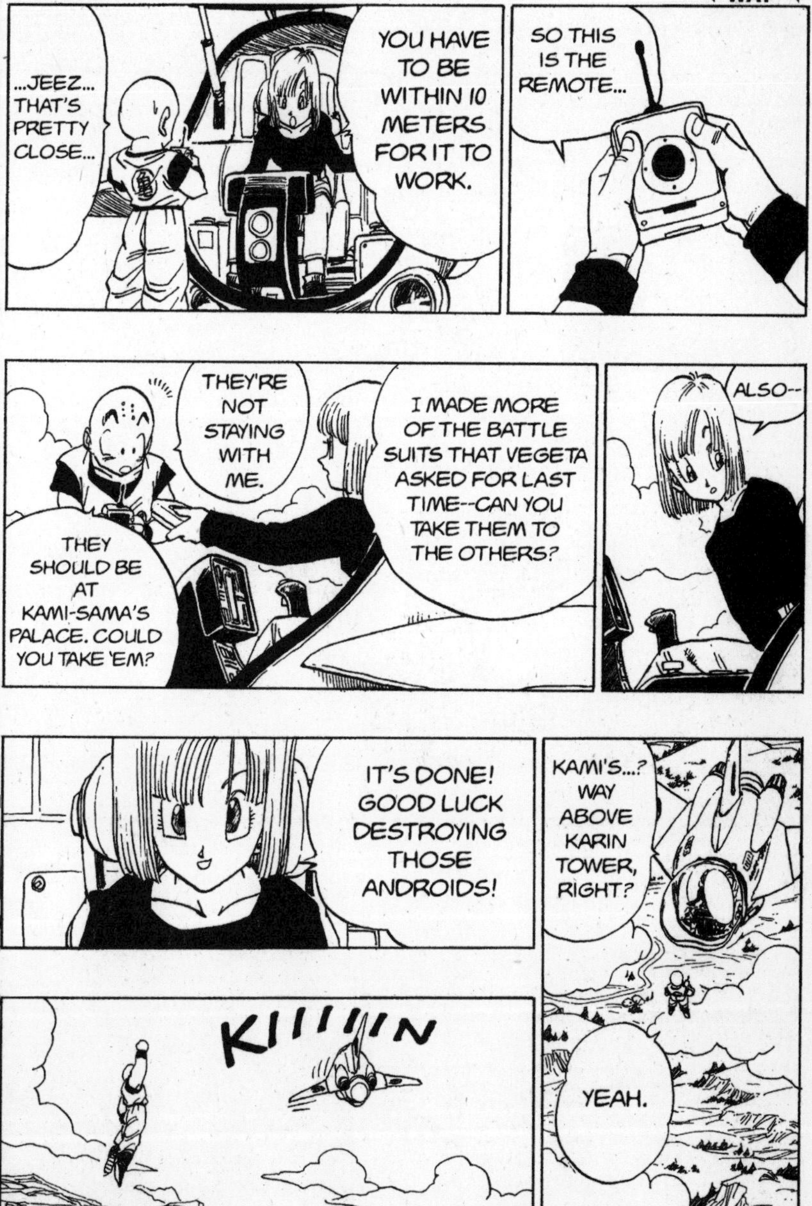

SO THIS IS THE REMOTE...
YOU HAVE TO BE WITHIN 10 METERS FOR IT TO WORK.
...JEEZ... THAT'S PRETTY CLOSE...
ALSO--
I MADE MORE OF THE BATTLE SUITS THAT VEGETA ASKED FOR LAST TIME--CAN YOU TAKE THEM TO THE OTHERS?
THEY'RE NOT STAYING WITH ME.
THEY SHOULD BE AT KAMI-SAMA'S PALACE. COULD YOU TAKE 'EM?
KAMI'S...? WAY ABOVE KARIN TOWER, RIGHT?
YEAH.
IT'S DONE! GOOD LUCK DESTROYING THOSE ANDROIDS!
KIIIIIN

READ THIS WAY

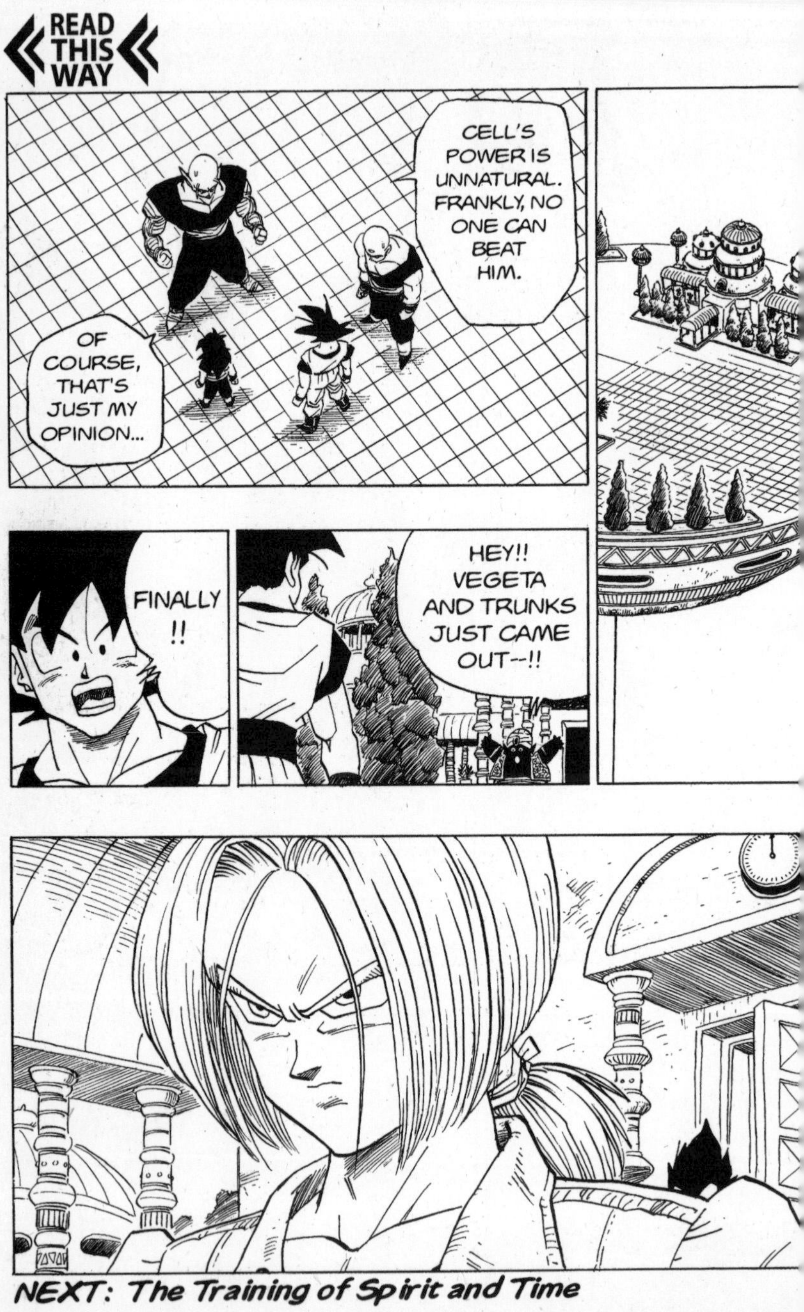

CELL'S POWER IS UNNATURAL. FRANKLY, NO ONE CAN BEAT HIM.
OF COURSE, THAT'S JUST MY OPINION...
HEY!! VEGETA AND TRUNKS JUST CAME OUT--!!
FINALLY !!

NEXT: The Training of Spirit and Time

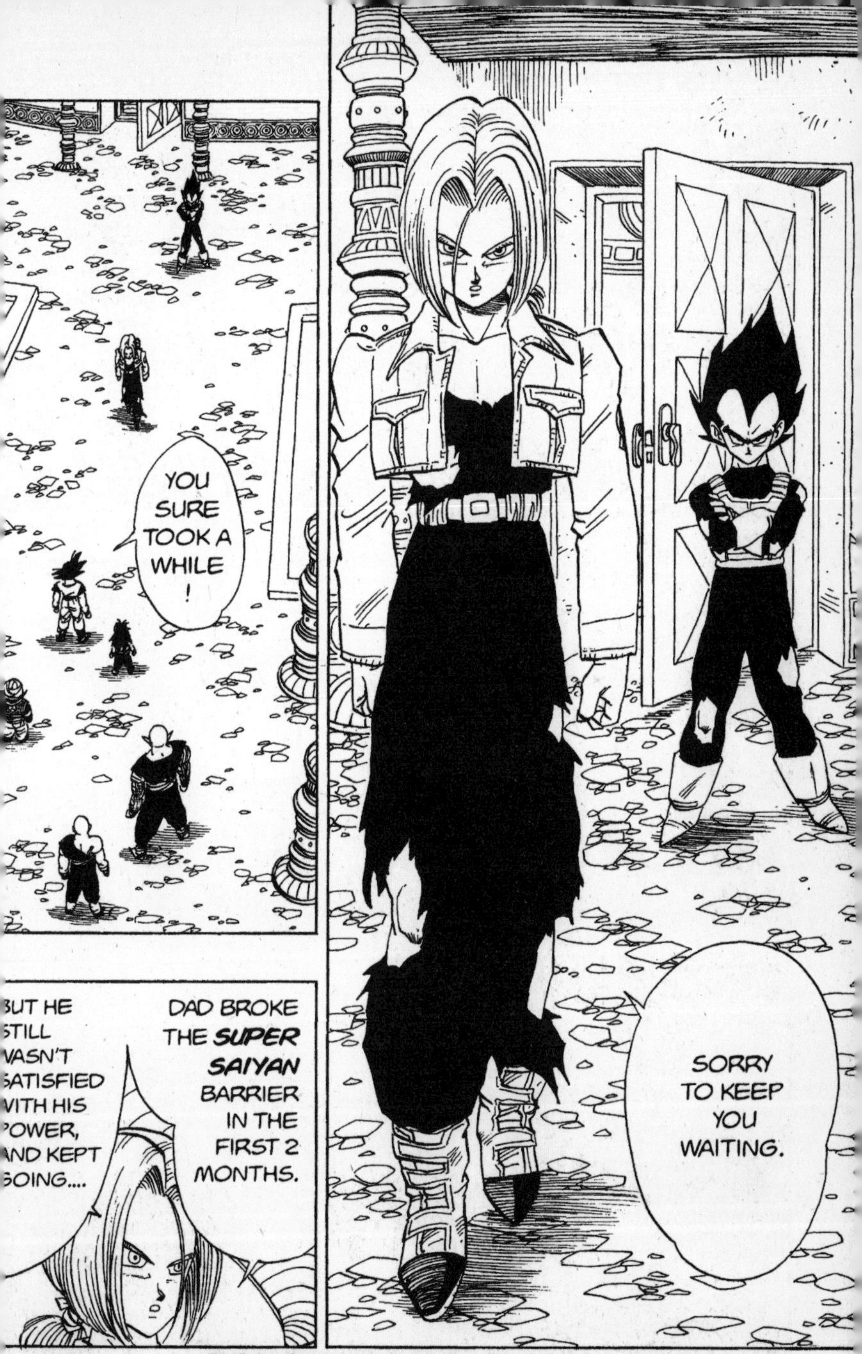

SORRY TO KEEP YOU WAITING.
YOU SURE TOOK A WHILE!
DAD BROKE THE *SUPER SAIYAN* BARRIER IN THE FIRST 2 MONTHS.
BUT HE STILL WASN'T SATISFIED WITH HIS POWER, AND KEPT GOING....

READ THIS WAY

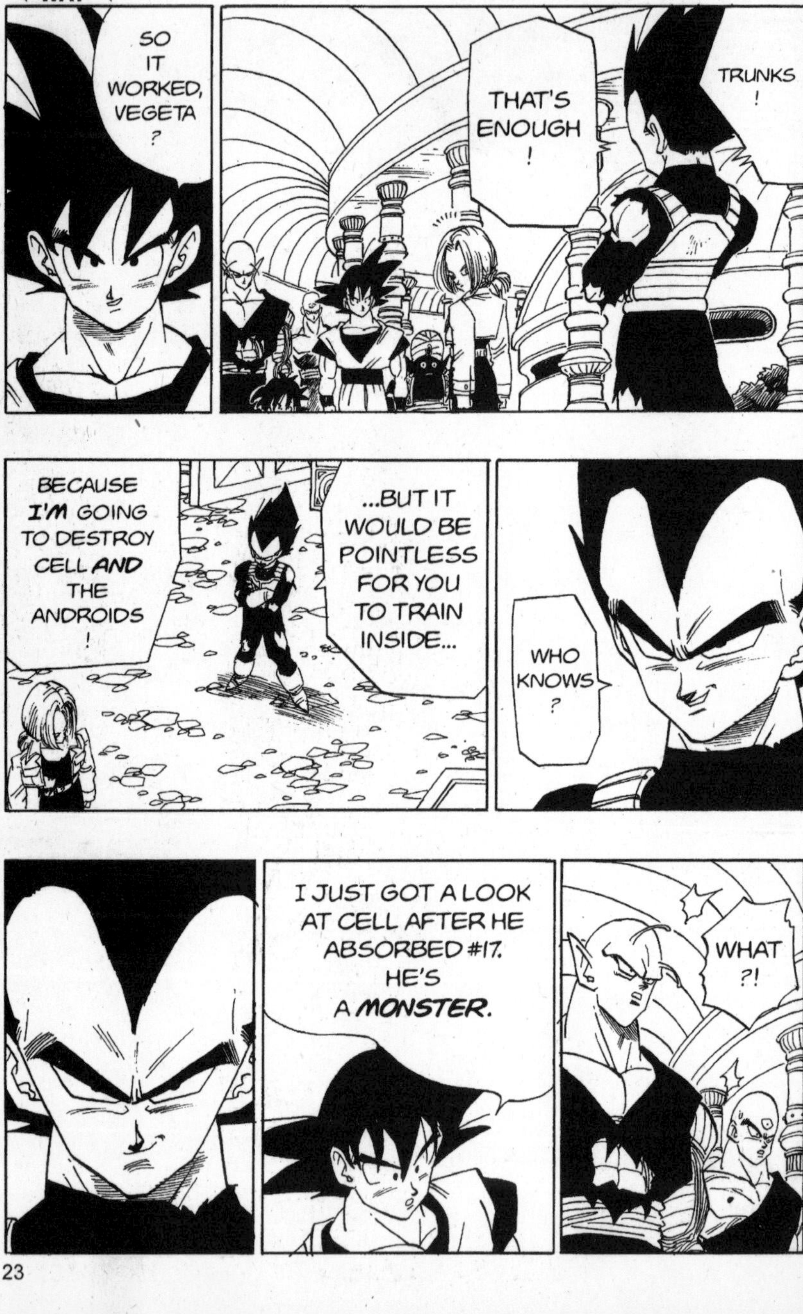

TRUNKS!
THAT'S ENOUGH!
SO IT WORKED, VEGETA?
WHO KNOWS?
...BUT IT WOULD BE POINTLESS FOR YOU TO TRAIN INSIDE...
BECAUSE I'M GOING TO DESTROY CELL AND THE ANDROIDS!
WHAT?!
I JUST GOT A LOOK AT CELL AFTER HE ABSORBED #17. HE'S A MONSTER.

READ THIS WAY

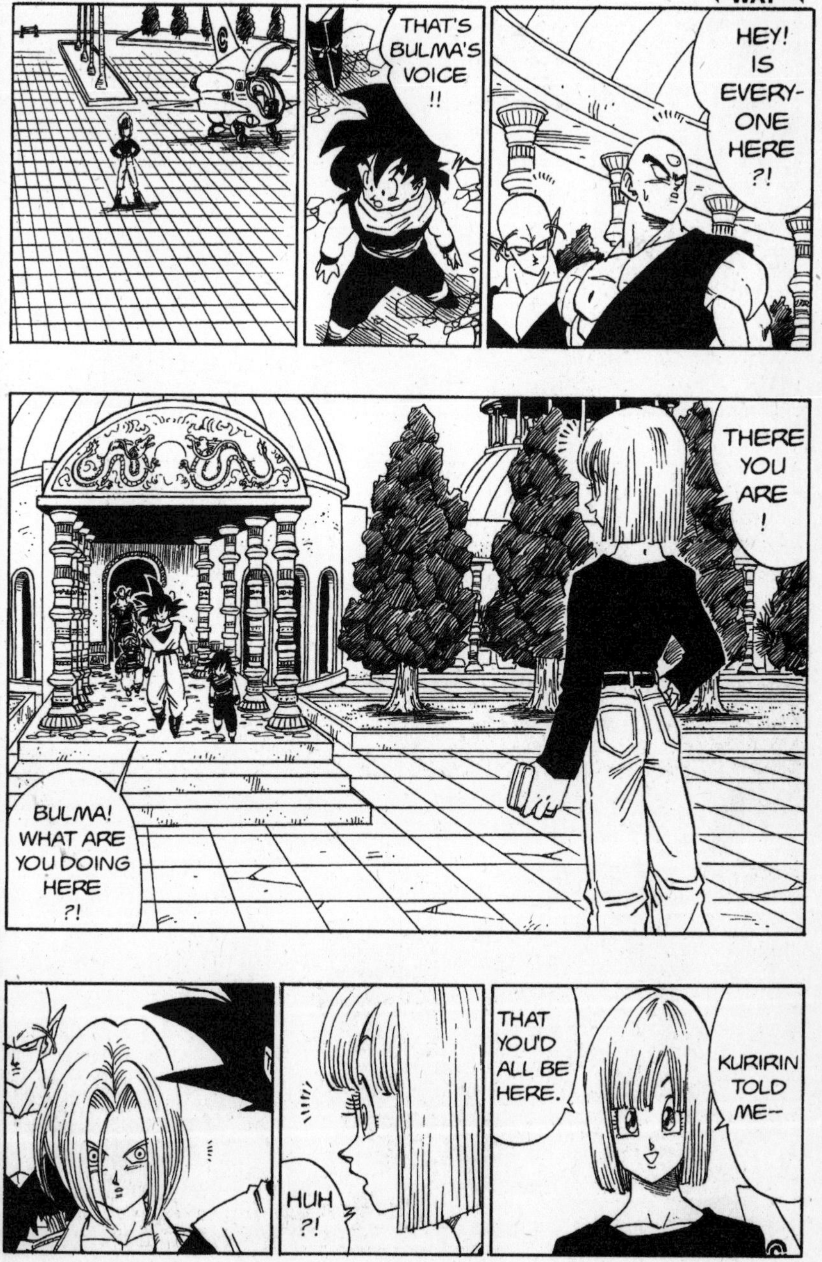
HEY! IS EVERYONE HERE ?!
THAT'S BULMA'S VOICE !!
THERE YOU ARE !
BULMA! WHAT ARE YOU DOING HERE ?!
KURIRIN TOLD ME--
THAT YOU'D ALL BE HERE.
HUH ?!

READ THIS WAY

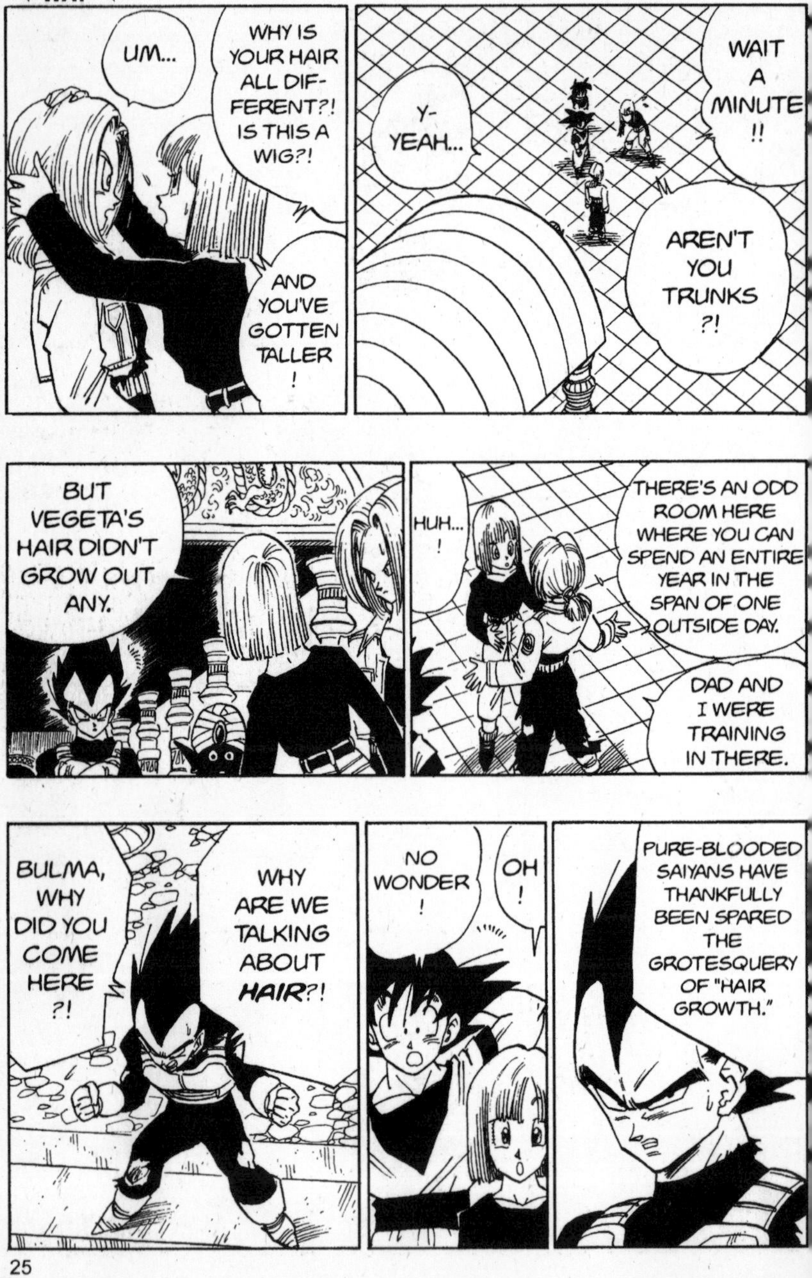
WAIT A MINUTE!!
AREN'T YOU TRUNKS?!
Y-YEAH...
WHY IS YOUR HAIR ALL DIF-FERENT?! IS THIS A WIG?!
AND YOU'VE GOTTEN TALLER!
UM...
THERE'S AN ODD ROOM HERE WHERE YOU CAN SPEND AN ENTIRE YEAR IN THE SPAN OF ONE OUTSIDE DAY.
DAD AND I WERE TRAINING IN THERE.
HUH...!
BUT VEGETA'S HAIR DIDN'T GROW OUT ANY.
PURE-BLOODED SAIYANS HAVE THANKFULLY BEEN SPARED THE GROTESQUERY OF "HAIR GROWTH."
OH!
NO WONDER!
WHY ARE WE TALKING ABOUT *HAIR*?!
BULMA, WHY DID YOU COME HERE?!

READ THIS WAY

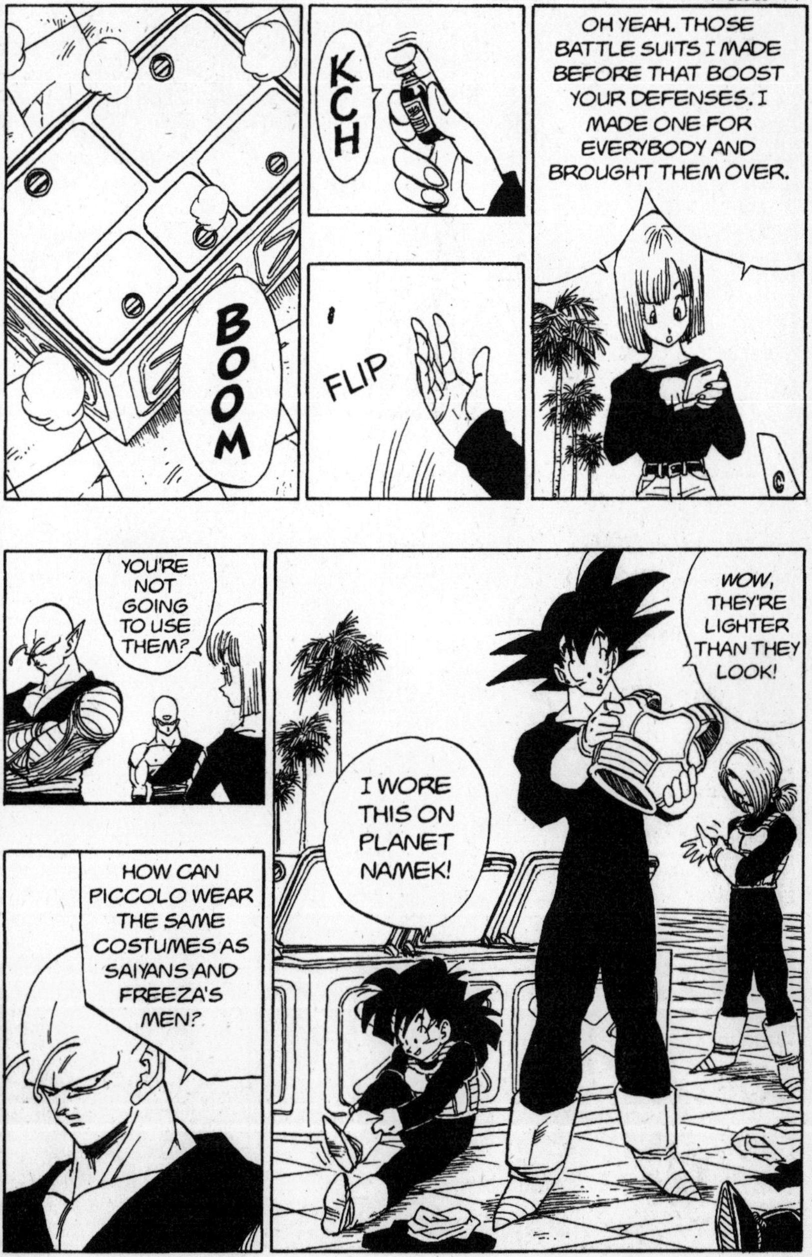
OH YEAH. THOSE BATTLE SUITS I MADE BEFORE THAT BOOST YOUR DEFENSES. I MADE ONE FOR EVERYBODY AND BROUGHT THEM OVER.
KCH
FLIP
BOOM
WOW, THEY'RE LIGHTER THAN THEY LOOK!
I WORE THIS ON PLANET NAMEK!
YOU'RE NOT GOING TO USE THEM?
HOW CAN PICCOLO WEAR THE SAME COSTUMES AS SAIYANS AND FREEZA'S MEN?

READ THIS WAY

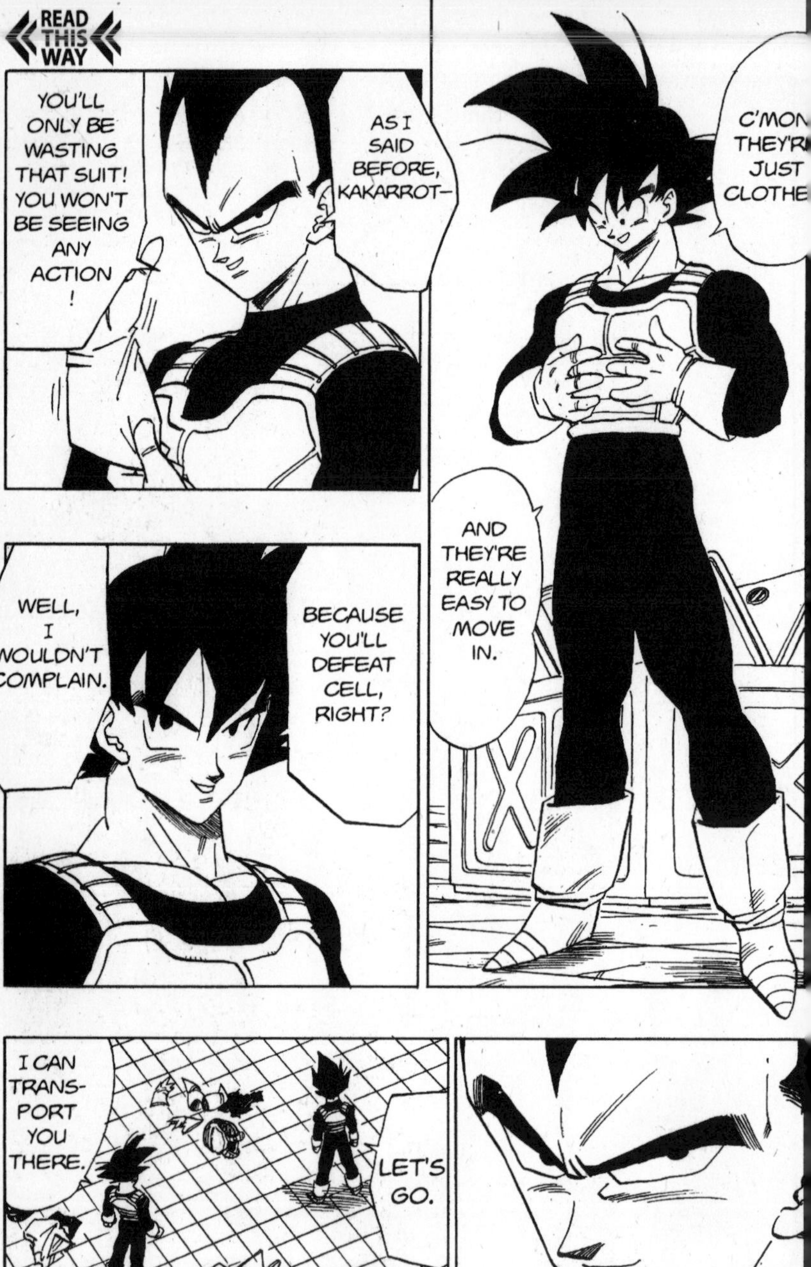

C'MON THEY'R JUST CLOTHE
AND THEY'RE REALLY EASY TO MOVE IN.
AS I SAID BEFORE, KAKARROT—
YOU'LL ONLY BE WASTING THAT SUIT! YOU WON'T BE SEEING ANY ACTION!
BECAUSE YOU'LL DEFEAT CELL, RIGHT?
WELL, I WOULDN'T COMPLAIN.
LET'S GO.
I CAN TRANSPORT YOU THERE.

READ THIS WAY

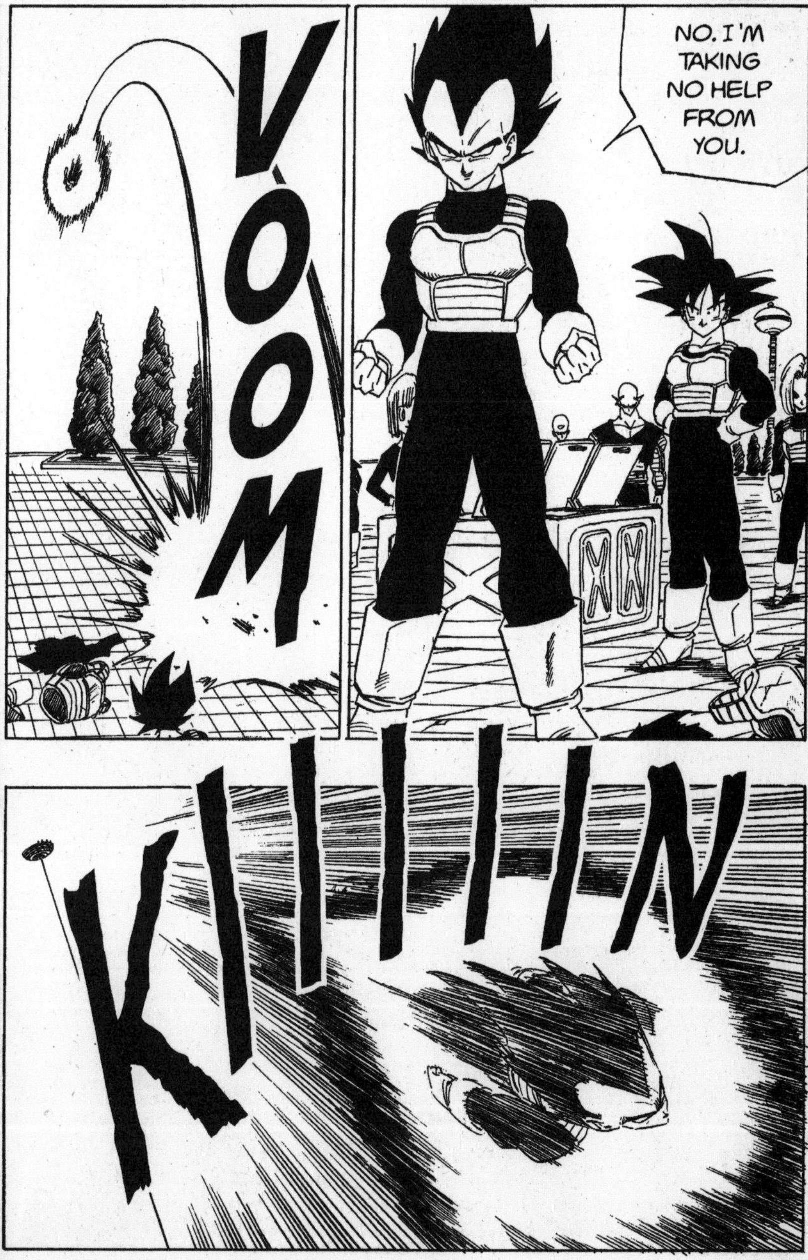
NO. I'M TAKING NO HELP FROM YOU.
VOOM
KIIIIN

READ THIS WAY

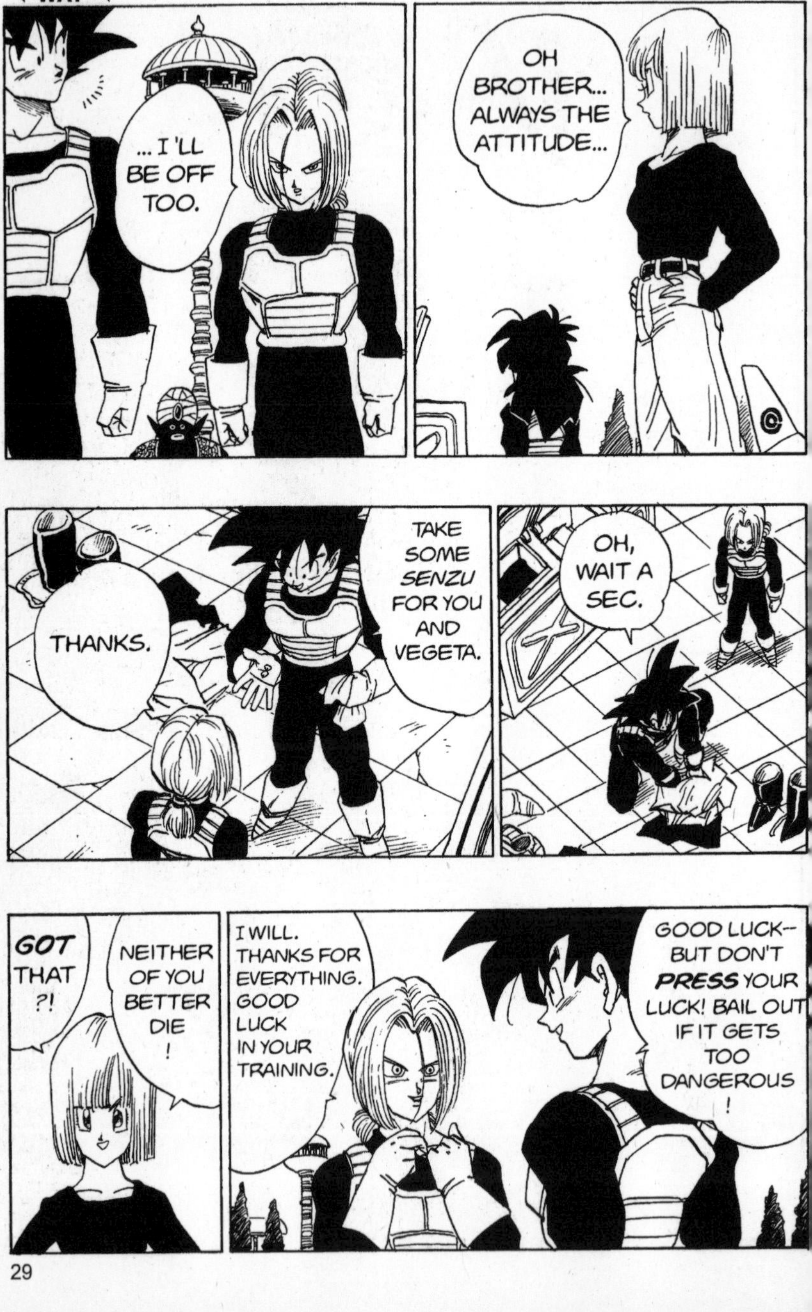
OH BROTHER... ALWAYS THE ATTITUDE...
... I'LL BE OFF TOO.
OH, WAIT A SEC.
TAKE SOME SENZU FOR YOU AND VEGETA.
THANKS.
GOOD LUCK-- BUT DON'T **PRESS** YOUR LUCK! BAIL OUT IF IT GETS TOO DANGEROUS!
I WILL. THANKS FOR EVERYTHING. GOOD LUCK IN YOUR TRAINING.
NEITHER OF YOU BETTER DIE!
GOT THAT?!

READ THIS WAY

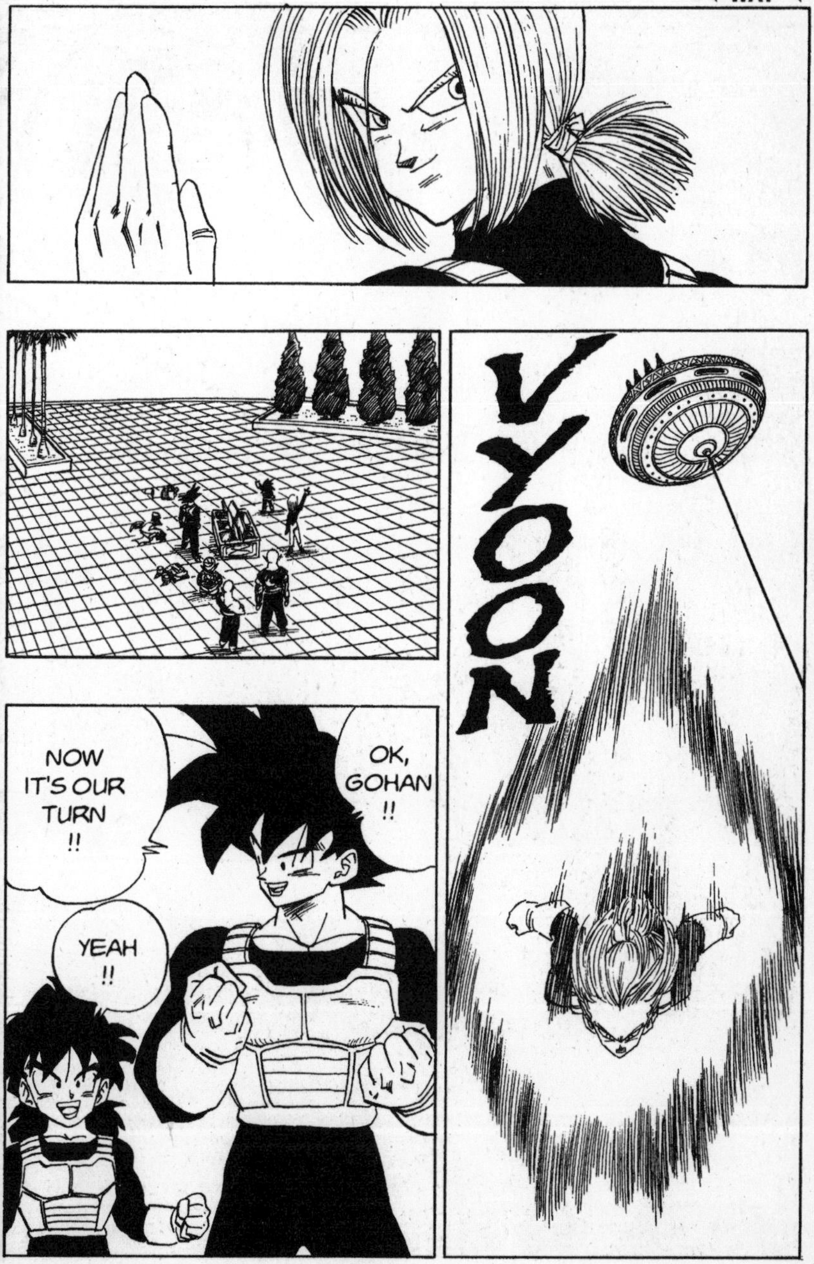
VYOON
OK, GOHAN!!
NOW IT'S OUR TURN!!
YEAH!!

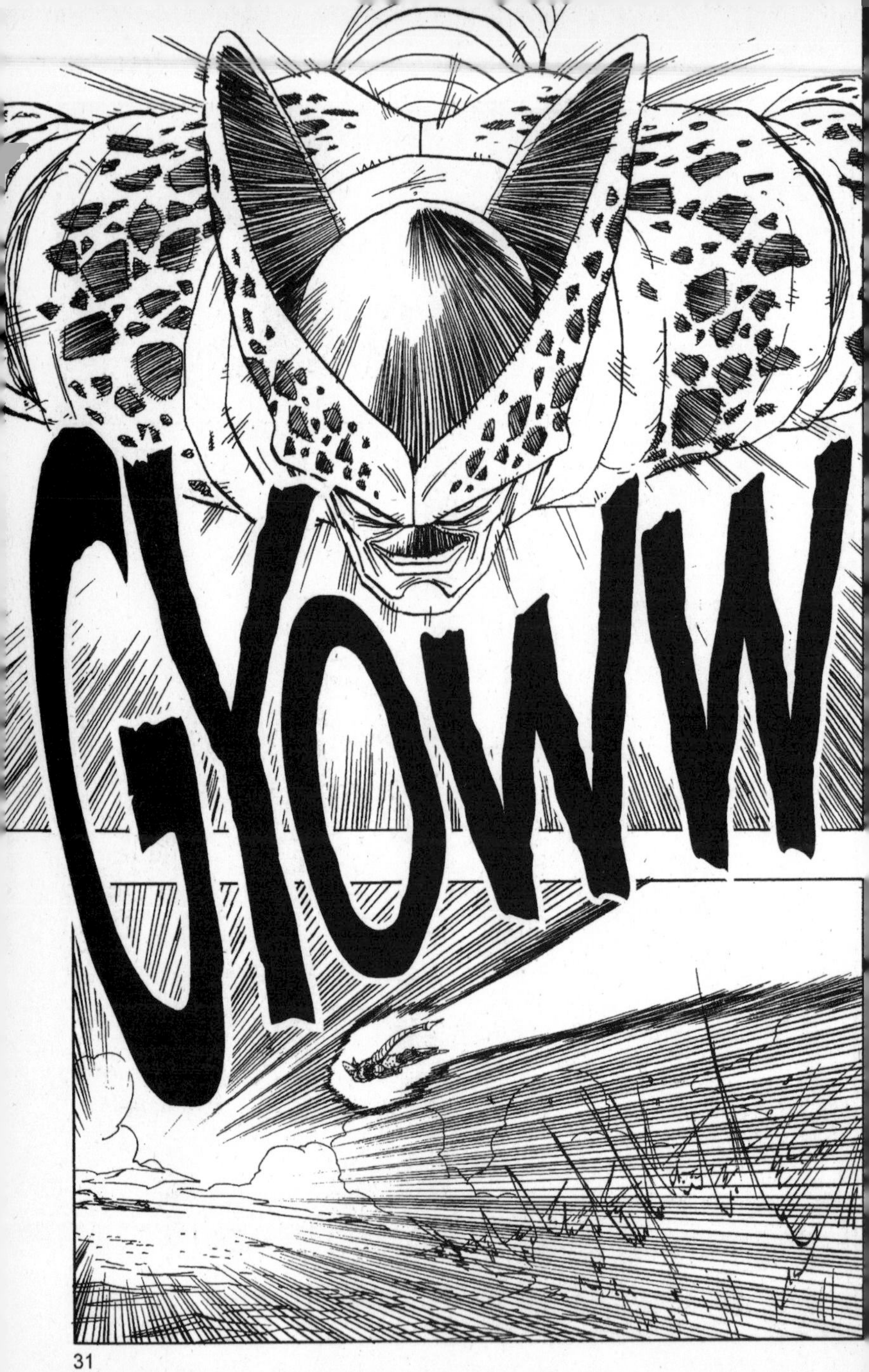
GYOWW

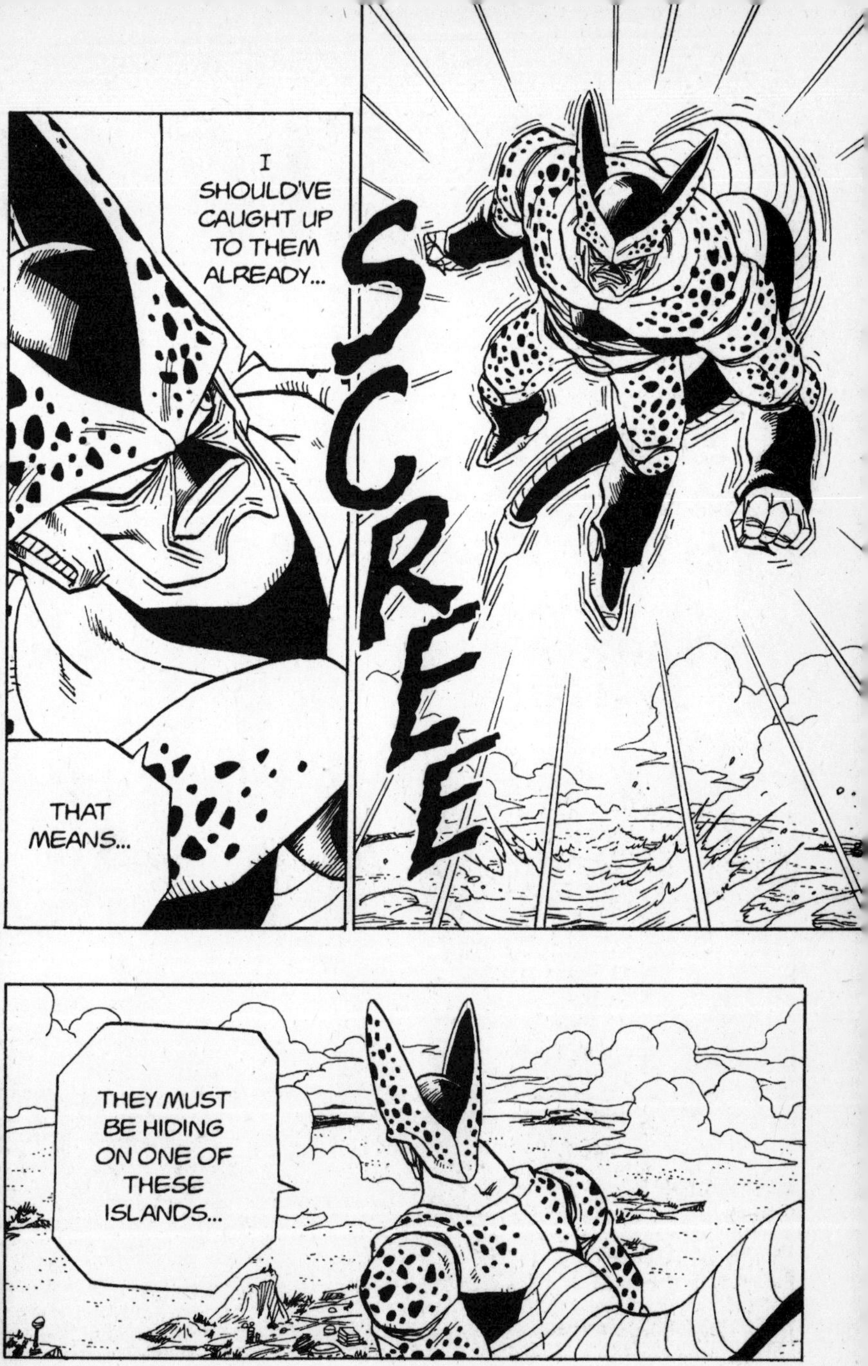
SCREEE
I SHOULD'VE CAUGHT UP TO THEM ALREADY...
THAT MEANS...
THEY MUST BE HIDING ON ONE OF THESE ISLANDS...

READ THIS WAY

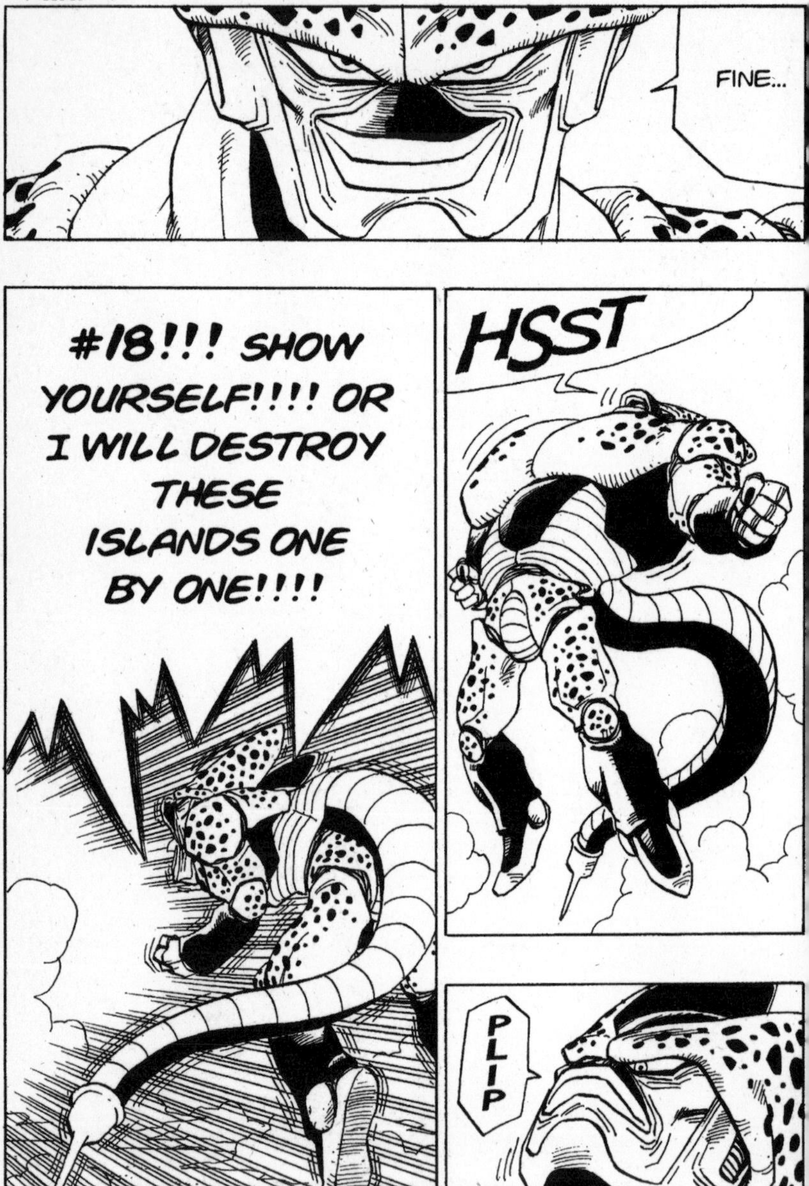

FINE...
HSST
PLIP
#18!!! SHOW YOURSELF!!!! OR I WILL DESTROY THESE ISLANDS ONE BY ONE!!!!

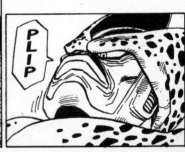

READ THIS WAY

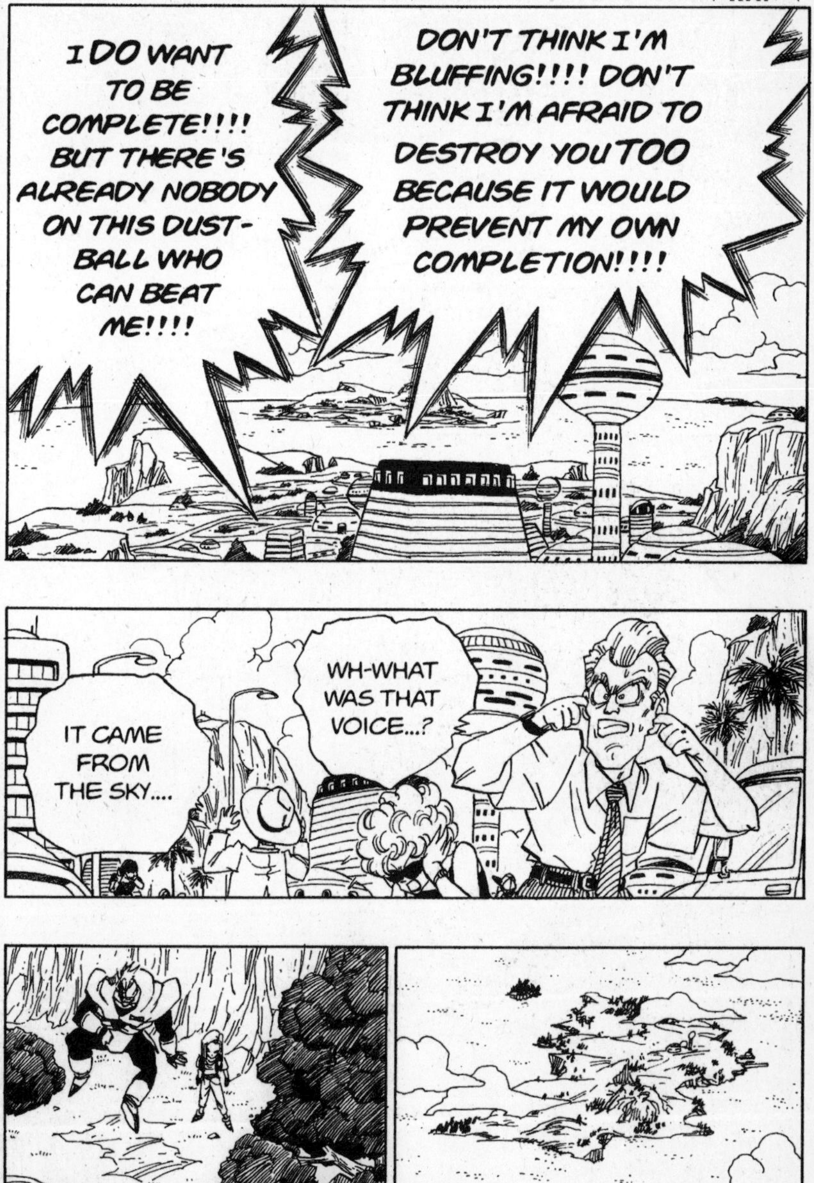

DON'T THINK I'M BLUFFING!!!! DON'T THINK I'M AFRAID TO DESTROY YOU TOO BECAUSE IT WOULD PREVENT MY OWN COMPLETION!!!!
I DO WANT TO BE COMPLETE!!!! BUT THERE'S ALREADY NOBODY ON THIS DUST-BALL WHO CAN BEAT ME!!!!
WH-WHAT WAS THAT VOICE...?
IT CAME FROM THE SKY....

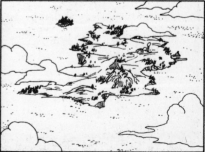

READ THIS WAY

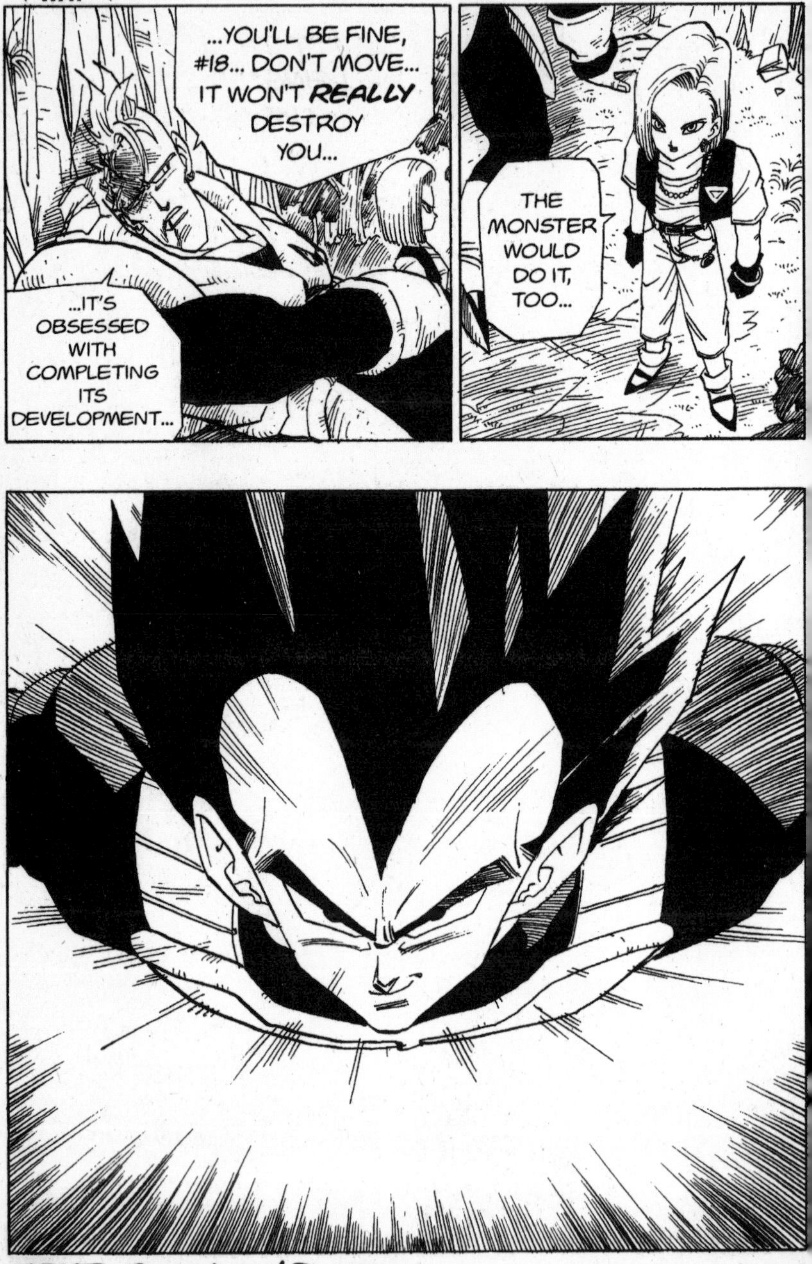
THE MONSTER WOULD DO IT, TOO...
...YOU'LL BE FINE, #18... DON'T MOVE... IT WON'T REALLY DESTROY YOU...
...IT'S OBSESSED WITH COMPLETING ITS DEVELOPMENT...

NEXT: Search and Destroy

DBZ:182 • Vegeta's Confidence

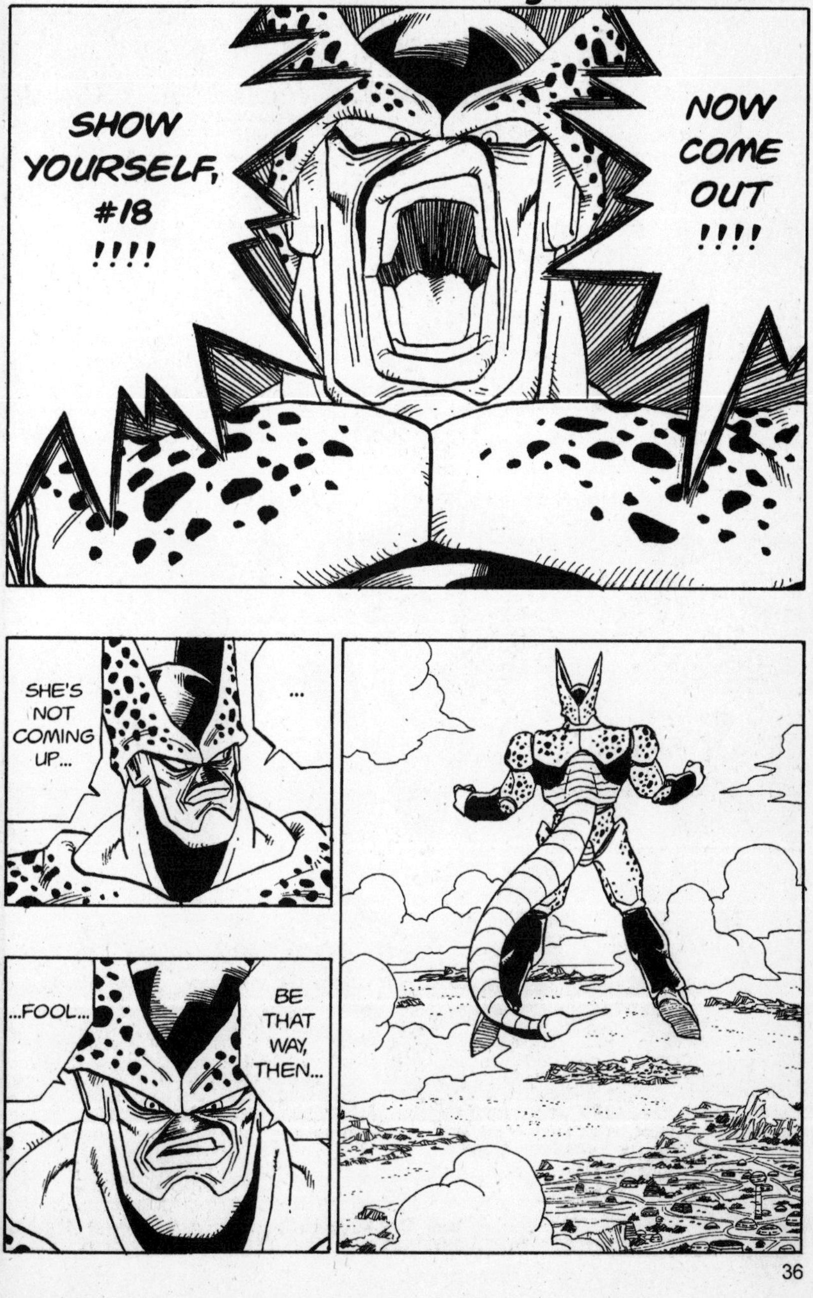
NOW COME OUT !!!!
SHOW YOURSELF, #18 !!!!
...
SHE'S NOT COMING UP...
BE THAT WAY, THEN...
...FOOL...

READ THIS WAY

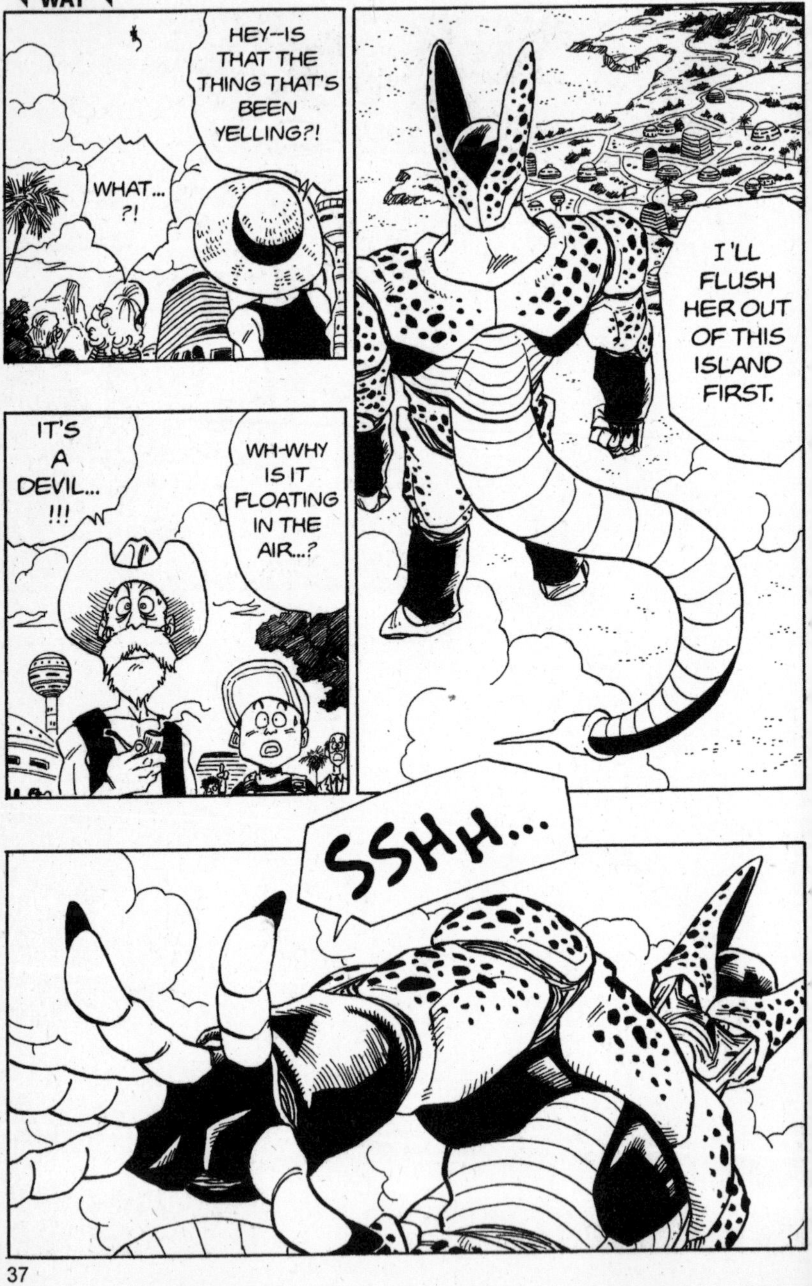

I'LL FLUSH HER OUT OF THIS ISLAND FIRST.
HEY--IS THAT THE THING THAT'S BEEN YELLING?!
WHAT... ?!
WH-WHY IS IT FLOATING IN THE AIR...?
IT'S A DEVIL... !!!
SSHH...

READ THIS WAY

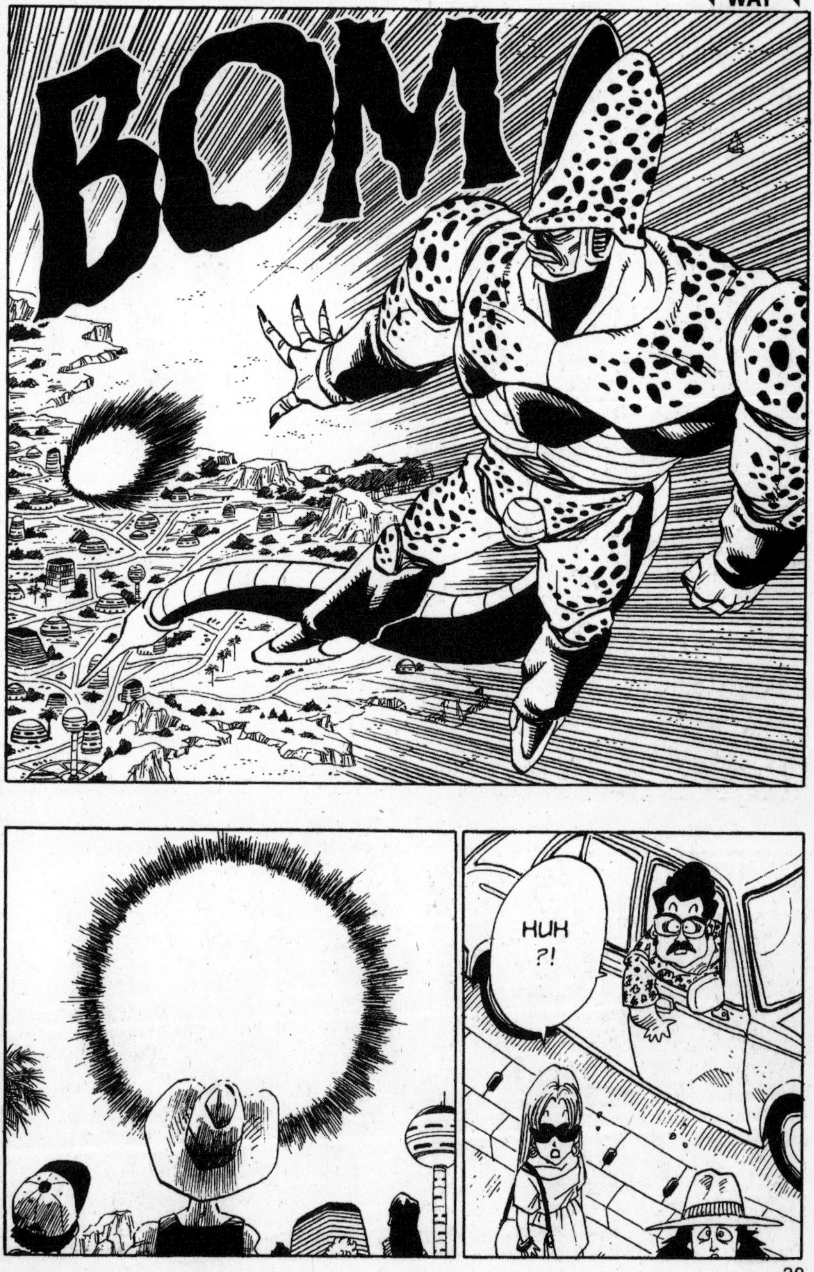
BOM
HUH ?!

READ THIS WAY

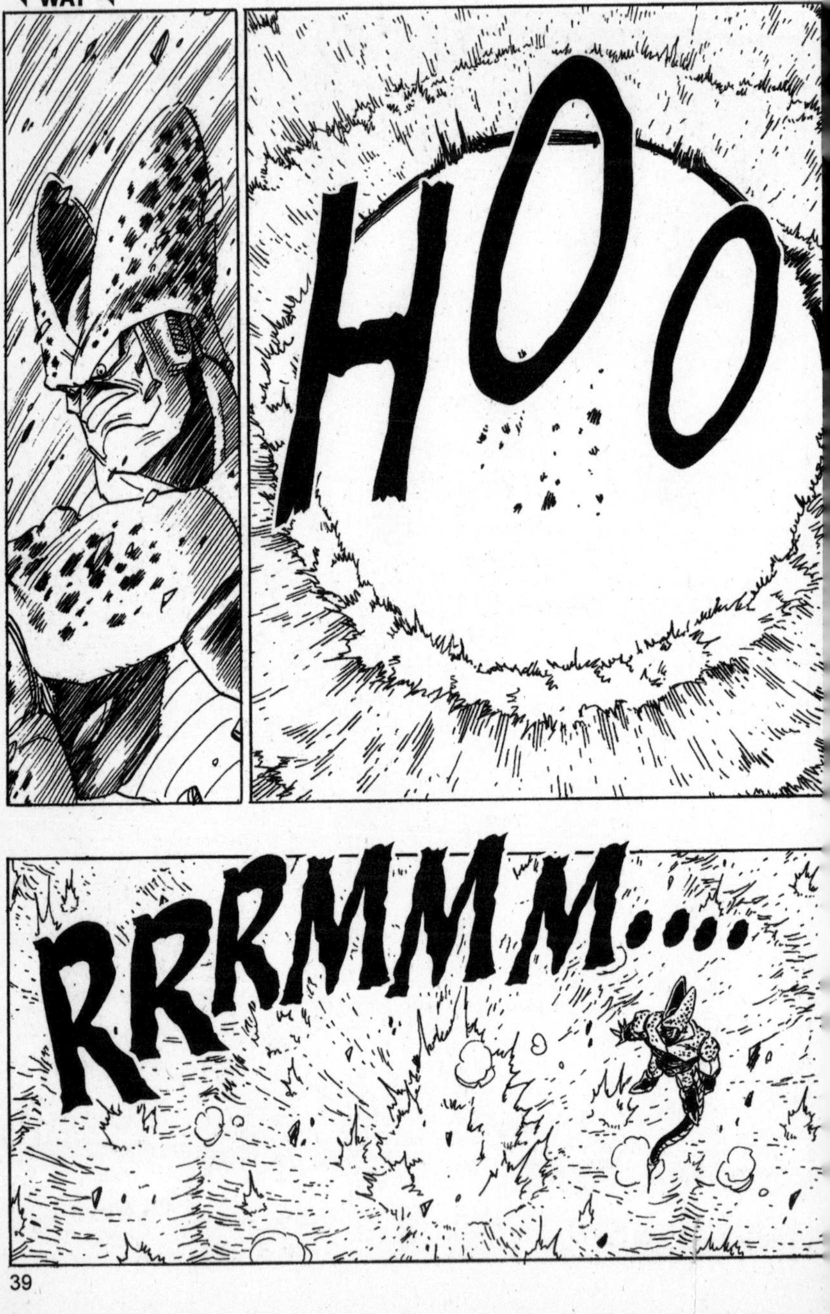
HOO
RRRMMM...

READ THIS WAY

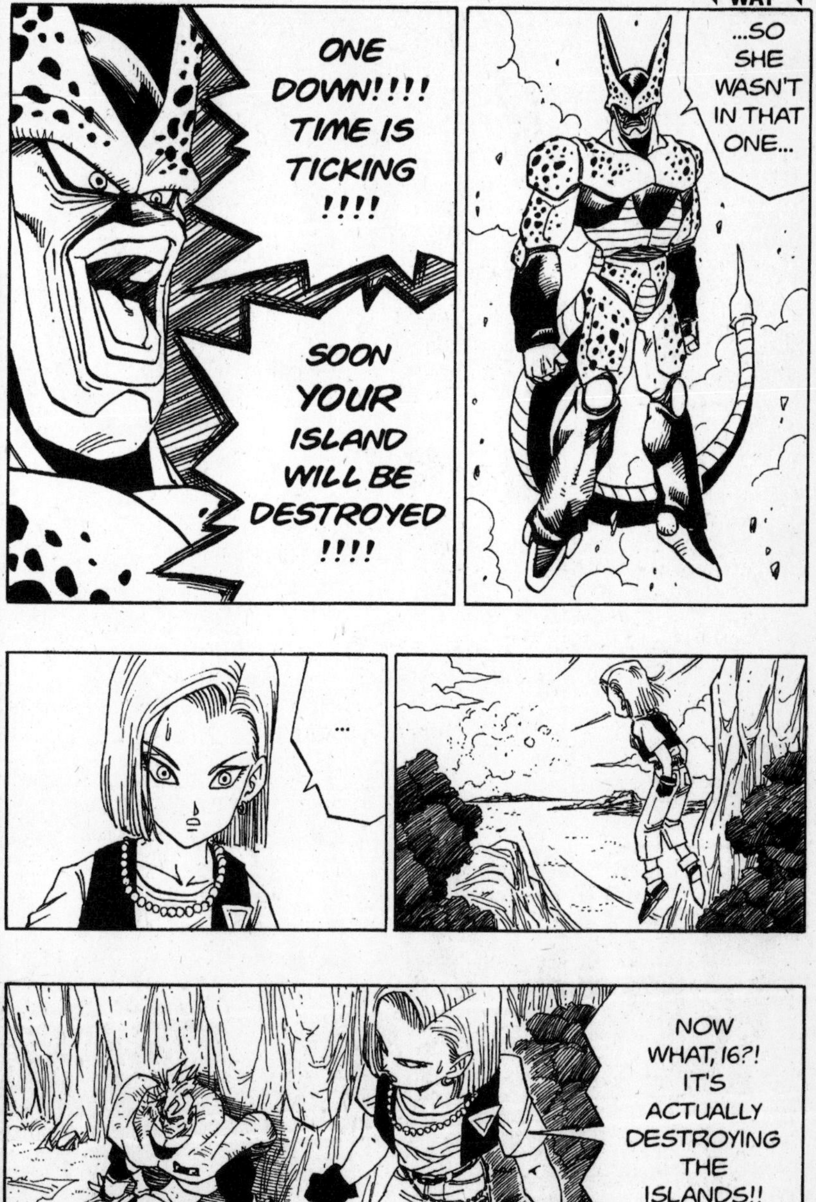
...SO SHE WASN'T IN THAT ONE...
ONE DOWN!!!! TIME IS TICKING !!!!
SOON YOUR ISLAND WILL BE DESTROYED !!!!
...
NOW WHAT, 16?! IT'S ACTUALLY DESTROYING THE ISLANDS!!

READ THIS WAY

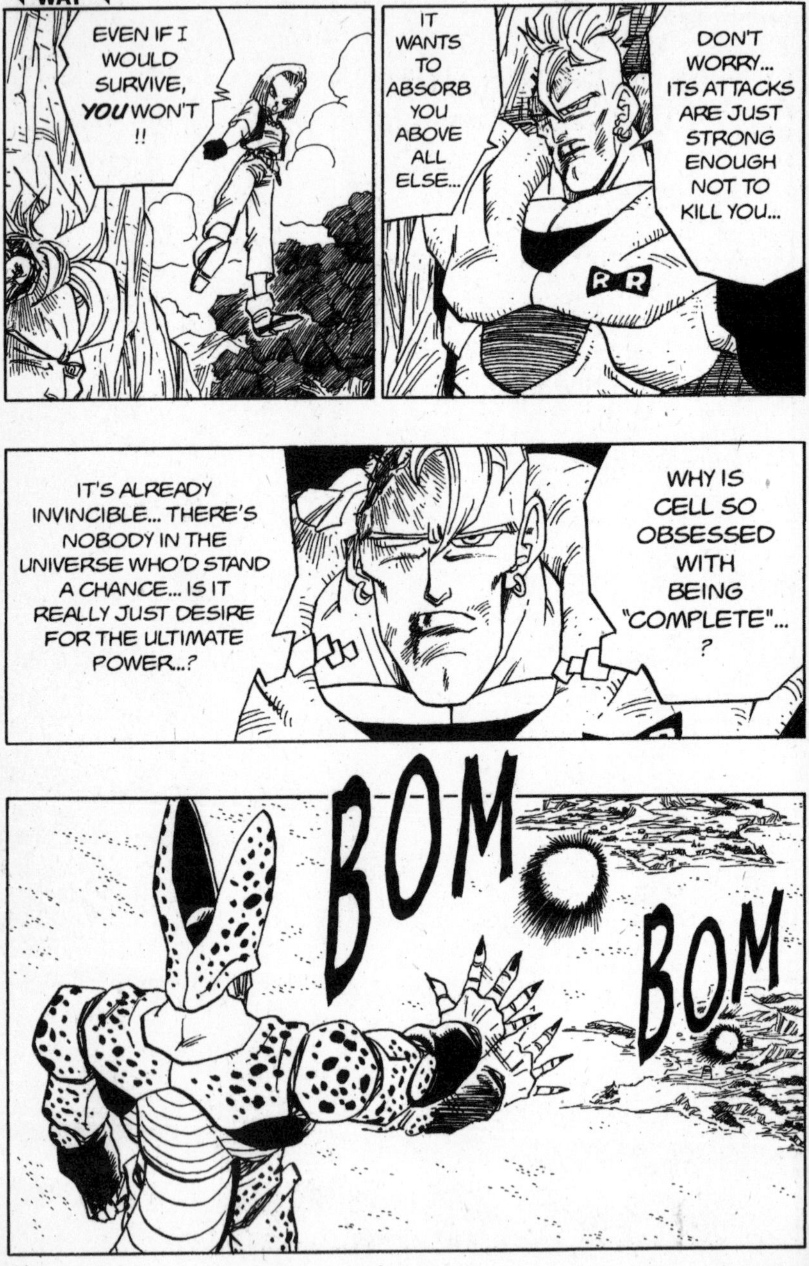

DON'T WORRY... ITS ATTACKS ARE JUST STRONG ENOUGH NOT TO KILL YOU...
IT WANTS TO ABSORB YOU ABOVE ALL ELSE...
EVEN IF I WOULD SURVIVE, **YOU** WON'T!!
WHY IS CELL SO OBSESSED WITH BEING "COMPLETE"...?
IT'S ALREADY INVINCIBLE... THERE'S NOBODY IN THE UNIVERSE WHO'D STAND A CHANCE... IS IT REALLY JUST DESIRE FOR THE ULTIMATE POWER...?
BOM
BOM

READ THIS WAY

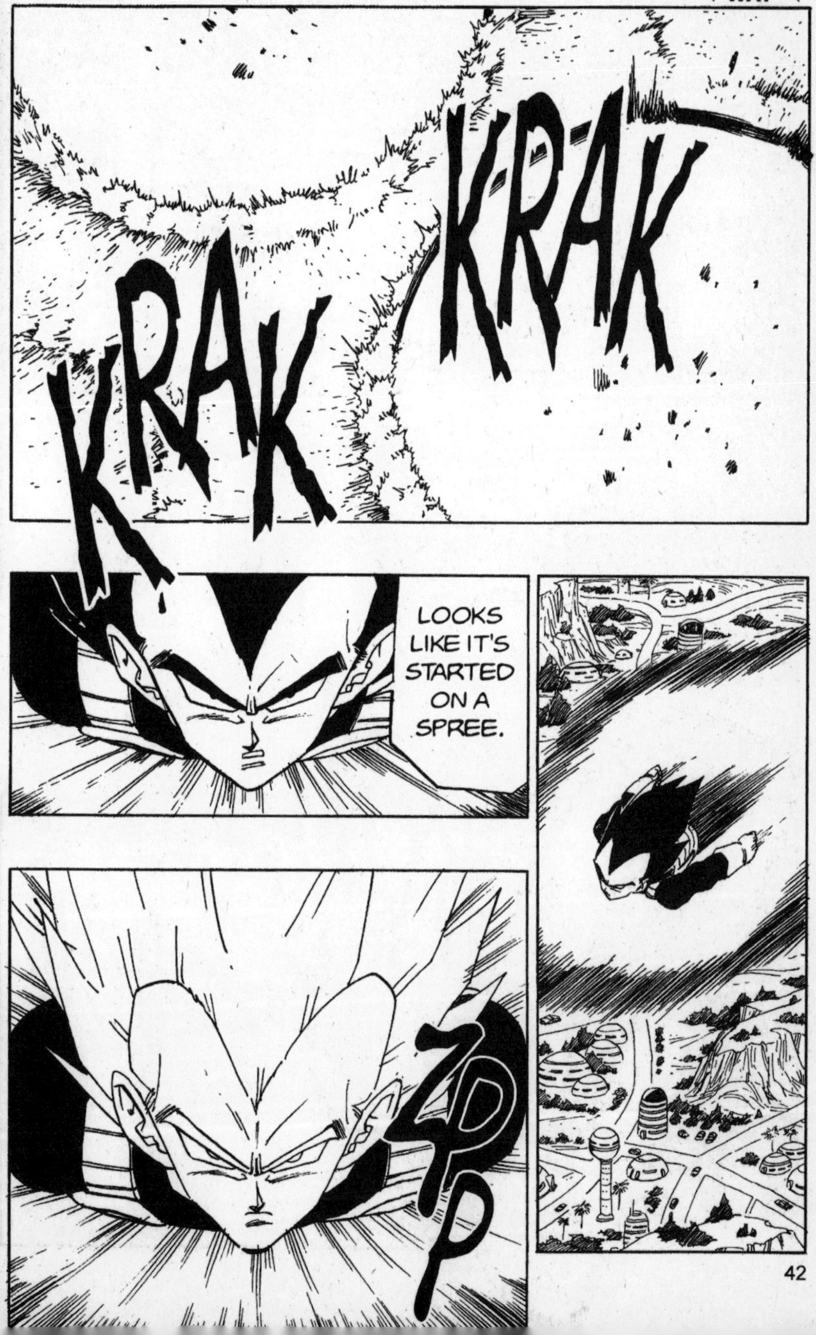
K-RAK
KRAK
LOOKS LIKE IT'S STARTED ON A SPREE.
ZOP

READ THIS WAY

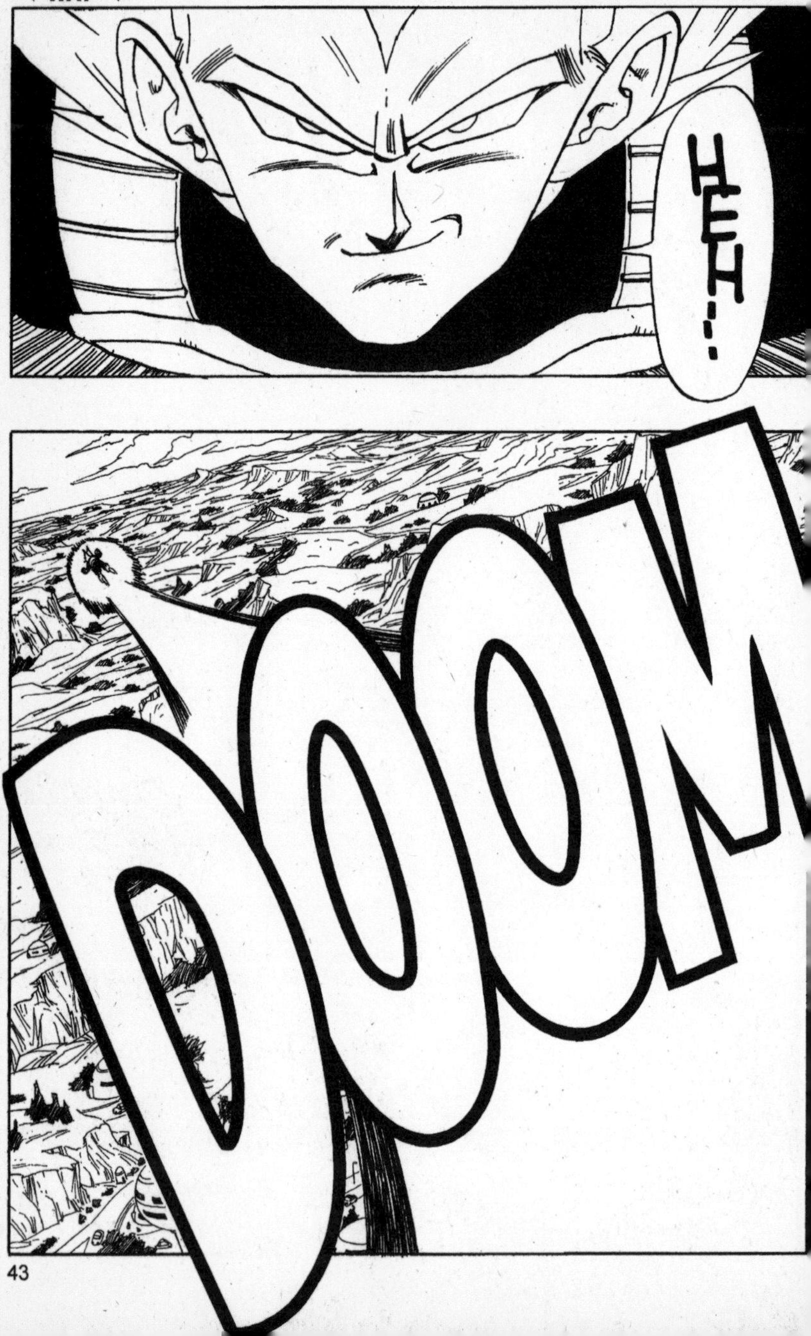
HEH...
DOOM

READ THIS WAY

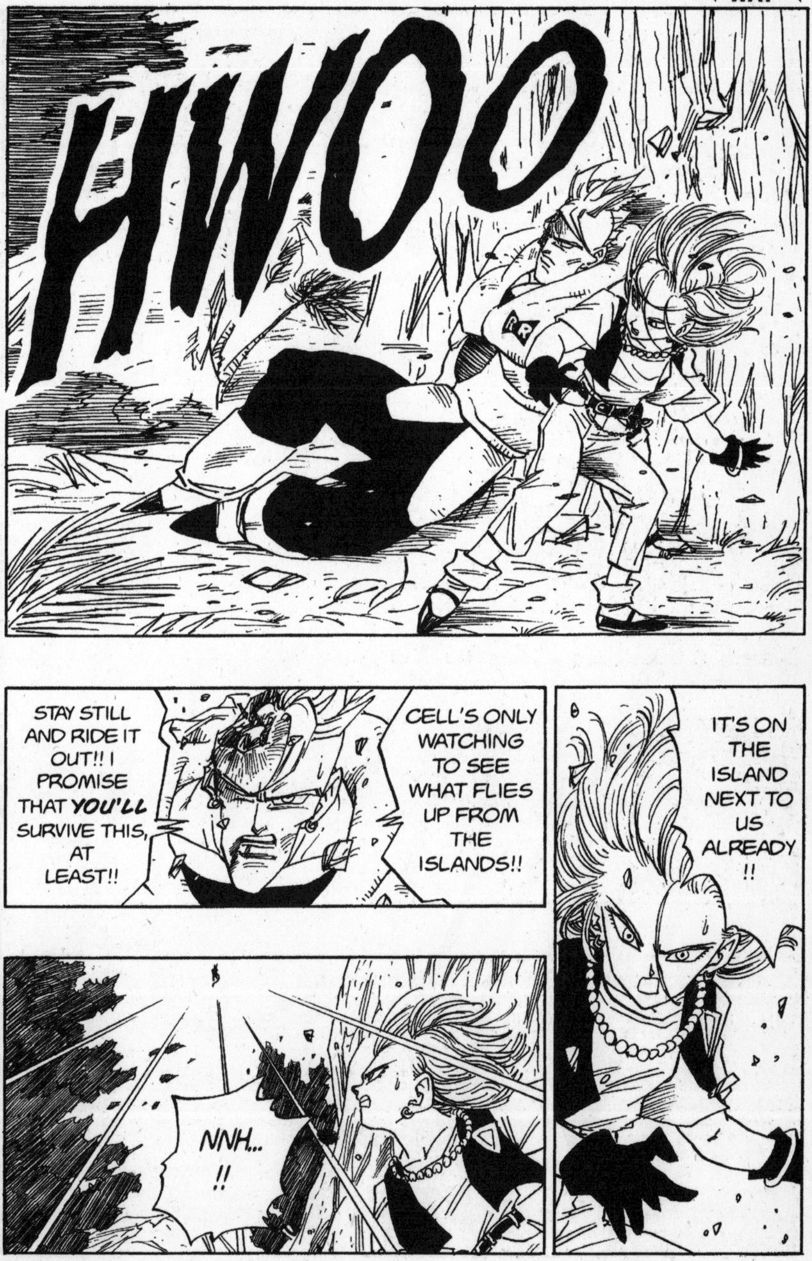

HWOO
IT'S ON THE ISLAND NEXT TO US ALREADY !!
CELL'S ONLY WATCHING TO SEE WHAT FLIES UP FROM THE ISLANDS!!
STAY STILL AND RIDE IT OUT!! I PROMISE THAT ***YOU'LL*** SURVIVE THIS, AT LEAST!!
NNH... !!

READ THIS WAY

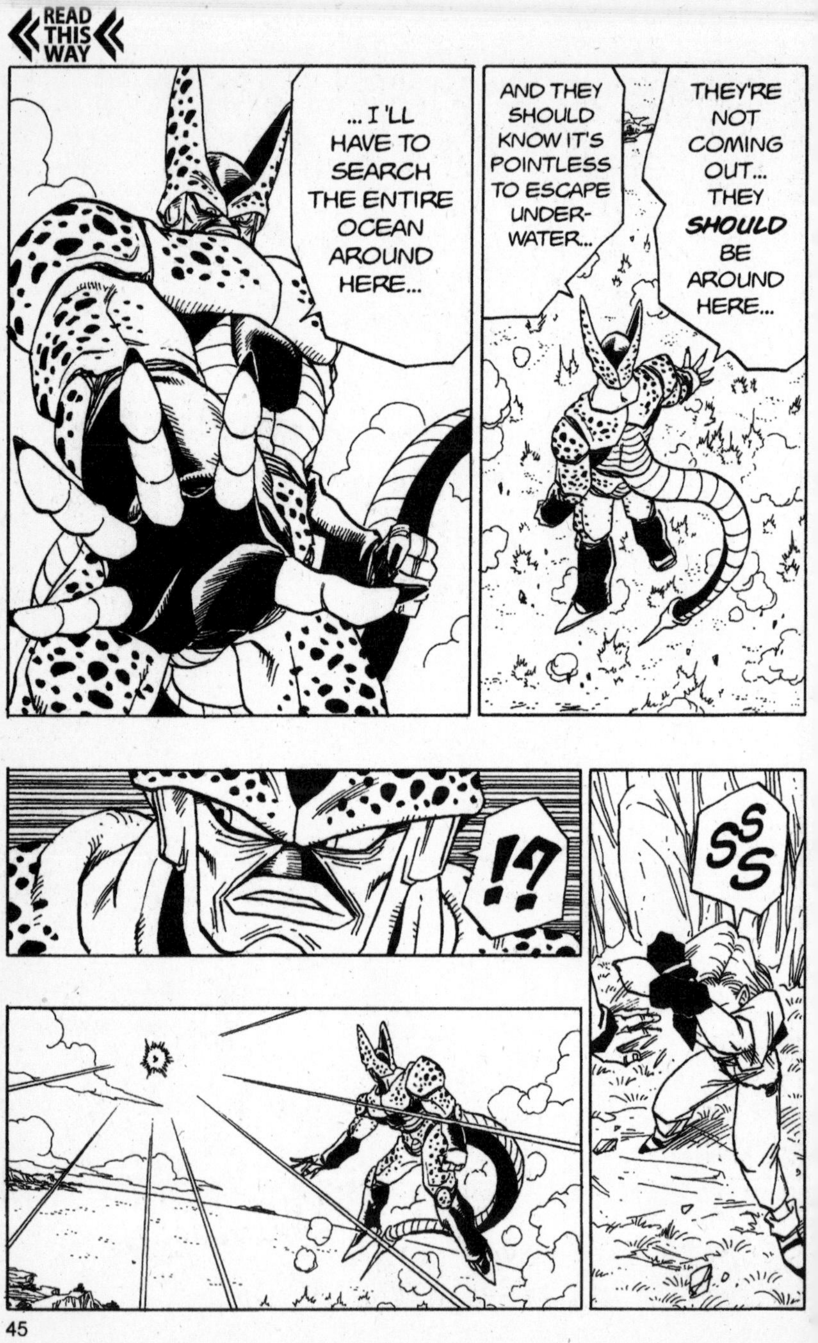

THEY'RE NOT COMING OUT... THEY SHOULD BE AROUND HERE...
AND THEY SHOULD KNOW IT'S POINTLESS TO ESCAPE UNDER-WATER...
... I'LL HAVE TO SEARCH THE ENTIRE OCEAN AROUND HERE...
SSS
!?

READ THIS WAY

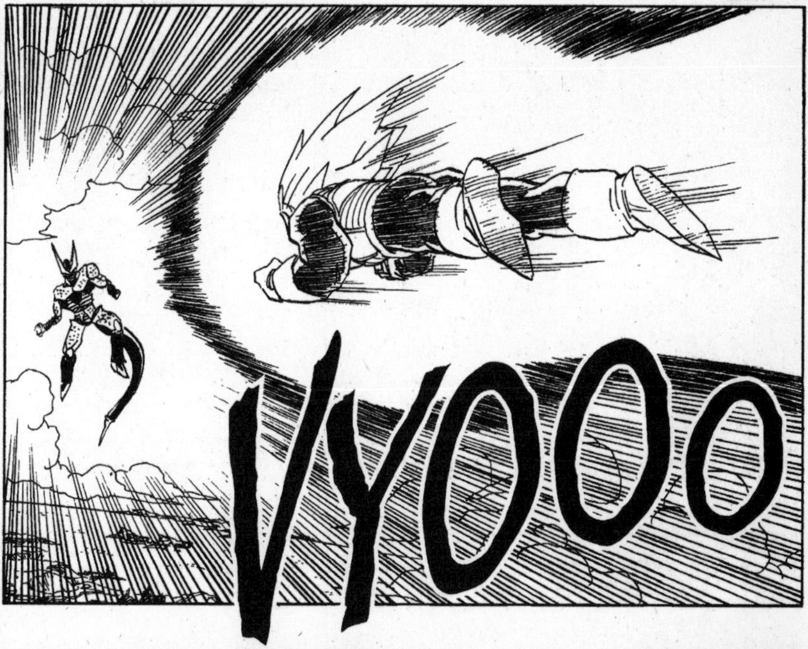

VYOOO

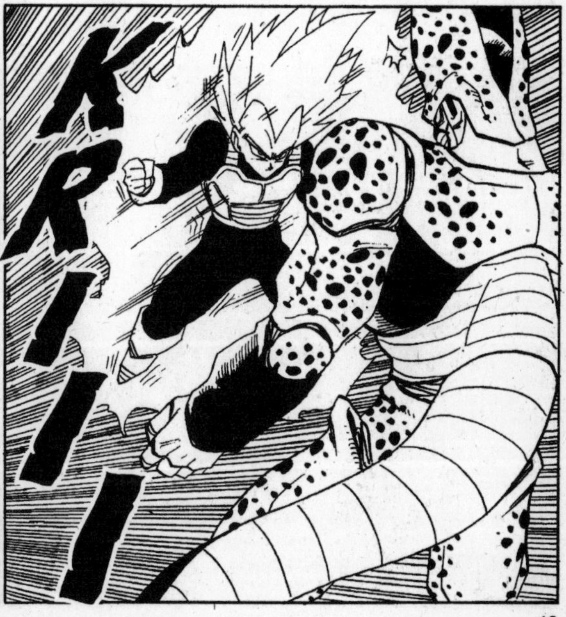

KRIII

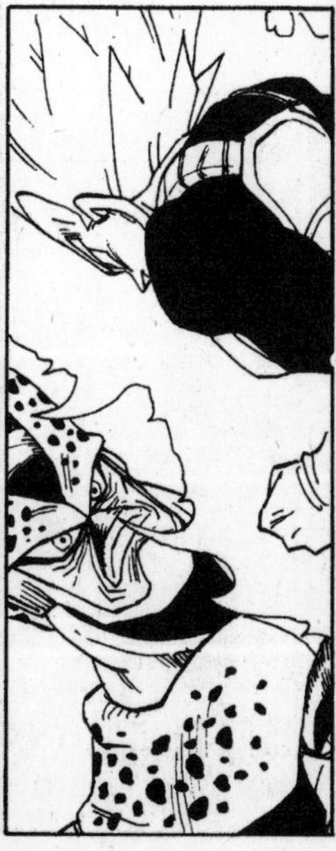

READ THIS WAY

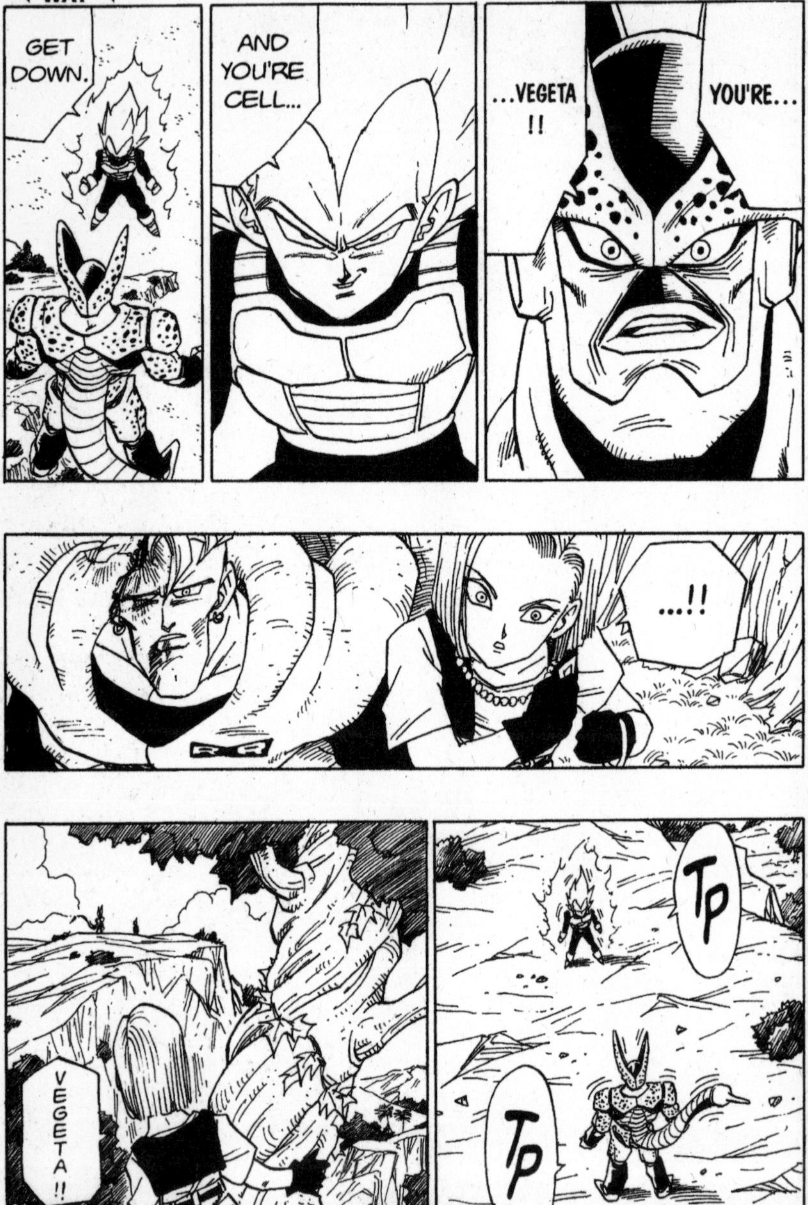
YOU'RE...
...VEGETA !!
AND YOU'RE CELL...
GET DOWN.
...!!
TP
TP
VEGETA!!

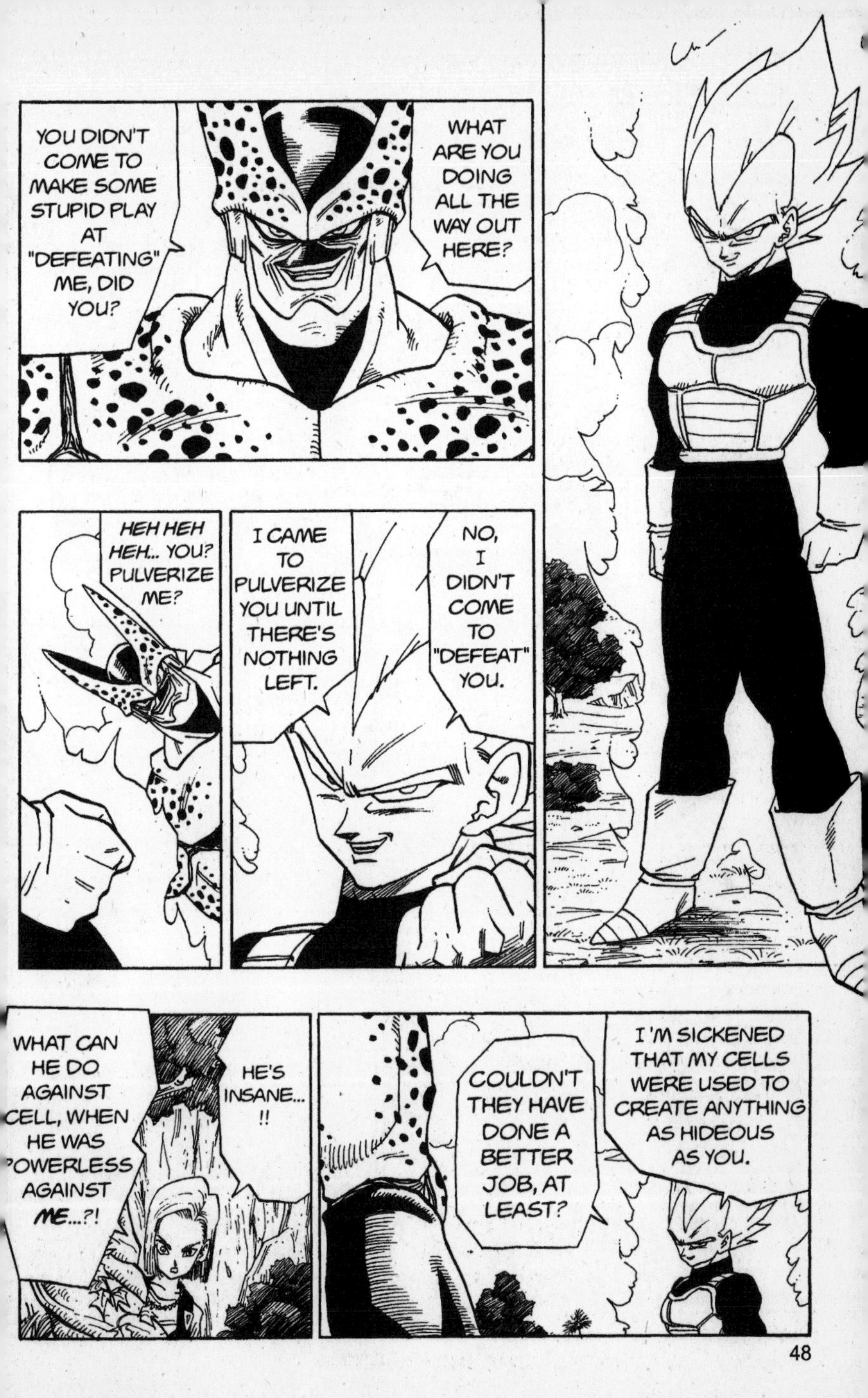
WHAT ARE YOU DOING ALL THE WAY OUT HERE?
YOU DIDN'T COME TO MAKE SOME STUPID PLAY AT "DEFEATING" ME, DID YOU?
NO, I DIDN'T COME TO "DEFEAT" YOU.
I CAME TO PULVERIZE YOU UNTIL THERE'S NOTHING LEFT.
HEH HEH HEH... YOU? PULVERIZE ME?
I'M SICKENED THAT MY CELLS WERE USED TO CREATE ANYTHING AS HIDEOUS AS YOU.
COULDN'T THEY HAVE DONE A BETTER JOB, AT LEAST?
HE'S INSANE... !!
WHAT CAN HE DO AGAINST CELL, WHEN HE WAS POWERLESS AGAINST *ME*...?!

READ THIS WAY

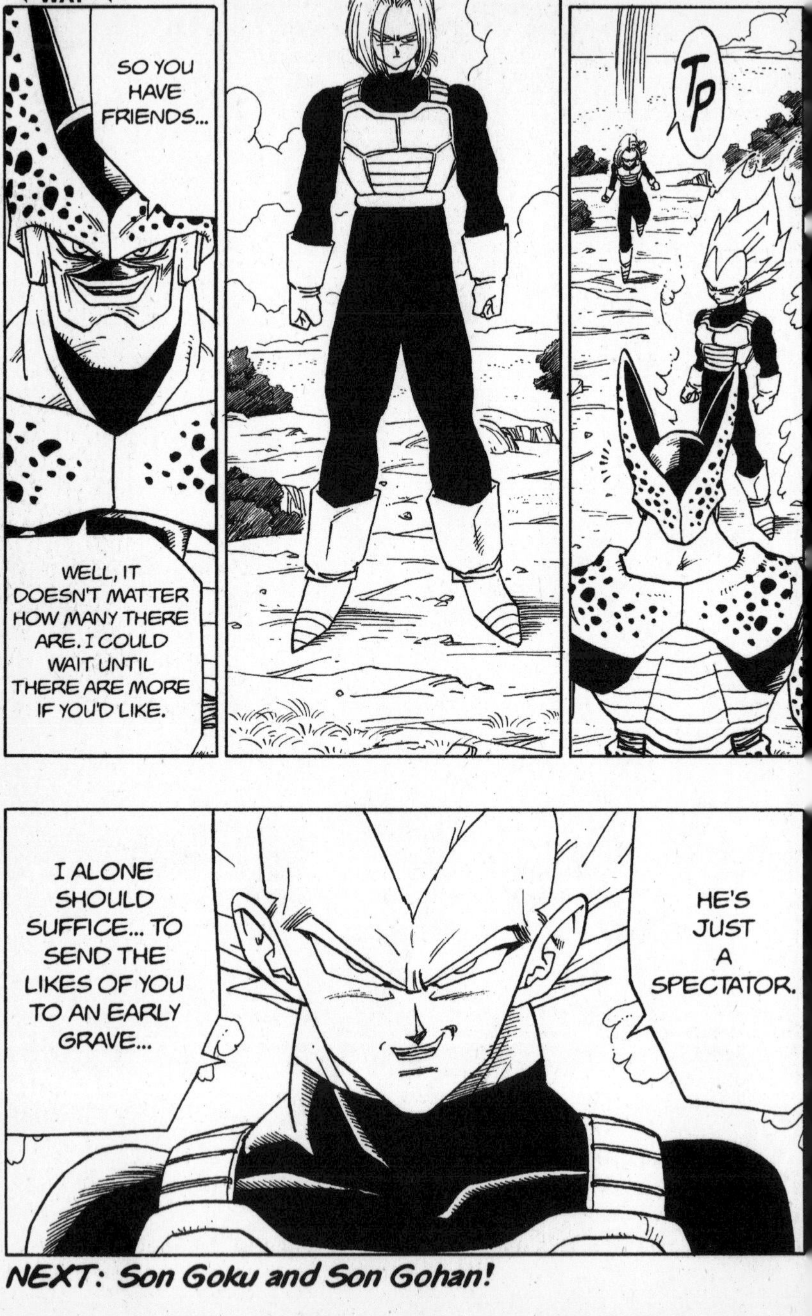
Tp
SO YOU HAVE FRIENDS...
WELL, IT DOESN'T MATTER HOW MANY THERE ARE. I COULD WAIT UNTIL THERE ARE MORE IF YOU'D LIKE.
HE'S JUST A SPECTATOR.
I ALONE SHOULD SUFFICE... TO SEND THE LIKES OF YOU TO AN EARLY GRAVE...

***NEXT*: Son Goku and Son Gohan!**

DBZ:183 • Beyond the Super Saiyan

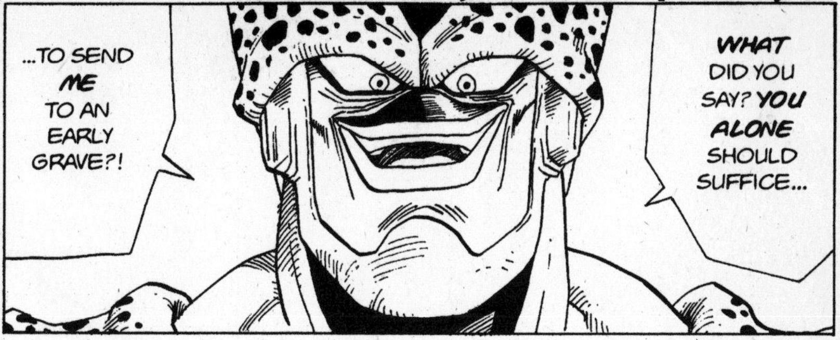
WHAT DID YOU SAY? YOU ALONE SHOULD SUFFICE...
...TO SEND ME TO AN EARLY GRAVE?!

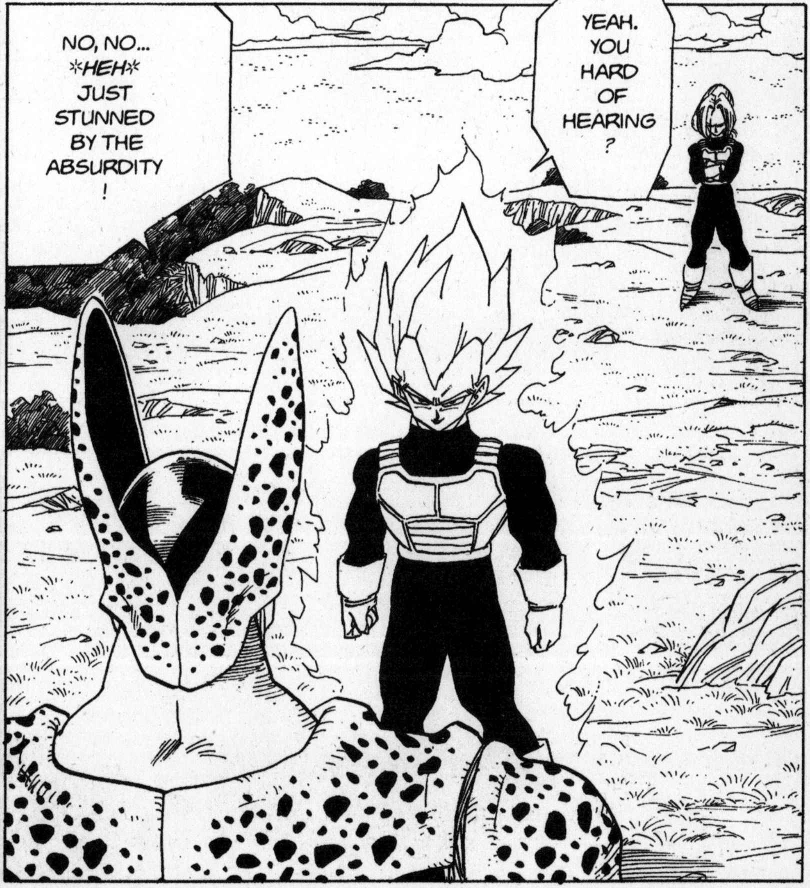
YEAH. YOU HARD OF HEARING?
NO, NO... *HEH* JUST STUNNED BY THE ABSURDITY!

READ THIS WAY

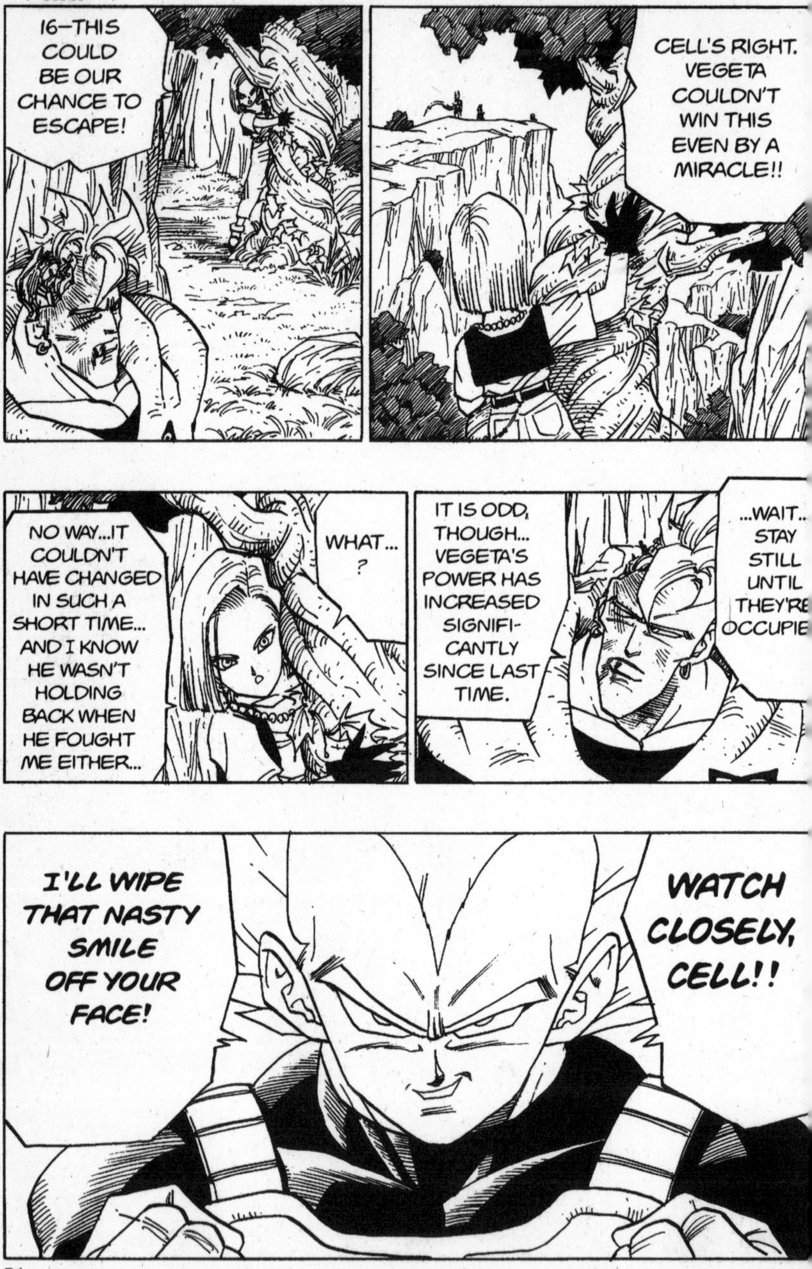
CELL'S RIGHT. VEGETA COULDN'T WIN THIS EVEN BY A MIRACLE!!
16—THIS COULD BE OUR CHANCE TO ESCAPE!
...WAIT... STAY STILL UNTIL THEY'RE OCCUPIE
IT IS ODD, THOUGH... VEGETA'S POWER HAS INCREASED SIGNIFI-CANTLY SINCE LAST TIME.
WHAT...?
NO WAY...IT COULDN'T HAVE CHANGED IN SUCH A SHORT TIME... AND I KNOW HE WASN'T HOLDING BACK WHEN HE FOUGHT ME EITHER...
WATCH CLOSELY, CELL!!
I'LL WIPE THAT NASTY SMILE OFF YOUR FACE!

READ THIS WAY

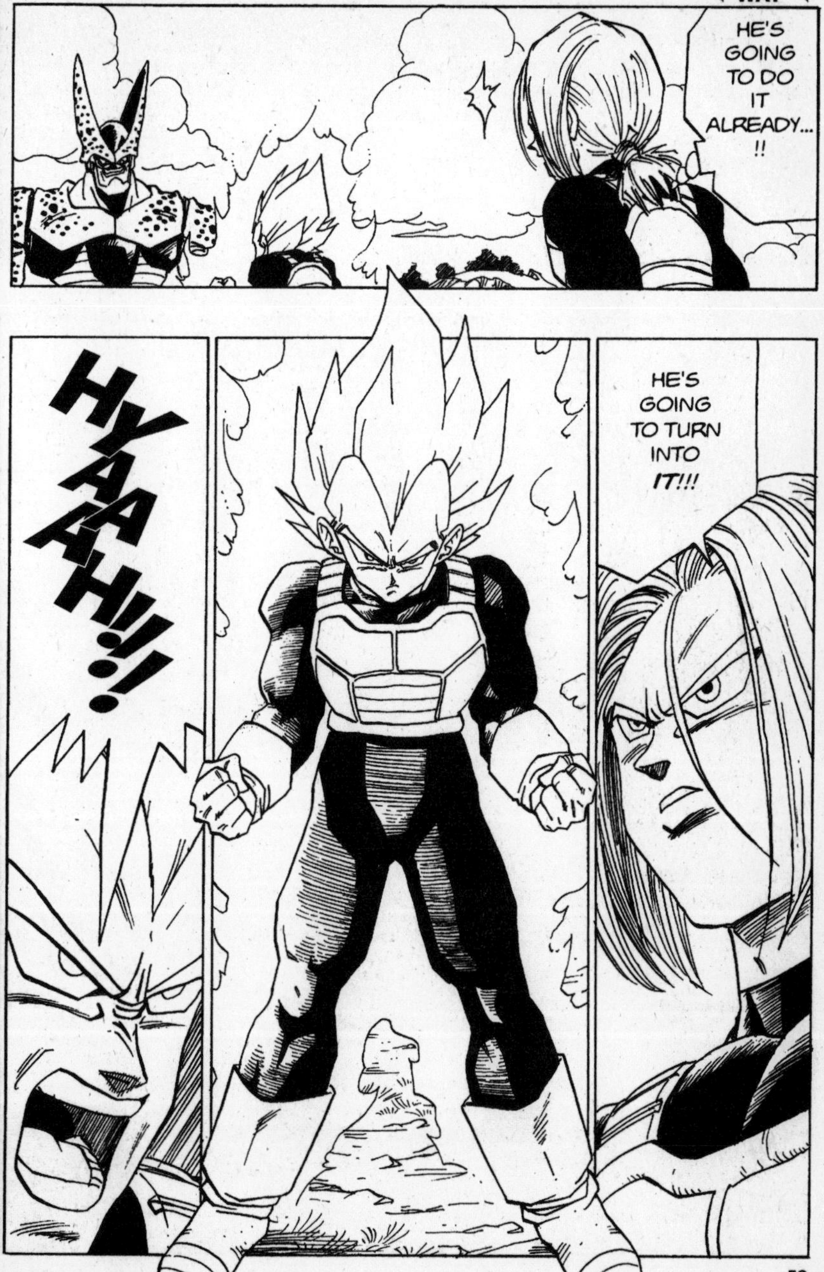
HE'S GOING TO DO IT ALREADY...!!
HE'S GOING TO TURN INTO *IT*!!!
HYAAAH!!!!!

READ THIS WAY

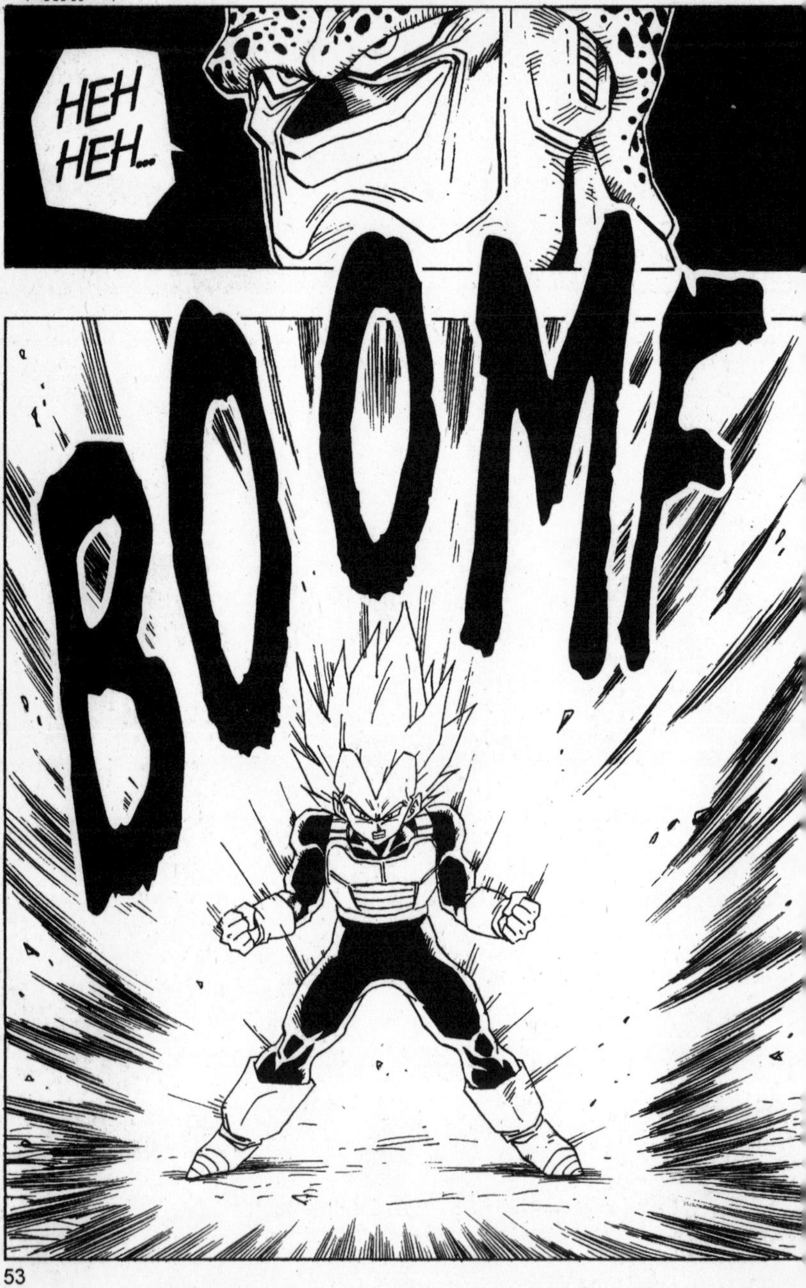
HEH HEH...
BOOMF

READ THIS WAY

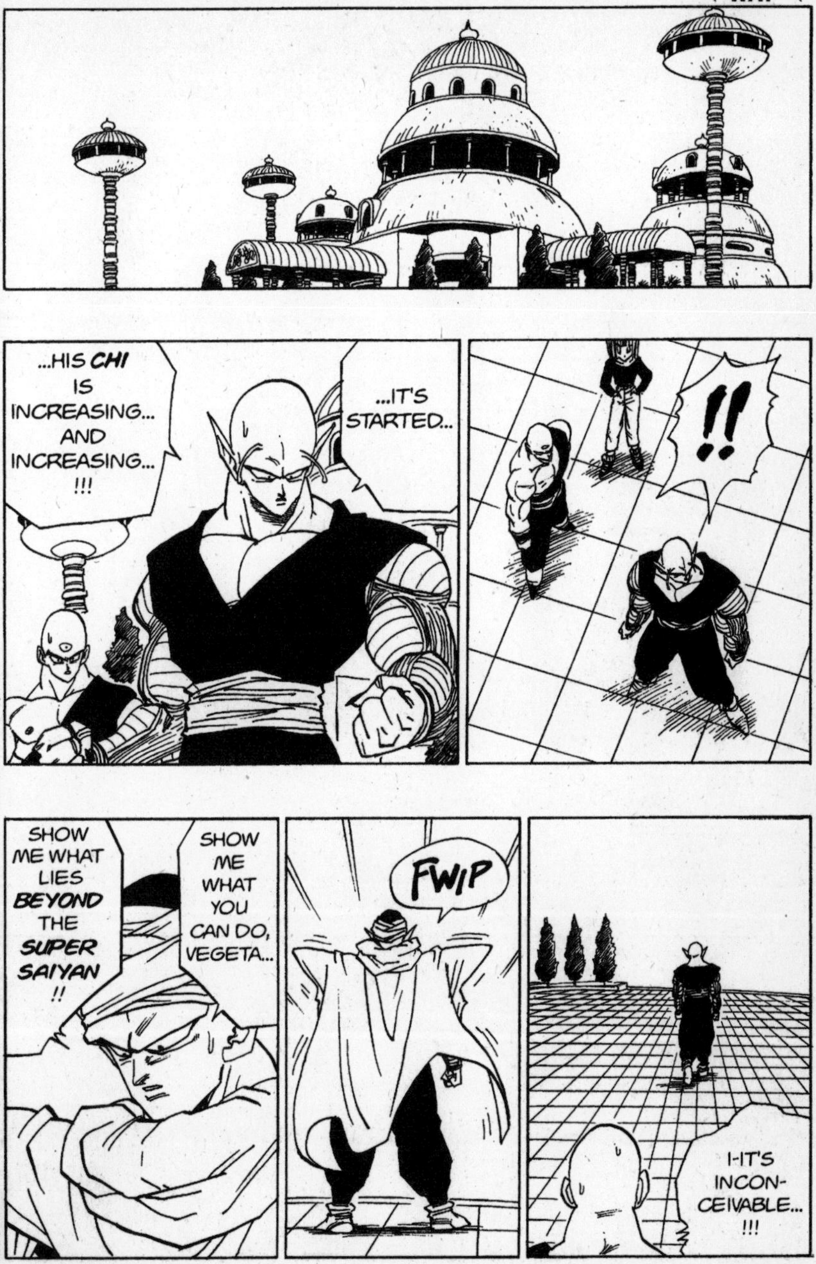

!!
...IT'S STARTED...
...HIS **CHI** IS INCREASING... AND INCREASING... !!!
I-IT'S INCONCEIVABLE... !!!
FWIP
SHOW ME WHAT YOU CAN DO, VEGETA...
SHOW ME WHAT LIES **BEYOND** THE **SUPER SAIYAN** !!

READ THIS WAY

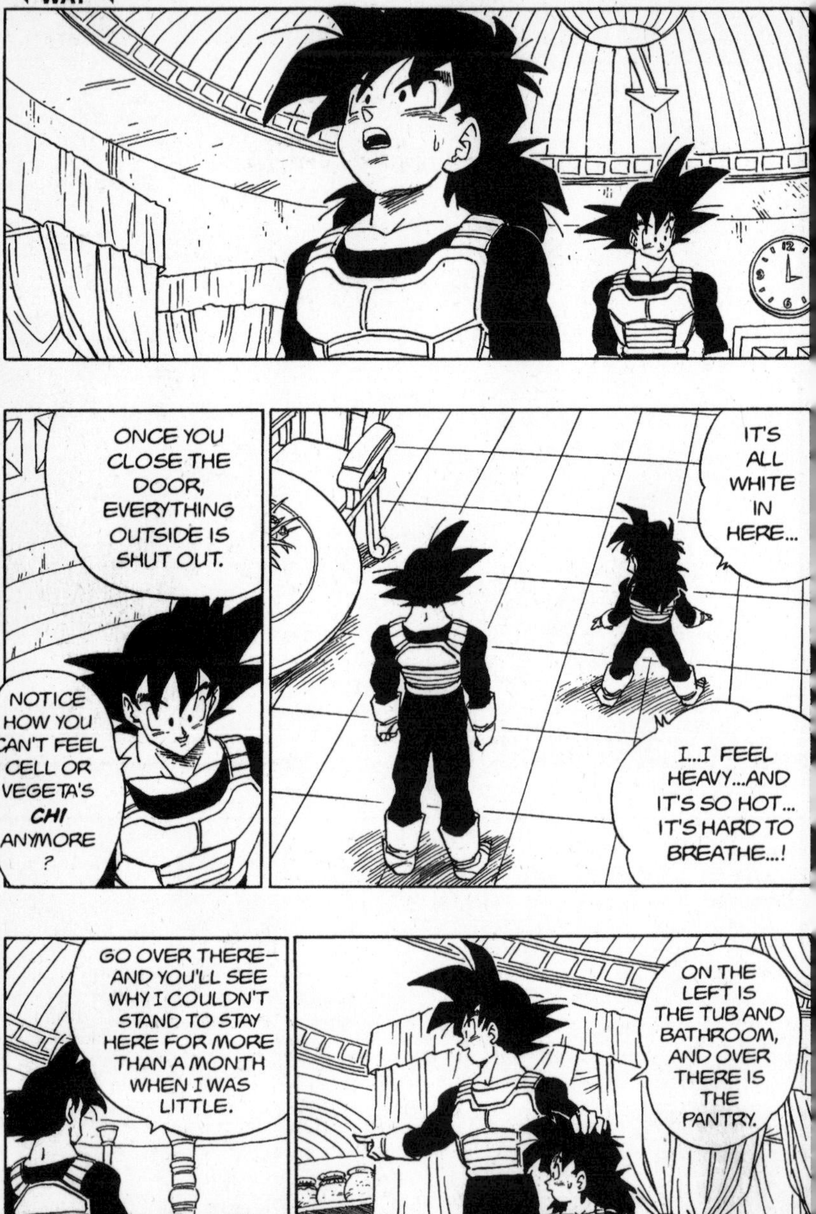

IT'S ALL WHITE IN HERE...
I...I FEEL HEAVY...AND IT'S SO HOT... IT'S HARD TO BREATHE...!
ONCE YOU CLOSE THE DOOR, EVERYTHING OUTSIDE IS SHUT OUT.
NOTICE HOW YOU CAN'T FEEL CELL OR VEGETA'S *CHI* ANYMORE ?
ON THE LEFT IS THE TUB AND BATHROOM, AND OVER THERE IS THE PANTRY.
GO OVER THERE— AND YOU'LL SEE WHY I COULDN'T STAND TO STAY HERE FOR MORE THAN A MONTH WHEN I WAS LITTLE.

READ THIS WAY

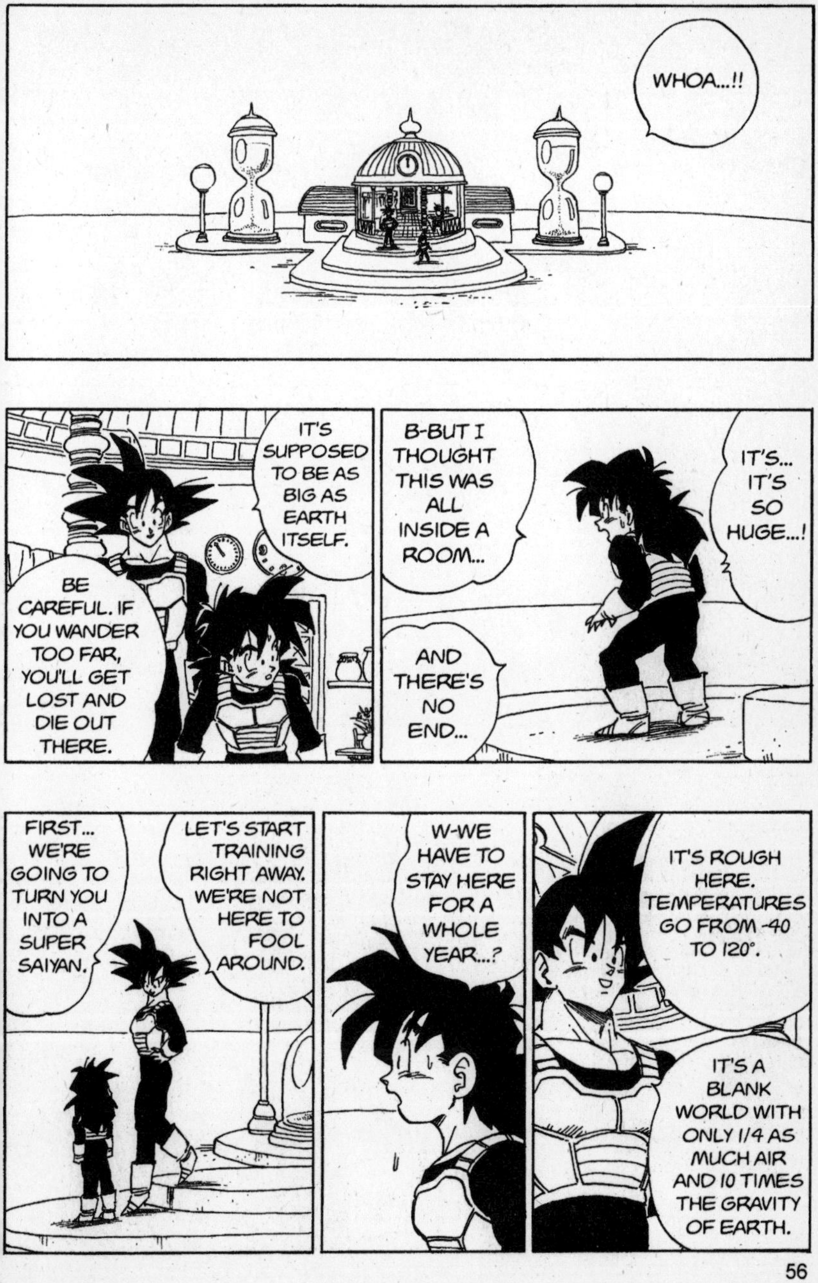
WHOA...!!
IT'S... IT'S SO HUGE...!
B-BUT I THOUGHT THIS WAS ALL INSIDE A ROOM...
AND THERE'S NO END...
IT'S SUPPOSED TO BE AS BIG AS EARTH ITSELF.
BE CAREFUL. IF YOU WANDER TOO FAR, YOU'LL GET LOST AND DIE OUT THERE.
IT'S ROUGH HERE. TEMPERATURES GO FROM -40 TO 120°.
IT'S A BLANK WORLD WITH ONLY 1/4 AS MUCH AIR AND 10 TIMES THE GRAVITY OF EARTH.
W-WE HAVE TO STAY HERE FOR A WHOLE YEAR...?
LET'S START TRAINING RIGHT AWAY. WE'RE NOT HERE TO FOOL AROUND.
FIRST... WE'RE GOING TO TURN YOU INTO A SUPER SAIYAN.

READ THIS WAY

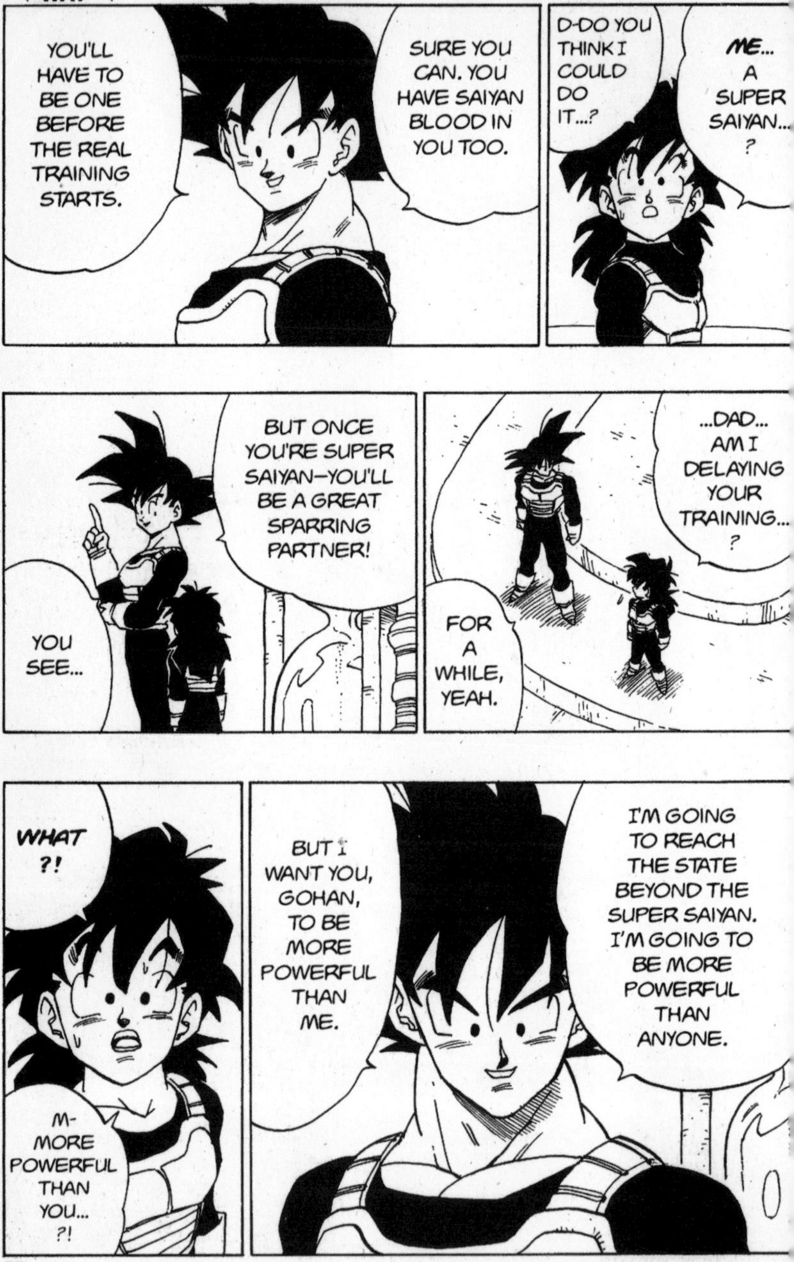
ME... A SUPER SAIYAN...?
D-DO YOU THINK I COULD DO IT...?
SURE YOU CAN. YOU HAVE SAIYAN BLOOD IN YOU TOO.
YOU'LL HAVE TO BE ONE BEFORE THE REAL TRAINING STARTS.
...DAD... AM I DELAYING YOUR TRAINING...?
FOR A WHILE, YEAH.
BUT ONCE YOU'RE SUPER SAIYAN—YOU'LL BE A GREAT SPARRING PARTNER!
YOU SEE...
I'M GOING TO REACH THE STATE BEYOND THE SUPER SAIYAN. I'M GOING TO BE MORE POWERFUL THAN ANYONE.
BUT I WANT YOU, GOHAN, TO BE MORE POWERFUL THAN ME.
WHAT?!
M-MORE POWERFUL THAN YOU...?!

READ THIS WAY

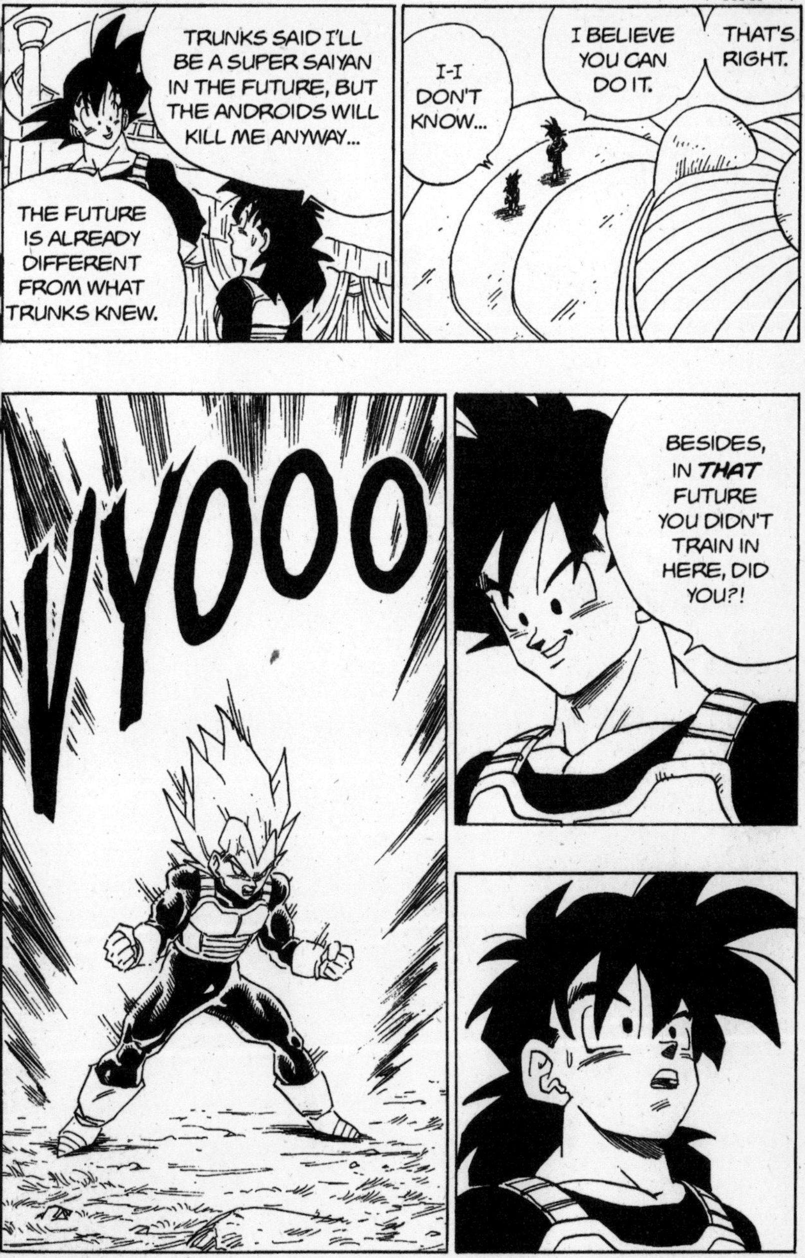
THAT'S RIGHT.
I BELIEVE YOU CAN DO IT.
I-I DON'T KNOW...
TRUNKS SAID I'LL BE A SUPER SAIYAN IN THE FUTURE, BUT THE ANDROIDS WILL KILL ME ANYWAY...
THE FUTURE IS ALREADY DIFFERENT FROM WHAT TRUNKS KNEW.
BESIDES, IN *THAT* FUTURE YOU DIDN'T TRAIN IN HERE, DID YOU?!
VYOOO

READ THIS WAY

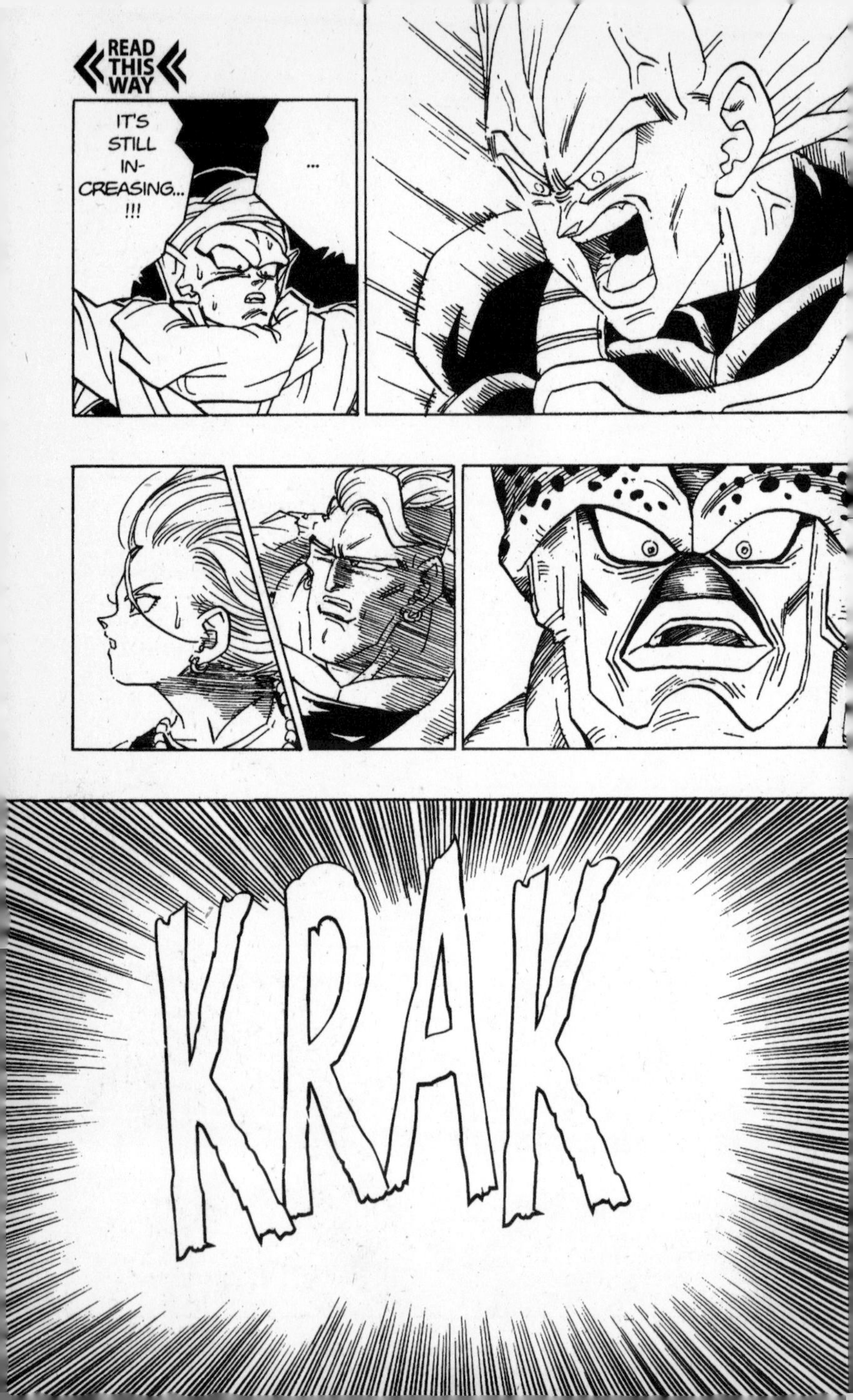
...
IT'S STILL IN-CREASING... !!!
KRAK

READ THIS WAY

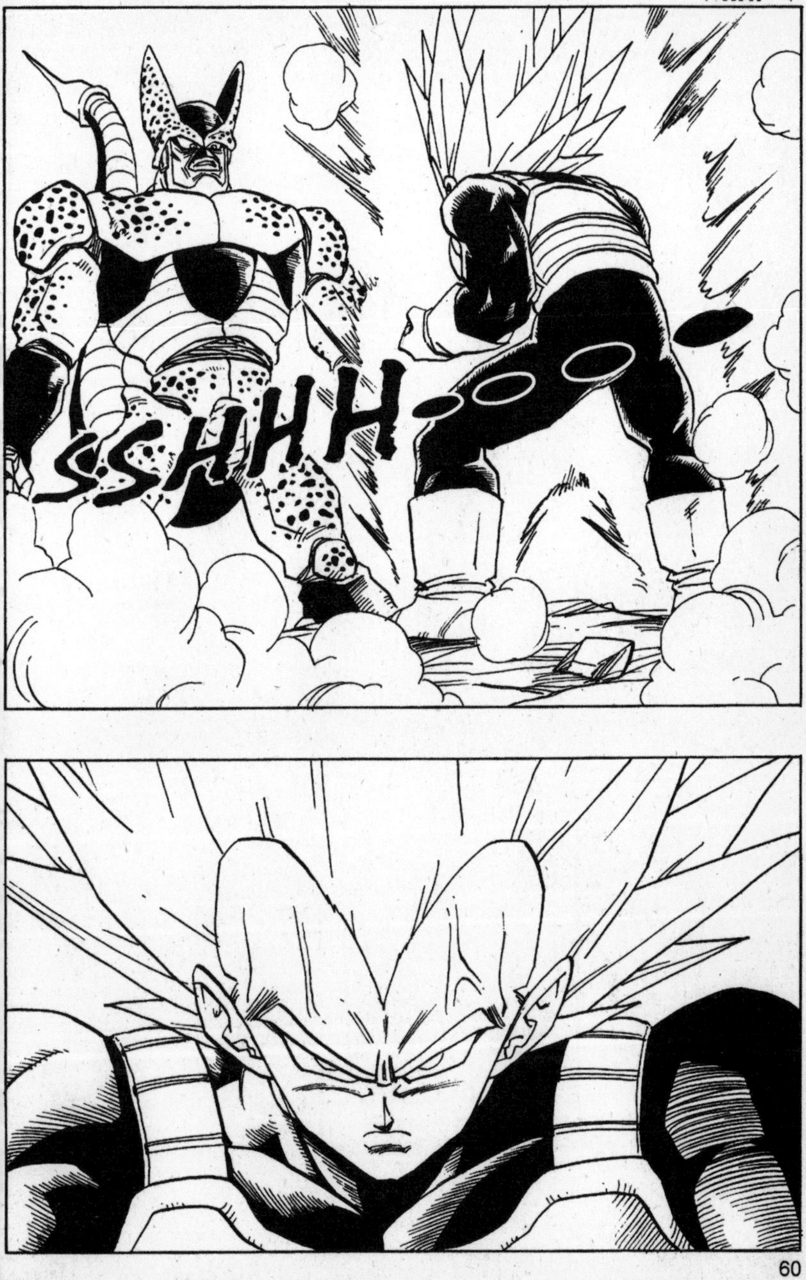
SSHHH-OOO

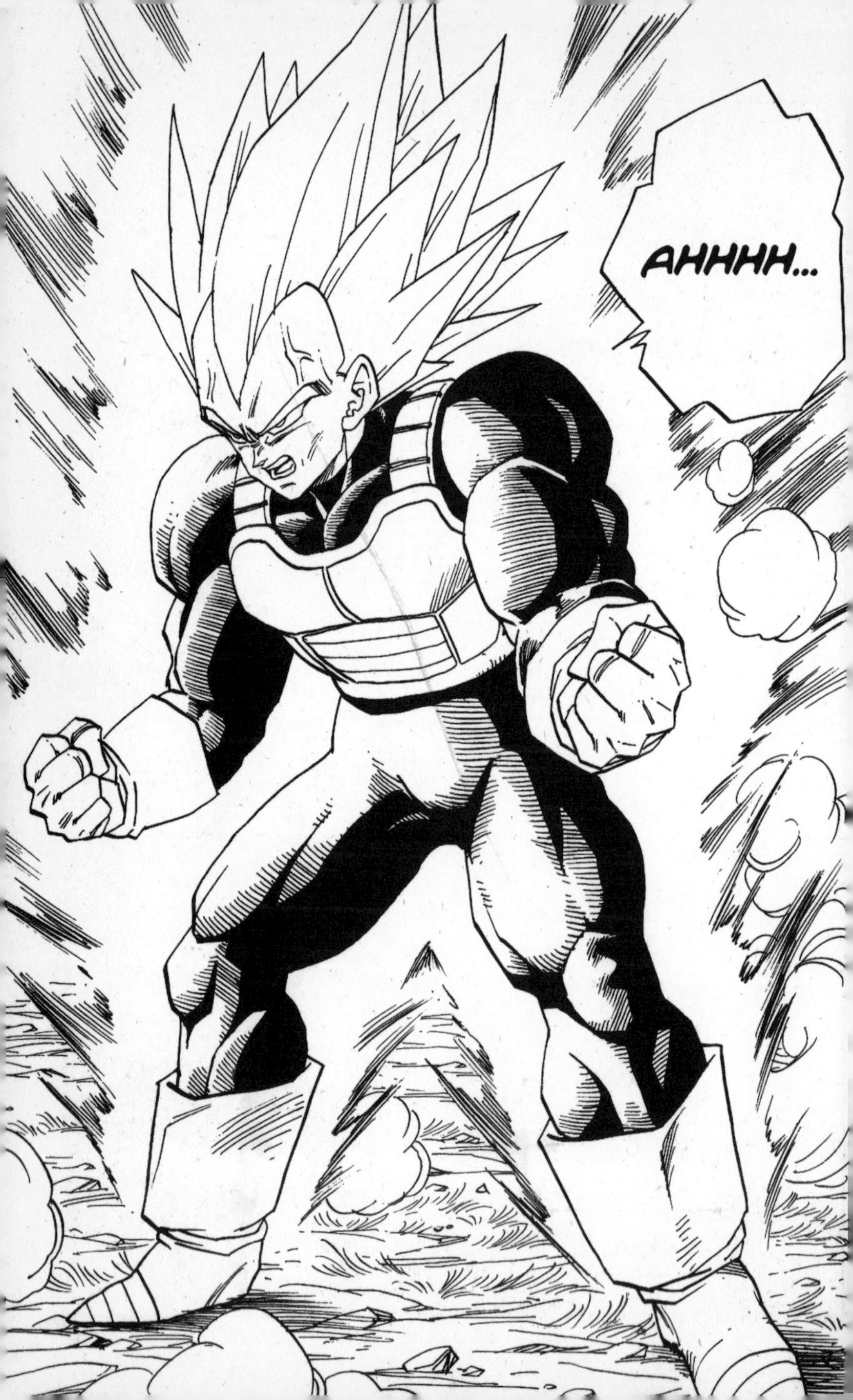
AHHHH...

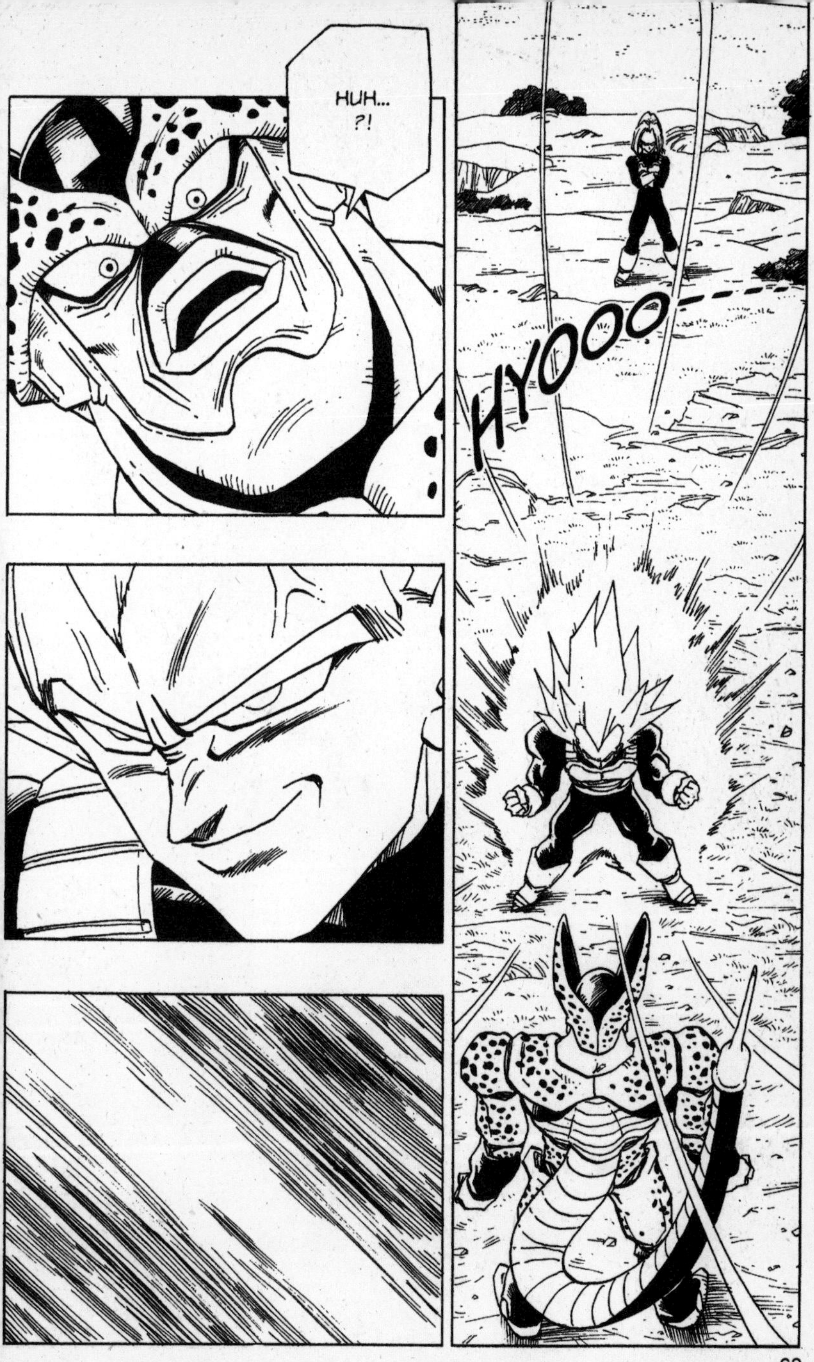
HYOOO
HUH... ?!

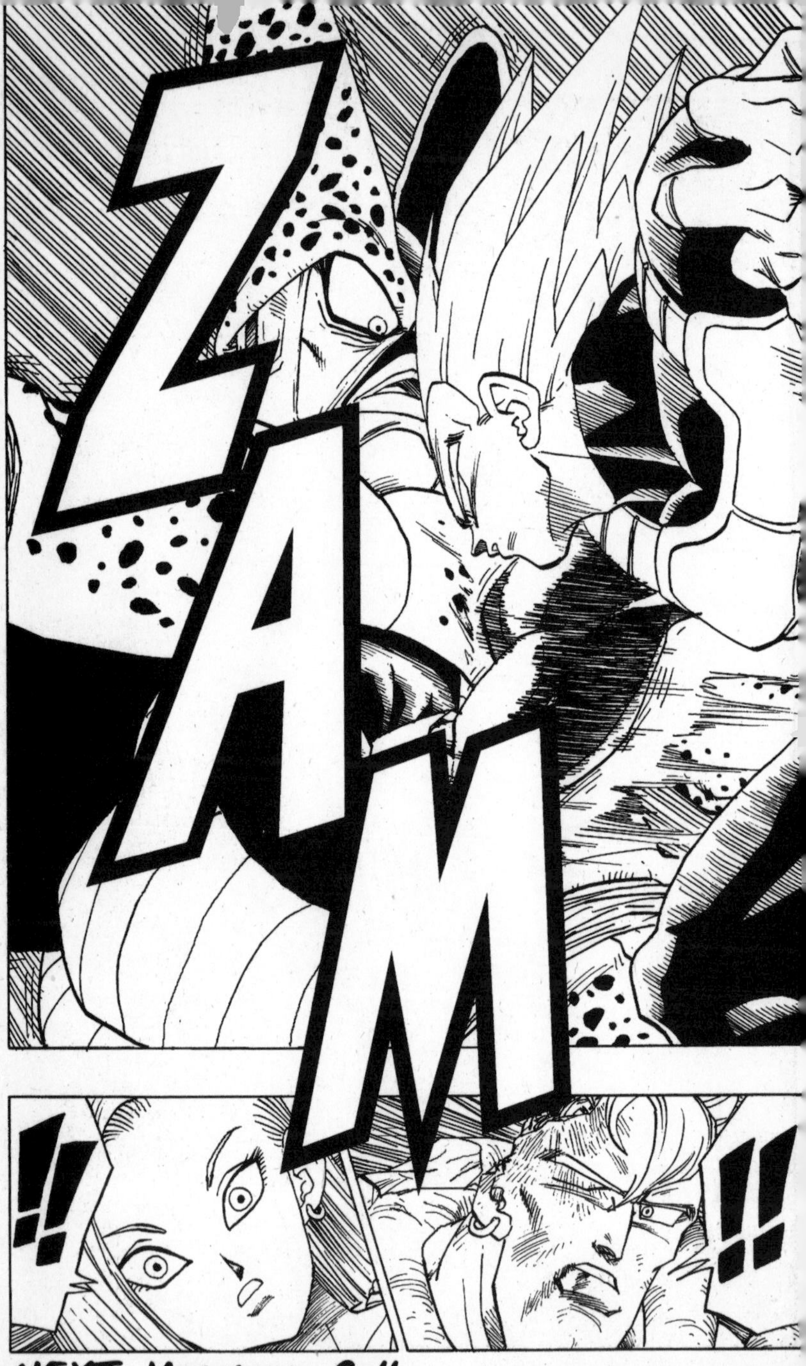
ZAM
!!
!!

NEXT: Vegeta vs. Cell

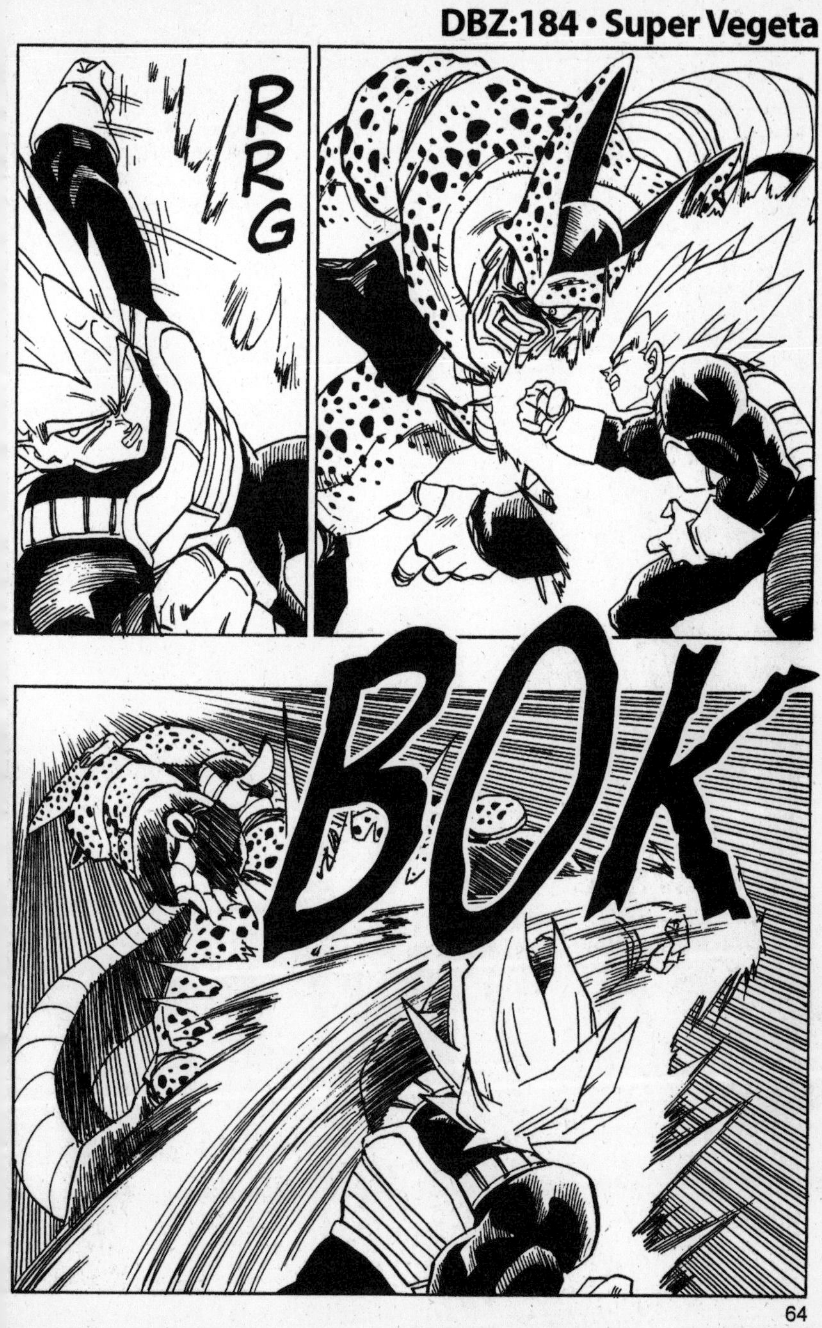
RRG
BOK

READ THIS WAY

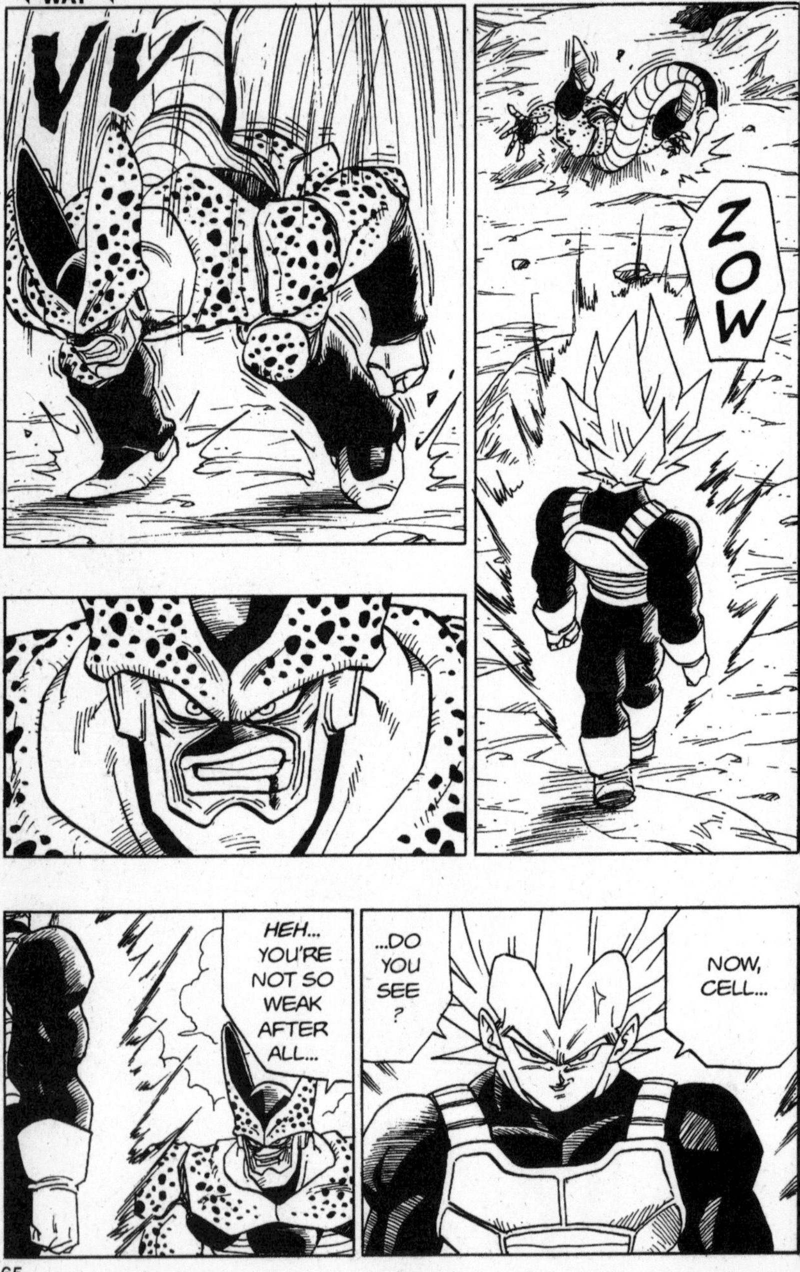
ZOW
VV
NOW, CELL...
...DO YOU SEE?
HEH... YOU'RE NOT SO WEAK AFTER ALL...

READ THIS WAY

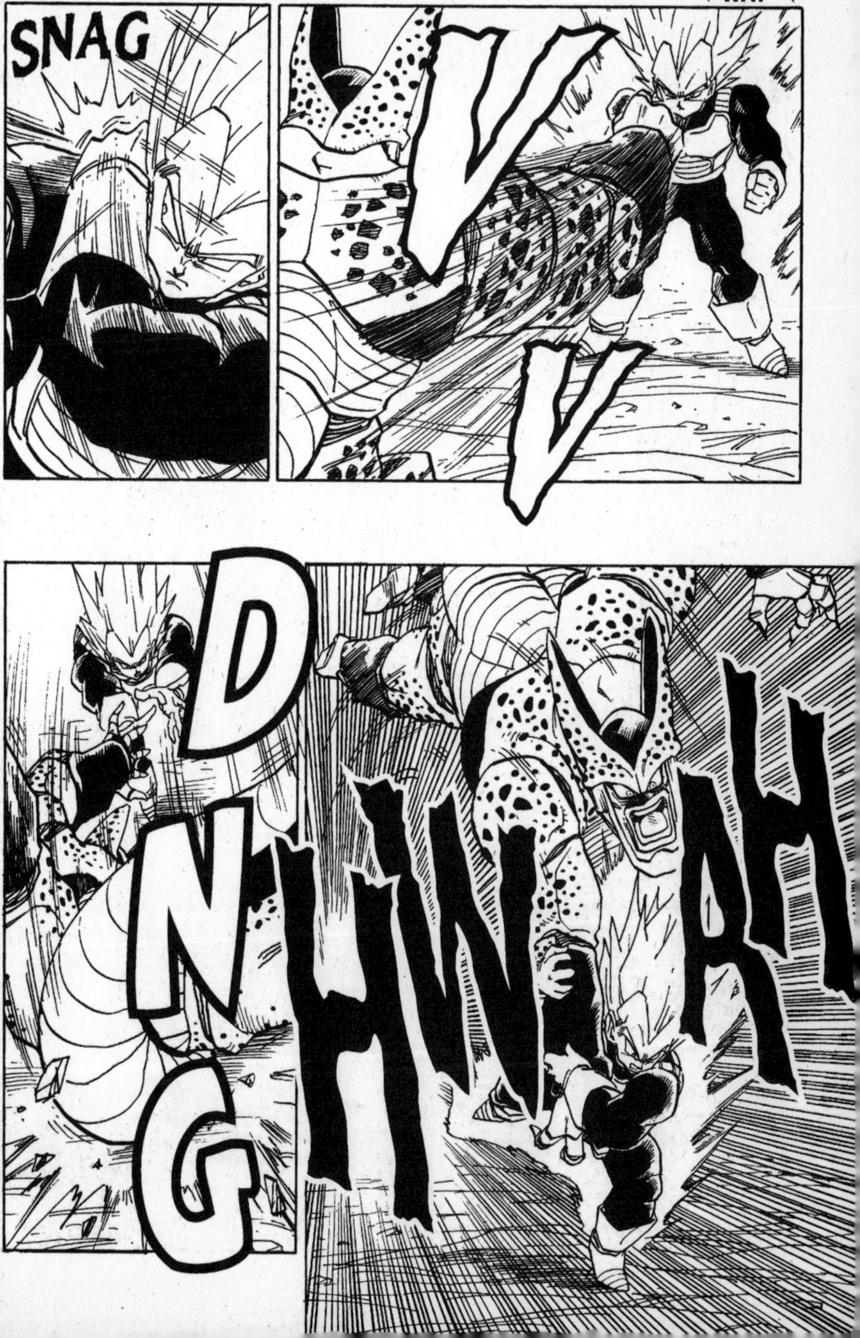
VV
SNAG
HNAH
DNG

READ THIS WAY

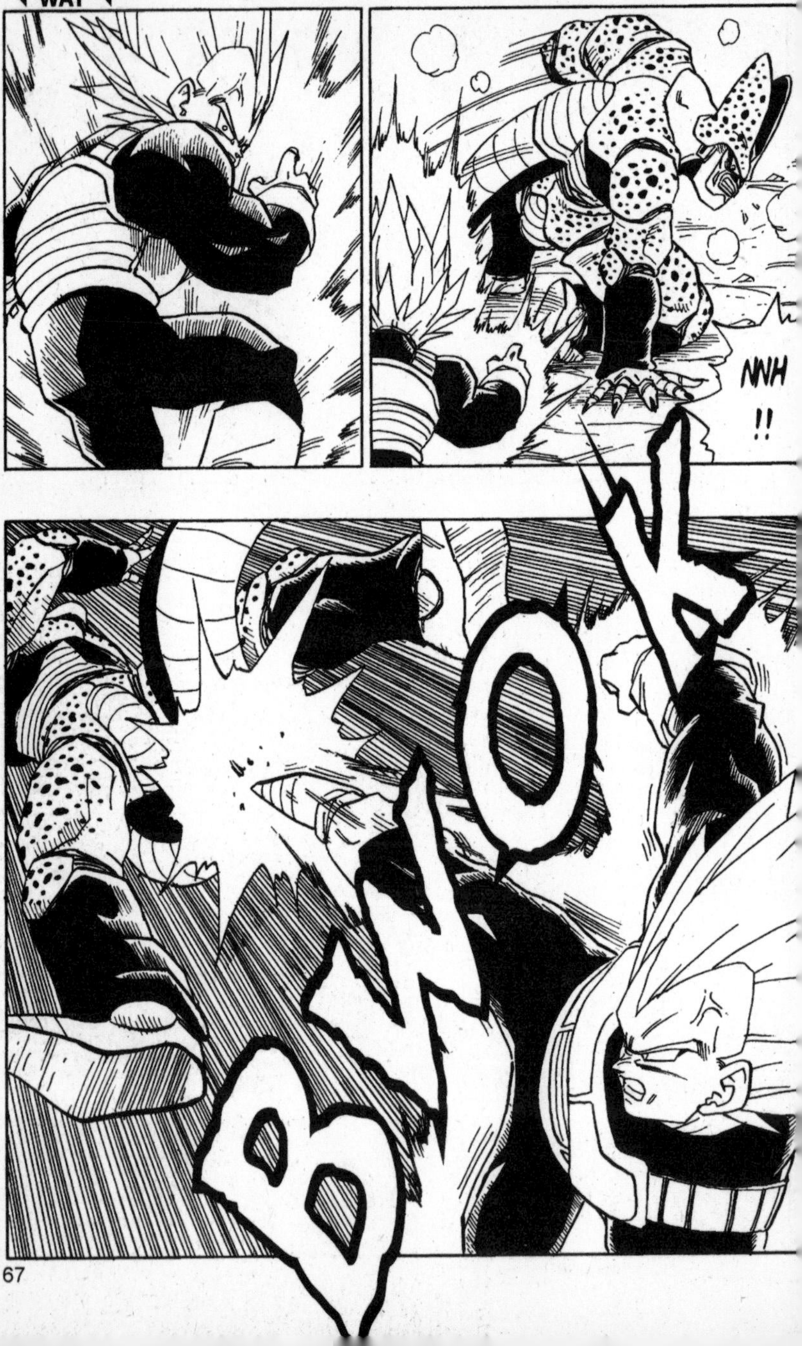
NNH !!
BWOK

READ THIS WAY

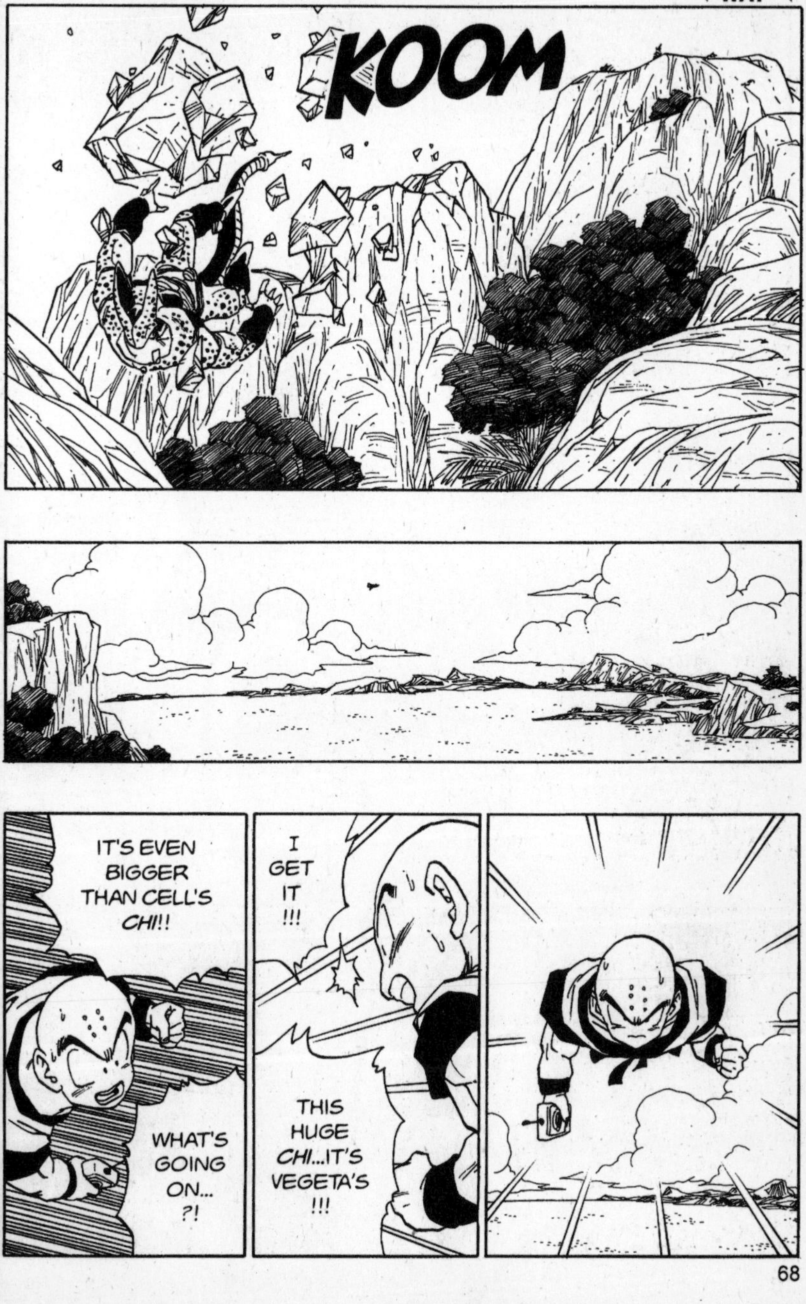
KOOM
I GET IT!!!
THIS HUGE *CHI*...IT'S VEGETA'S!!!
IT'S EVEN BIGGER THAN CELL'S *CHI*!!
WHAT'S GOING ON...?!

READ THIS WAY

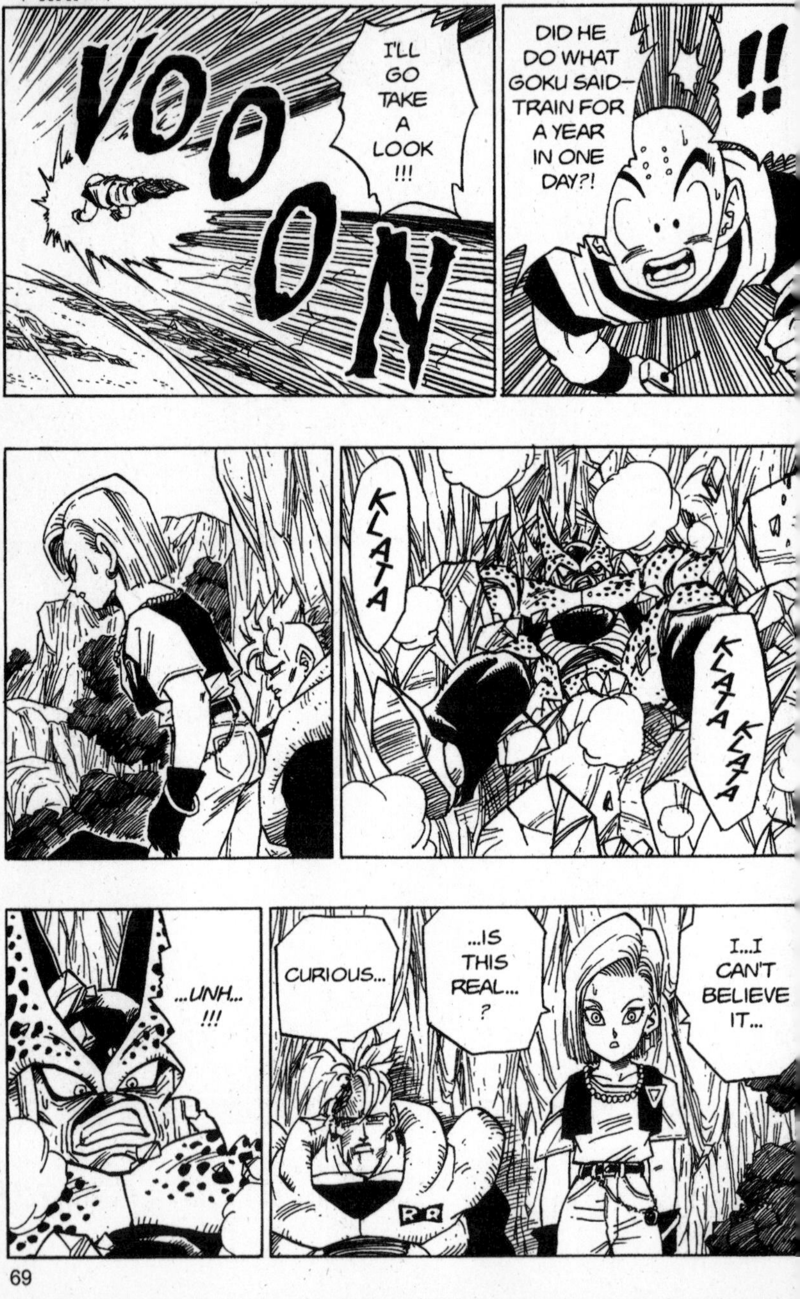

DID HE DO WHAT GOKU SAID— TRAIN FOR A YEAR IN ONE DAY?!
!!
I'LL GO TAKE A LOOK !!!
VOOOON
KLATA
KLATA
KLATA
I...I CAN'T BELIEVE IT...
...IS THIS REAL... ?
CURIOUS...
...UNH... !!!

READ THIS WAY

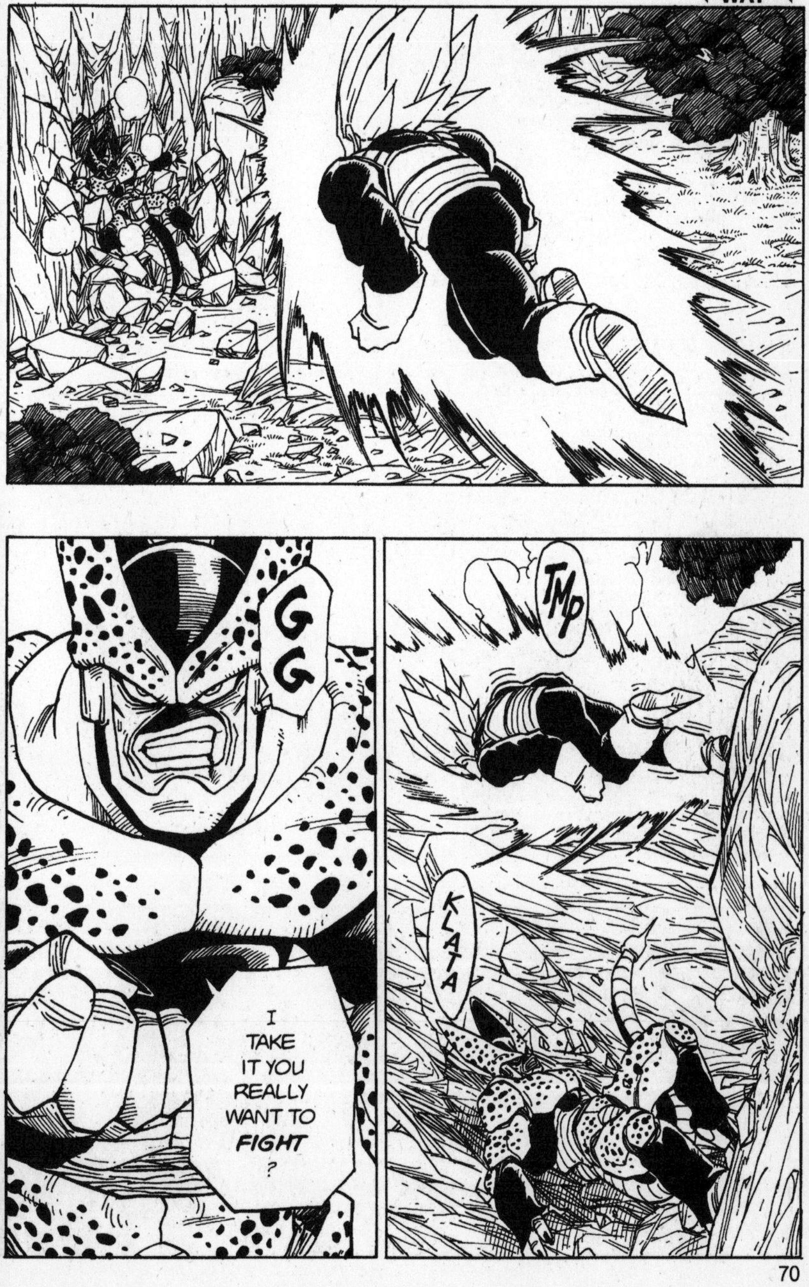
TMP
KLATA
GG
I TAKE IT YOU REALLY WANT TO *FIGHT* ?

READ THIS WAY

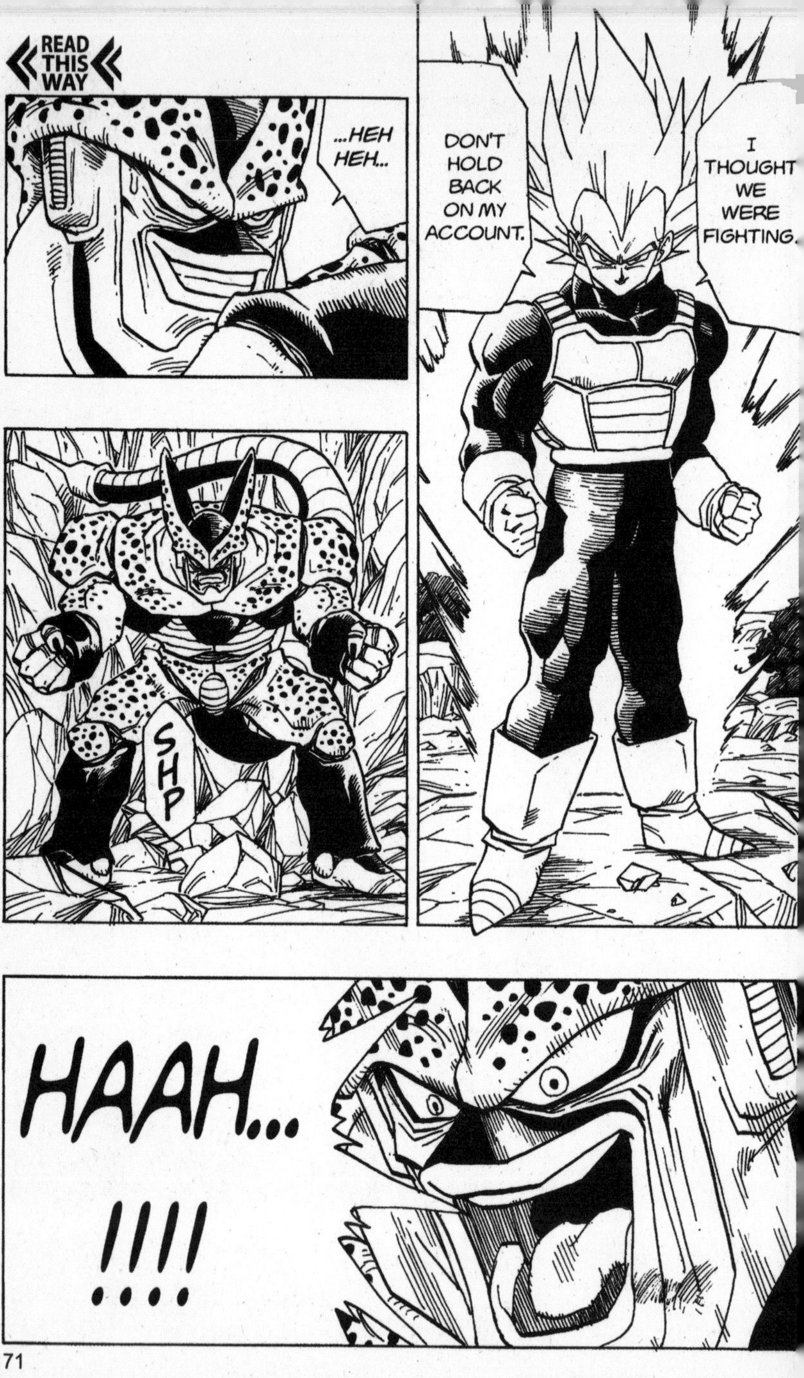

I THOUGHT WE WERE FIGHTING.
DON'T HOLD BACK ON MY ACCOUNT.
...HEH HEH...
SHP
HAAH... !!!!

READ THIS WAY

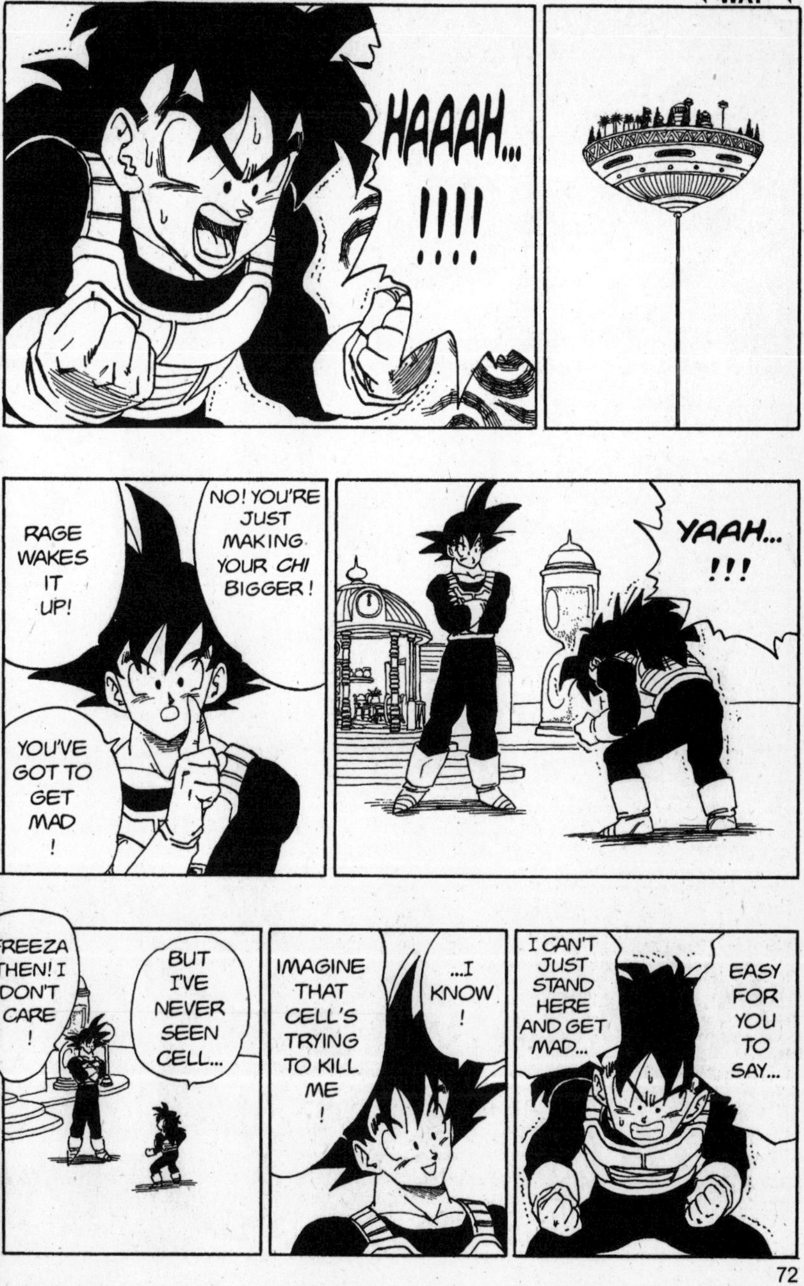

HAAAH... !!!!
YAAH... !!!
NO! YOU'RE JUST MAKING YOUR *CHI* BIGGER!
RAGE WAKES IT UP!
YOU'VE GOT TO GET MAD!
EASY FOR YOU TO SAY...
I CAN'T JUST STAND HERE AND GET MAD...
...I KNOW!
IMAGINE THAT CELL'S TRYING TO KILL ME!
BUT I'VE NEVER SEEN CELL...
FREEZA THEN! I DON'T CARE!

READ THIS WAY

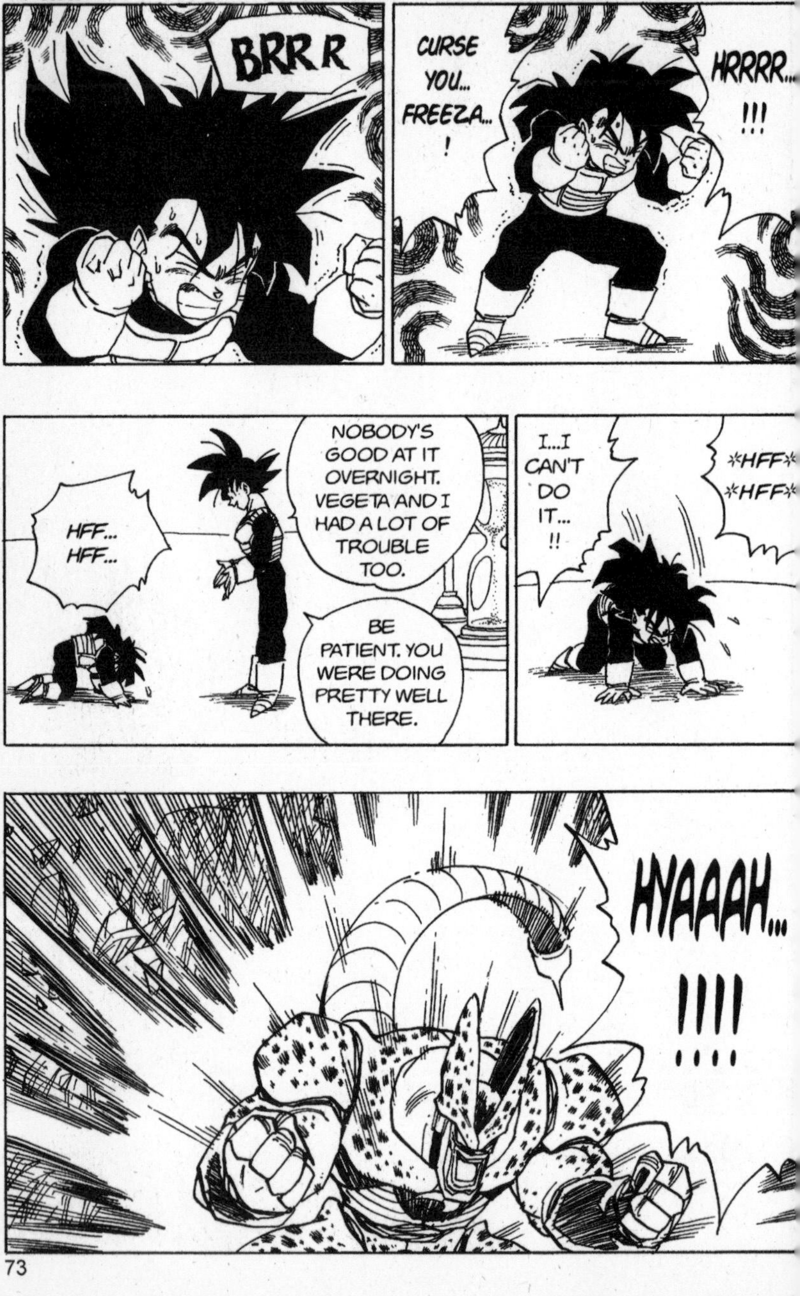

HRRRR... !!!
CURSE YOU... FREEZA... !
BRR R
HFF *HFF*
I...I CAN'T DO IT... !!
NOBODY'S GOOD AT IT OVERNIGHT. VEGETA AND I HAD A LOT OF TROUBLE TOO.
BE PATIENT. YOU WERE DOING PRETTY WELL THERE.
HFF... HFF...
HYAAAH... !!!! !!!!

READ THIS WAY

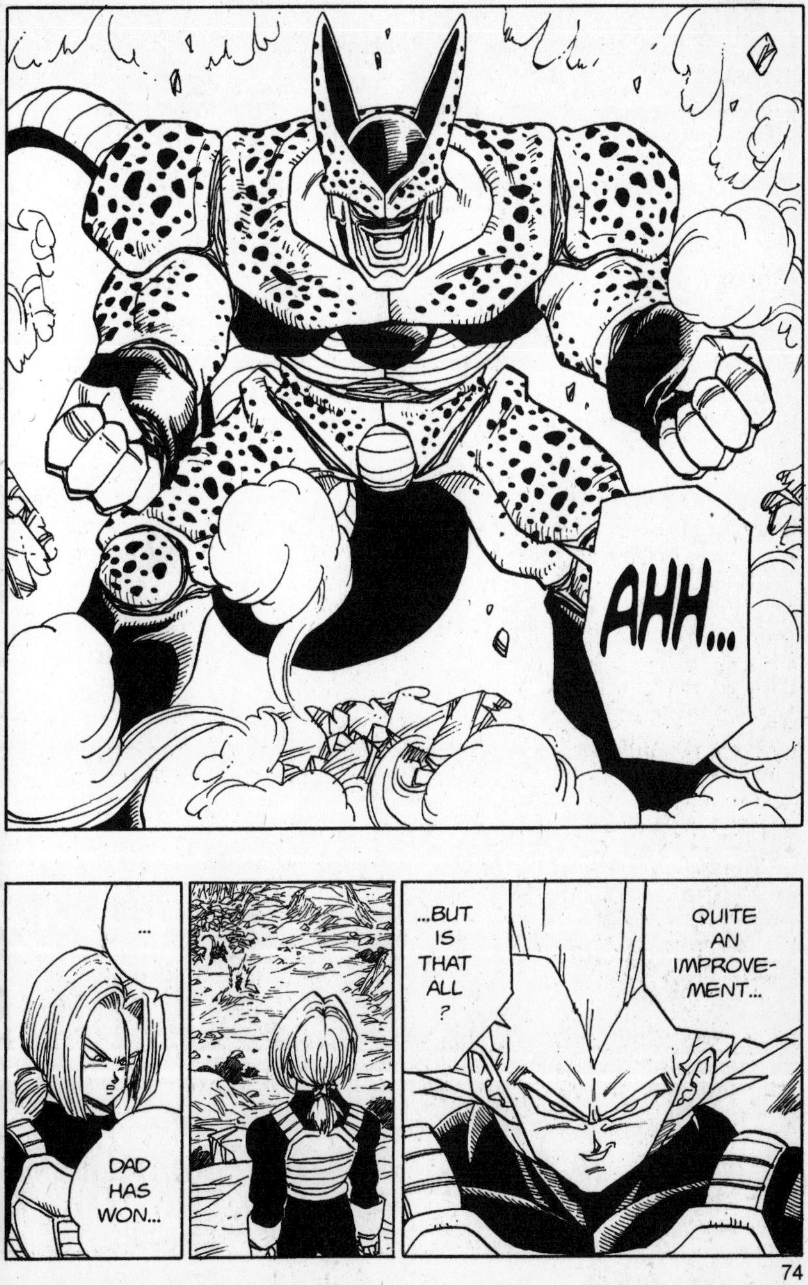
AHH...
QUITE AN IMPROVEMENT...
...BUT IS THAT ALL?
...
DAD HAS WON...

READ THIS WAY

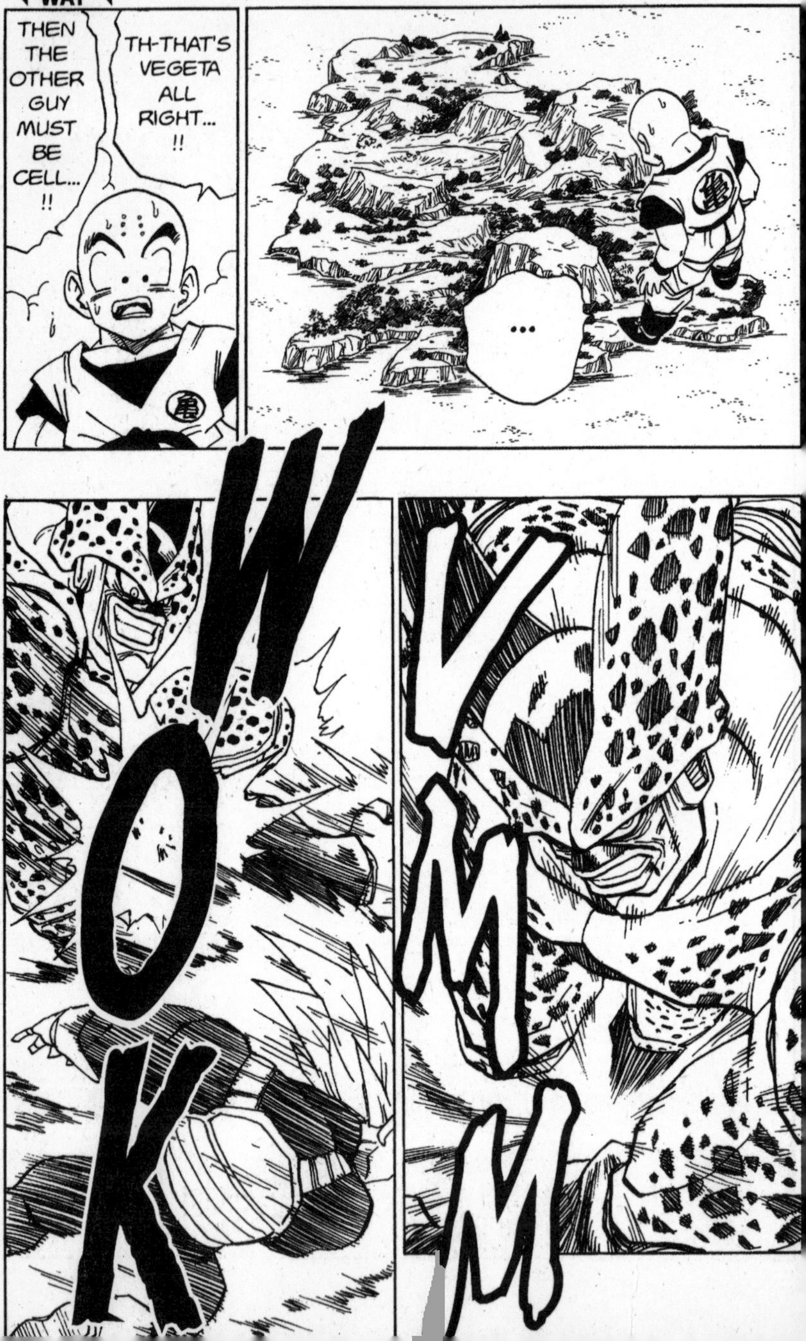
...
TH-THAT'S VEGETA ALL RIGHT... !!
THEN THE OTHER GUY MUST BE CELL... !!
VMMM
WOK

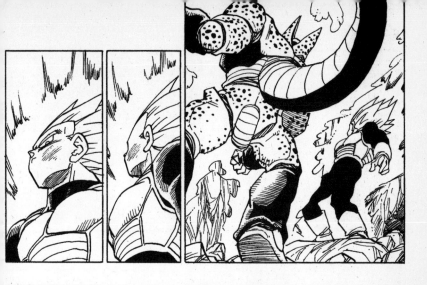

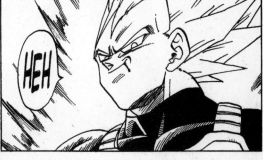

I GUESS THAT'S ALL THERE IS...

HEH

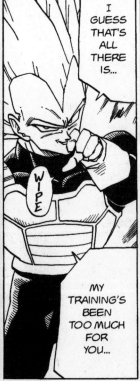

WIPE

MY TRAINING'S BEEN TOO MUCH FOR YOU...

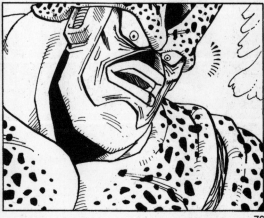

READ THIS WAY

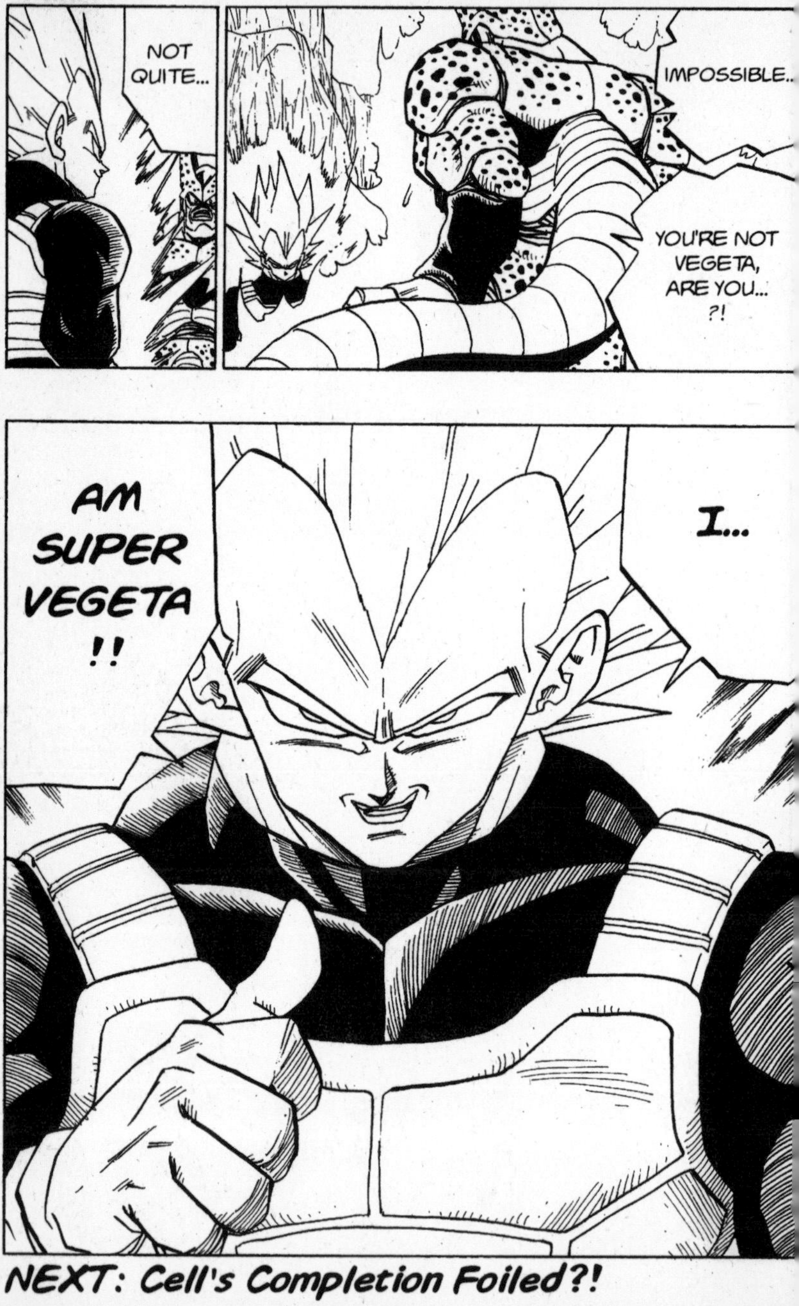
IMPOSSIBLE..
YOU'RE NOT VEGETA, ARE YOU... ?!
NOT QUITE...
I...
AM SUPER VEGETA !!

NEXT: Cell's Completion Foiled?!

DBZ:185 • Cell's Last Chance

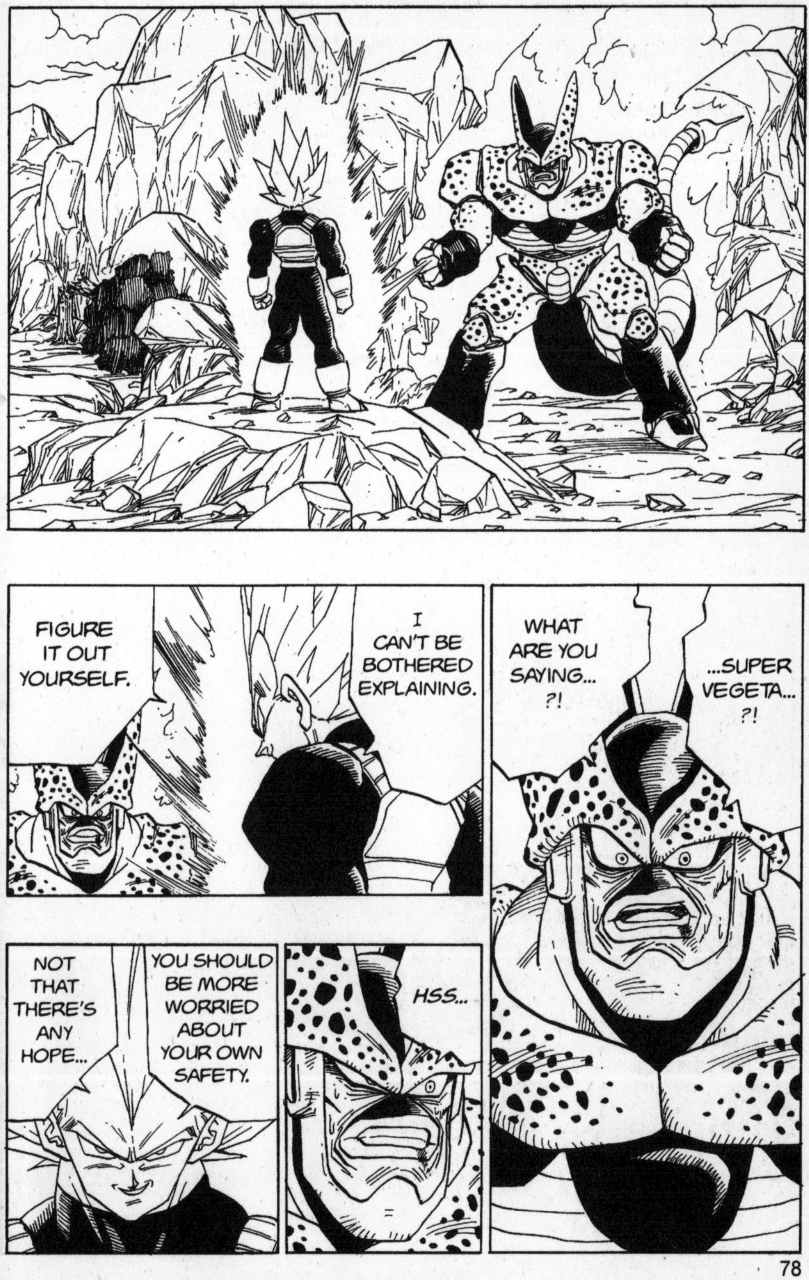

WHAT ARE YOU SAYING...?!
...SUPER VEGETA...?!
I CAN'T BE BOTHERED EXPLAINING.
FIGURE IT OUT YOURSELF.
HSS...
YOU SHOULD BE MORE WORRIED ABOUT YOUR OWN SAFETY.
NOT THAT THERE'S ANY HOPE...

READ THIS WAY

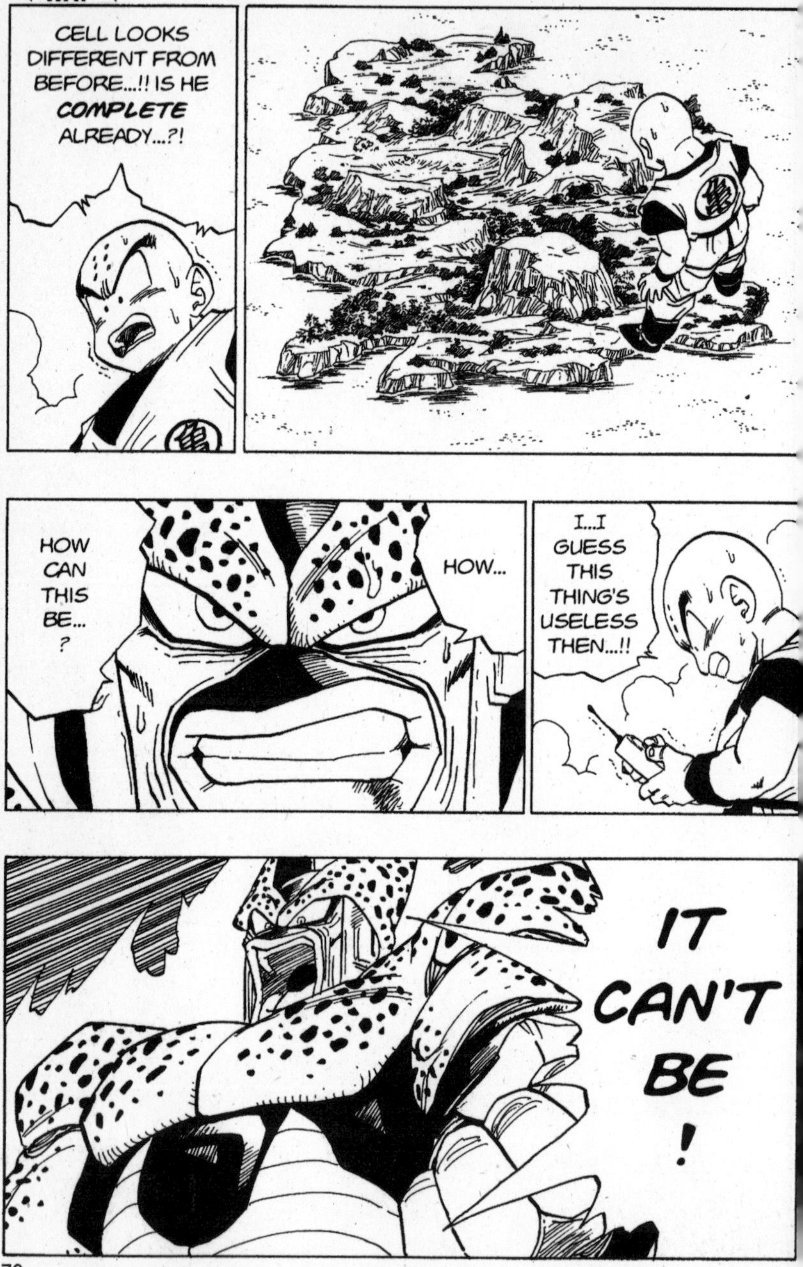
CELL LOOKS DIFFERENT FROM BEFORE...!! IS HE *COMPLETE* ALREADY...?!
I...I GUESS THIS THING'S USELESS THEN...!!
HOW...
HOW CAN THIS BE...?
IT CAN'T BE!

READ THIS WAY

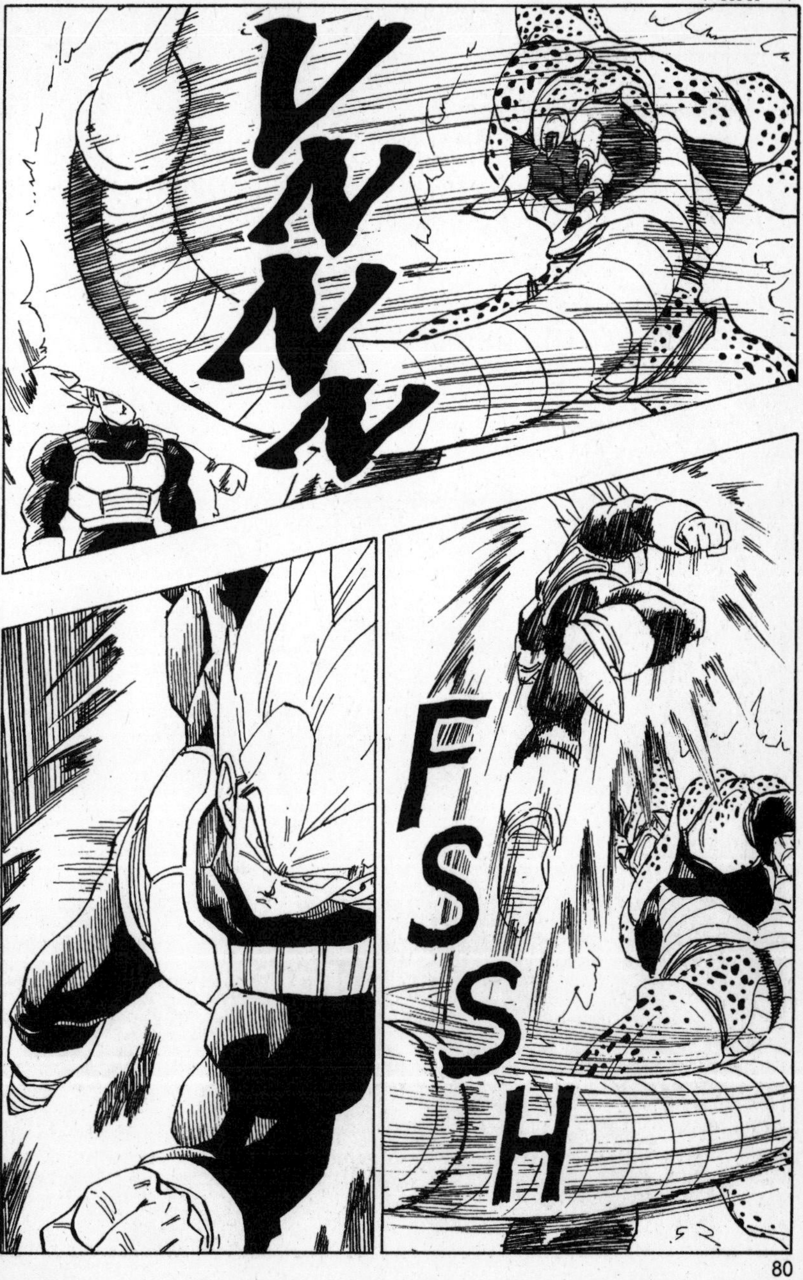
VNNN
FSSH

READ THIS WAY

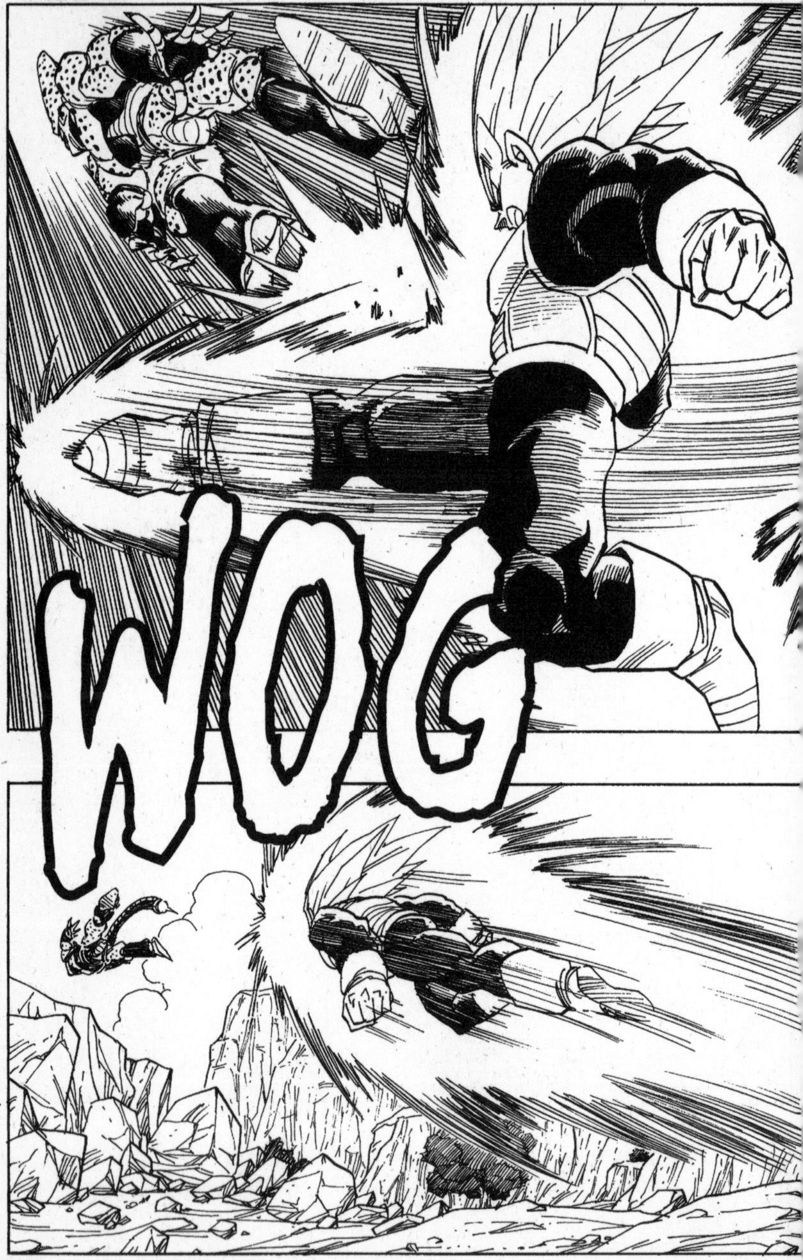
WOG

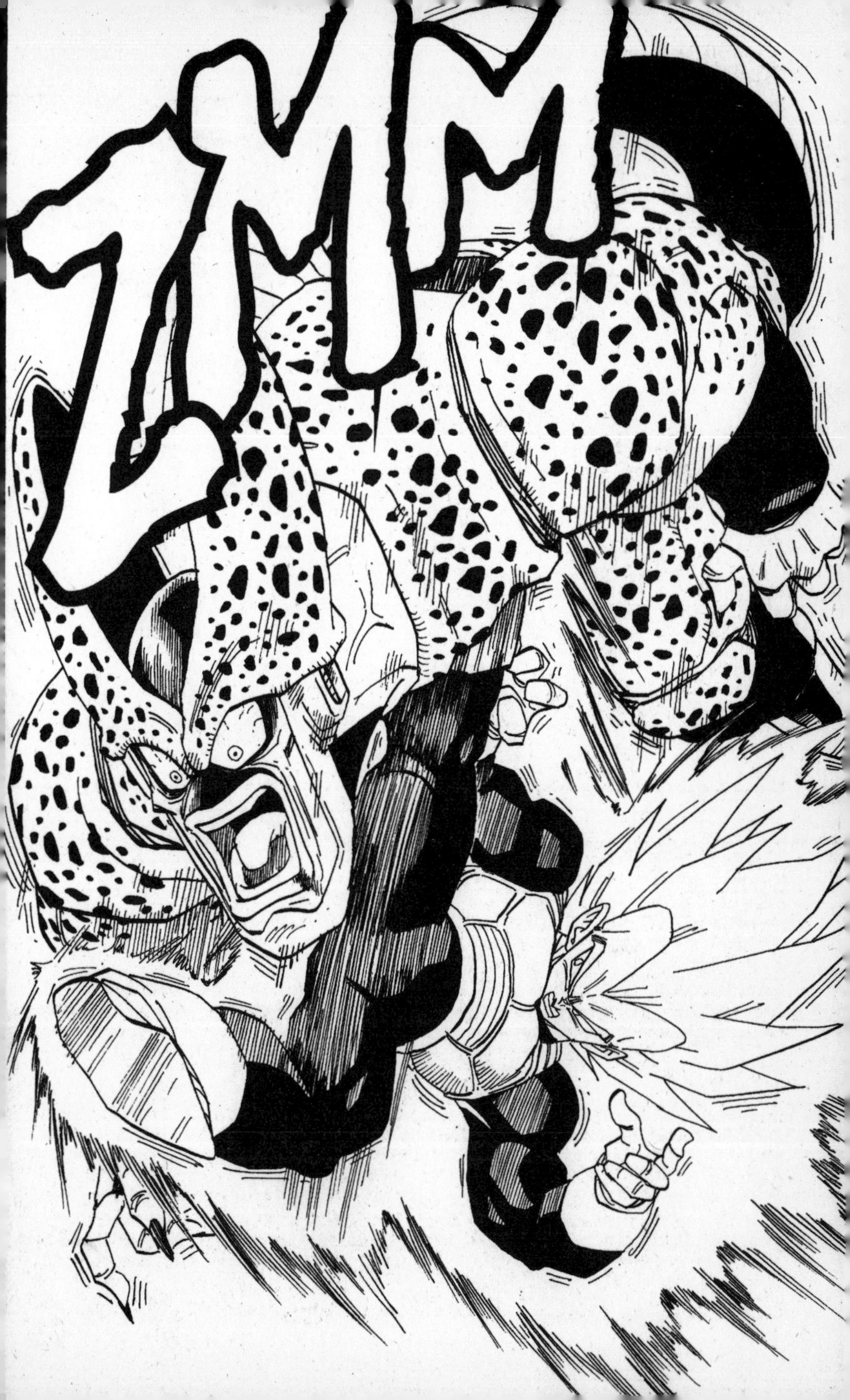

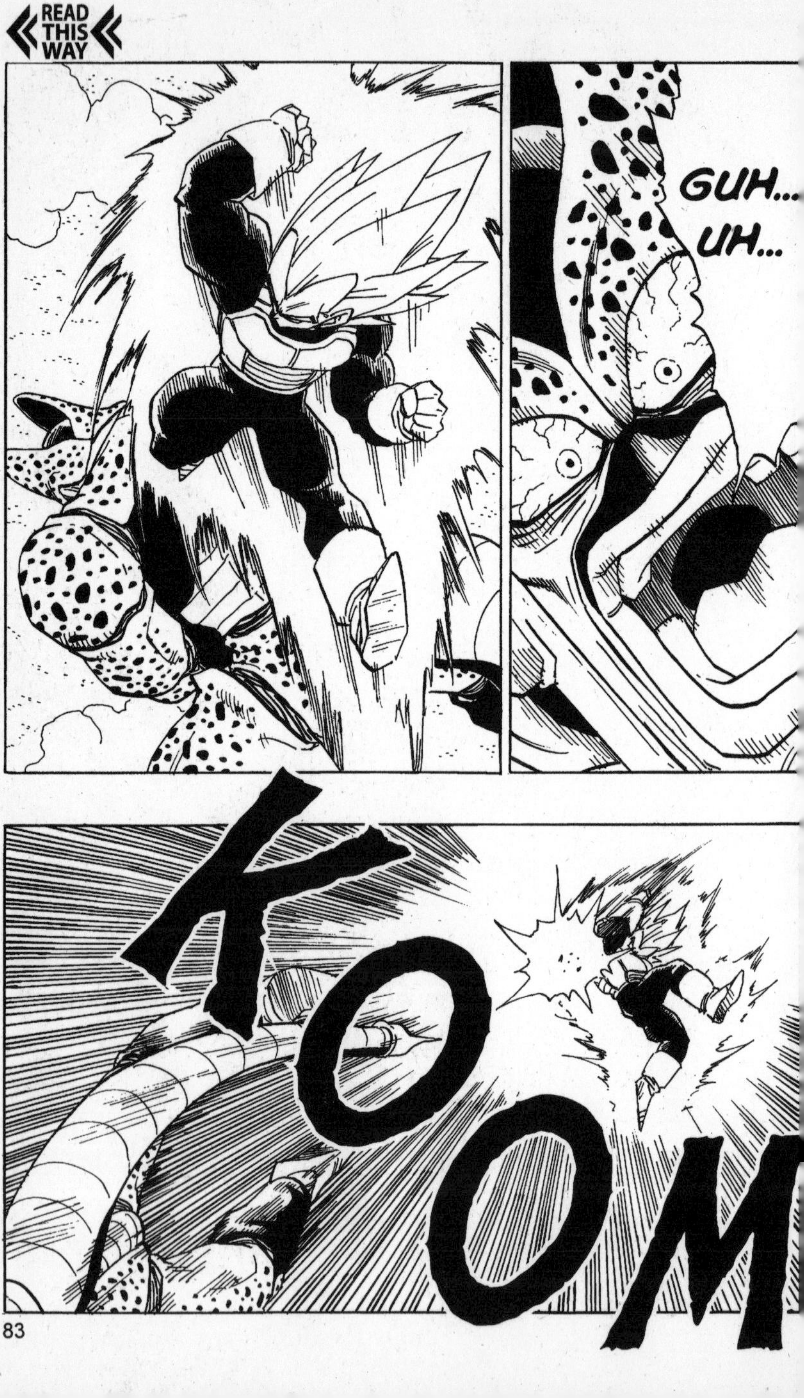
READ THIS WAY
GUH... UH...
KOOM

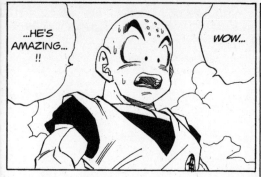

...HE'S AMAZING...!!

WOW...

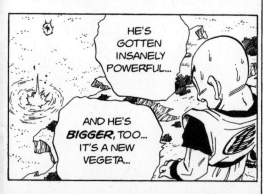

HE'S GOTTEN INSANELY POWERFUL...

AND HE'S *BIGGER*, TOO... IT'S A NEW VEGETA...

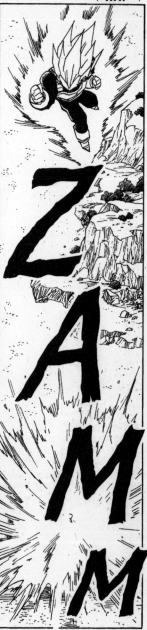

Z
A
M
M

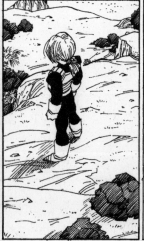

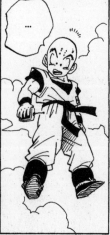

...

READ THIS WAY

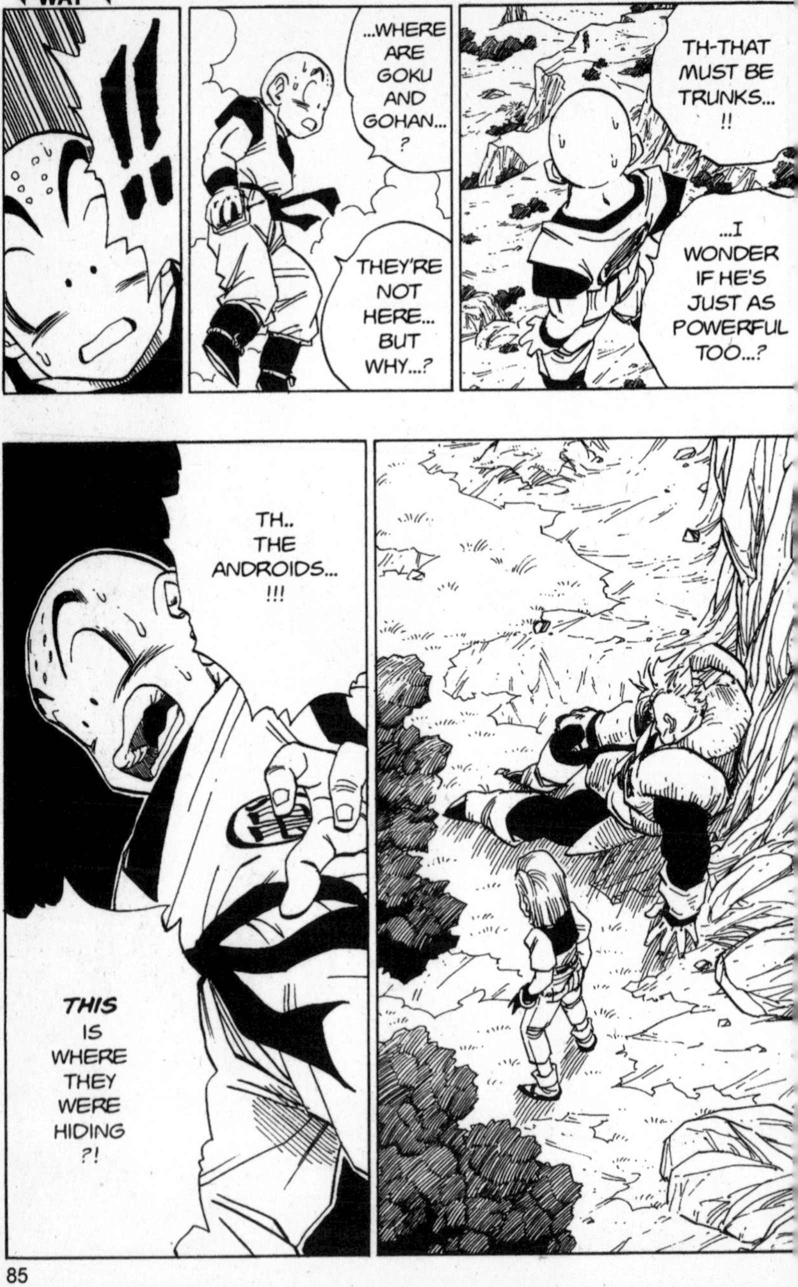

TH-THAT MUST BE TRUNKS... !!
...I WONDER IF HE'S JUST AS POWERFUL TOO...?
...WHERE ARE GOKU AND GOHAN... ?
THEY'RE NOT HERE... BUT WHY...?
!!
TH.. THE ANDROIDS... !!!
THIS IS WHERE THEY WERE HIDING ?!

READ THIS WAY

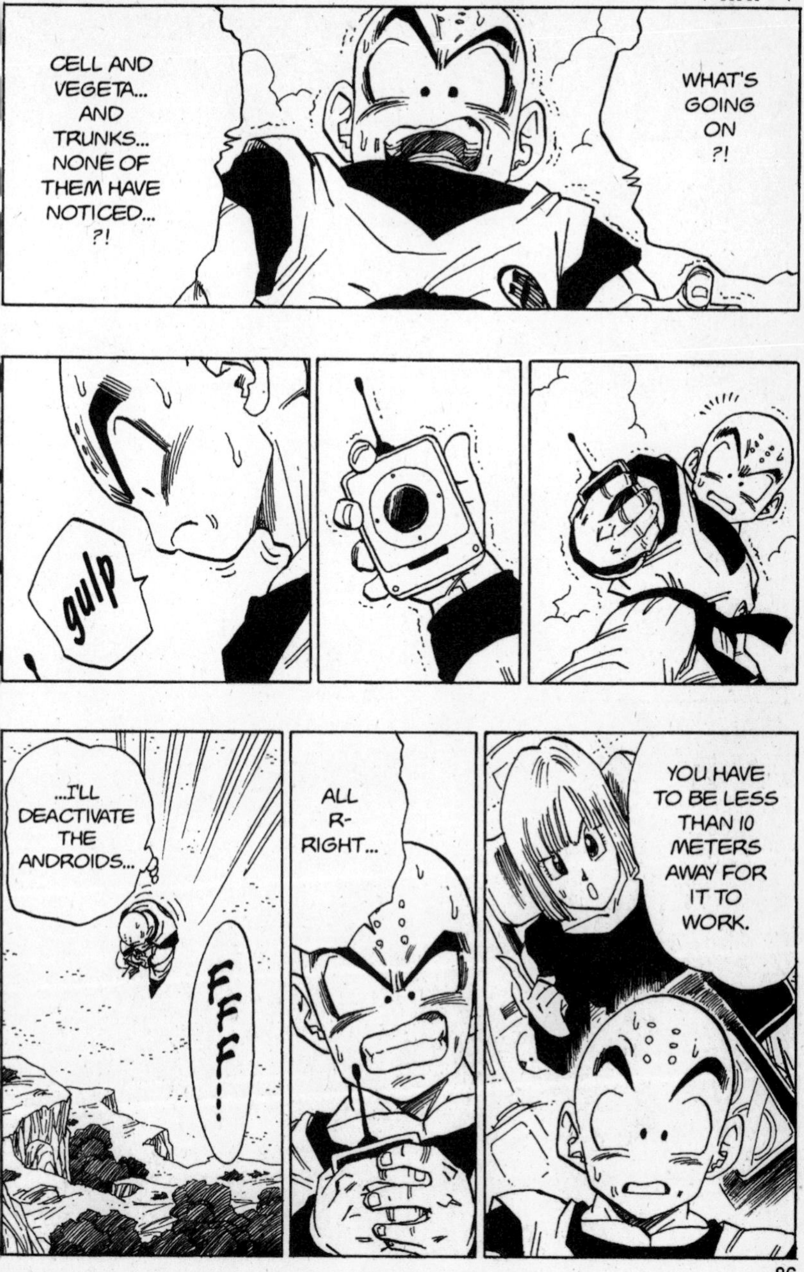
WHAT'S GOING ON ?!
CELL AND VEGETA... AND TRUNKS... NONE OF THEM HAVE NOTICED... ?!
gulp
YOU HAVE TO BE LESS THAN 10 METERS AWAY FOR IT TO WORK.
ALL R-RIGHT...
...I'LL DEACTIVATE THE ANDROIDS...
FFF...

READ THIS WAY

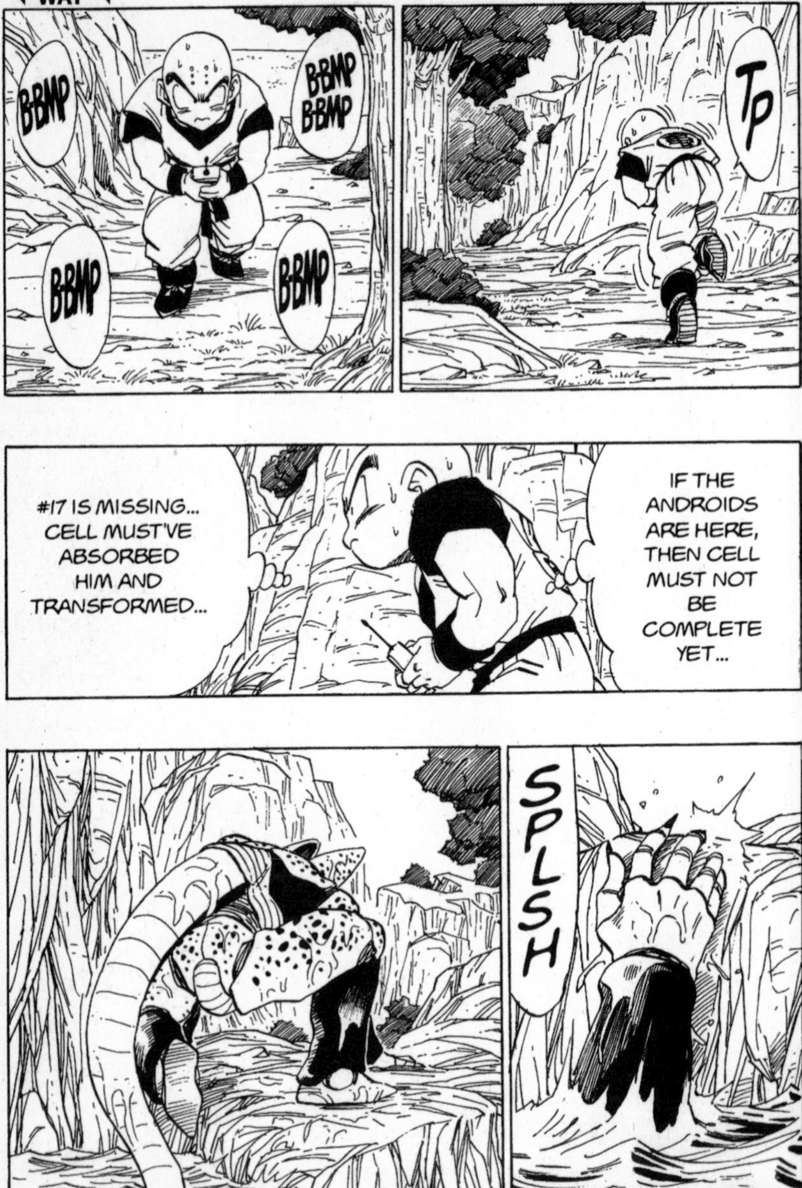
TP
B-BMP
B-BMP B-BMP
B-BMP
B-BMP
IF THE ANDROIDS ARE HERE, THEN CELL MUST NOT BE COMPLETE YET...
#17 IS MISSING... CELL MUST'VE ABSORBED HIM AND TRANSFORMED...
SPLSH

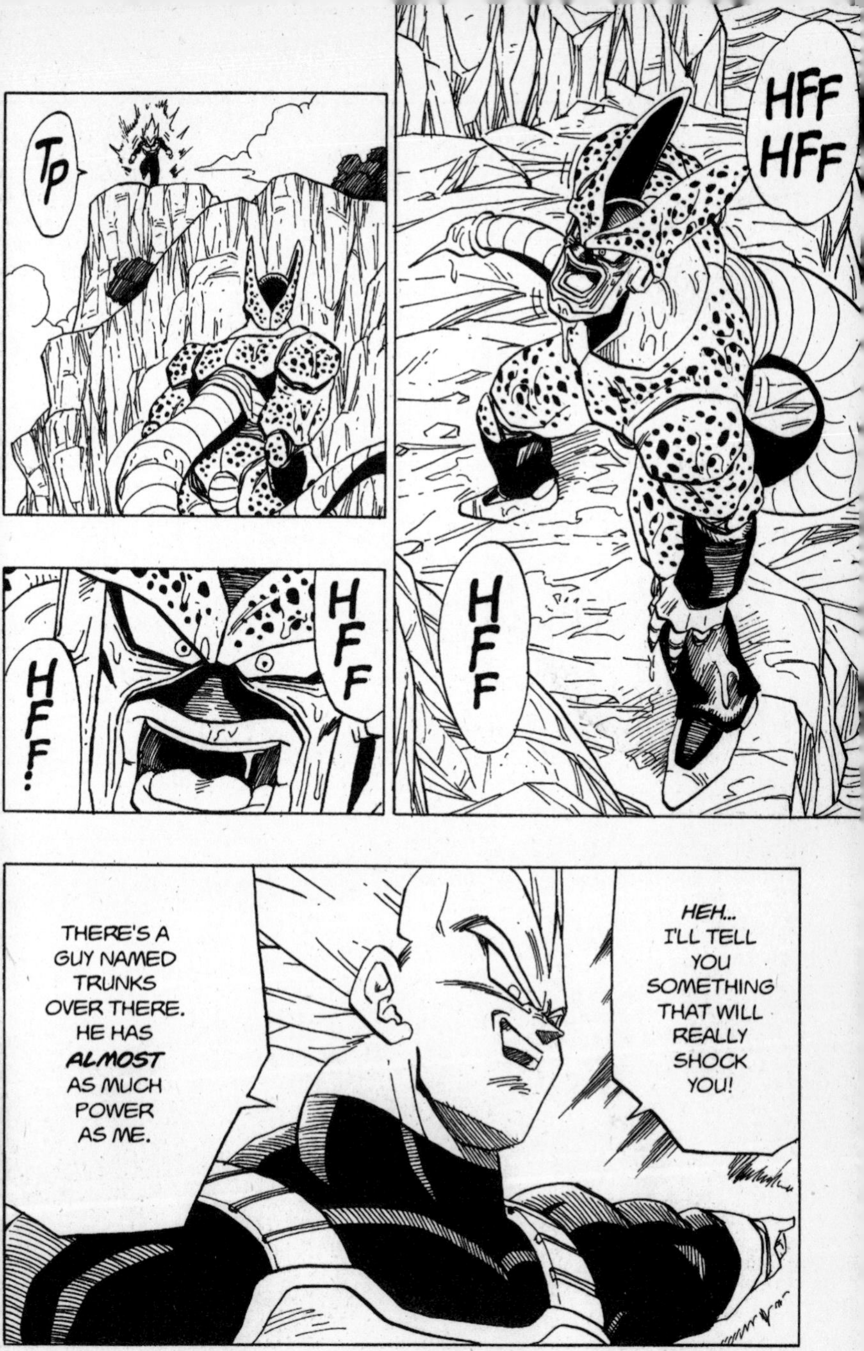
HFF HFF
HFF
TP
HFF
HFF...
HEH... I'LL TELL YOU SOMETHING THAT WILL REALLY SHOCK YOU!
THERE'S A GUY NAMED TRUNKS OVER THERE. HE HAS ALMOST AS MUCH POWER AS ME.

READ THIS WAY

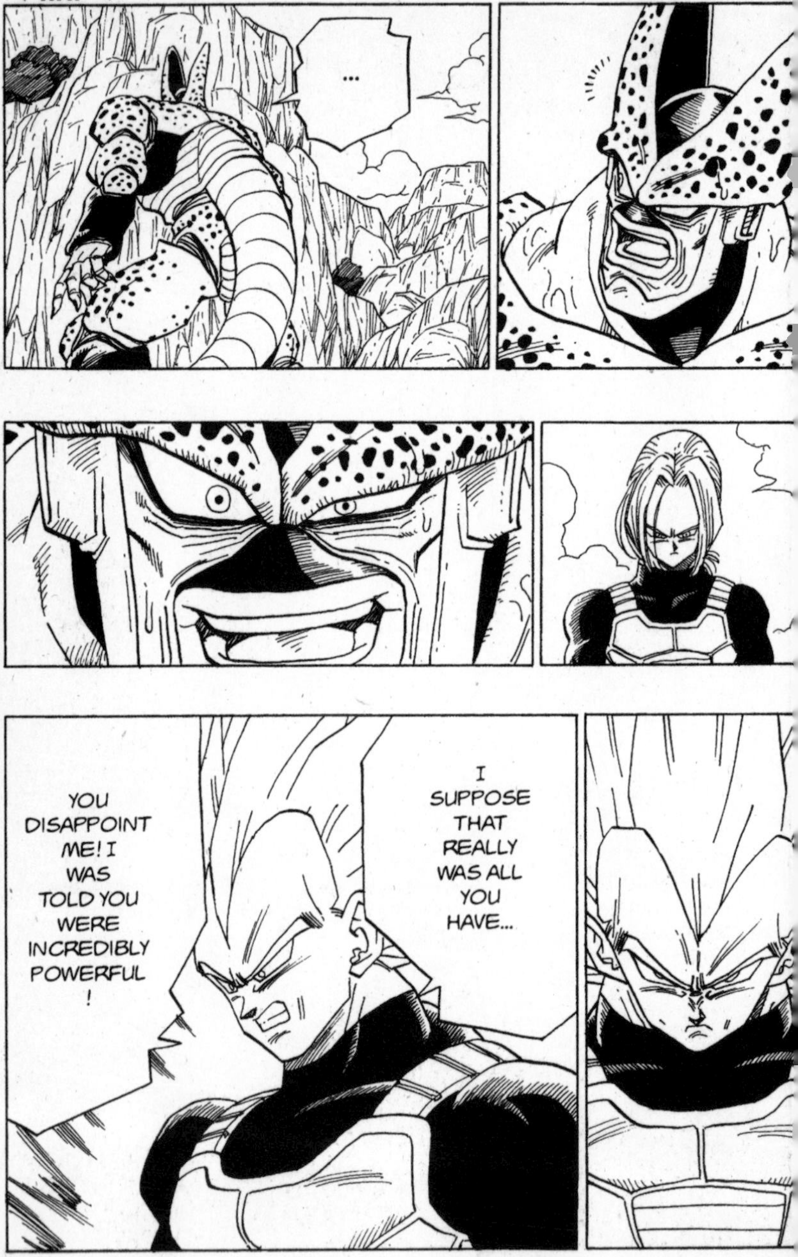
...
I SUPPOSE THAT REALLY WAS ALL YOU HAVE...
YOU DISAPPOINT ME! I WAS TOLD YOU WERE INCREDIBLY POWERFUL!

READ THIS WAY

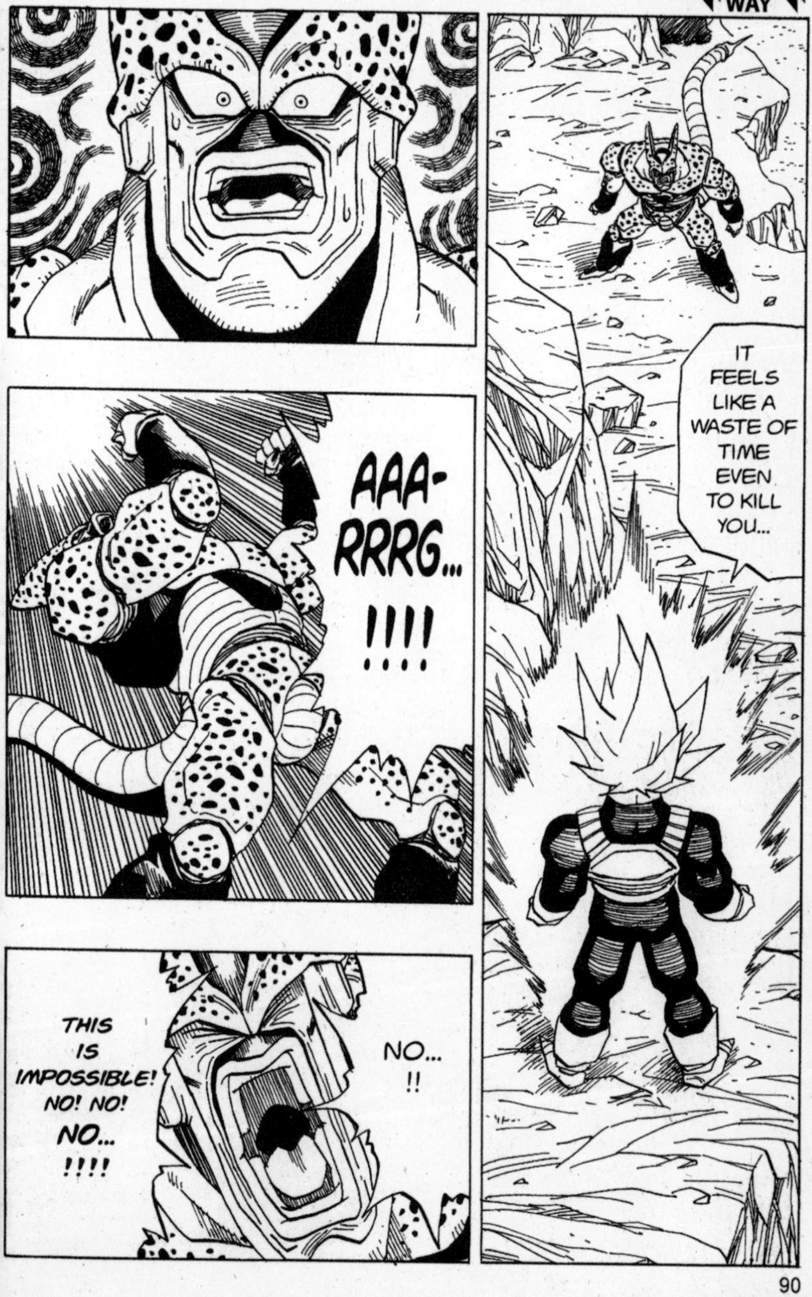
IT FEELS LIKE A WASTE OF TIME EVEN TO KILL YOU...
AAA-RRRG... !!!!
NO... !!
THIS IS IMPOSSIBLE! NO! NO! NO... !!!!

READ THIS WAY

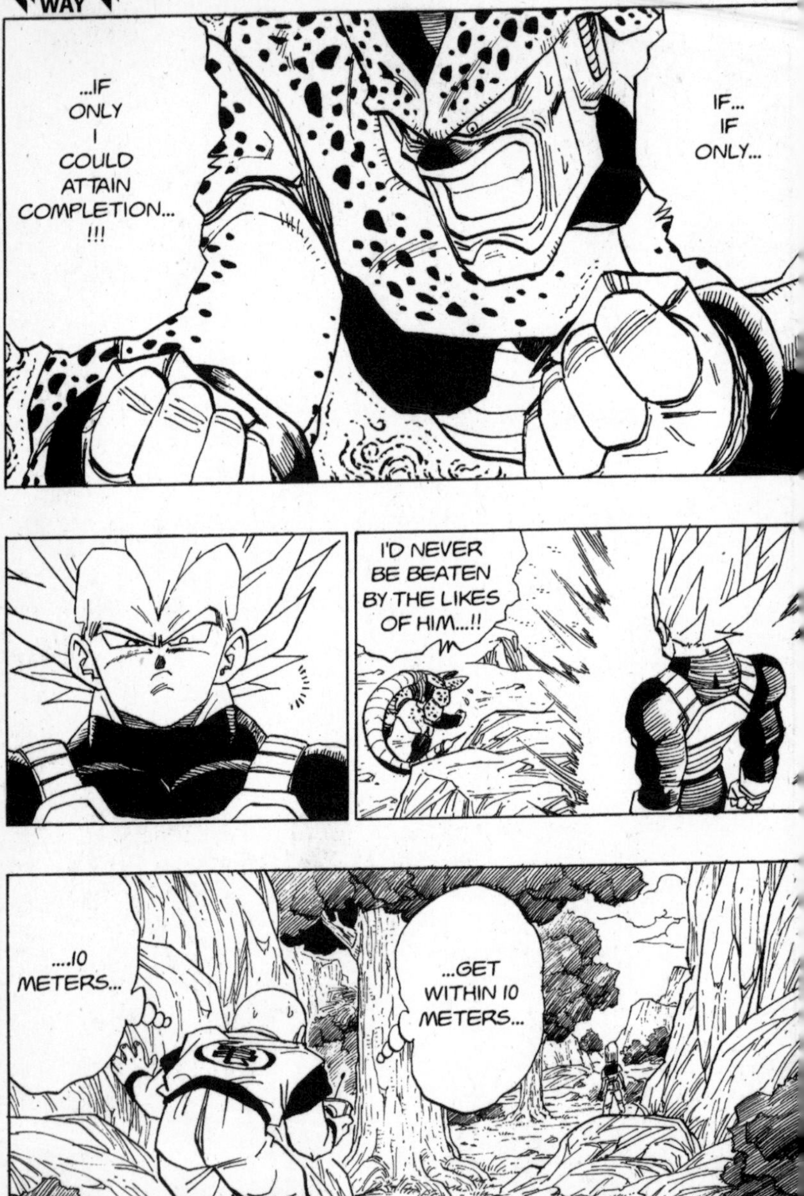
IF... IF ONLY...
...IF ONLY I COULD ATTAIN COMPLETION... !!!
I'D NEVER BE BEATEN BY THE LIKES OF HIM...!!
...GET WITHIN 10 METERS...
....10 METERS...

NEXT: Run, #18!!

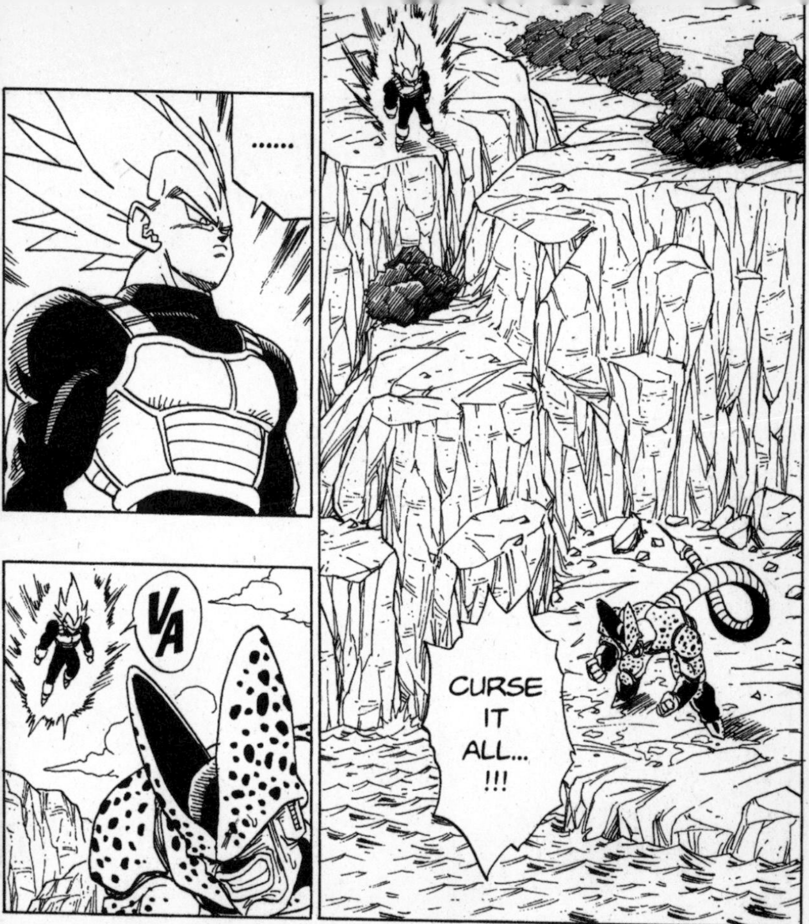
CURSE IT ALL... !!!
......
VA

DBZ:186 • The Evil Truce

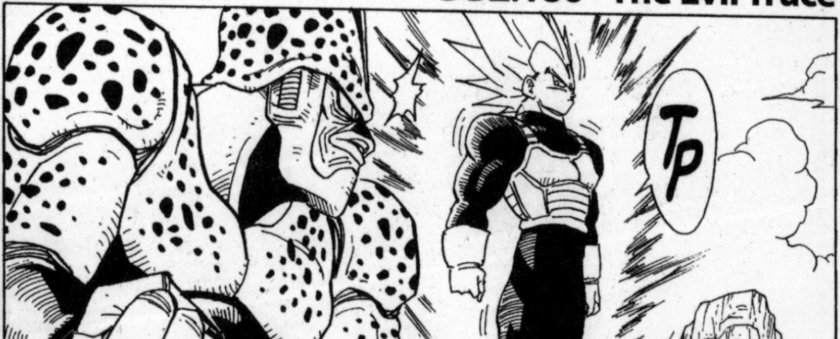
TP

READ THIS WAY

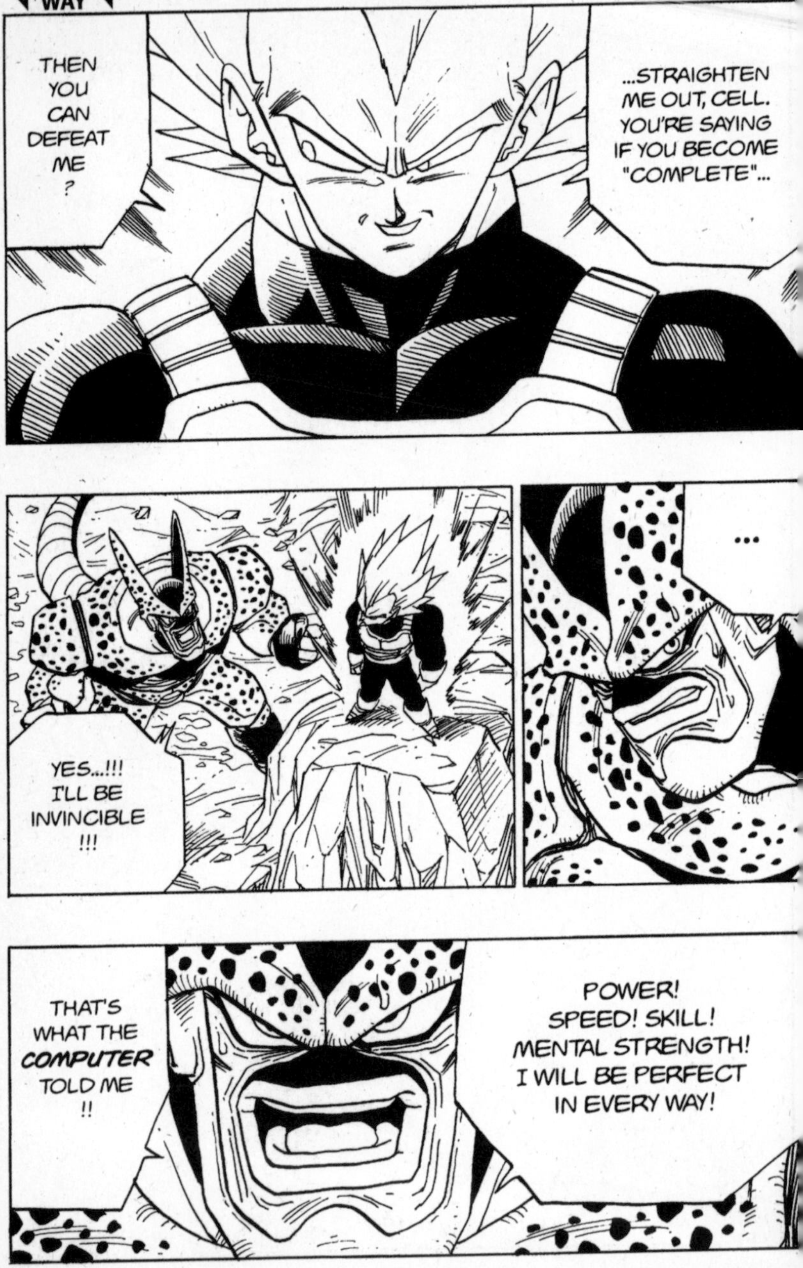
...STRAIGHTEN ME OUT, CELL. YOU'RE SAYING IF YOU BECOME "COMPLETE"...
THEN YOU CAN DEFEAT ME?
...
YES...!!! I'LL BE INVINCIBLE!!!
POWER! SPEED! SKILL! MENTAL STRENGTH! I WILL BE PERFECT IN EVERY WAY!
THAT'S WHAT THE *COMPUTER* TOLD ME!!

READ THIS WAY

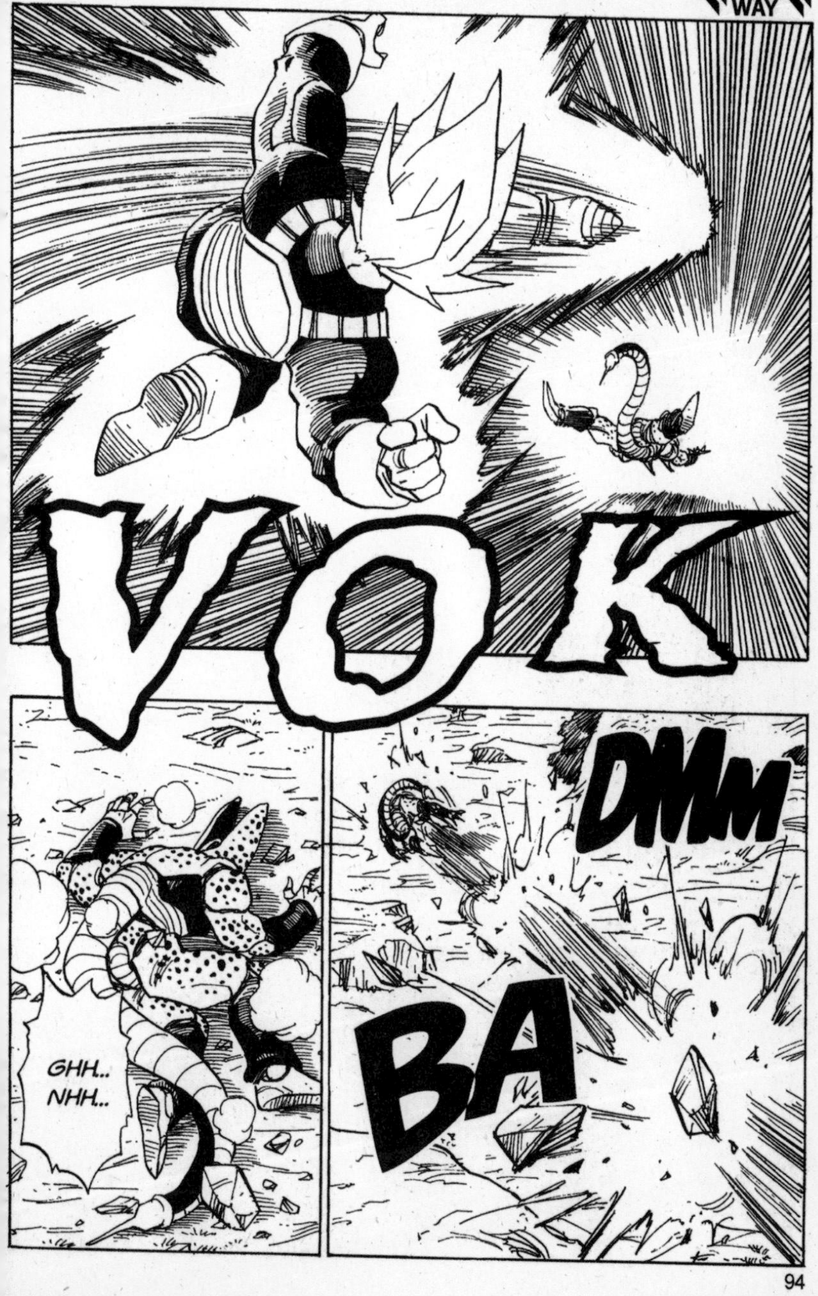
VOK
DMM
BA
GHH...
NHH...

READ THIS WAY

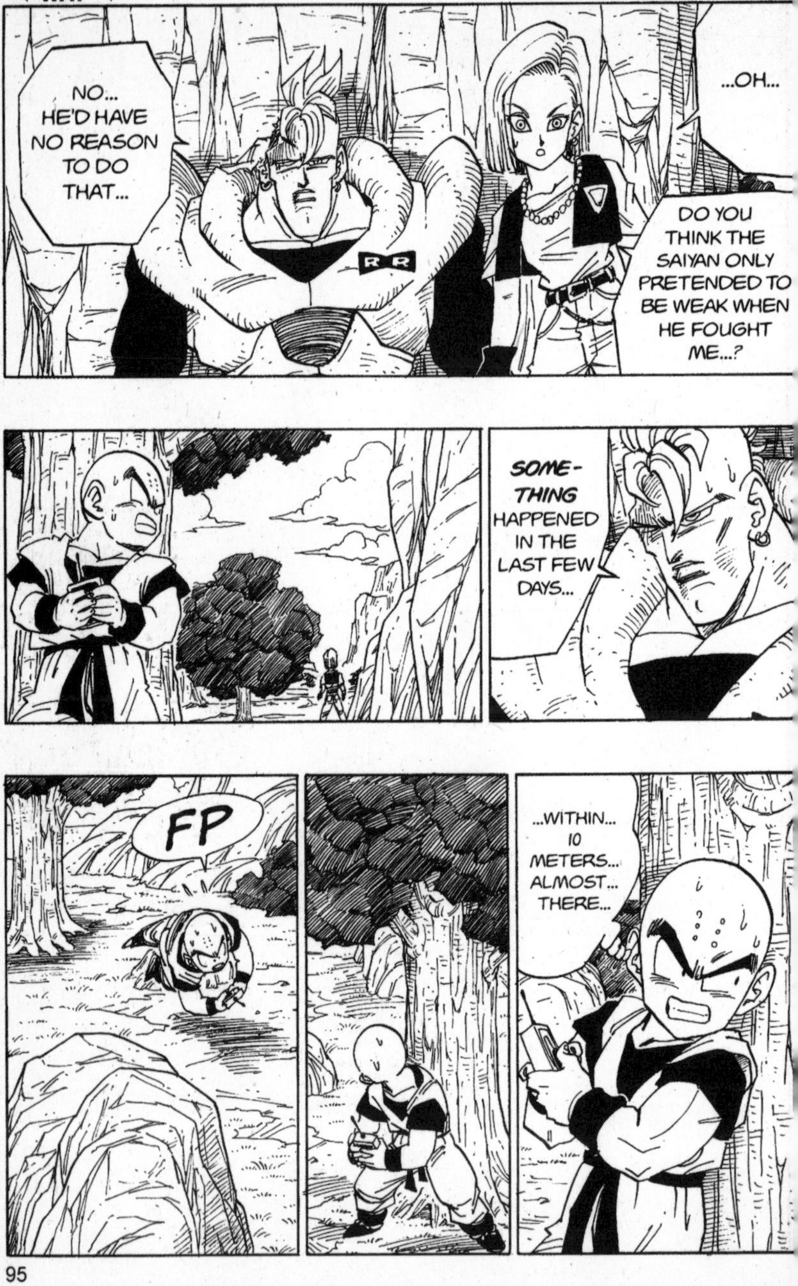
...OH...
DO YOU THINK THE SAIYAN ONLY PRETENDED TO BE WEAK WHEN HE FOUGHT ME...?
NO... HE'D HAVE NO REASON TO DO THAT...
SOME-THING HAPPENED IN THE LAST FEW DAYS...
...WITHIN... 10 METERS... ALMOST... THERE...
FP

READ THIS WAY

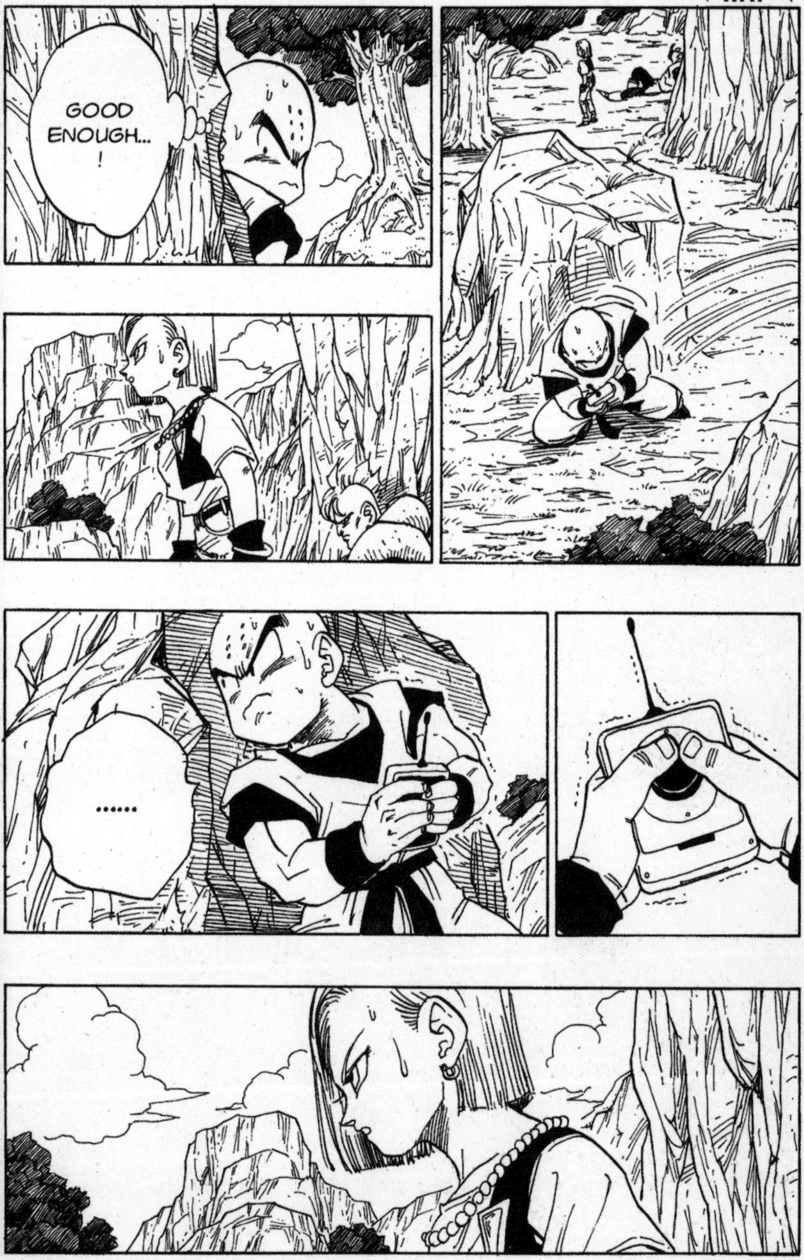
GOOD ENOUGH... !
......

READ THIS WAY

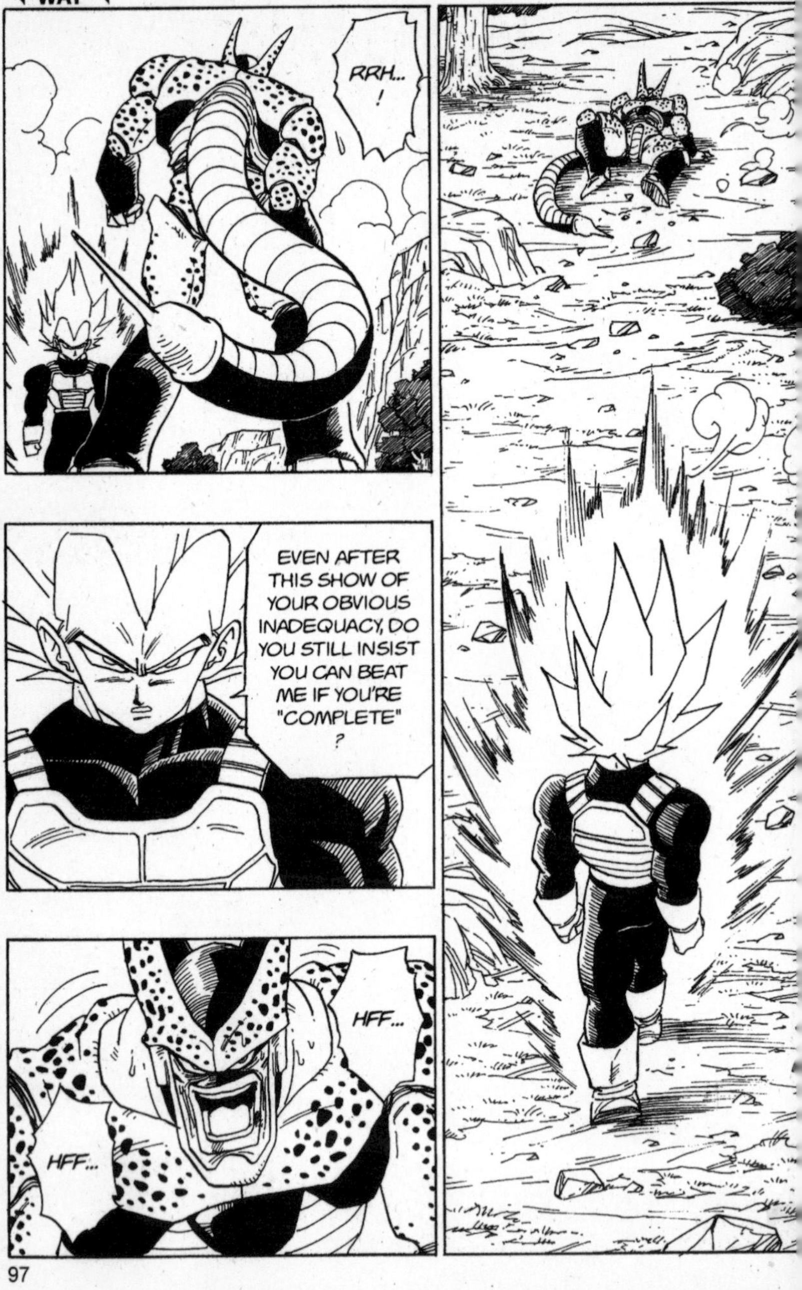
RRH... !
EVEN AFTER THIS SHOW OF YOUR OBVIOUS INADEQUACY, DO YOU STILL INSIST YOU CAN BEAT ME IF YOU'RE "COMPLETE" ?
HFF...
HFF...

READ THIS WAY

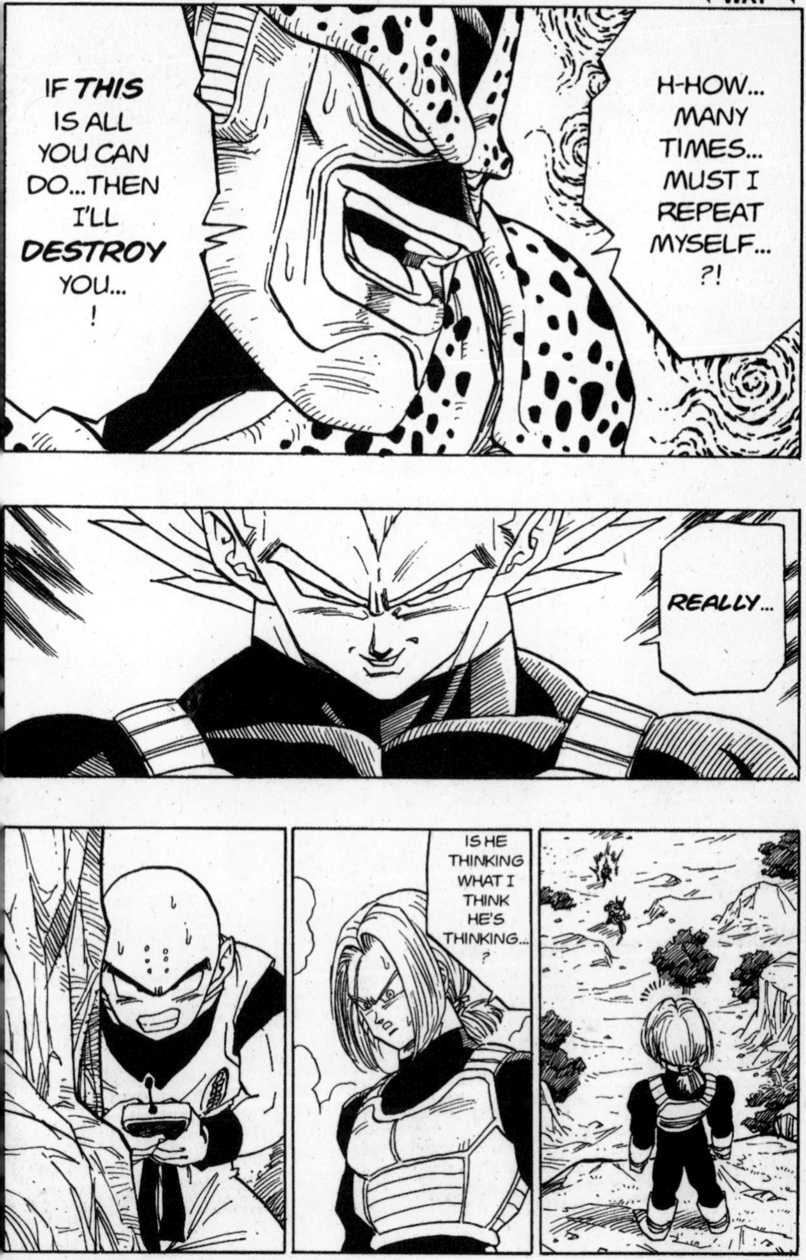
H-HOW... MANY TIMES... MUST I REPEAT MYSELF... ?!
IF **THIS** IS ALL YOU CAN DO...THEN I'LL **DESTROY** YOU... !
REALLY...
IS HE THINKING WHAT I THINK HE'S THINKING... ?

READ THIS WAY

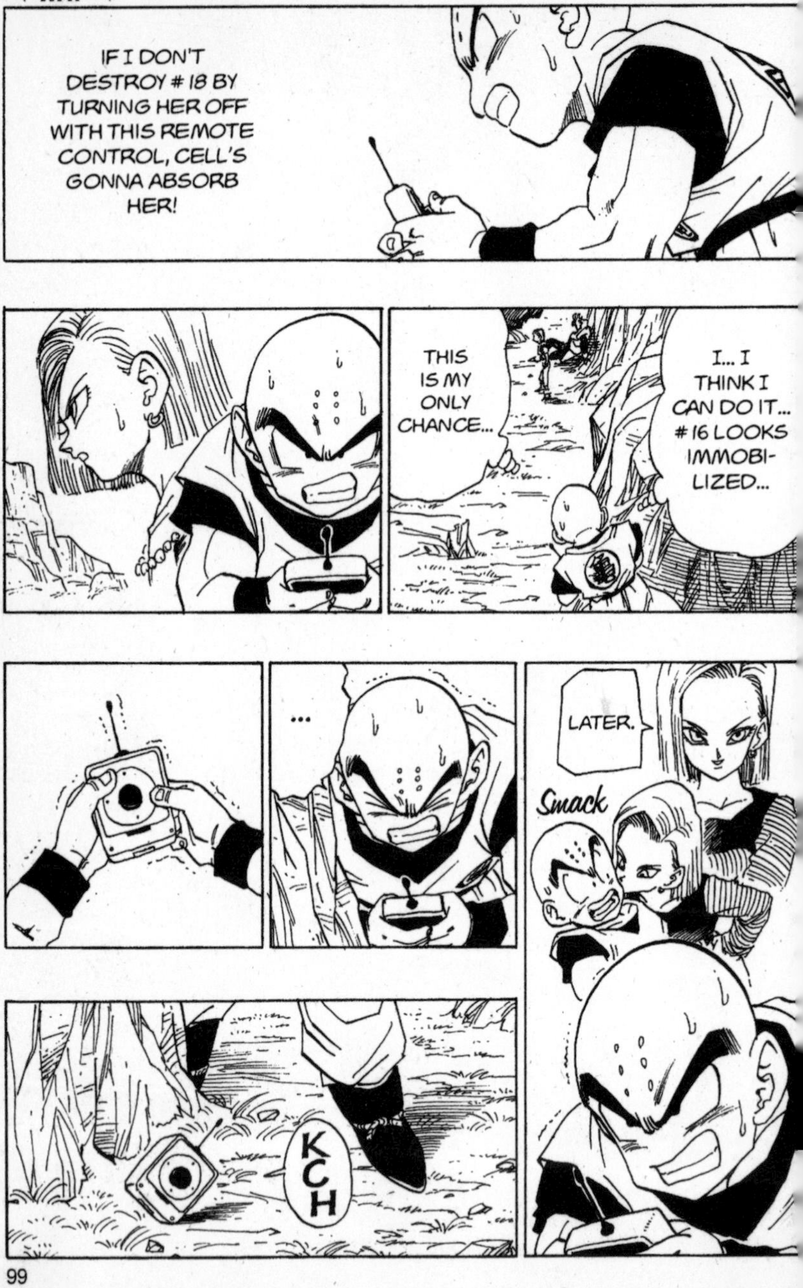

IF I DON'T DESTROY #18 BY TURNING HER OFF WITH THIS REMOTE CONTROL, CELL'S GONNA ABSORB HER!
I... I THINK I CAN DO IT... #16 LOOKS IMMOBI-LIZED...
THIS IS MY ONLY CHANCE...
LATER.
Smack
...
KCH

READ THIS WAY

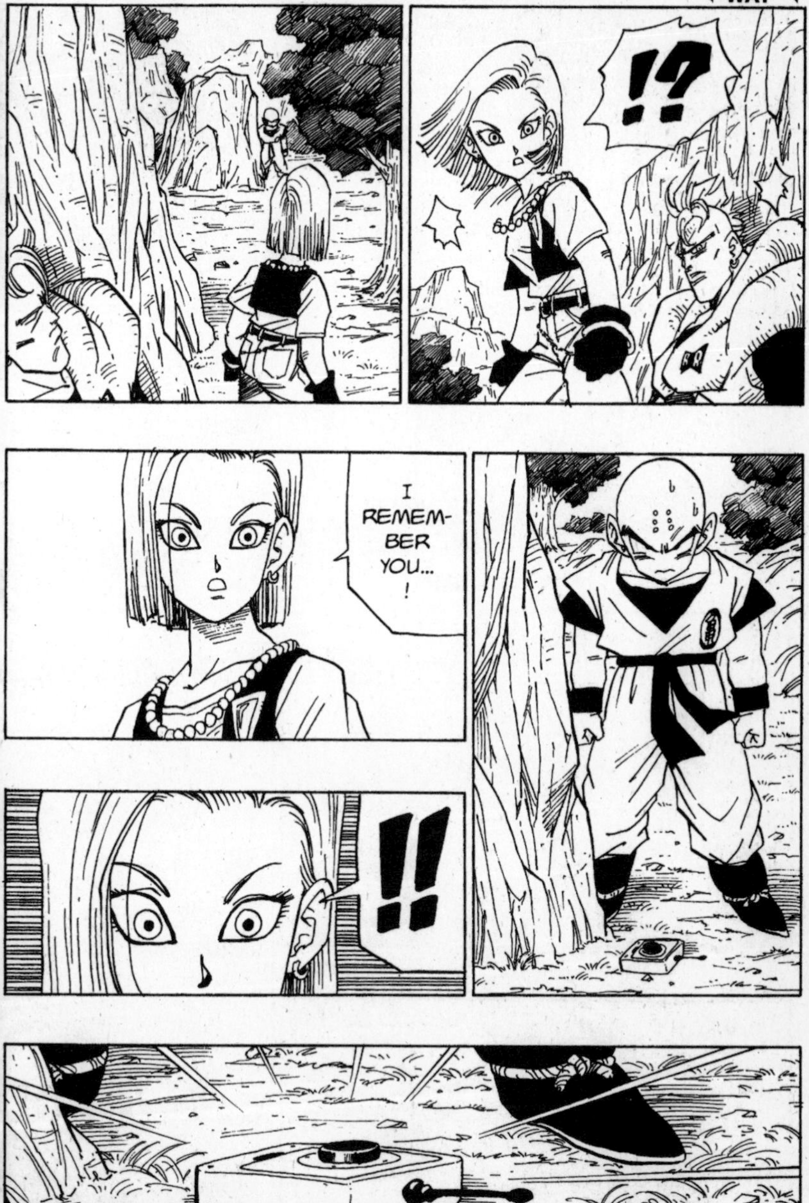
!?
I REMEMBER YOU...!
!!

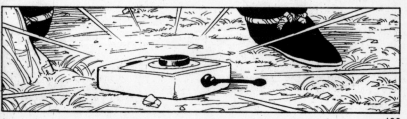

READ THIS WAY

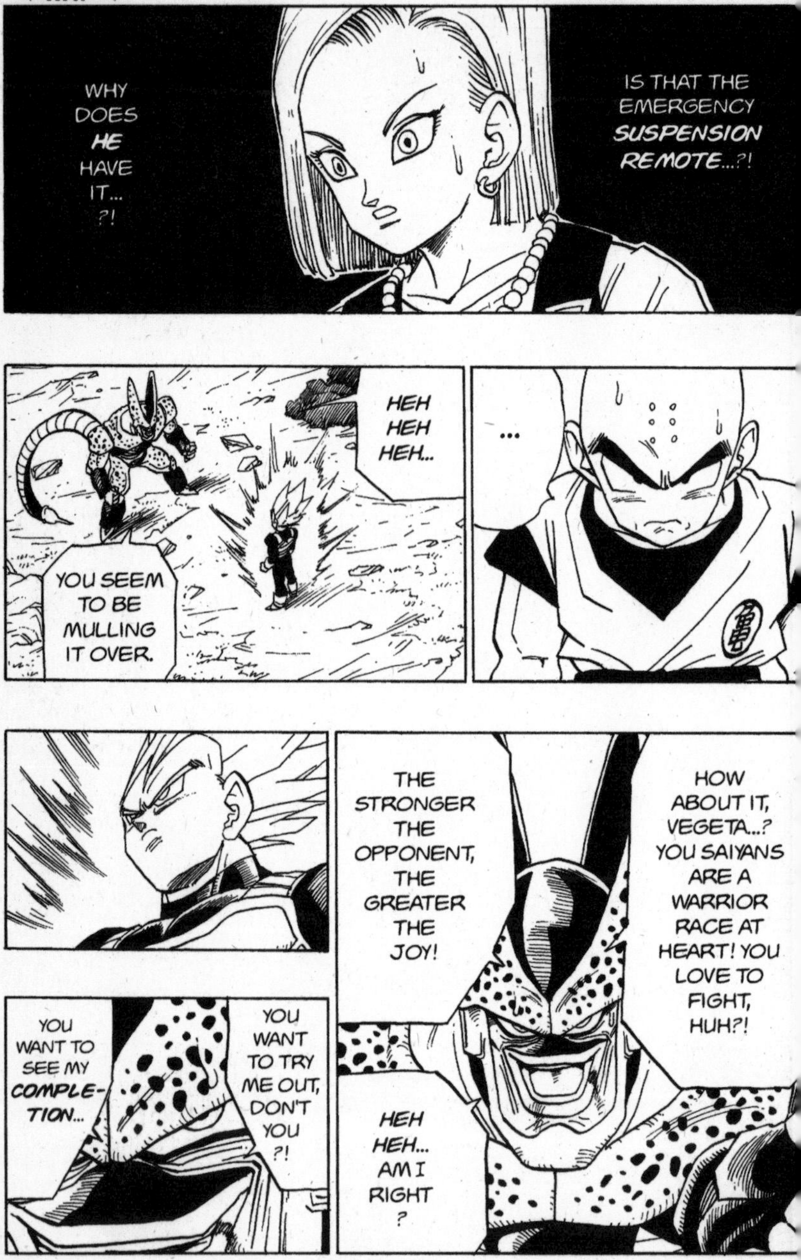
IS THAT THE EMERGENCY *SUSPENSION REMOTE*...?!
WHY DOES *HE* HAVE IT...?!
...
HEH HEH HEH...
YOU SEEM TO BE MULLING IT OVER.
HOW ABOUT IT, VEGETA...? YOU SAIYANS ARE A WARRIOR RACE AT HEART! YOU LOVE TO FIGHT, HUH?!
THE STRONGER THE OPPONENT, THE GREATER THE JOY!
HEH HEH... AM I RIGHT?
YOU WANT TO TRY ME OUT, DON'T YOU?!
YOU WANT TO SEE MY *COMPLETION*...

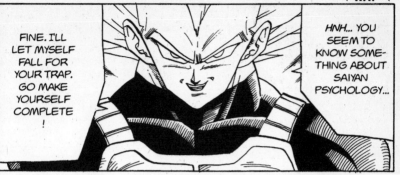

HNH... YOU SEEM TO KNOW SOMETHING ABOUT SAIYAN PSYCHOLOGY...

FINE. I'LL LET MYSELF FALL FOR YOUR TRAP. GO MAKE YOURSELF COMPLETE!

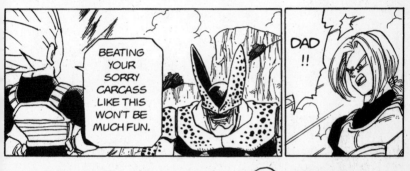

BEATING YOUR SORRY CARCASS LIKE THIS WON'T BE MUCH FUN.

DAD!!

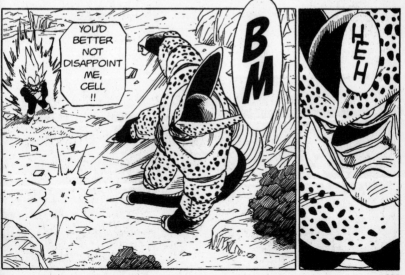

YOU'D BETTER NOT DISAPPOINT ME, CELL!!

B M

HEH

102

READ THIS WAY

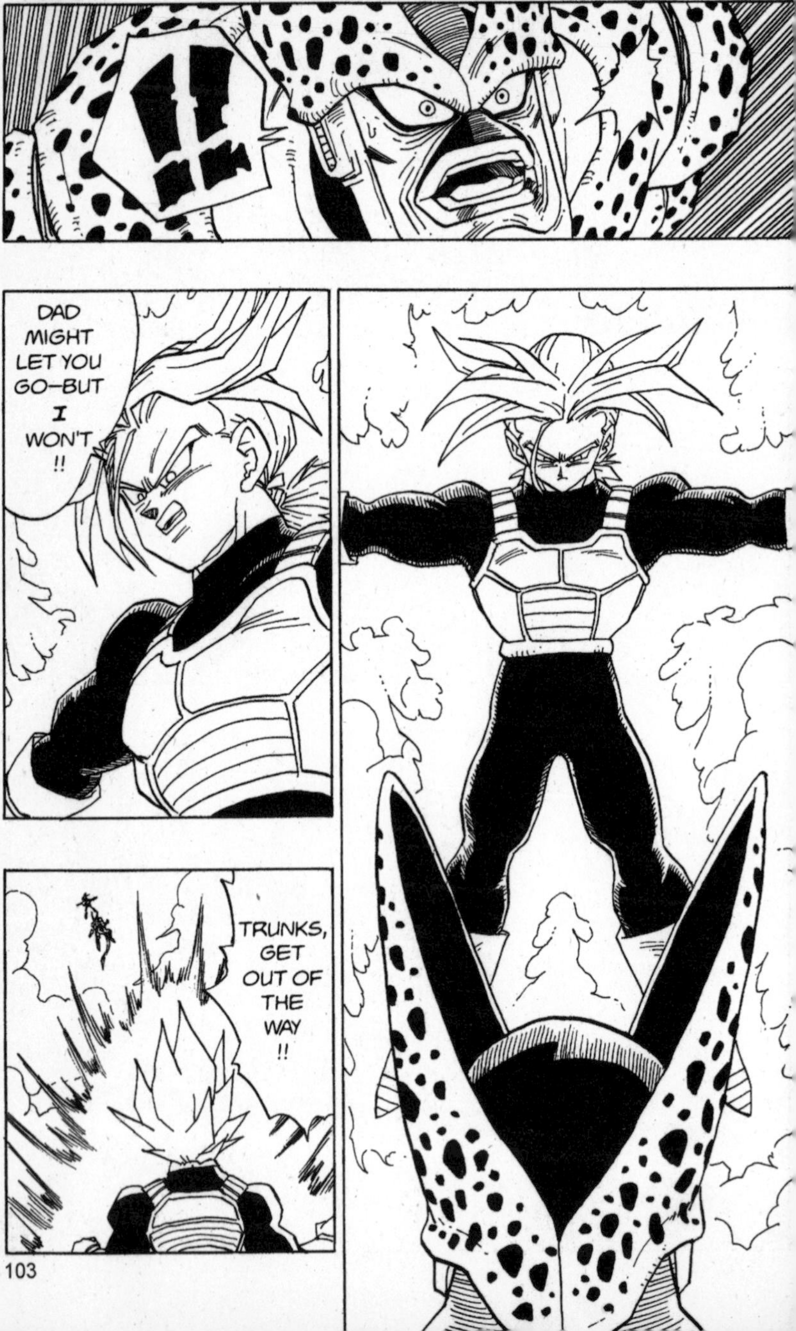
!!
DAD MIGHT LET YOU GO—BUT I WON'T !!
TRUNKS, GET OUT OF THE WAY !!

READ THIS WAY

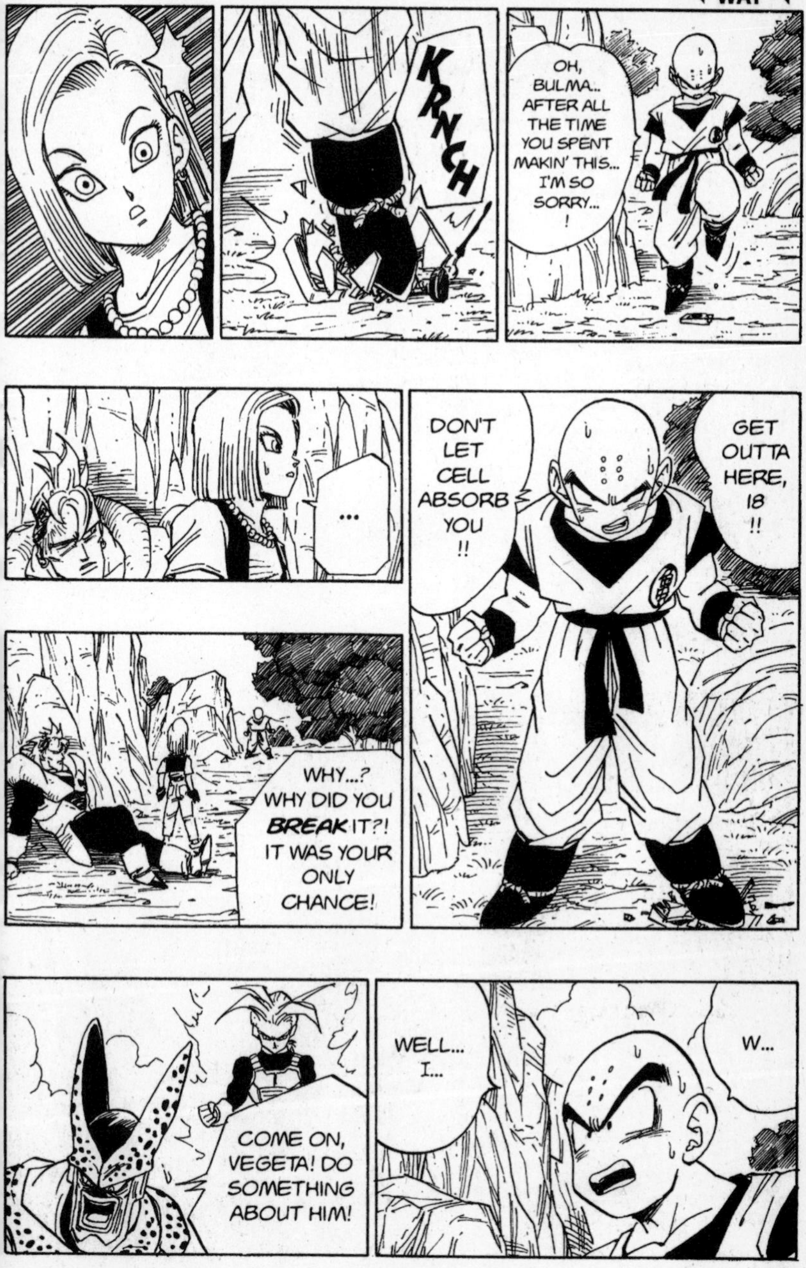
OH, BULMA.. AFTER ALL THE TIME YOU SPENT MAKIN' THIS... I'M SO SORRY... !
KRNCH
GET OUTTA HERE, 18 !!
DON'T LET CELL ABSORB YOU !!
...
WHY...? WHY DID YOU *BREAK* IT?! IT WAS YOUR ONLY CHANCE!
W...
WELL... I...
COME ON, VEGETA! DO SOMETHING ABOUT HIM!

READ THIS WAY

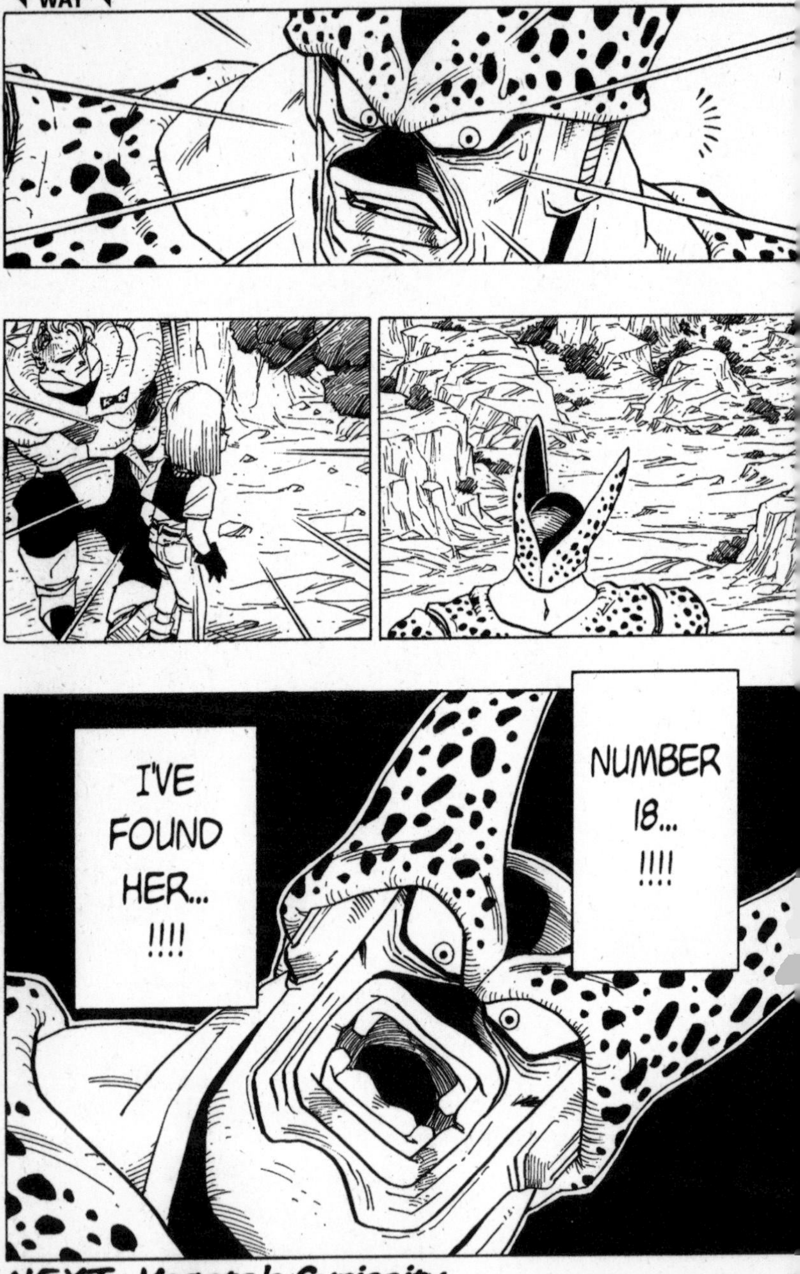
NUMBER 18... !!!!
I'VE FOUND HER... !!!!

NEXT: Vegeta's Curiosity

DBZ:187 • Vegeta vs.Trunks?

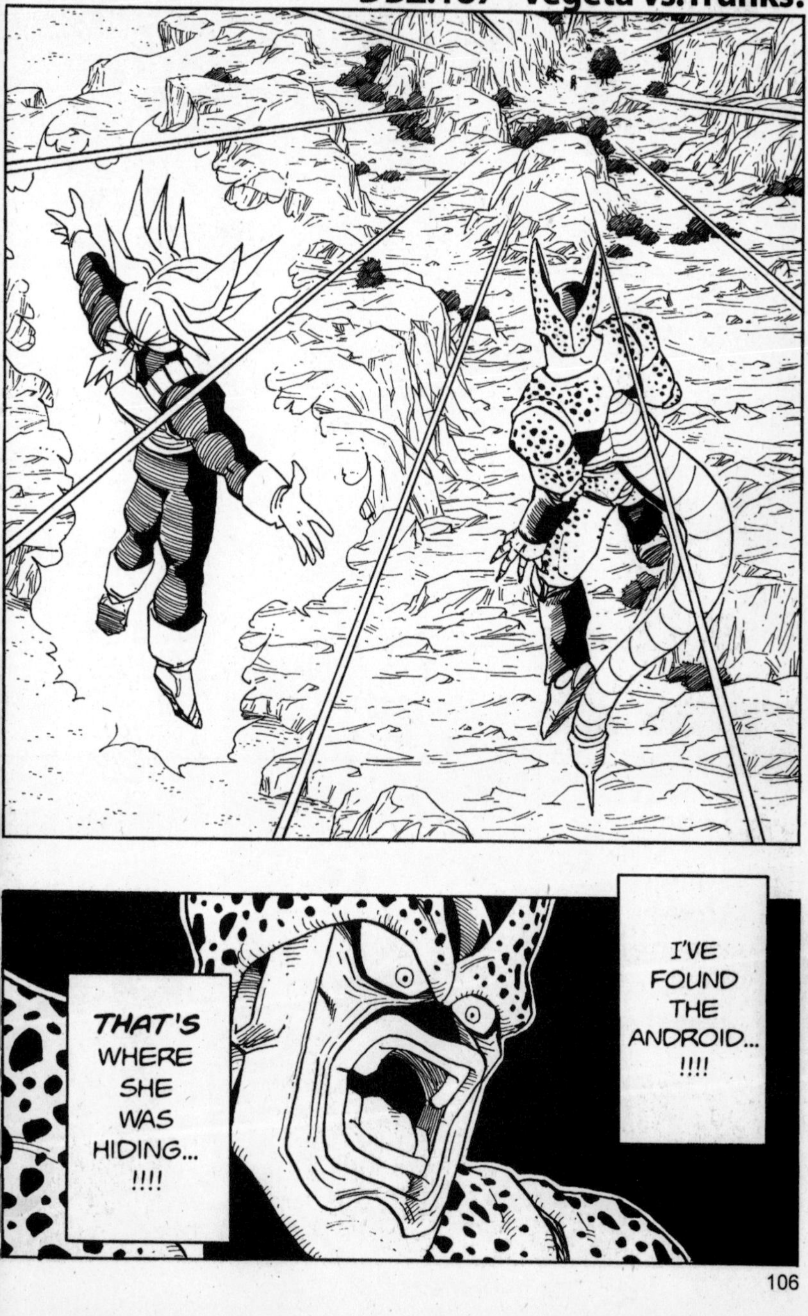
I'VE FOUND THE ANDROID... !!!!
THAT'S WHERE SHE WAS HIDING... !!!!

READ THIS WAY

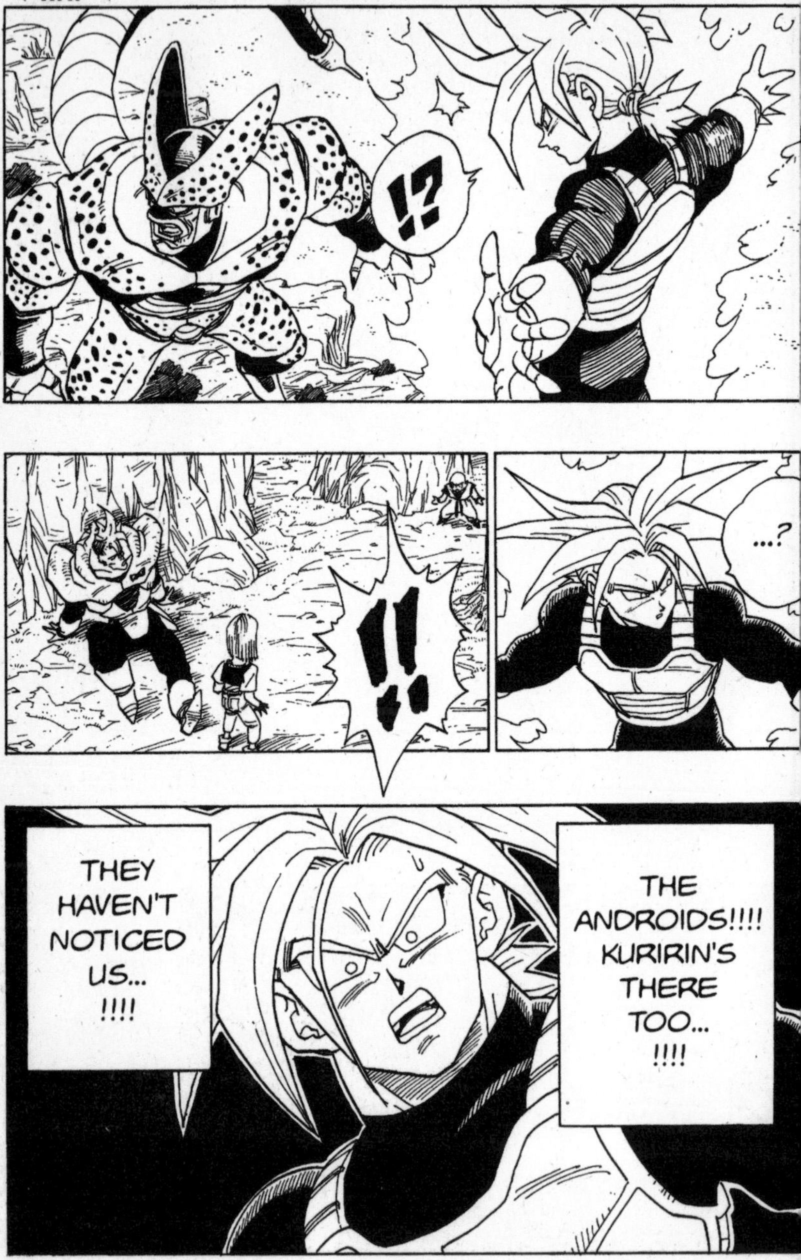
!?
...?
!!
THE ANDROIDS!!!! KURIRIN'S THERE TOO... !!!!
THEY HAVEN'T NOTICED US... !!!!

READ THIS WAY

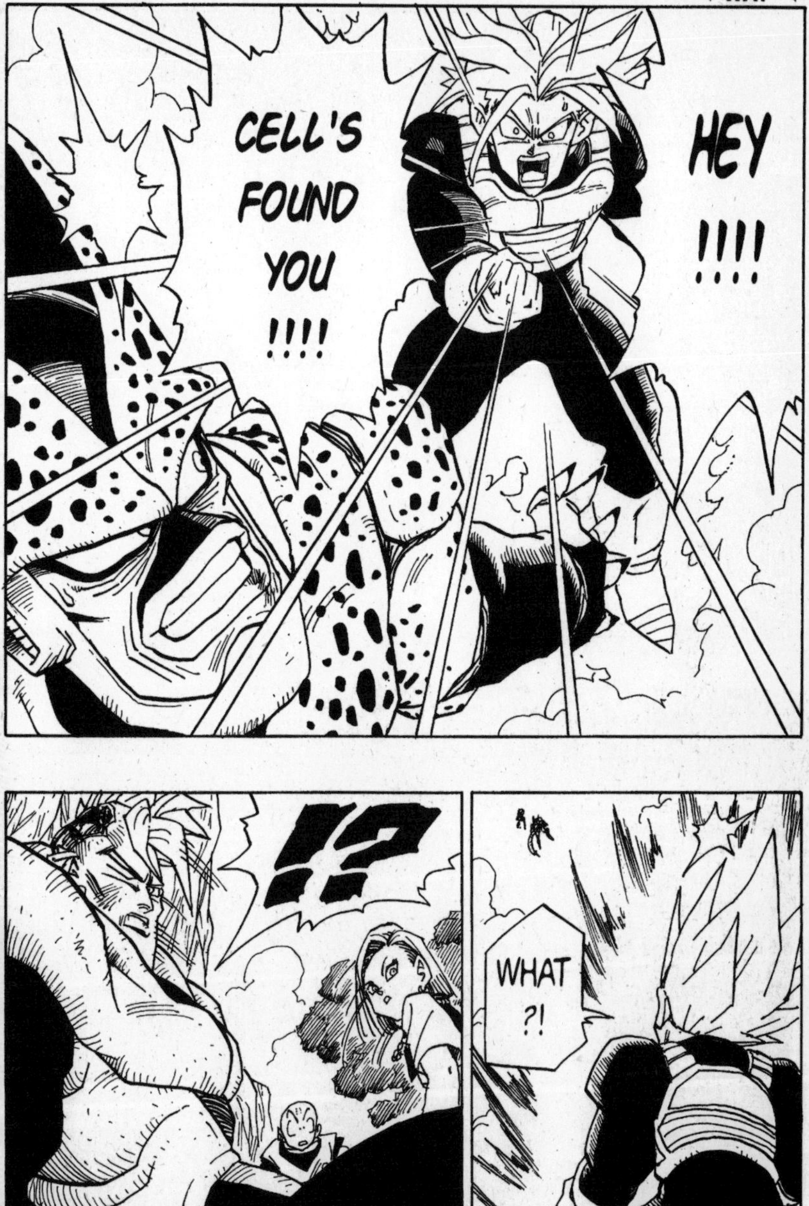
HEY !!!!
CELL'S FOUND YOU !!!!
WHAT ?!
!?

READ THIS WAY

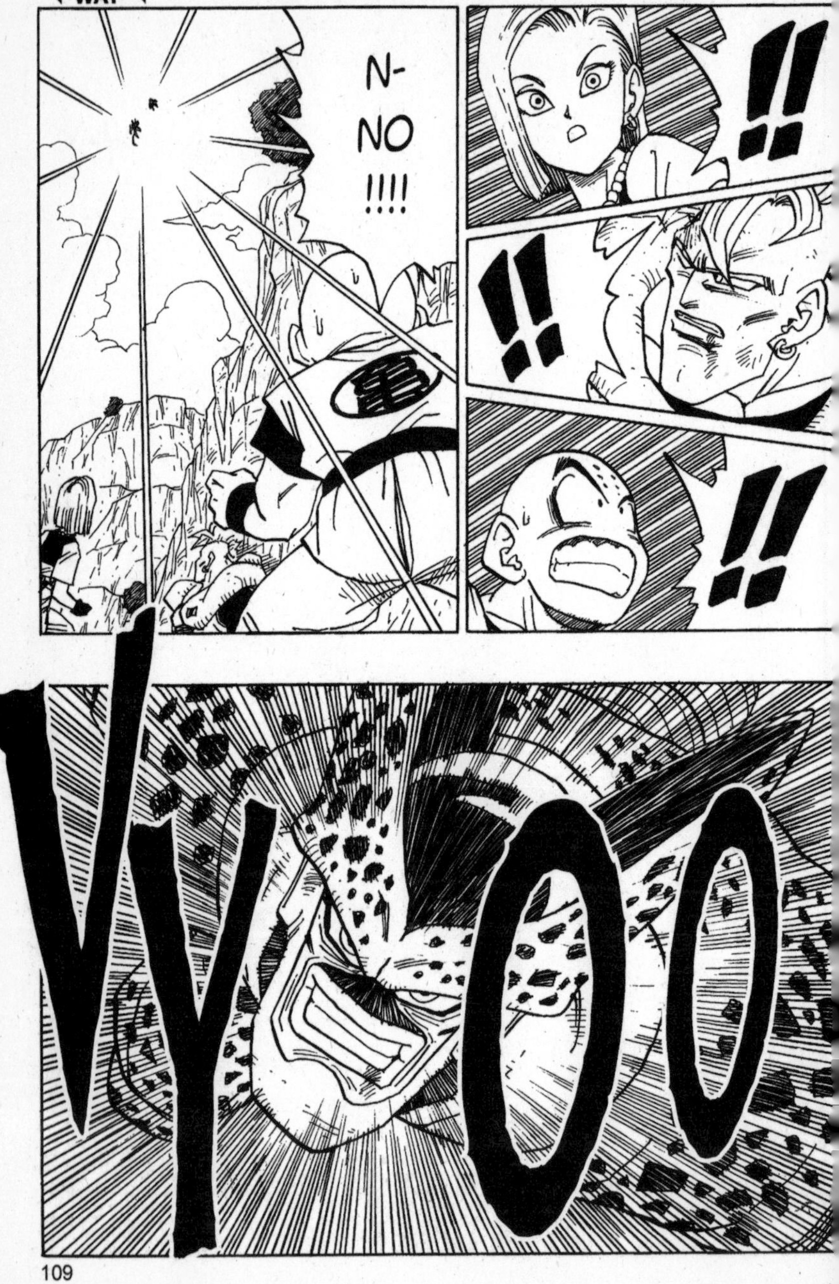
!!
!!
!!
N-NO!!!!
VYOO

READ THIS WAY

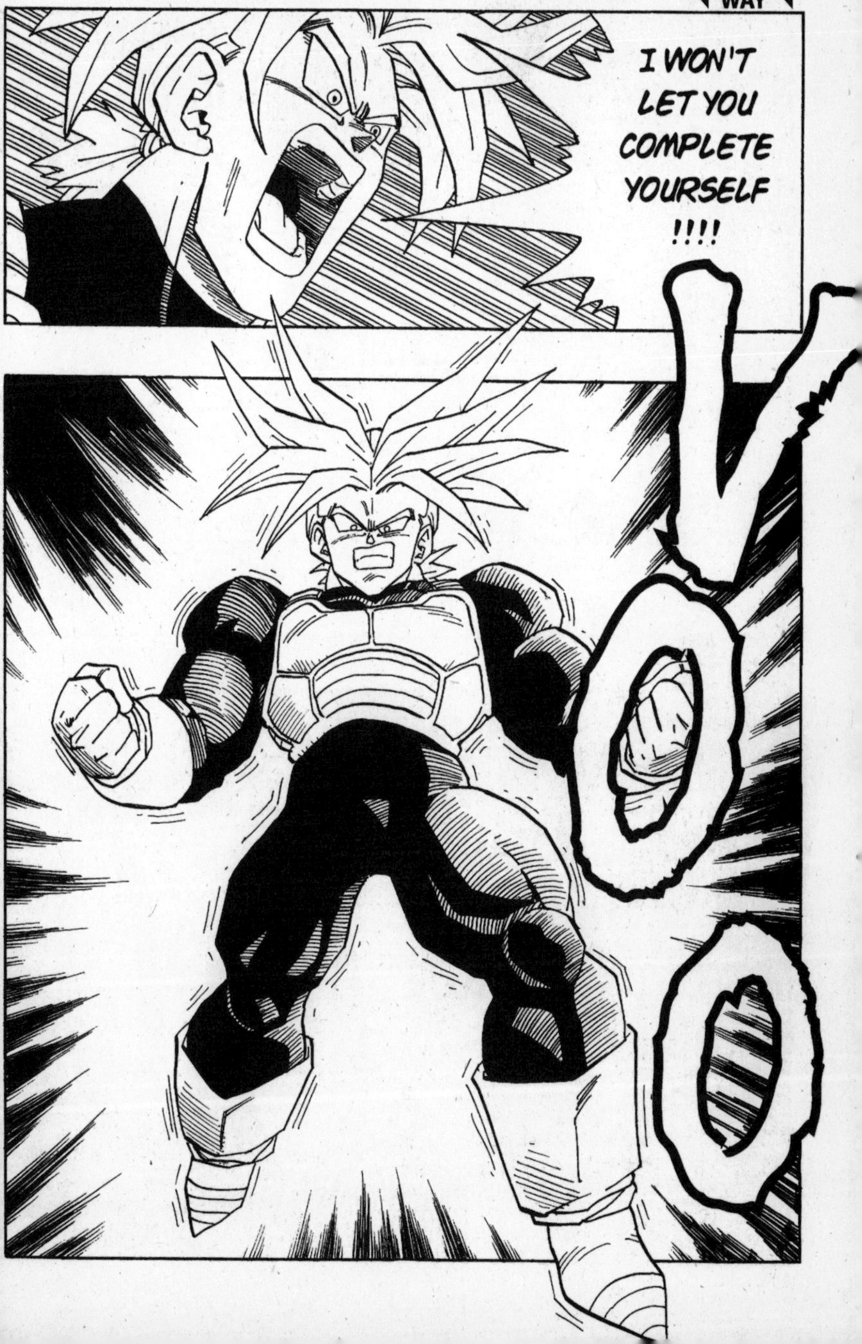
I WON'T LET YOU COMPLETE YOURSELF !!!!

READ THIS WAY

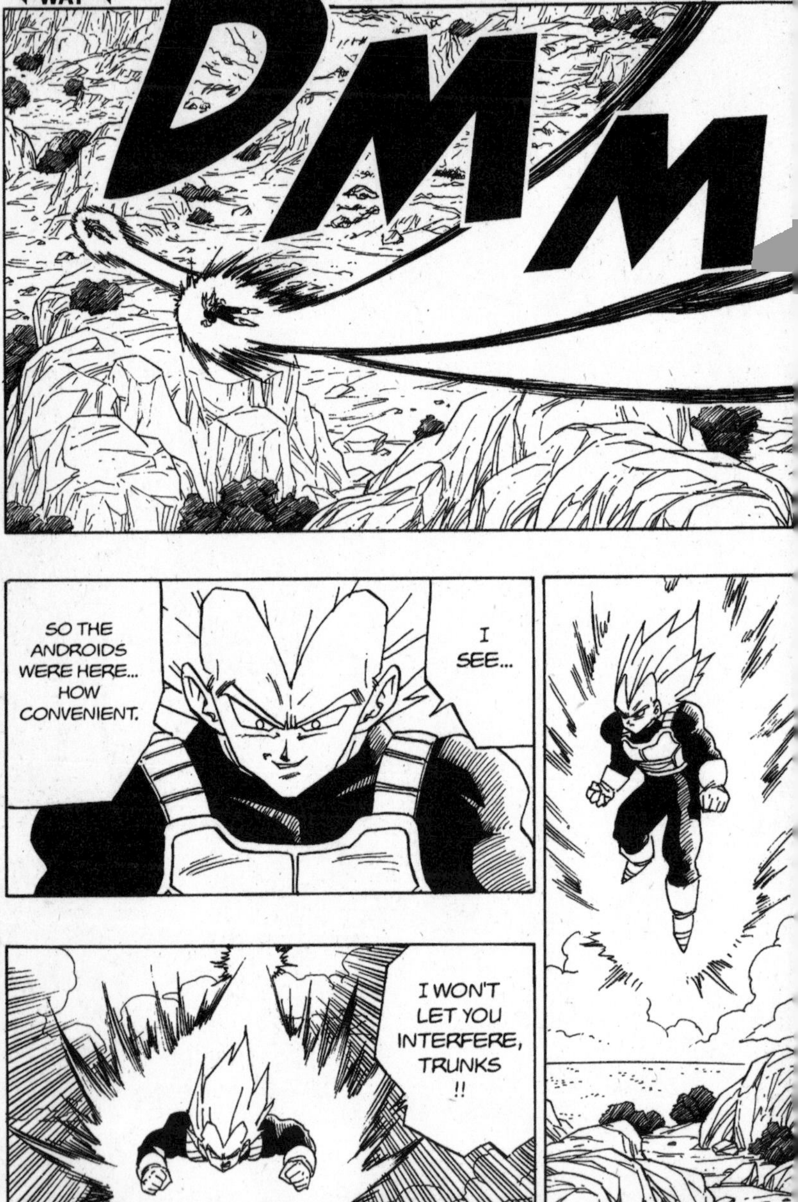
DMM
I SEE...
SO THE ANDROIDS WERE HERE... HOW CONVENIENT.
I WON'T LET YOU INTERFERE, TRUNKS !!

READ THIS WAY

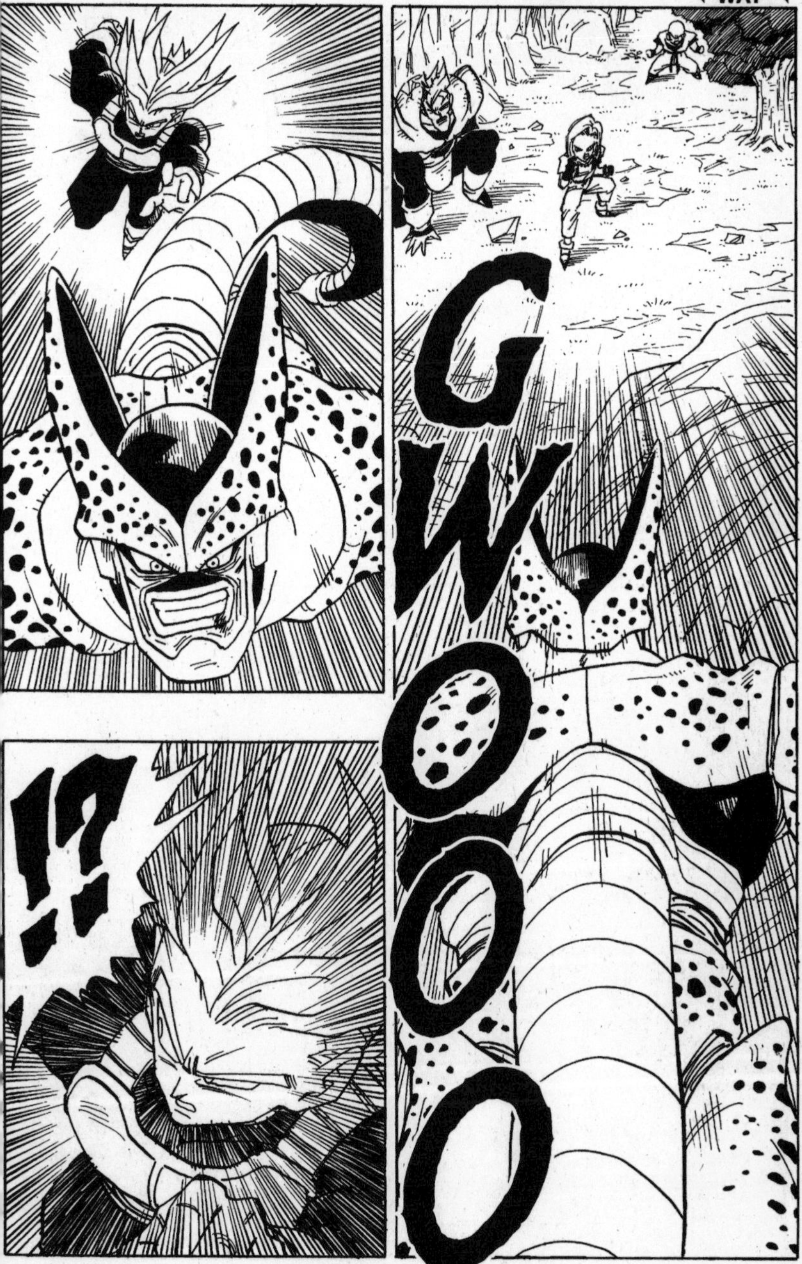
GWOOO
!?

READ THIS WAY

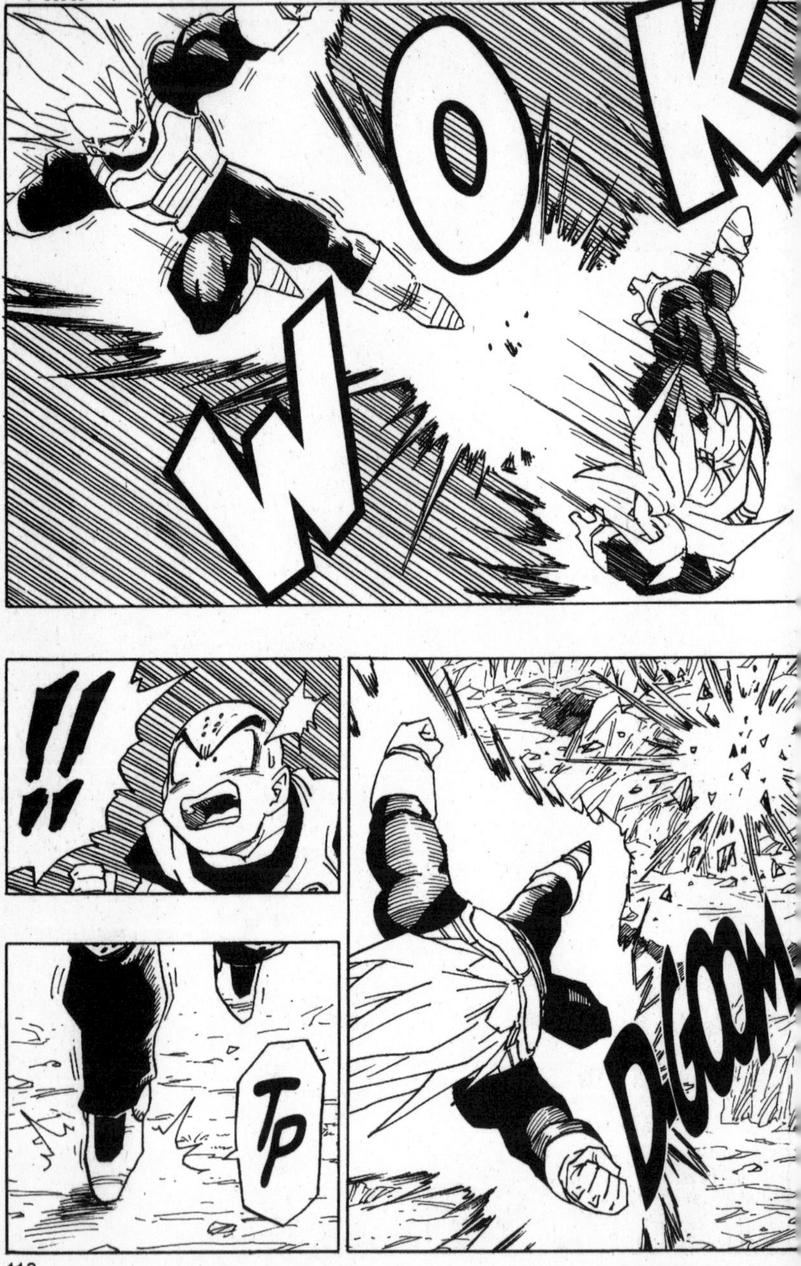
WOK
DGOOM
!!
TP

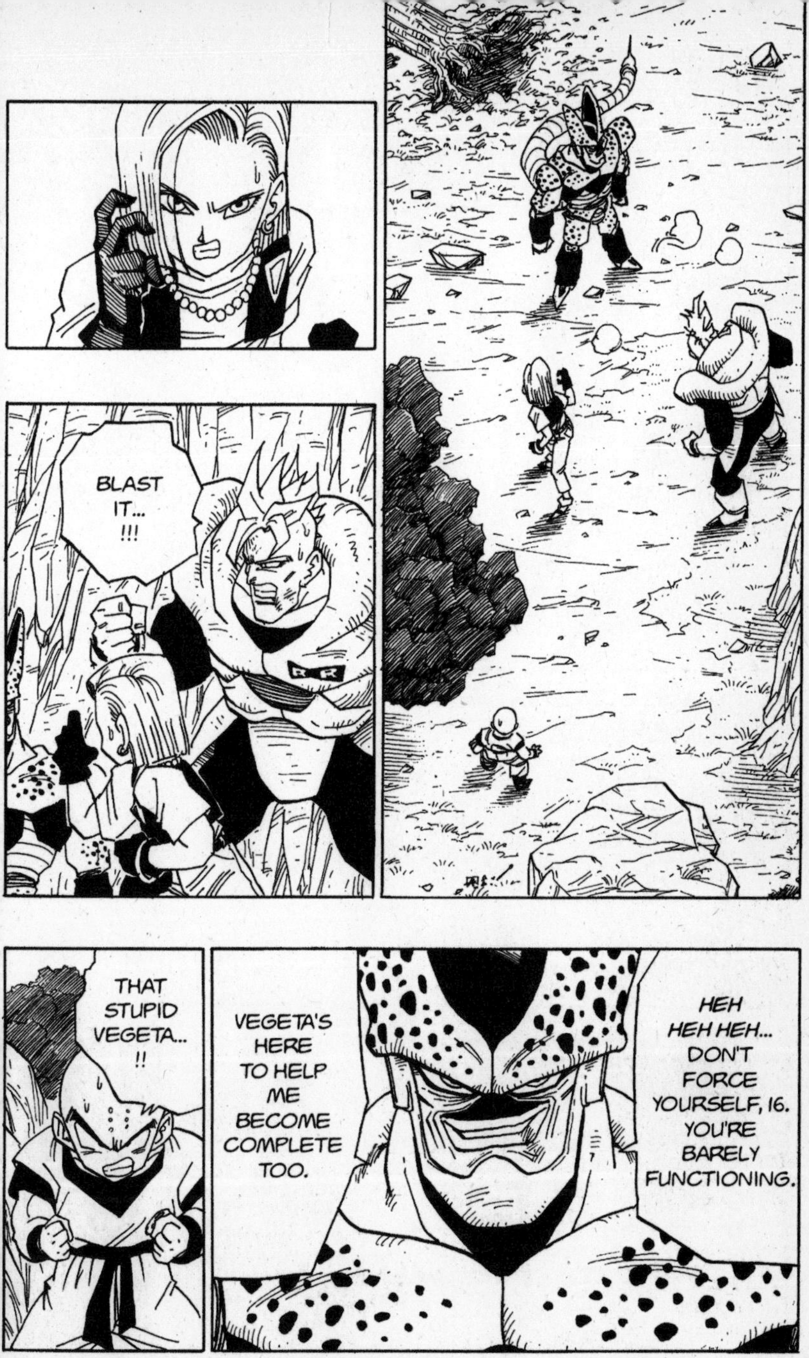
BLAST IT... !!!
HEH HEH HEH... DON'T FORCE YOURSELF, 16. YOU'RE BARELY FUNCTIONING.
VEGETA'S HERE TO HELP ME BECOME COMPLETE TOO.
THAT STUPID VEGETA... !!

« READ THIS WAY «

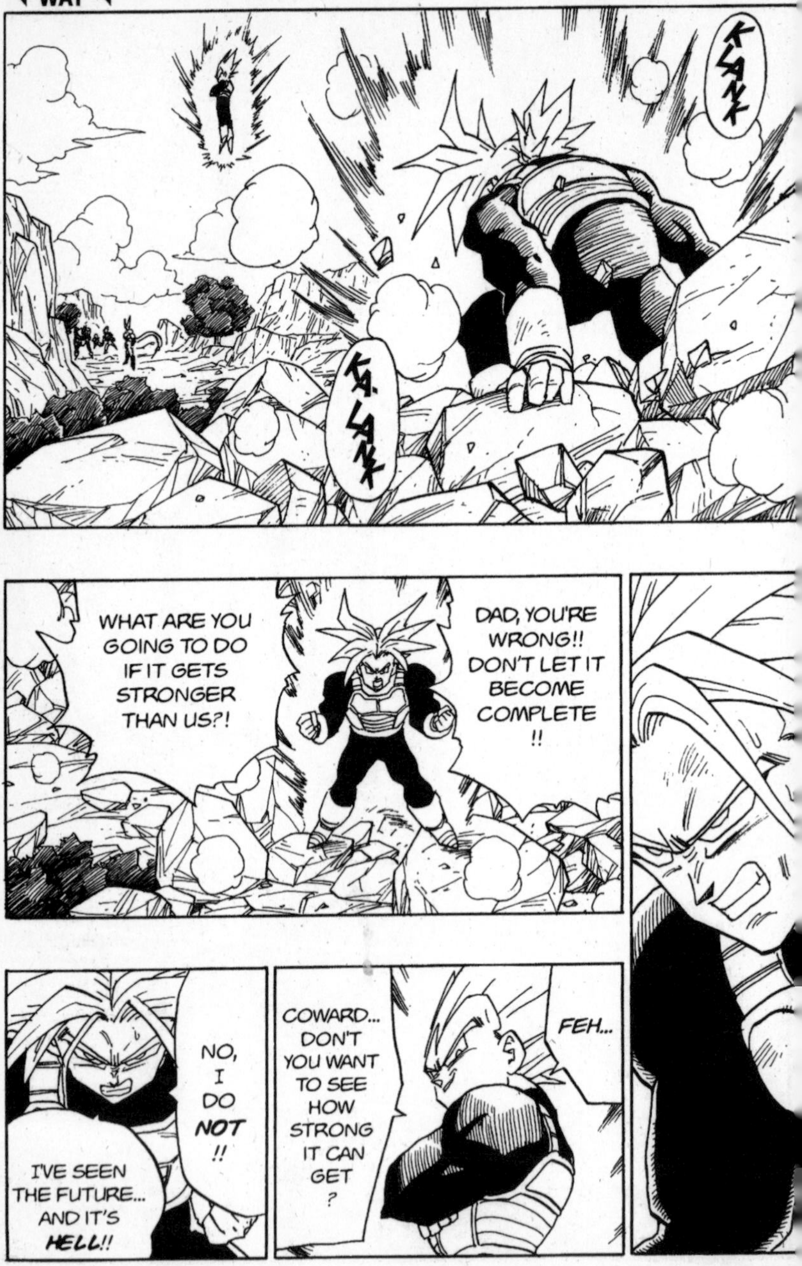
KSANK
KA-LANK
DAD, YOU'RE WRONG!! DON'T LET IT BECOME COMPLETE !!
WHAT ARE YOU GOING TO DO IF IT GETS STRONGER THAN US?!
FEH...
COWARD... DON'T YOU WANT TO SEE HOW STRONG IT CAN GET ?
NO, I DO ***NOT*** !!
I'VE SEEN THE FUTURE... AND IT'S ***HELL!!***

READ THIS WAY

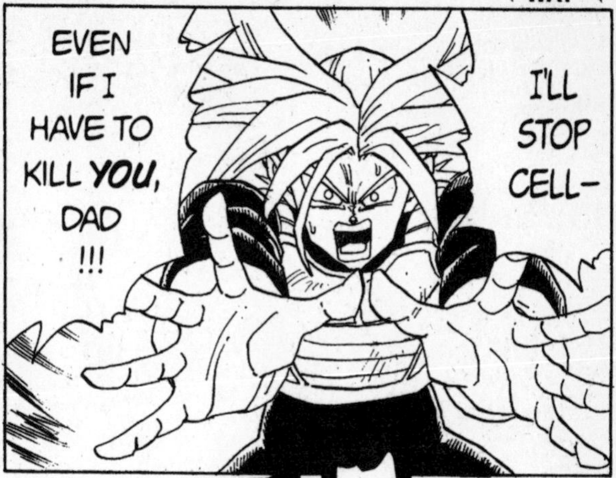
I'LL STOP CELL-
EVEN IF I HAVE TO KILL YOU, DAD !!!

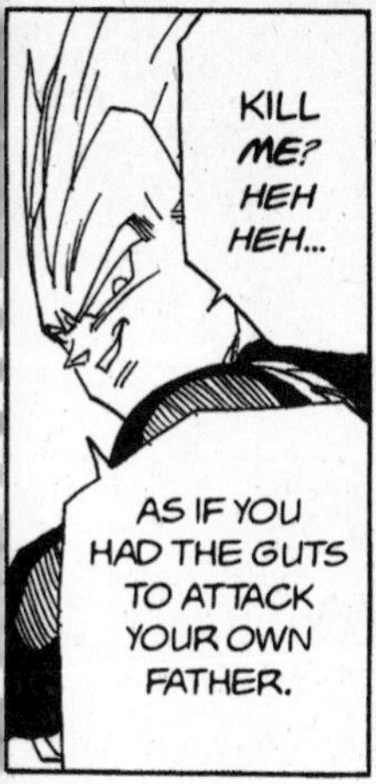
KILL ME? HEH HEH...
AS IF YOU HAD THE GUTS TO ATTACK YOUR OWN FATHER.

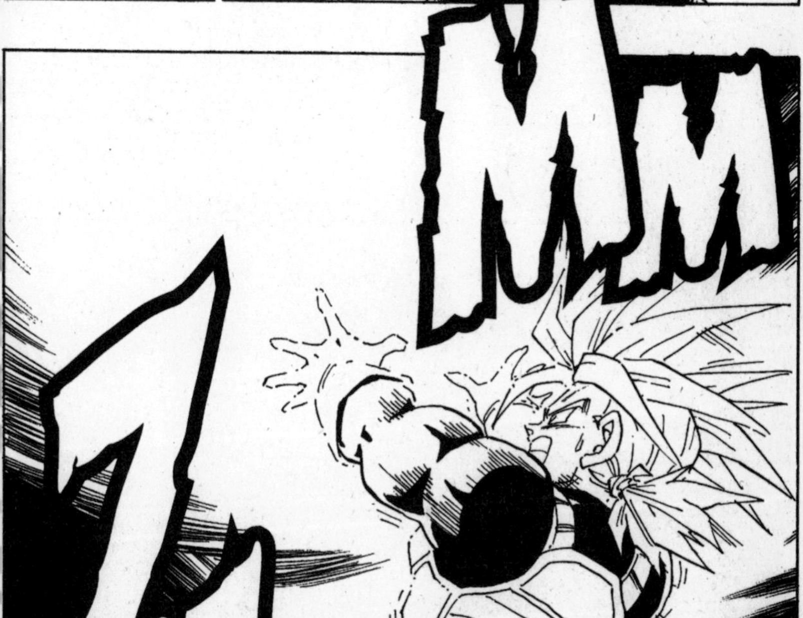
MM

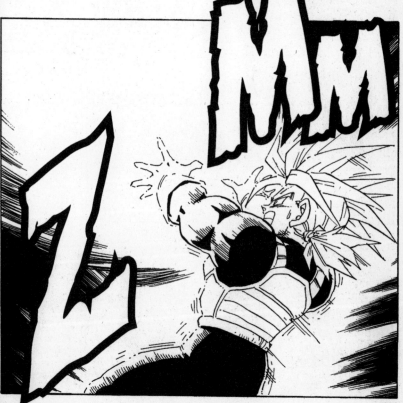

READ THIS WAY

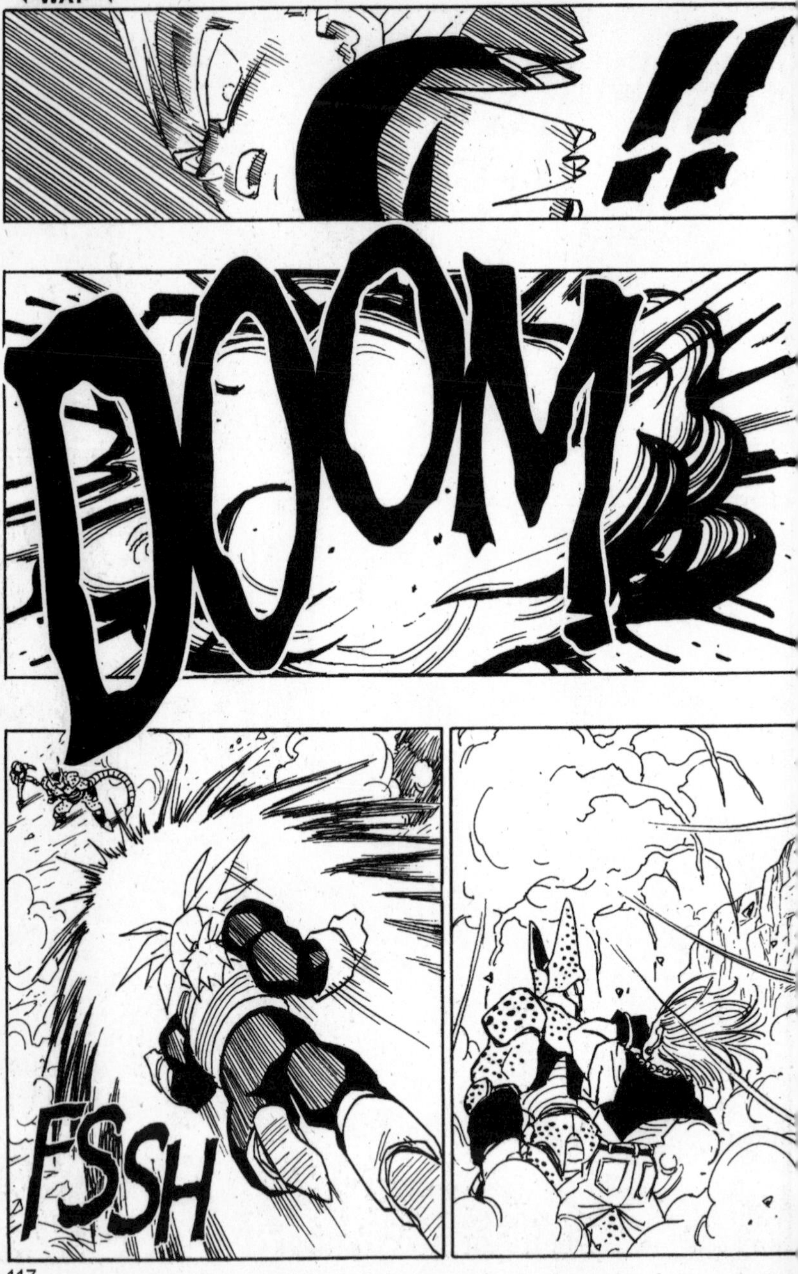
!!
DOOM
FSSH

READ THIS WAY

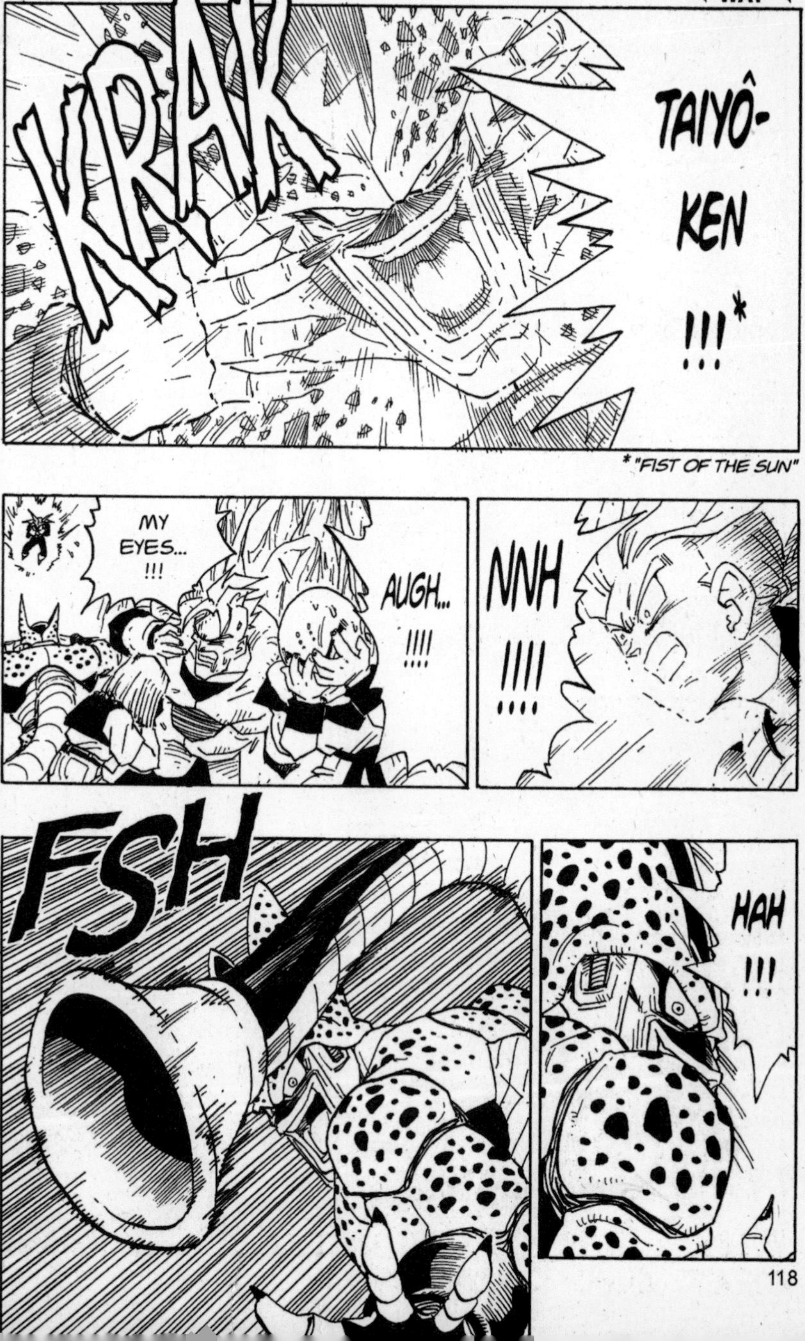
TAIYÔ-KEN!!!*
KRAK
NNH!!!!!!!!
AUGH...!!!!
MY EYES...!!!
HAH!!!
FSH

* "FIST OF THE SUN"

READ THIS WAY

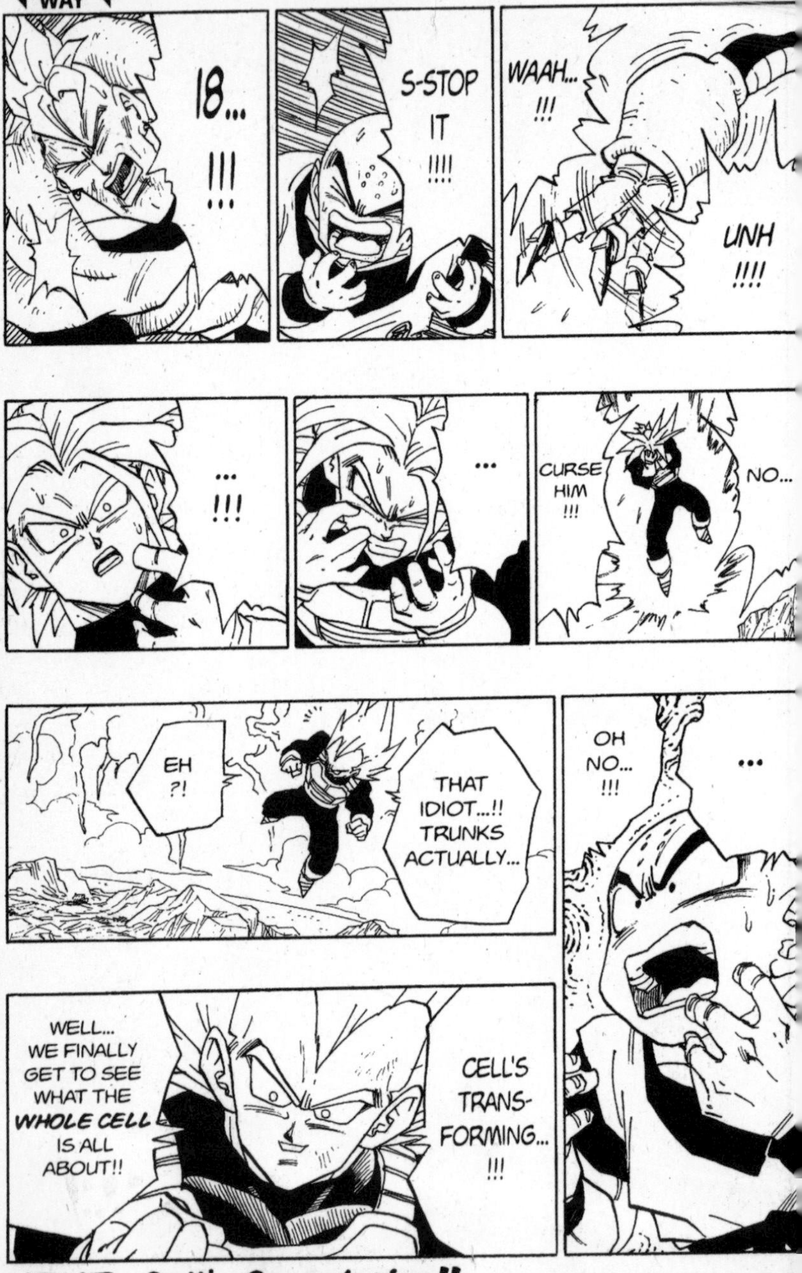
WAAH...!!!
UNH!!!!
S-STOP IT!!!!
18...!!!
NO...
CURSE HIM!!!
...
...!!!
...
OH NO...!!!
THAT IDIOT...!! TRUNKS ACTUALLY...
EH?!
CELL'S TRANS-FORMING...!!!
WELL... WE FINALLY GET TO SEE WHAT THE WHOLE CELL IS ALL ABOUT!!

NEXT: Cell's Completion!!

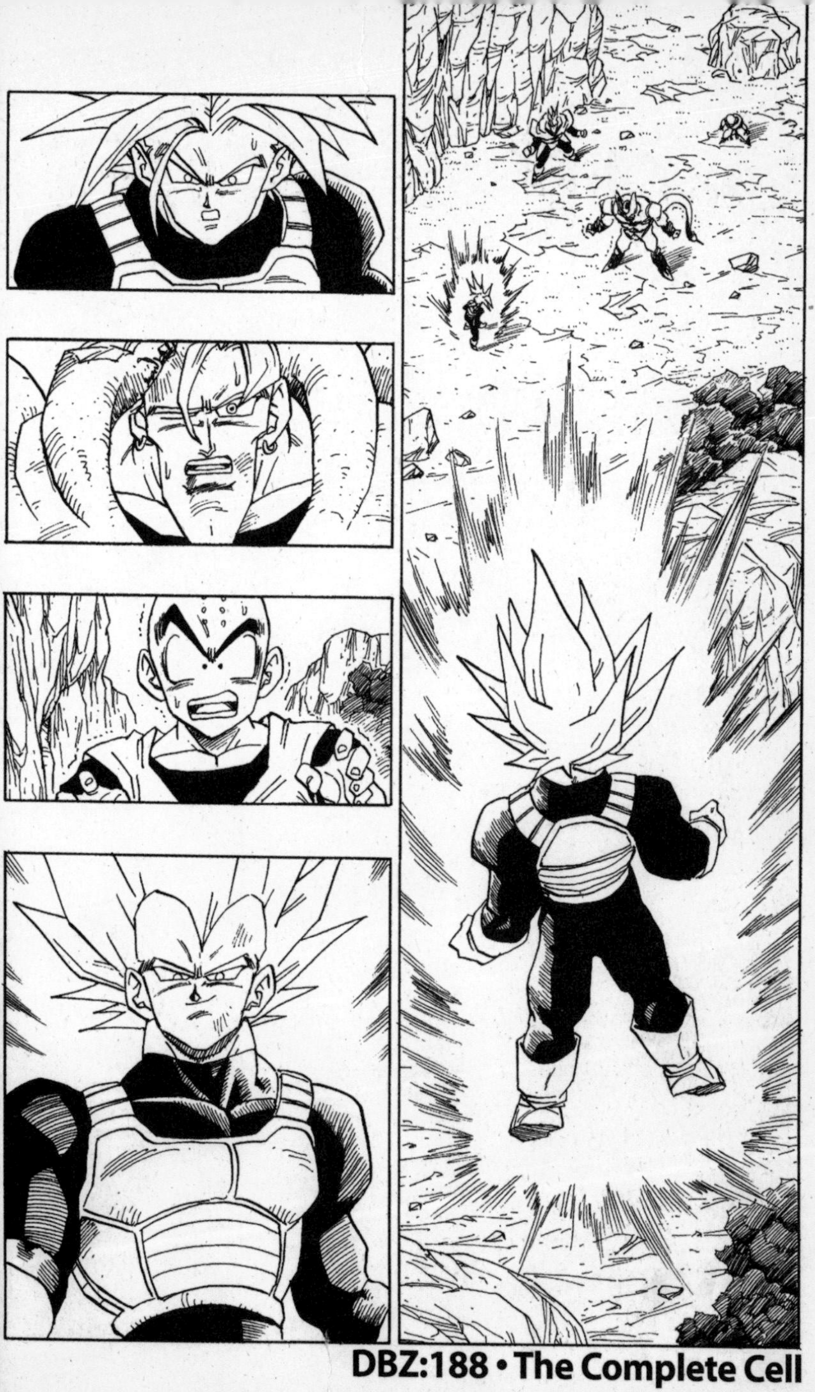

DBZ:188 • The Complete Cell

READ THIS WAY

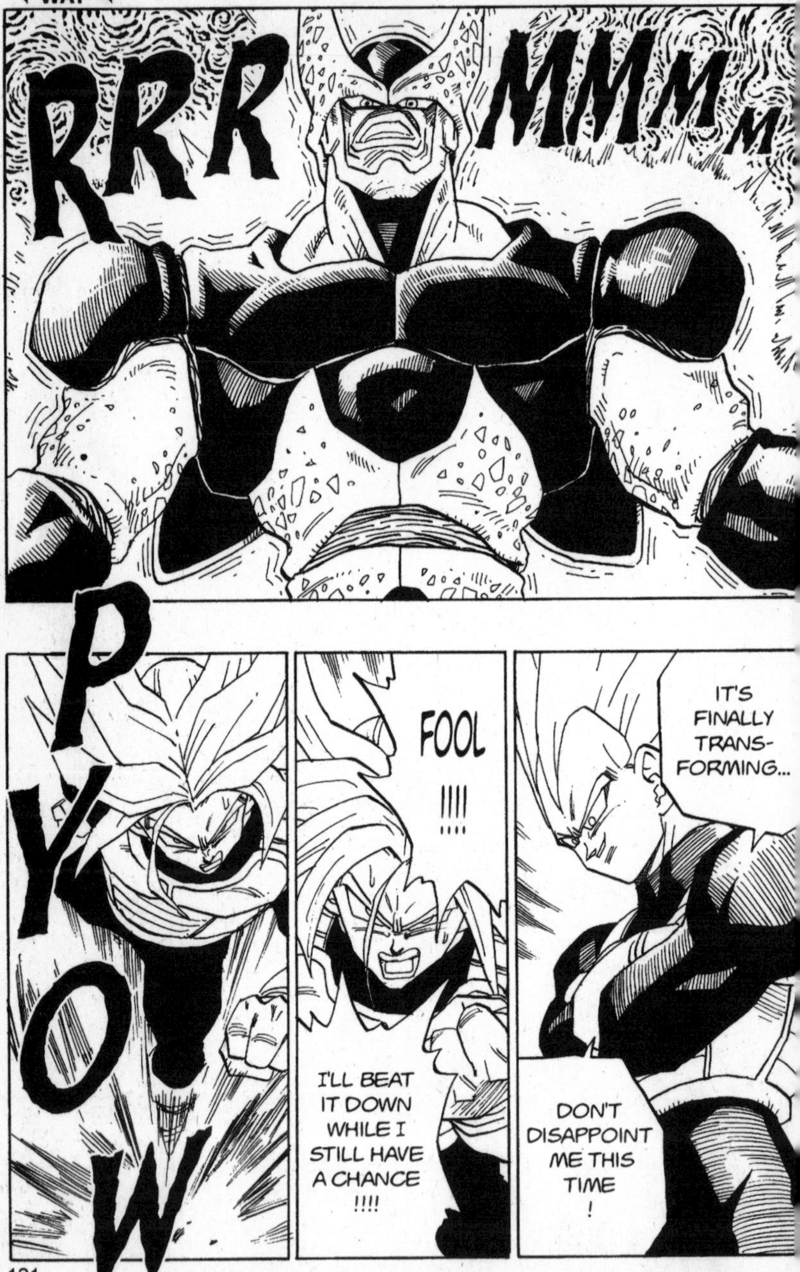
RRRMMMM
IT'S FINALLY TRANS- FORMING...
DON'T DISAPPOINT ME THIS TIME !
FOOL !!!!
I'LL BEAT IT DOWN WHILE I STILL HAVE A CHANCE !!!!
PYOOW

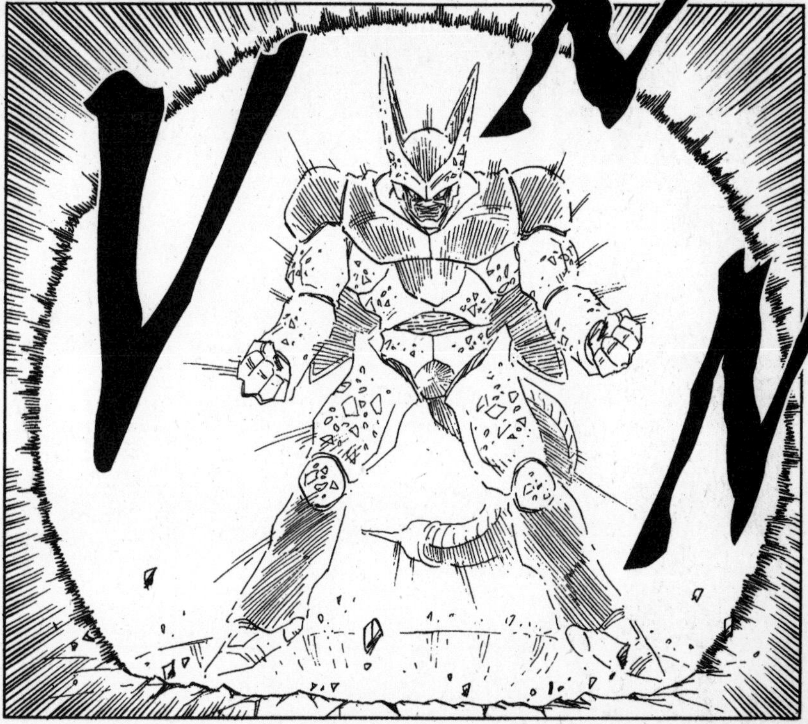
VNN

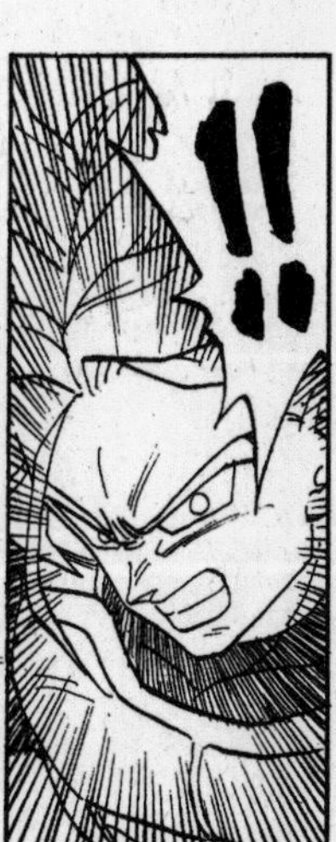
!!

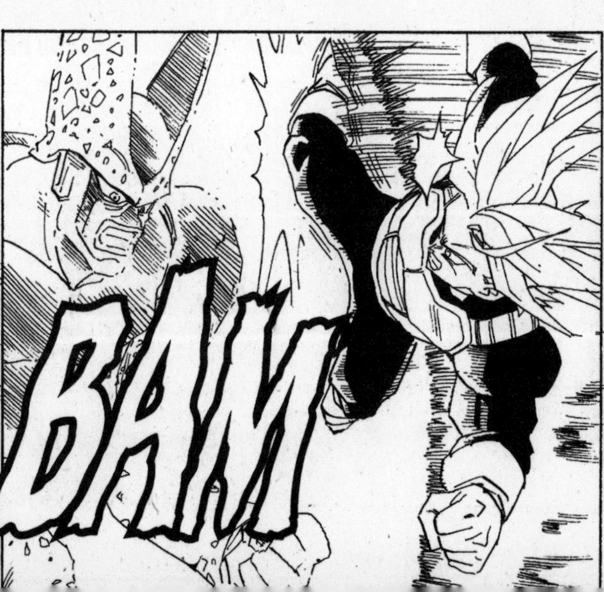
BAM

READ THIS WAY

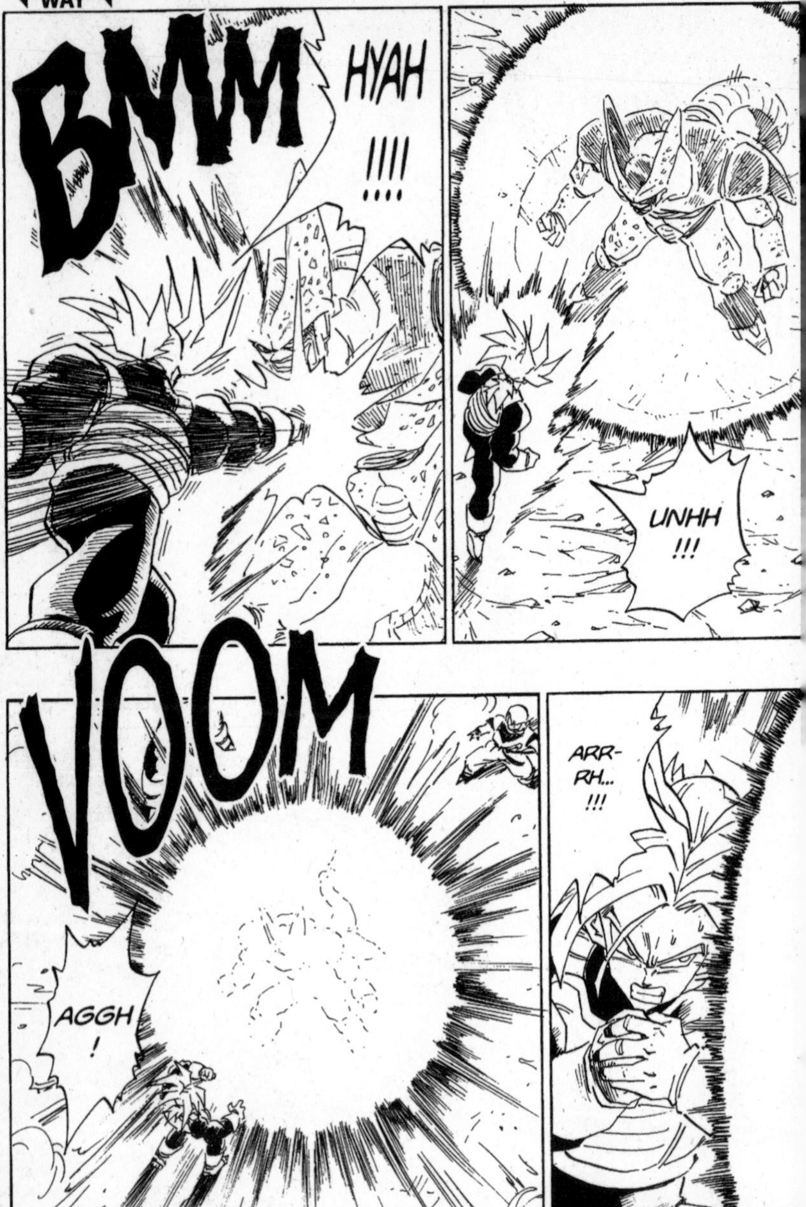
UNHH !!!
HYAH !!!!
BMM
ARR-RH... !!!
VOOM
AGGH !

READ THIS WAY

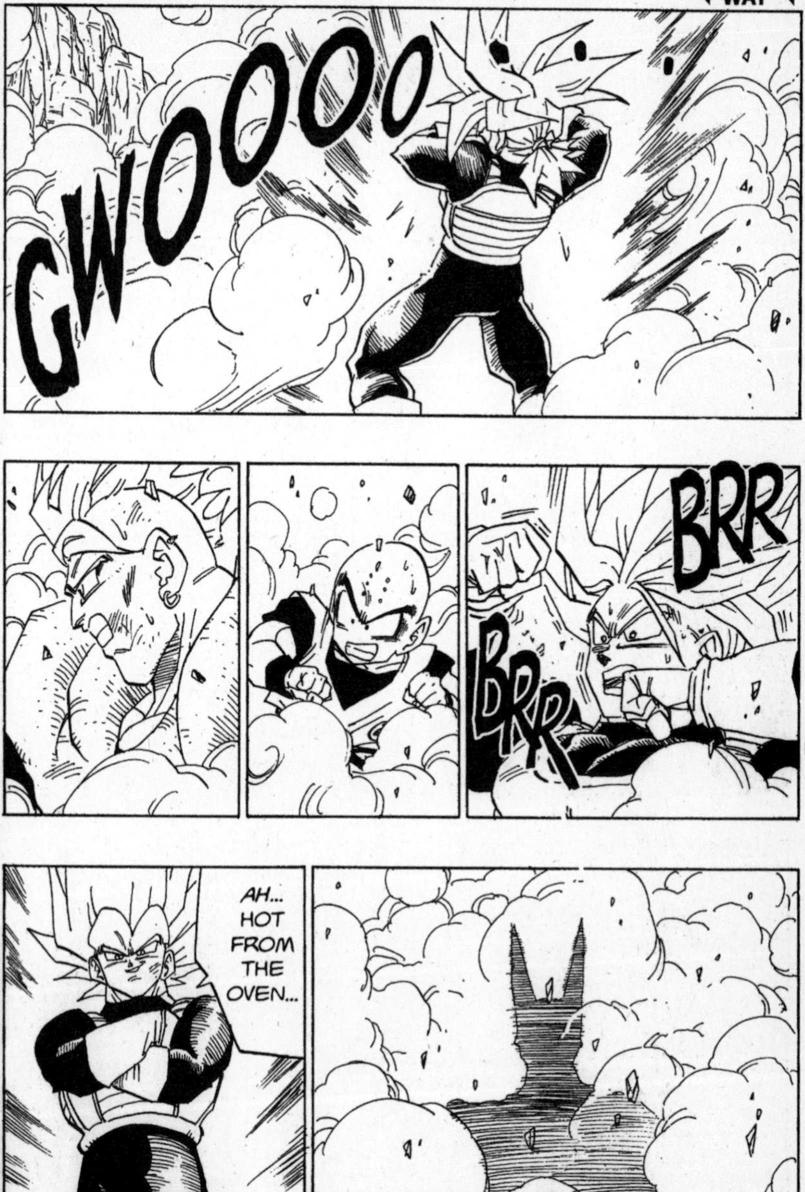
GWOOOOO
BRR
BRR
AH... HOT FROM THE OVEN...

READ THIS WAY

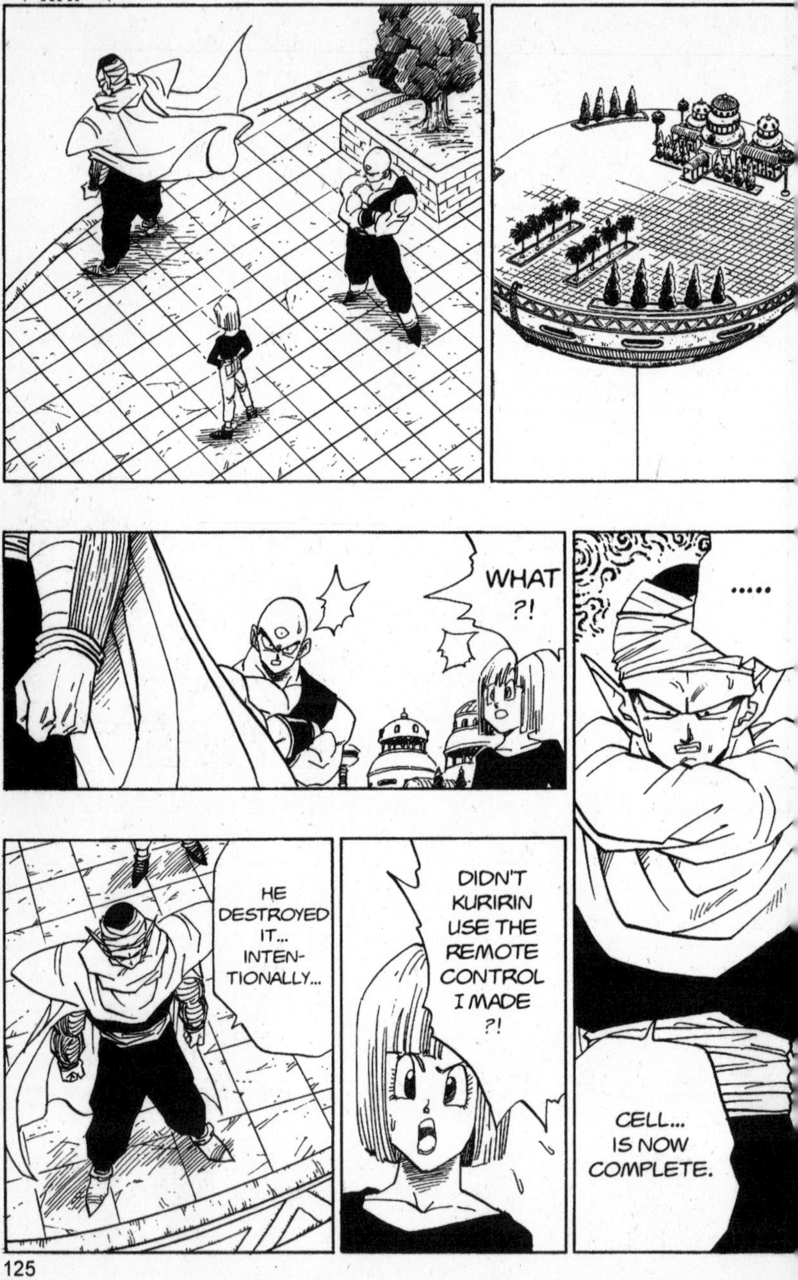

.....
CELL... IS NOW COMPLETE.
WHAT ?!
DIDN'T KURIRIN USE THE REMOTE CONTROL I MADE ?!
HE DESTROYED IT... INTEN-TIONALLY...

READ THIS WAY

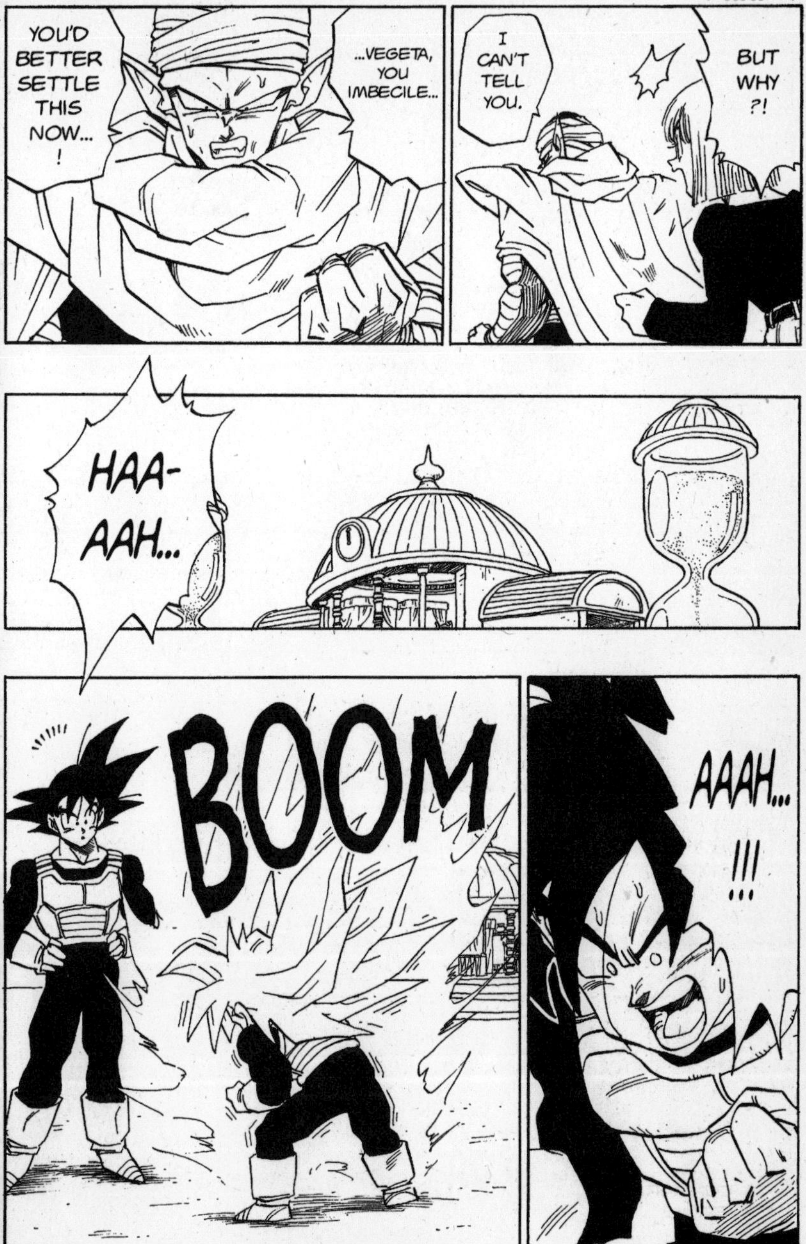
BUT WHY ?!
I CAN'T TELL YOU.
...VEGETA, YOU IMBECILE...
YOU'D BETTER SETTLE THIS NOW... !
HAA- AAH...
AAAH... !!!
BOOM

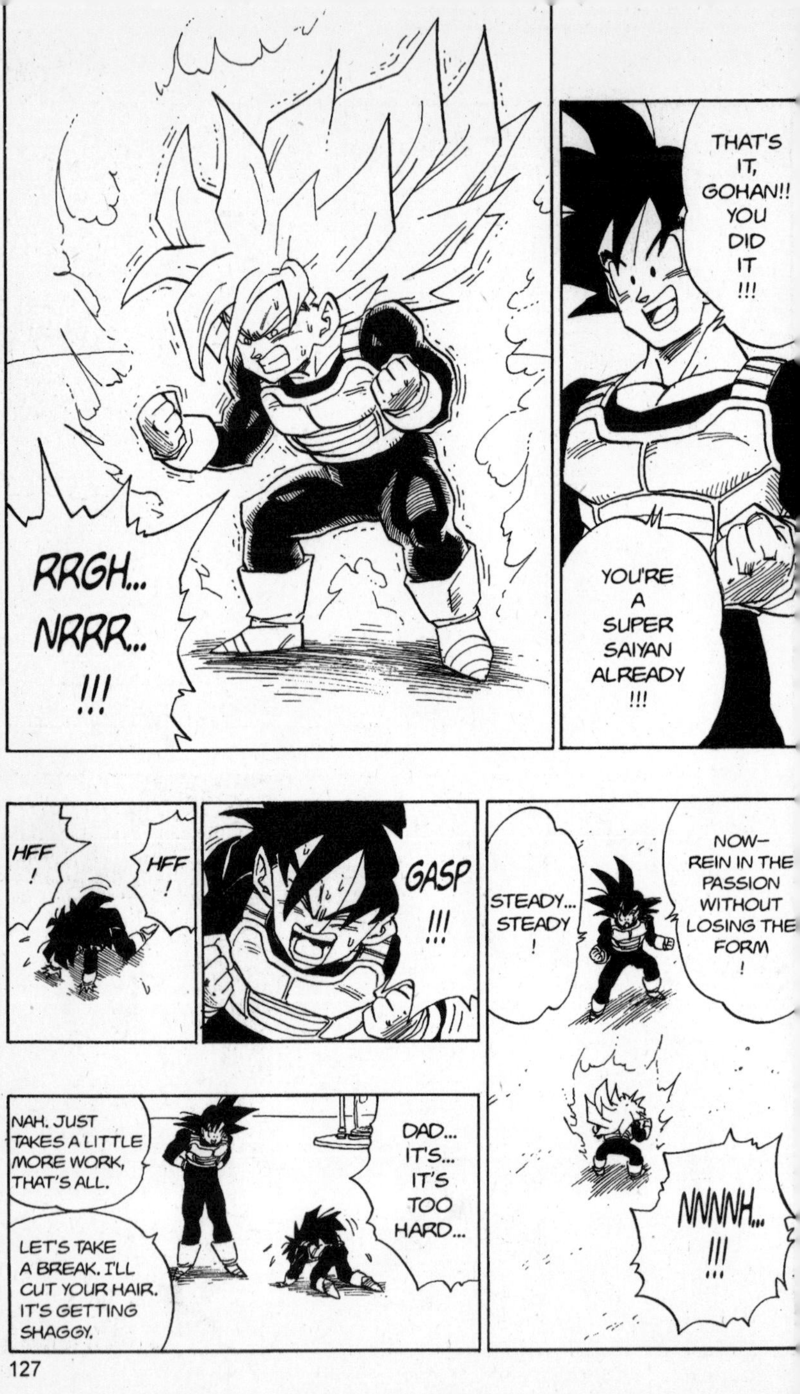
THAT'S IT, GOHAN!! YOU DID IT!!!
YOU'RE A SUPER SAIYAN ALREADY!!!
RRGH... NRRR... !!!
NOW— REIN IN THE PASSION WITHOUT LOSING THE FORM!
STEADY... STEADY!
NNNNH... !!!
GASP!!!
HFF!
HFF!
DAD... IT'S... IT'S TOO HARD...
NAH. JUST TAKES A LITTLE MORE WORK, THAT'S ALL.
LET'S TAKE A BREAK. I'LL CUT YOUR HAIR. IT'S GETTING SHAGGY.

READ THIS WAY

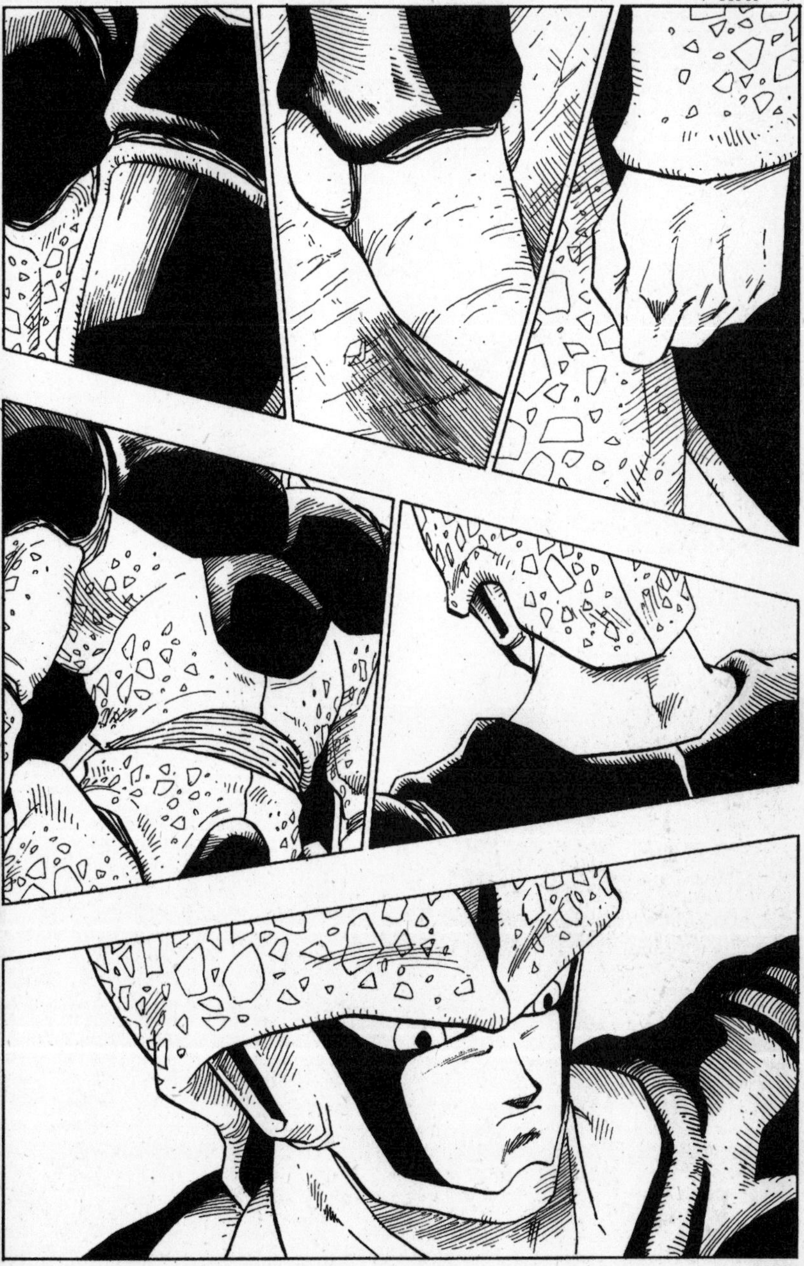

READ THIS WAY

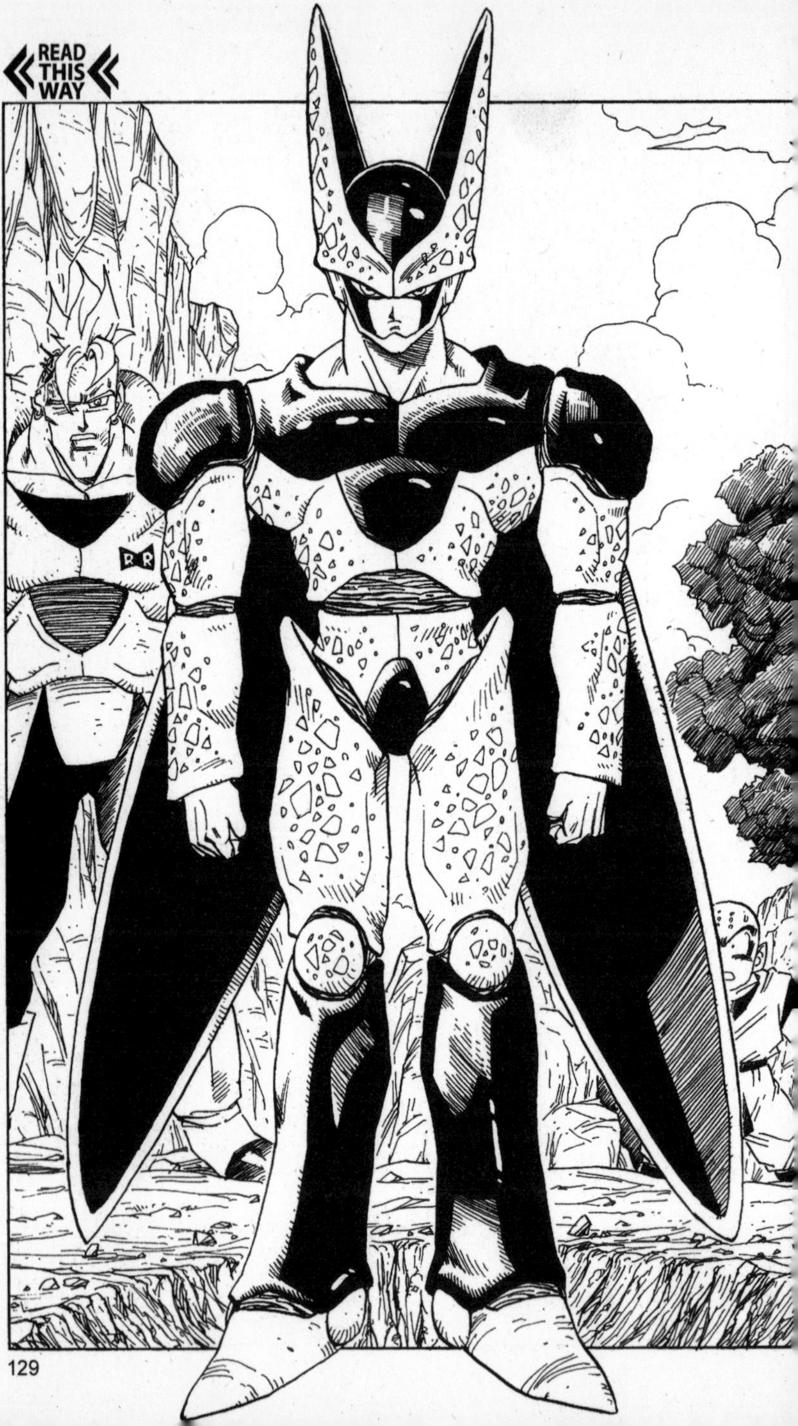

READ THIS WAY

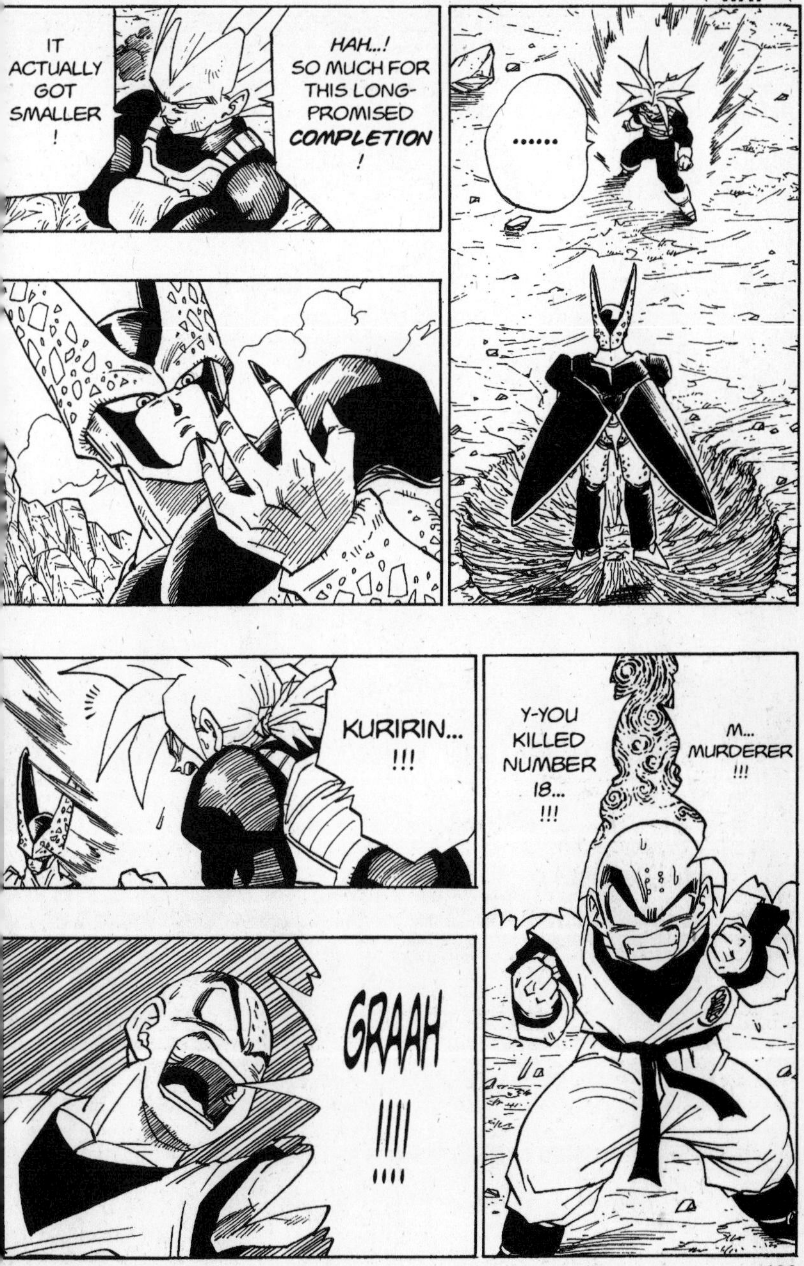

......
HAH...! SO MUCH FOR THIS LONG-PROMISED COMPLETION !
IT ACTUALLY GOT SMALLER !
M... MURDERER !!!
Y-YOU KILLED NUMBER 18... !!!
KURIRIN... !!!
GRAAH !!!!!!!!!

READ THIS WAY

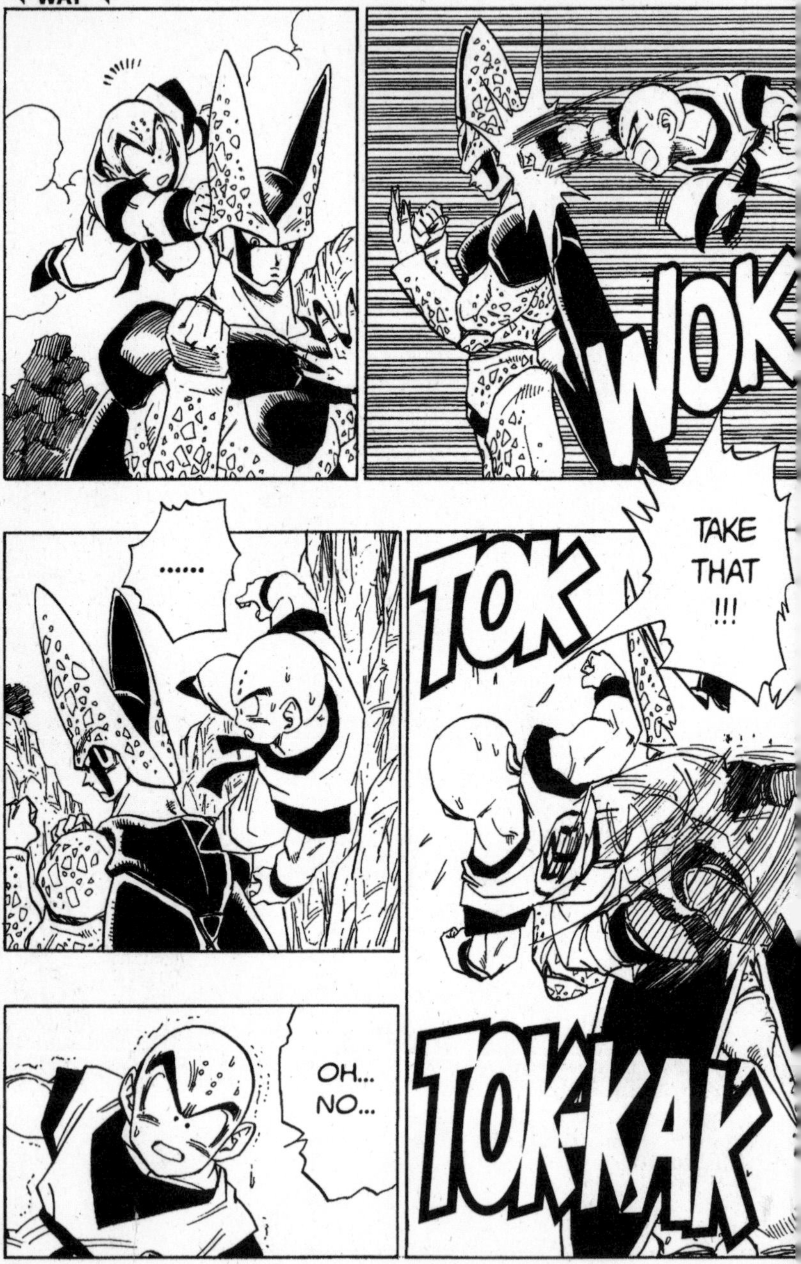
WOK
TAKE THAT !!!
TOK
TOK-KAK
......
OH... NO...

READ THIS WAY

WSH
SHHSHH
SHH
HEH
HYAH!!!!
VM

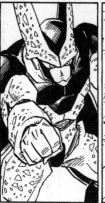

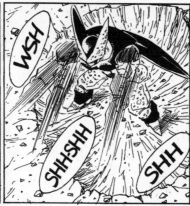

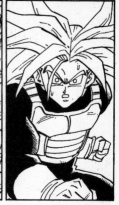

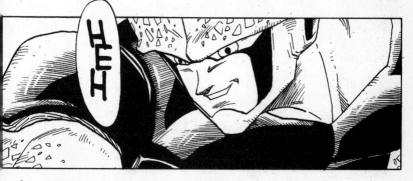

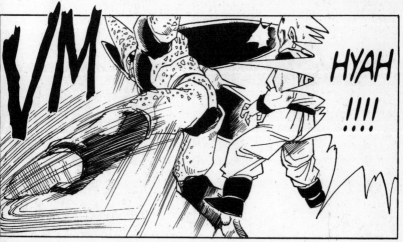

READ THIS WAY

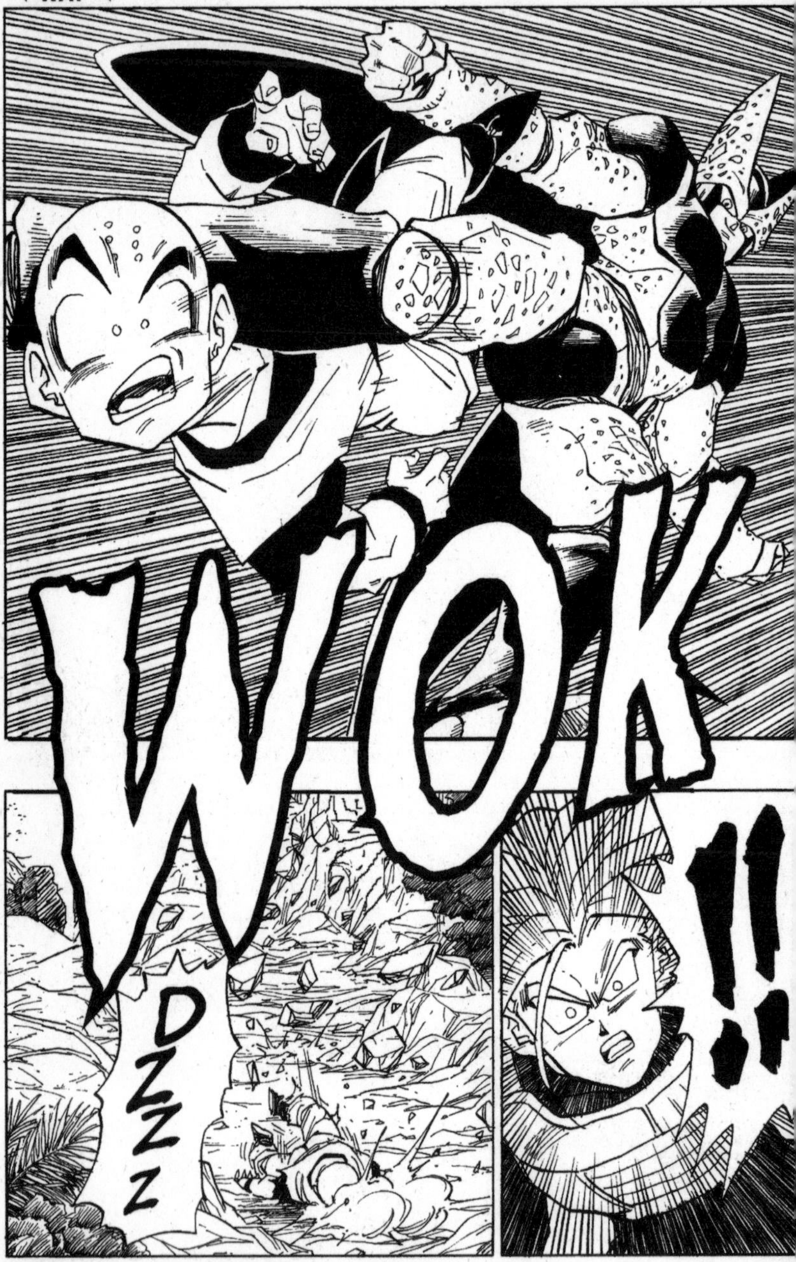
WOK!!
DZZZ

NEXT: The Tables Turn!!

DBZ:189 • A Reversal

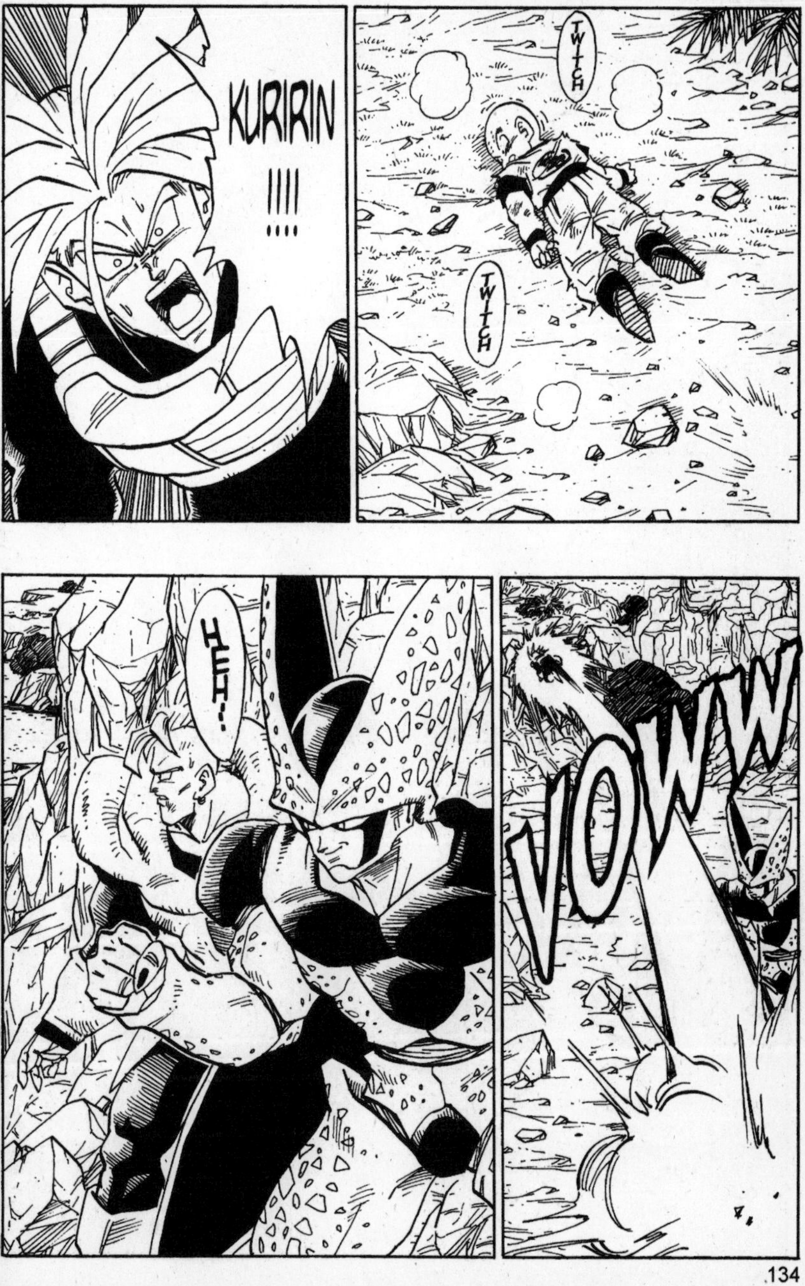
TWITCH
TWITCH
KURIRIN!!!!!!!!!
VOWW
HEH!!

READ THIS WAY

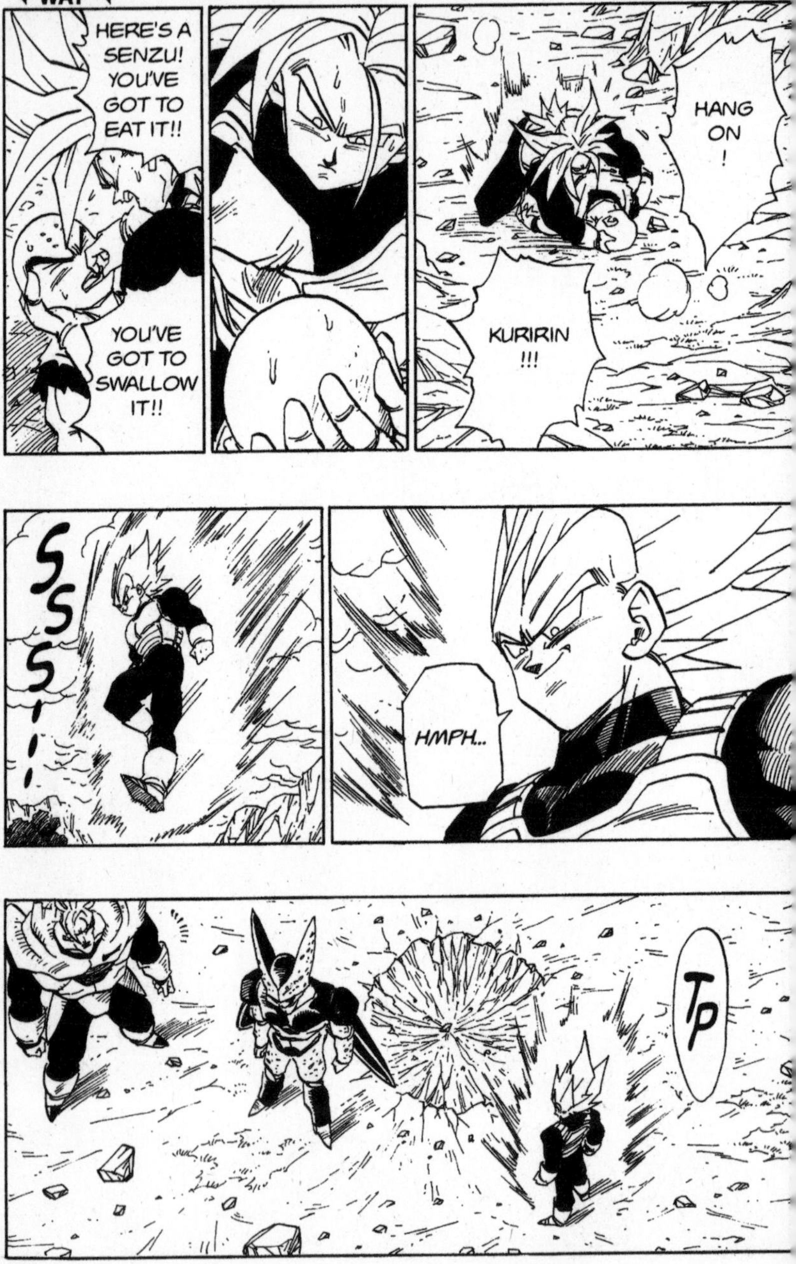
HANG ON!
KURIRIN!!!
HERE'S A SENZU! YOU'VE GOT TO EAT IT!!
YOU'VE GOT TO SWALLOW IT!!
HMPH...
SSS
TP

READ THIS WAY

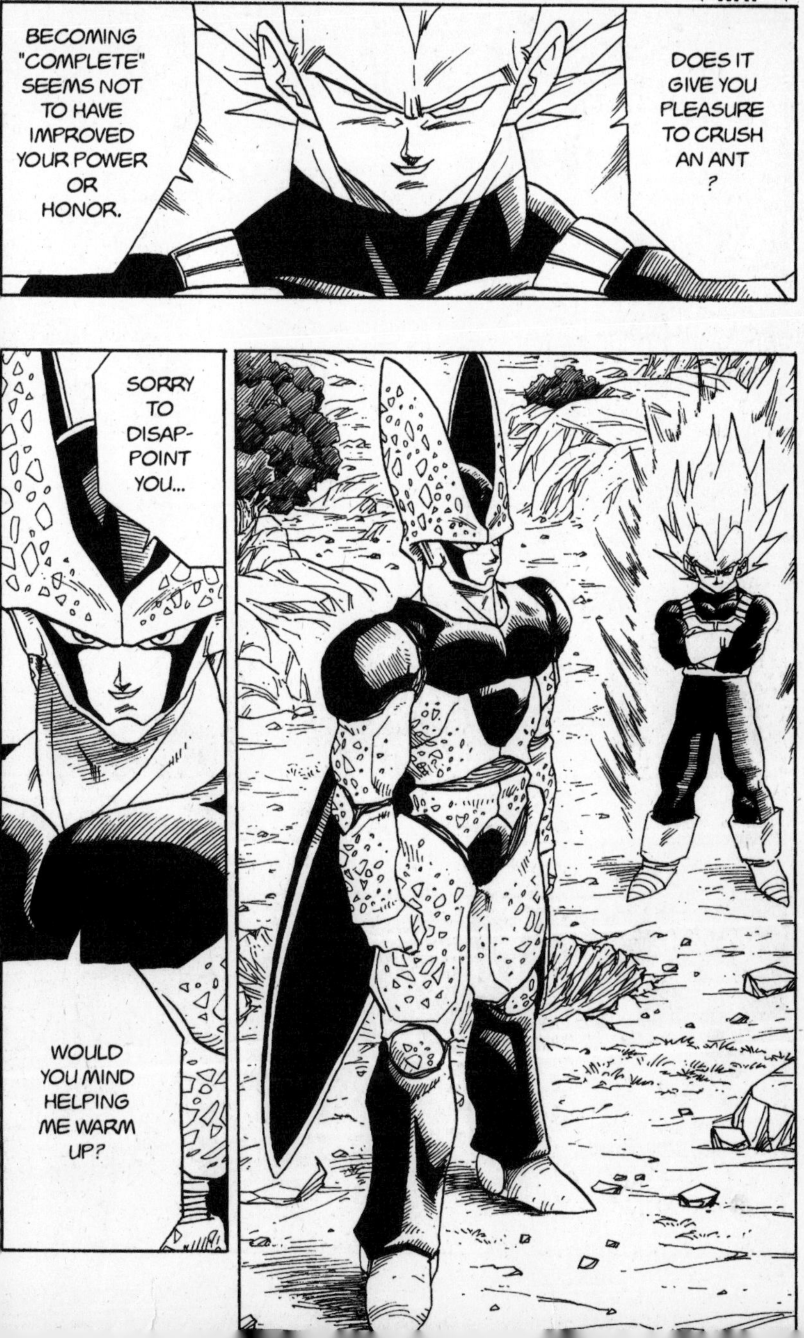
DOES IT GIVE YOU PLEASURE TO CRUSH AN ANT ?
BECOMING "COMPLETE" SEEMS NOT TO HAVE IMPROVED YOUR POWER OR HONOR.
SORRY TO DISAP-POINT YOU...
WOULD YOU MIND HELPING ME WARM UP?

READ THIS WAY

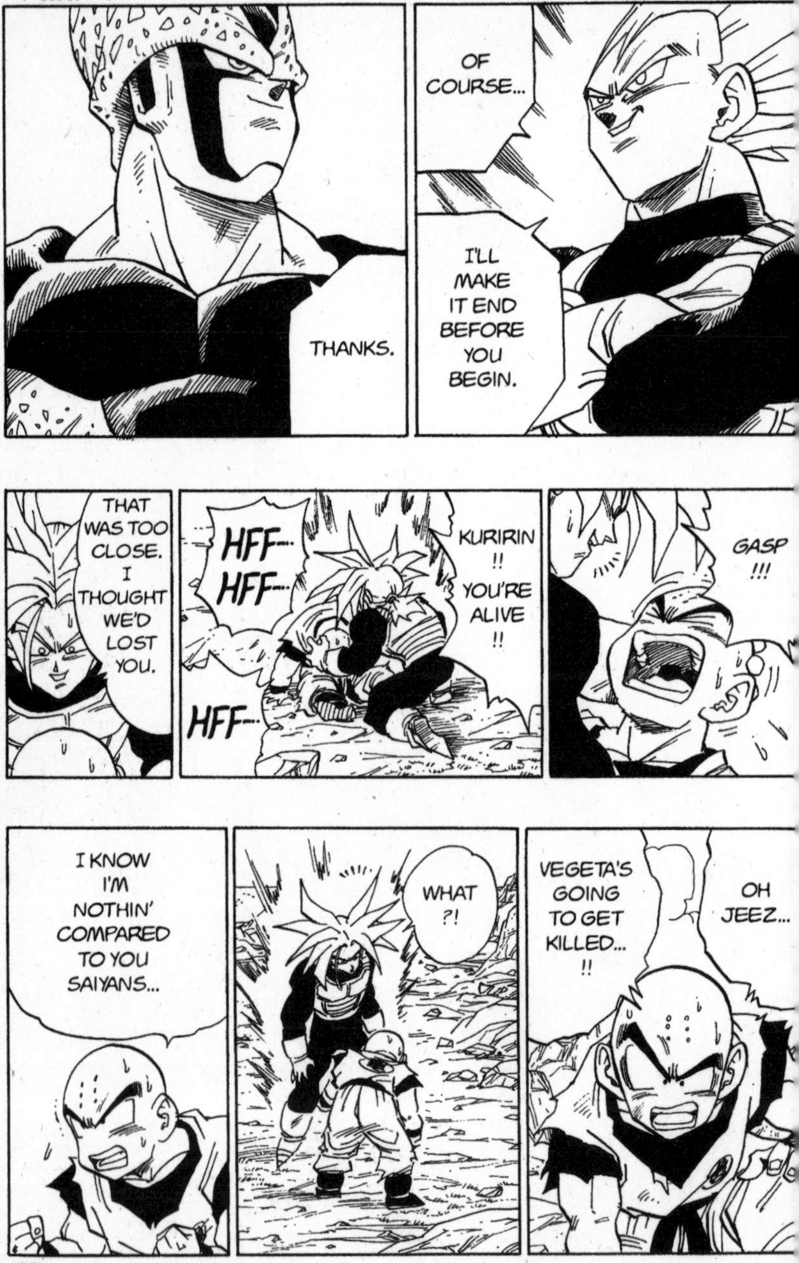
OF COURSE...
I'LL MAKE IT END BEFORE YOU BEGIN.
THANKS.
GASP !!!
KURIRIN !! YOU'RE ALIVE !!
HFF-- HFF--
HFF--
THAT WAS TOO CLOSE. I THOUGHT WE'D LOST YOU.
OH JEEZ...
VEGETA'S GOING TO GET KILLED... !!
WHAT ?!
I KNOW I'M NOTHIN' COMPARED TO YOU SAIYANS...

READ THIS WAY

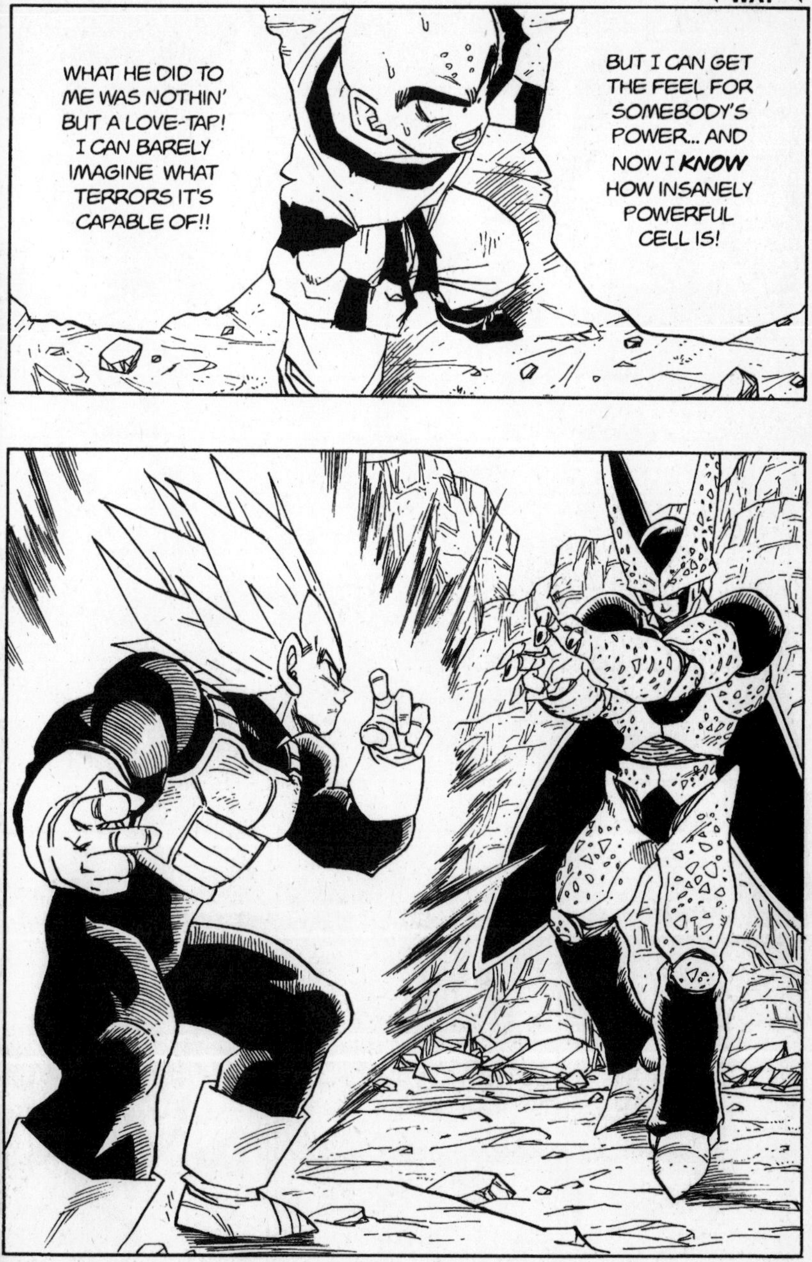
BUT I CAN GET THE FEEL FOR SOMEBODY'S POWER... AND NOW I **KNOW** HOW INSANELY POWERFUL CELL IS!
WHAT HE DID TO ME WAS NOTHIN' BUT A LOVE-TAP! I CAN BARELY IMAGINE WHAT TERRORS IT'S CAPABLE OF!!

READ THIS WAY

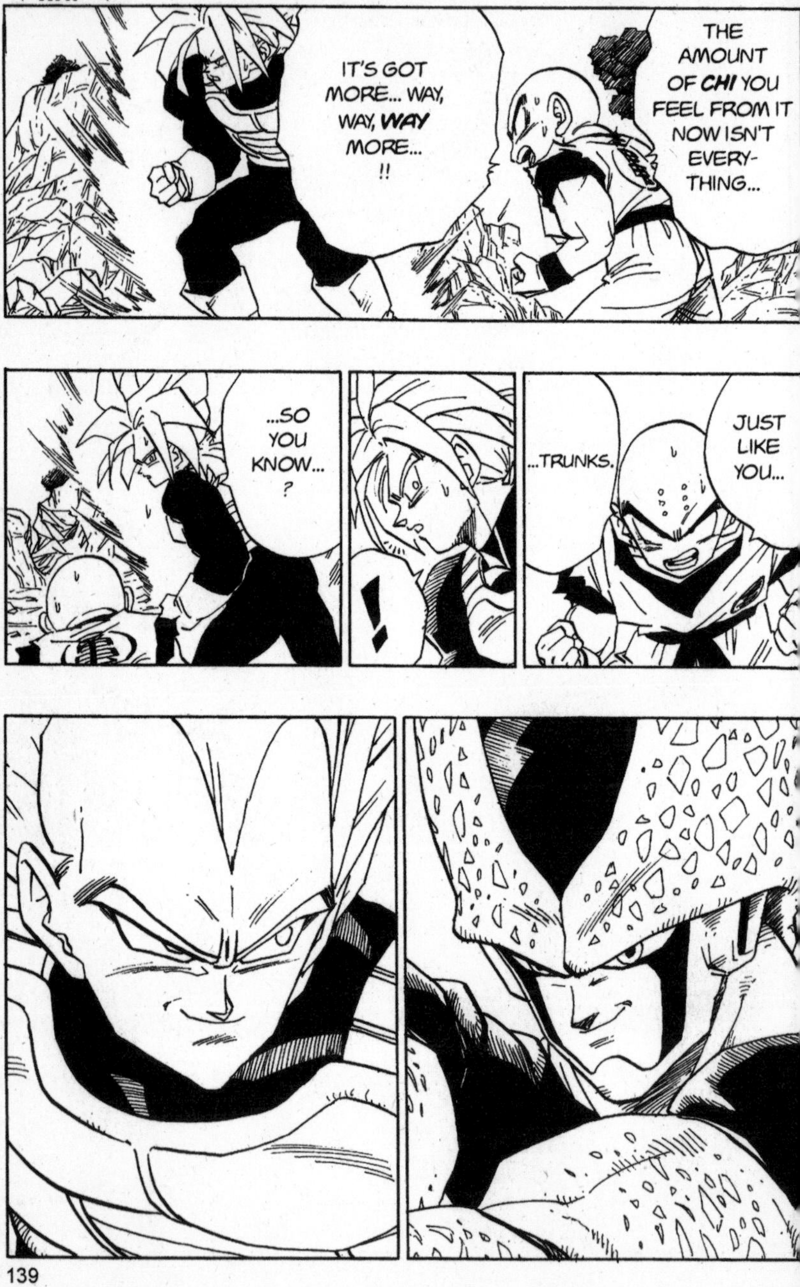

THE AMOUNT OF CHI YOU FEEL FROM IT NOW ISN'T EVERYTHING...
IT'S GOT MORE... WAY, WAY, WAY MORE... !!
JUST LIKE YOU...
...TRUNKS.
!
...SO YOU KNOW...?

READ THIS WAY

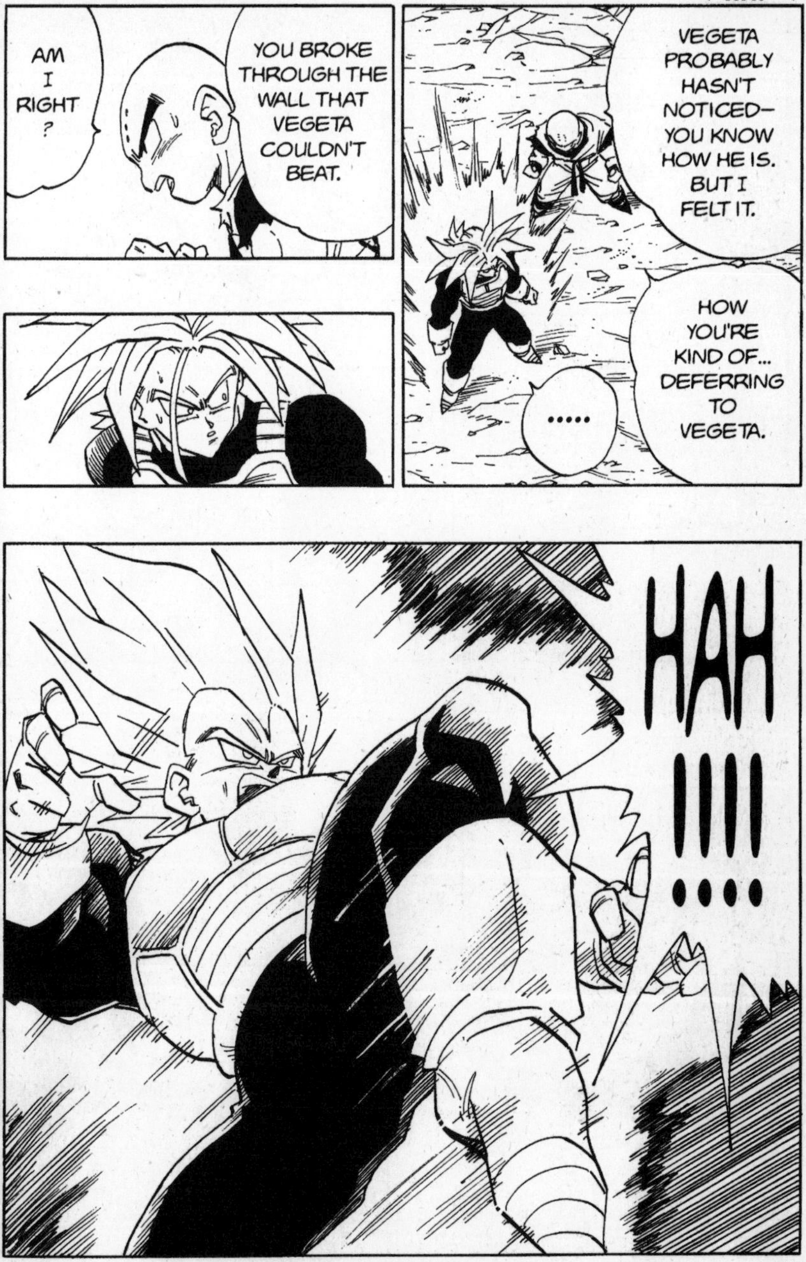
VEGETA PROBABLY HASN'T NOTICED— YOU KNOW HOW HE IS. BUT I FELT IT.
HOW YOU'RE KIND OF... DEFERRING TO VEGETA.
.....
YOU BROKE THROUGH THE WALL THAT VEGETA COULDN'T BEAT.
AM I RIGHT?
HAH!!!!....

READ THIS WAY

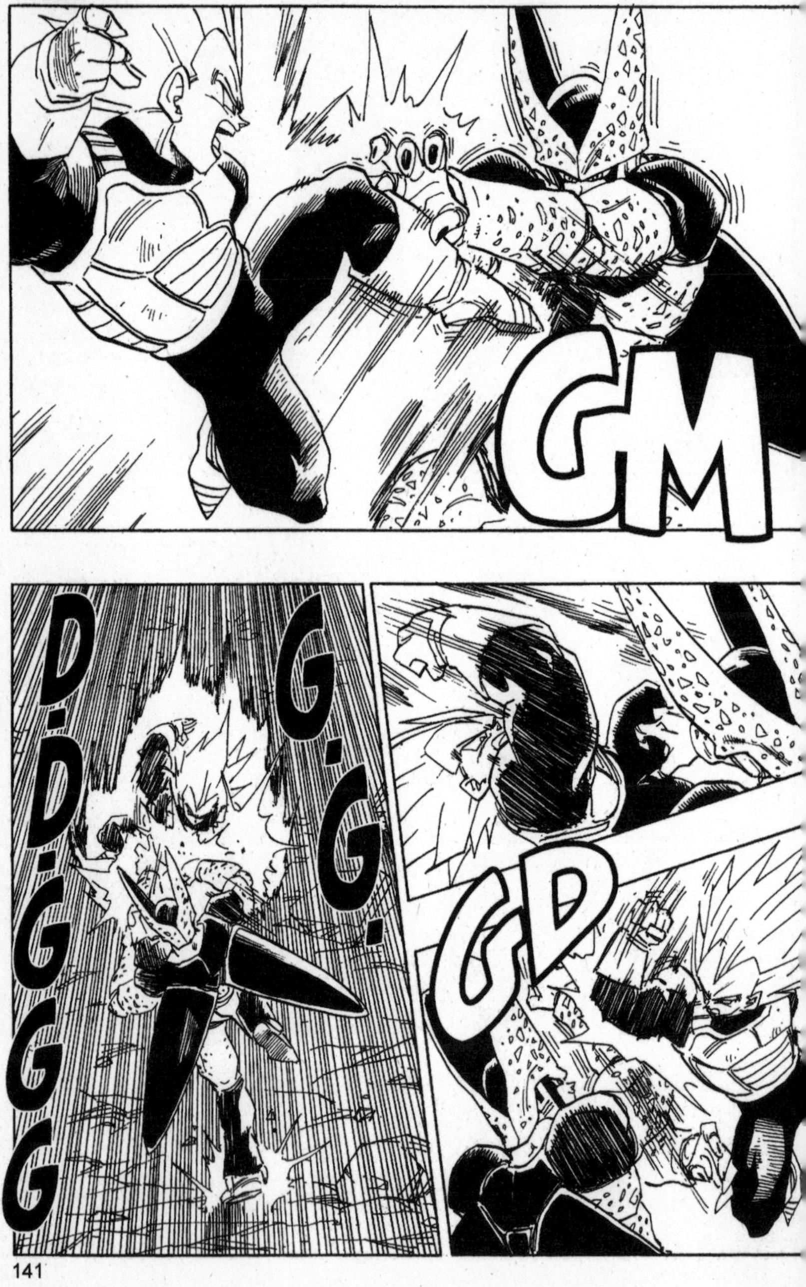
GM
GD
G.G.G.
D.D.GGGG

READ THIS WAY

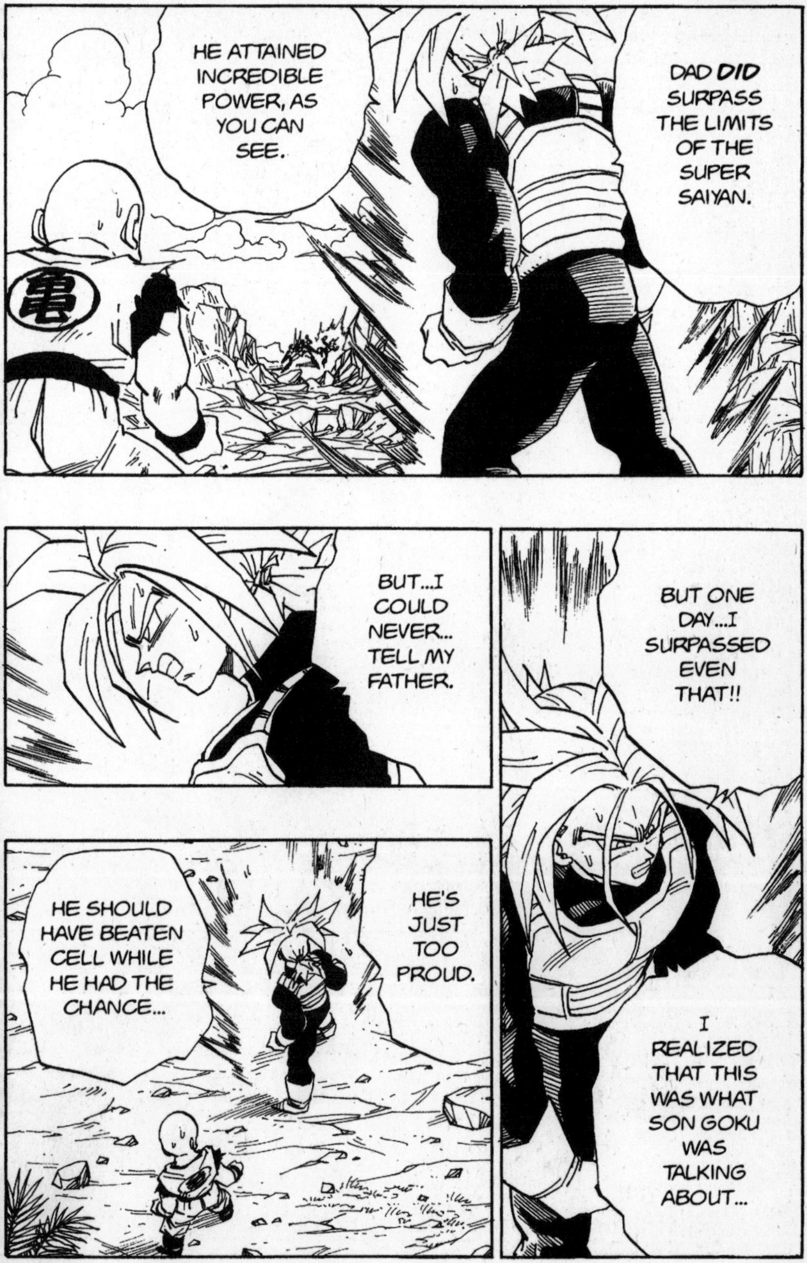
DAD DID SURPASS THE LIMITS OF THE SUPER SAIYAN.
HE ATTAINED INCREDIBLE POWER, AS YOU CAN SEE.
BUT ONE DAY...I SURPASSED EVEN THAT!!
I REALIZED THAT THIS WAS WHAT SON GOKU WAS TALKING ABOUT...
BUT...I COULD NEVER... TELL MY FATHER.
HE'S JUST TOO PROUD.
HE SHOULD HAVE BEATEN CELL WHILE HE HAD THE CHANCE...

READ THIS WAY

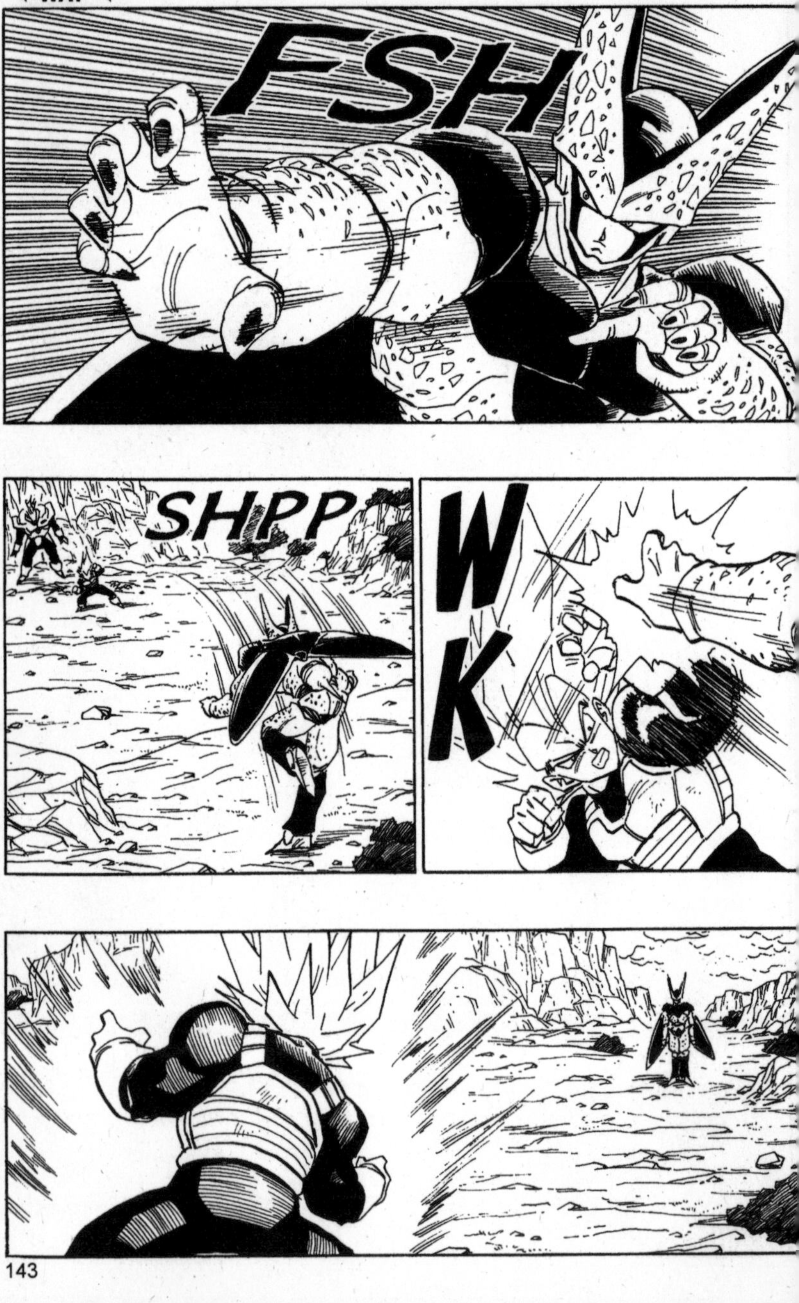
FSH
WK
SHPP

READ THIS WAY

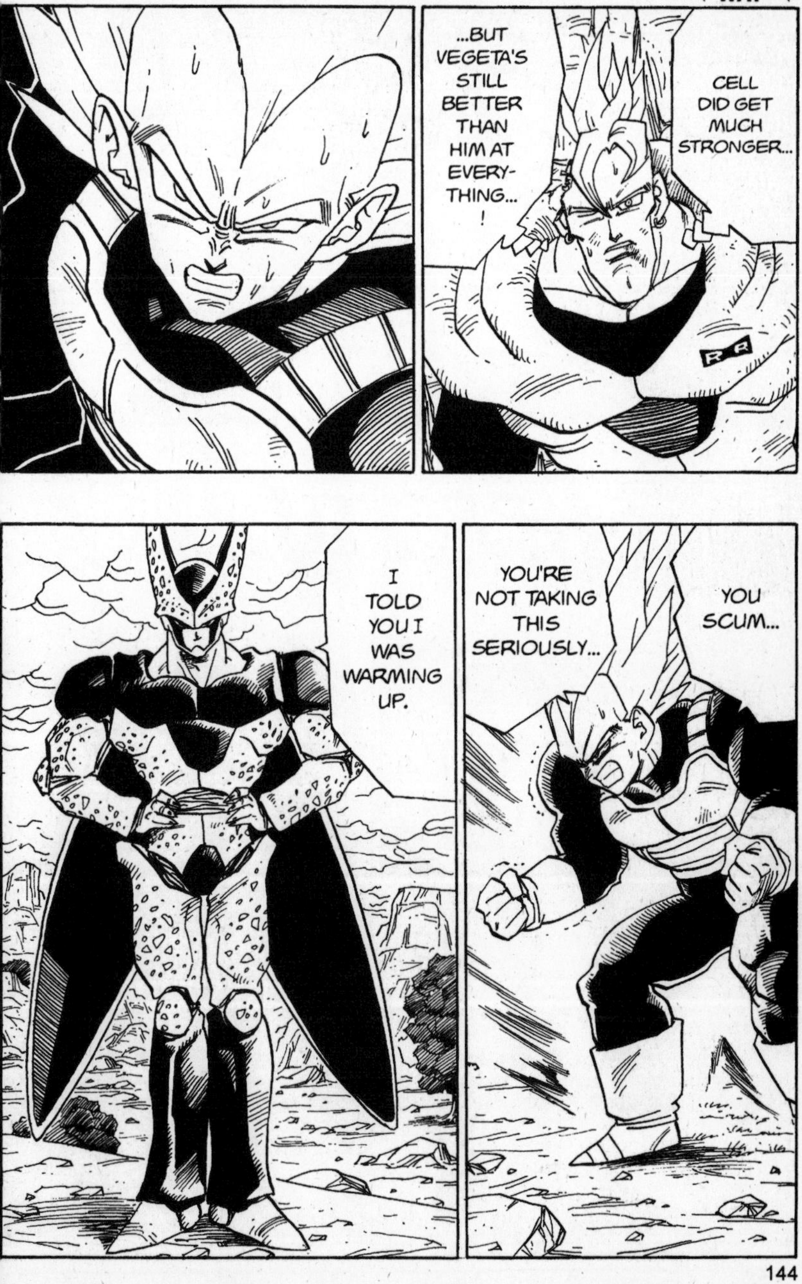
CELL DID GET MUCH STRONGER...
...BUT VEGETA'S STILL BETTER THAN HIM AT EVERY-THING...
!
YOU SCUM...
YOU'RE NOT TAKING THIS SERIOUSLY...
I TOLD YOU I WAS WARMING UP.

READ THIS WAY

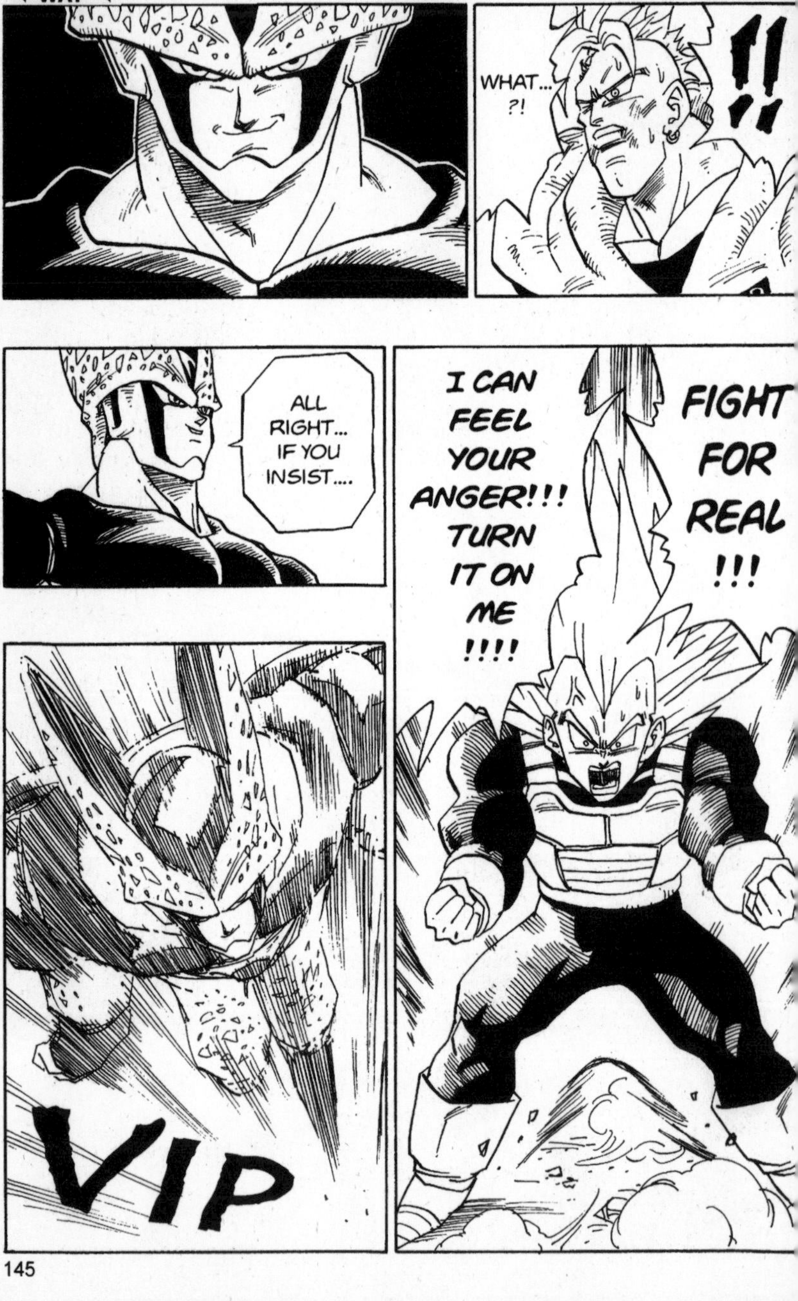

WHAT... ?!
!!
FIGHT FOR REAL!!!
I CAN FEEL YOUR ANGER!!! TURN IT ON ME!!!!
ALL RIGHT... IF YOU INSIST....
VIP

READ THIS WAY

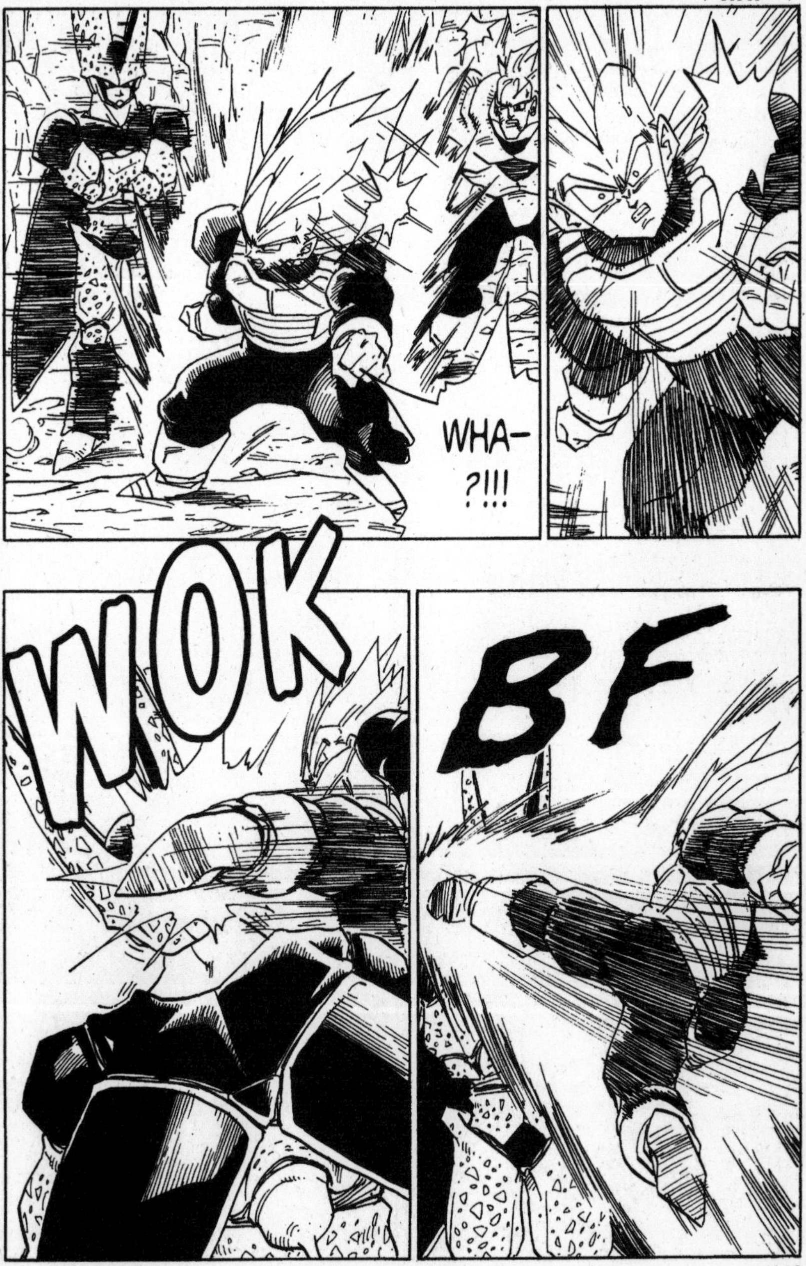
WHA-?!!!
BF
WOK

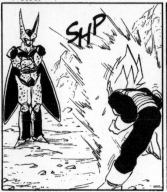

READ THIS WAY

HEH
SHP
HEH HEH HEH... "SUPER VEGETA," EH...?
A-AREN'T YOU GONNA SAVE HIM, WITH THIS POWER OF YOURS...?!
...DAD WOULD FIND IT MORE HUMILIATING TO BE RESCUED BY ME THAN LOSE TO CELL... THAT'S JUST WHO HE IS...

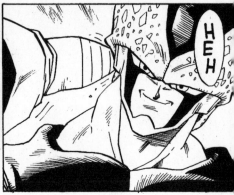

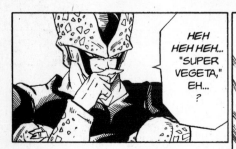

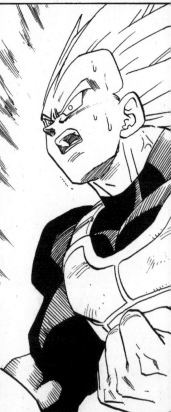

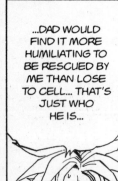

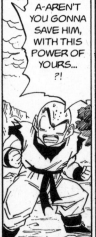

NEXT: Vegeta's Tenacity

DBZ:190 • The Final Flash

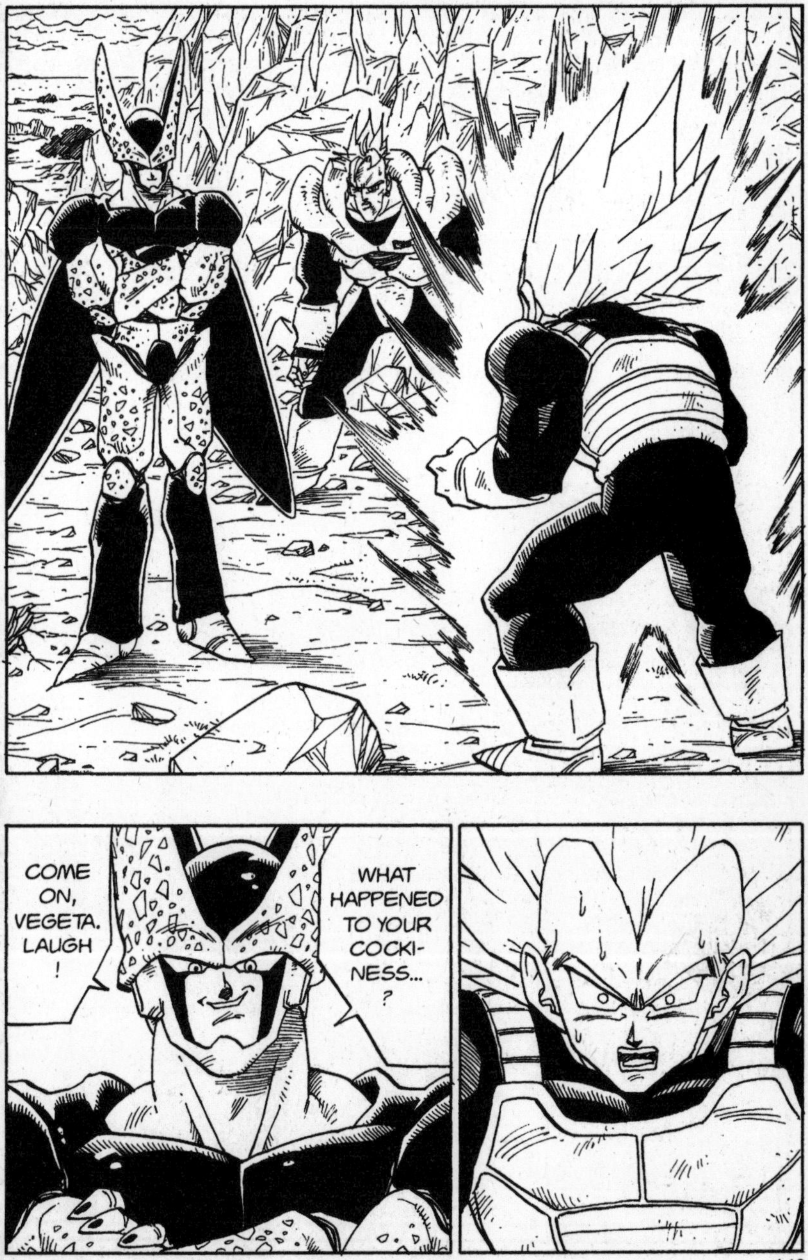
WHAT HAPPENED TO YOUR COCKI-NESS... ?
COME ON, VEGETA. LAUGH !

READ THIS WAY

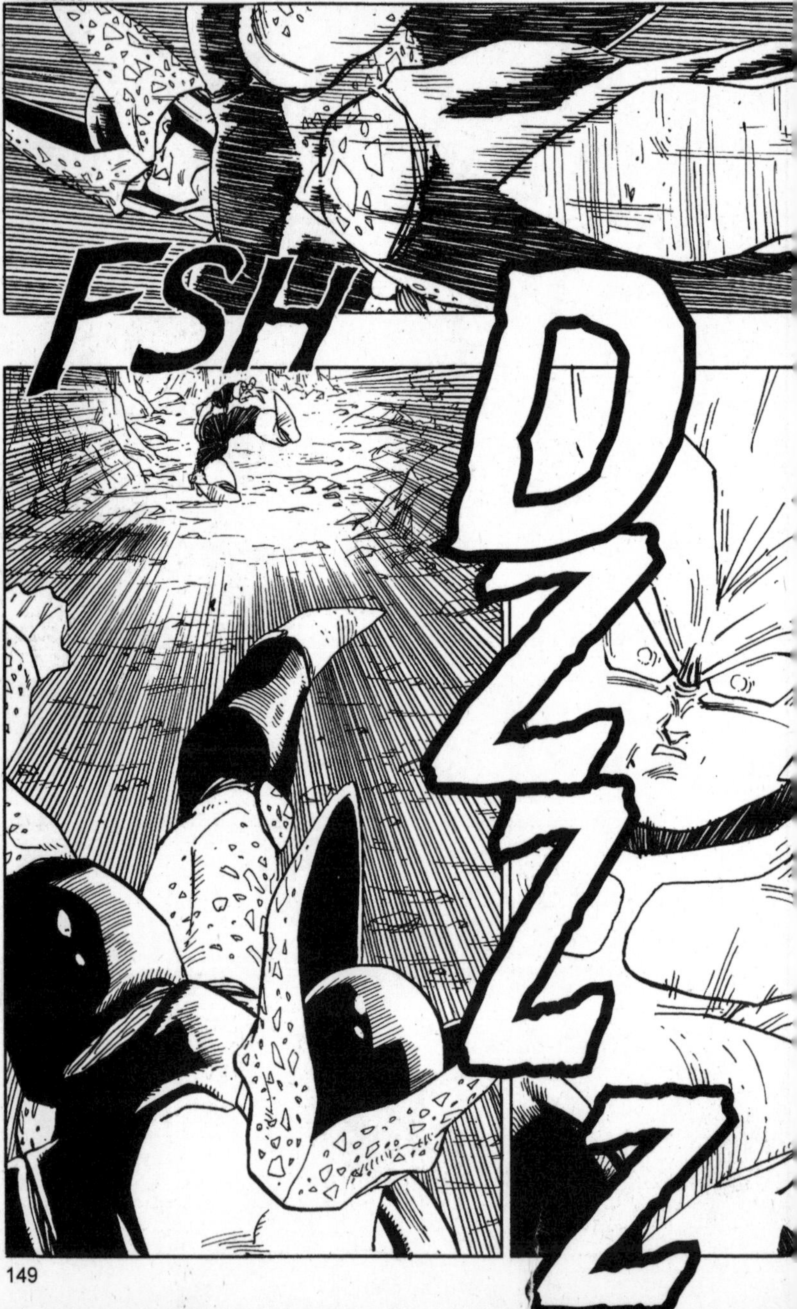
FSH
DZZZ

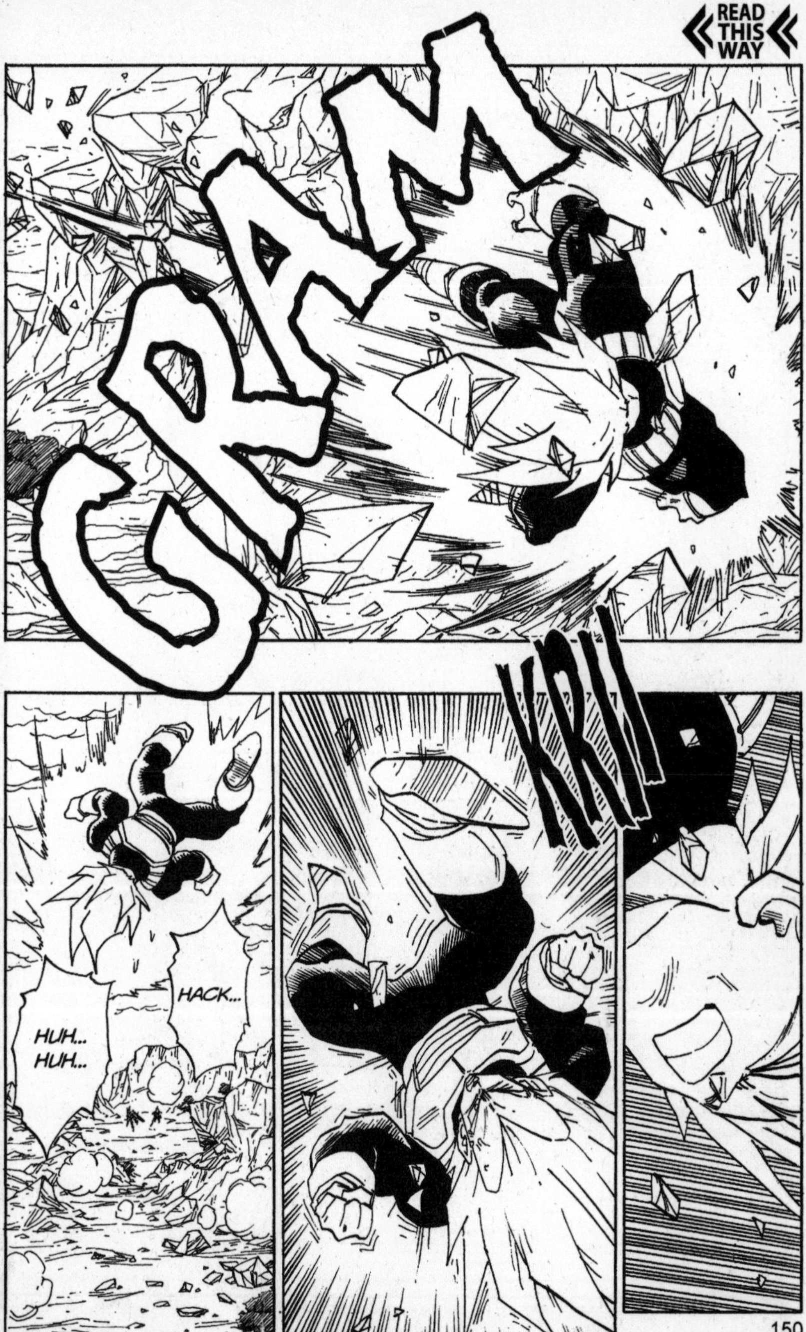
CRAM
KRII
HACK...
HUH... HUH...

READ THIS WAY

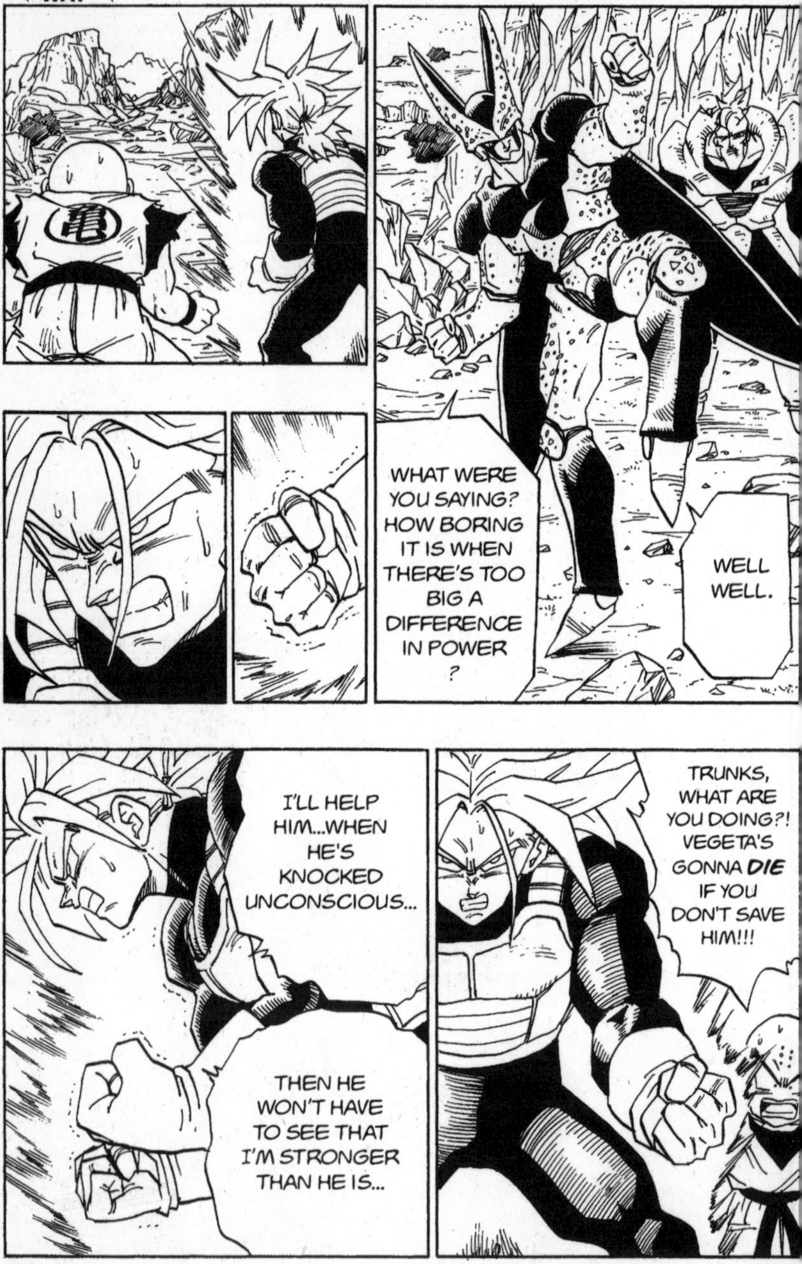
WELL WELL.
WHAT WERE YOU SAYING? HOW BORING IT IS WHEN THERE'S TOO BIG A DIFFERENCE IN POWER ?
TRUNKS, WHAT ARE YOU DOING?! VEGETA'S GONNA **DIE** IF YOU DON'T SAVE HIM!!!
I'LL HELP HIM...WHEN HE'S KNOCKED UNCONSCIOUS...
THEN HE WON'T HAVE TO SEE THAT I'M STRONGER THAN HE IS...

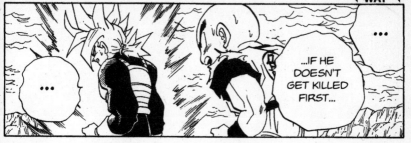

...

...IF HE DOESN'T GET KILLED FIRST...

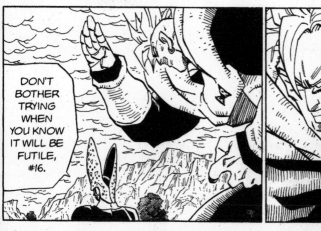

DON'T BOTHER TRYING WHEN YOU KNOW IT WILL BE FUTILE, #16.

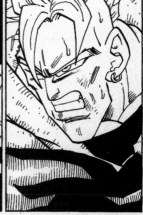

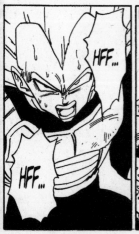

HFF...

HFF...

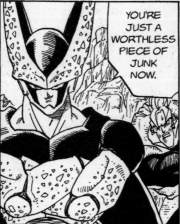

YOU'RE JUST A WORTHLESS PIECE OF JUNK NOW.

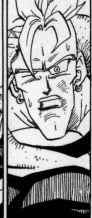

READ THIS WAY

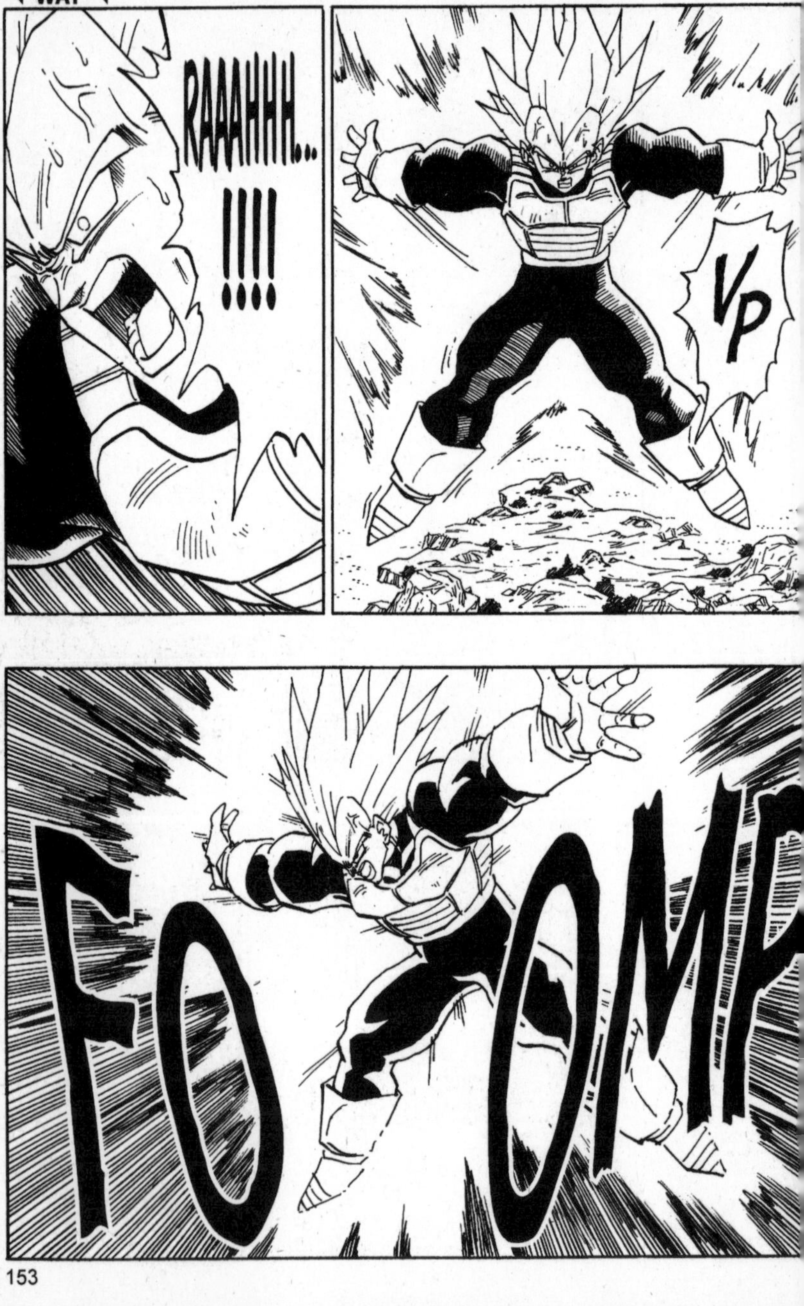
VP
RAAAHHH...
!!!!!
FOOMP

READ THIS WAY

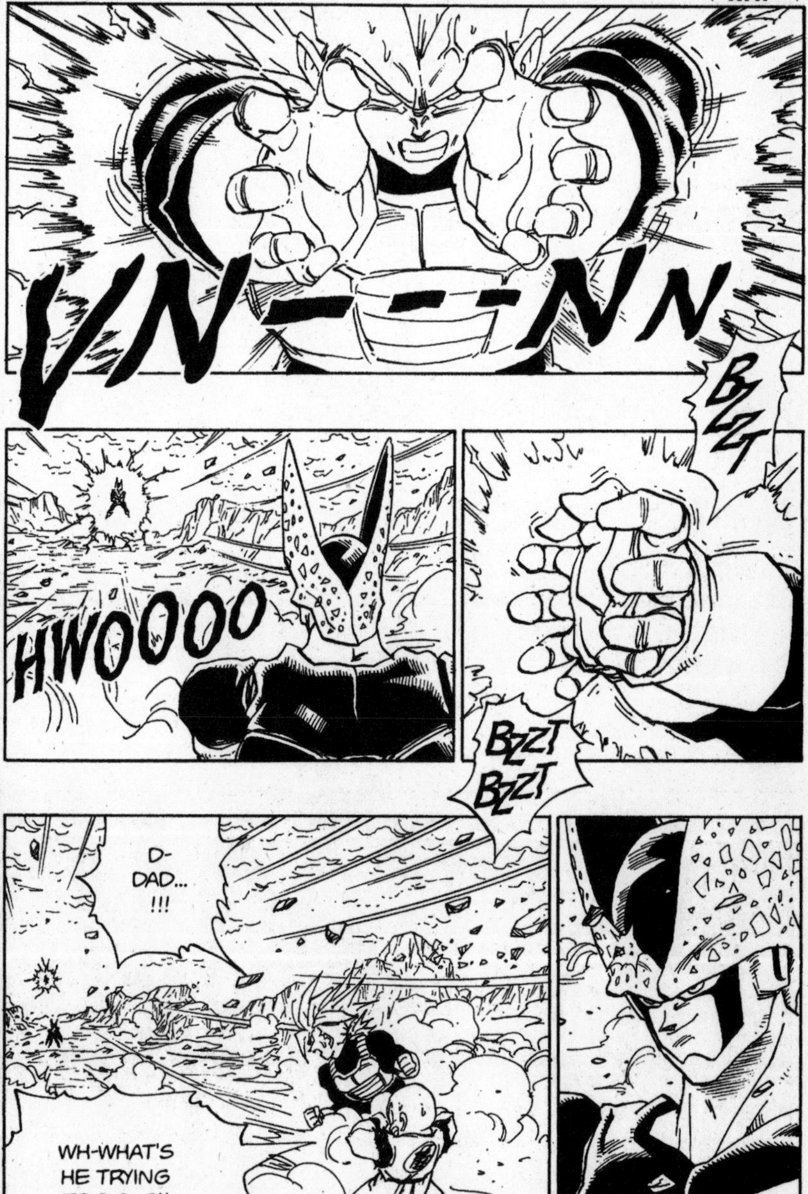
VN--NN
BZZT
BZZT
BZZT
HWOOOO
D-DAD... !!!
WH-WHAT'S HE TRYING TO DO...?!!

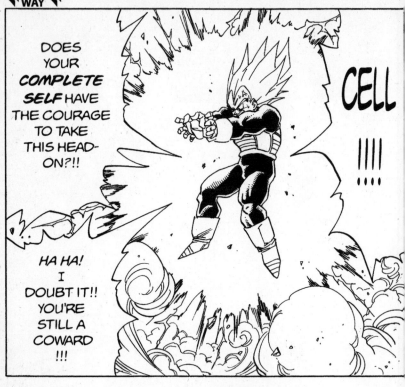

READ THIS WAY

CELL !!!!
DOES YOUR COMPLETE SELF HAVE THE COURAGE TO TAKE THIS HEAD-ON?!!
HA HA! I DOUBT IT!! YOU'RE STILL A COWARD !!!
HEH...
H-HE'S PROVOKING HIM...
SO HE WON'T DODGE...
HE CAN'T BE...!!! HE CAN'T BE FIRING THAT OFF ON EARTH... !!

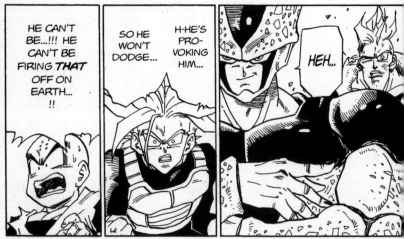

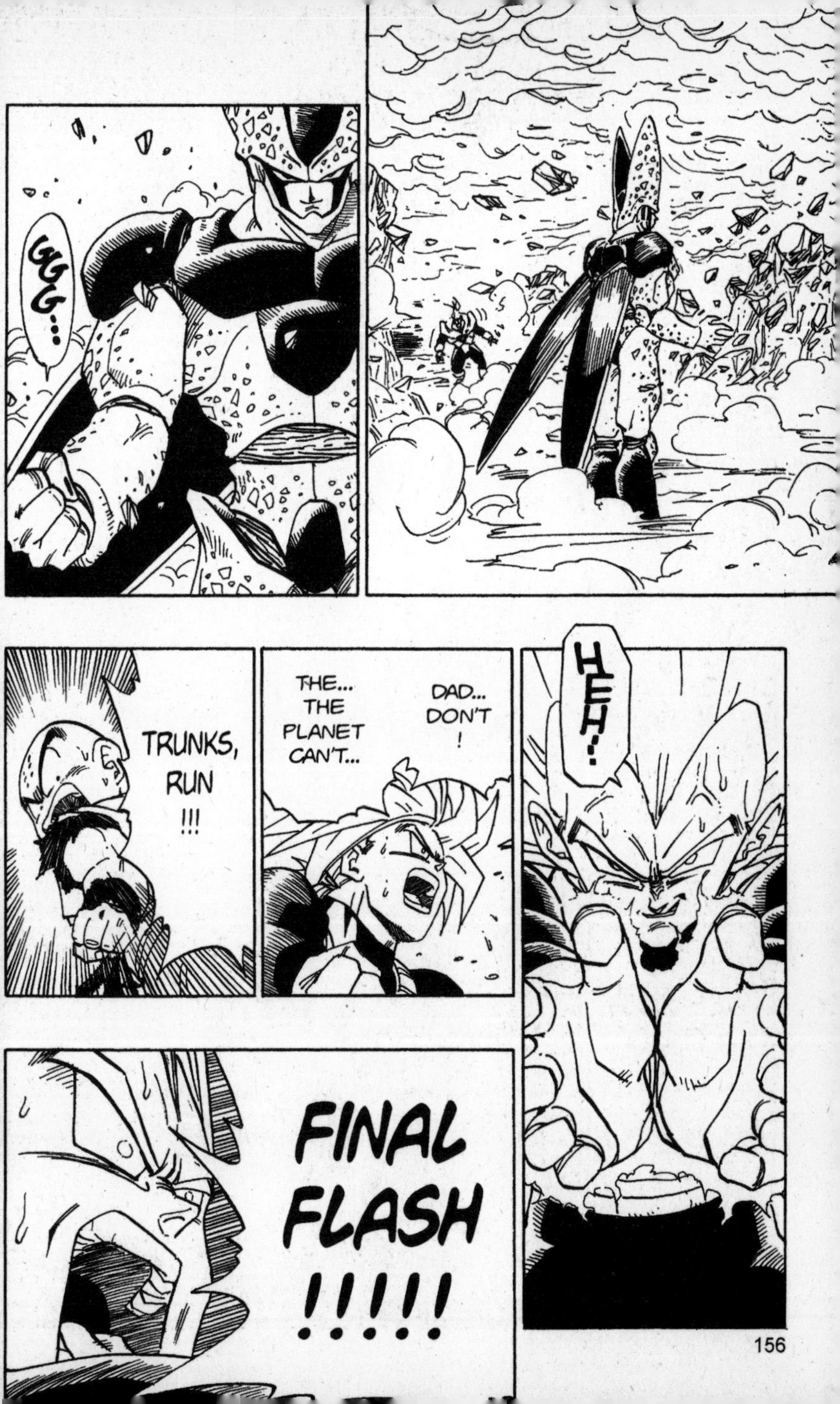
GGG...
HEH!!
DAD... DON'T !
THE... THE PLANET CAN'T...
TRUNKS, RUN !!!
FINAL FLASH !!!!!

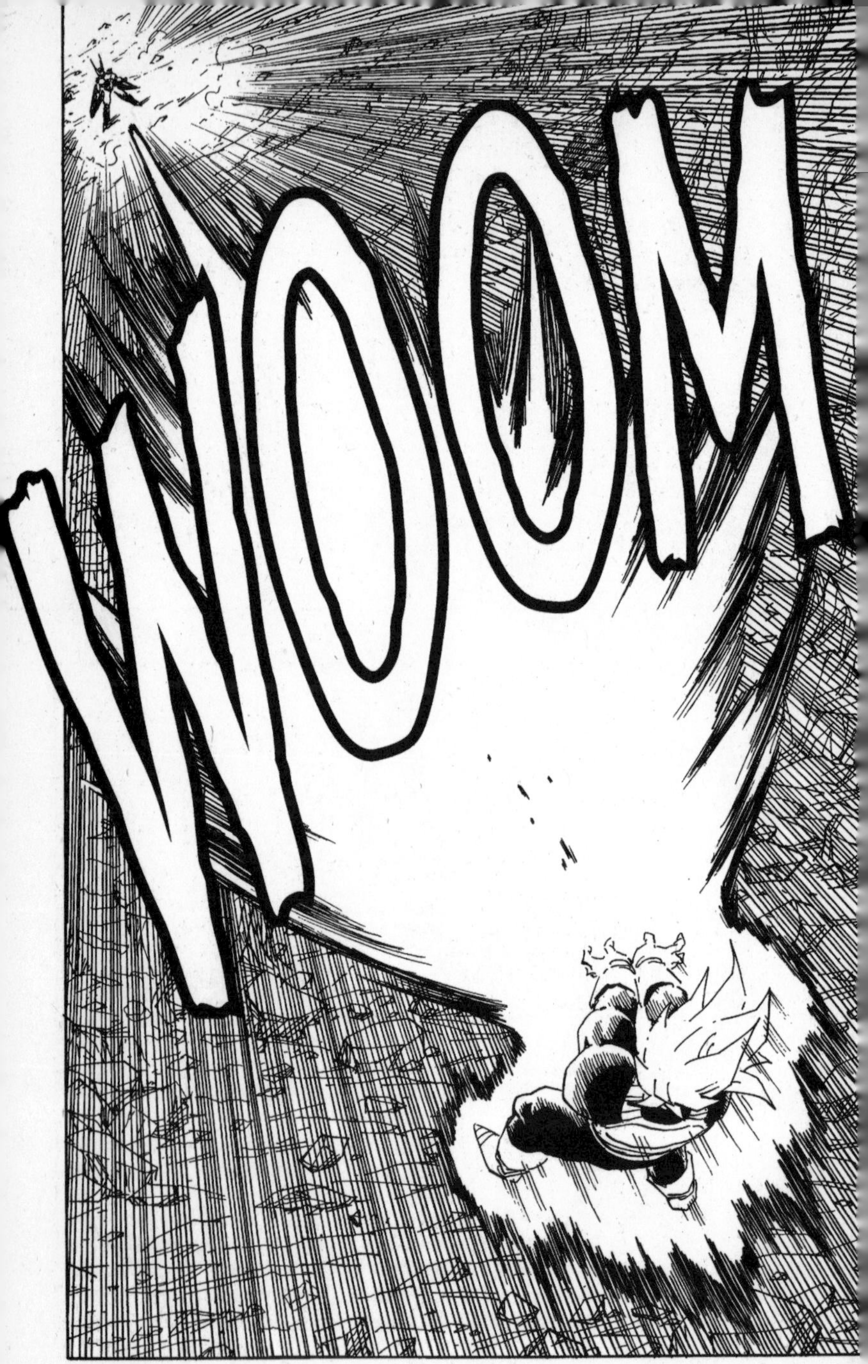
WOOM

READ THIS WAY

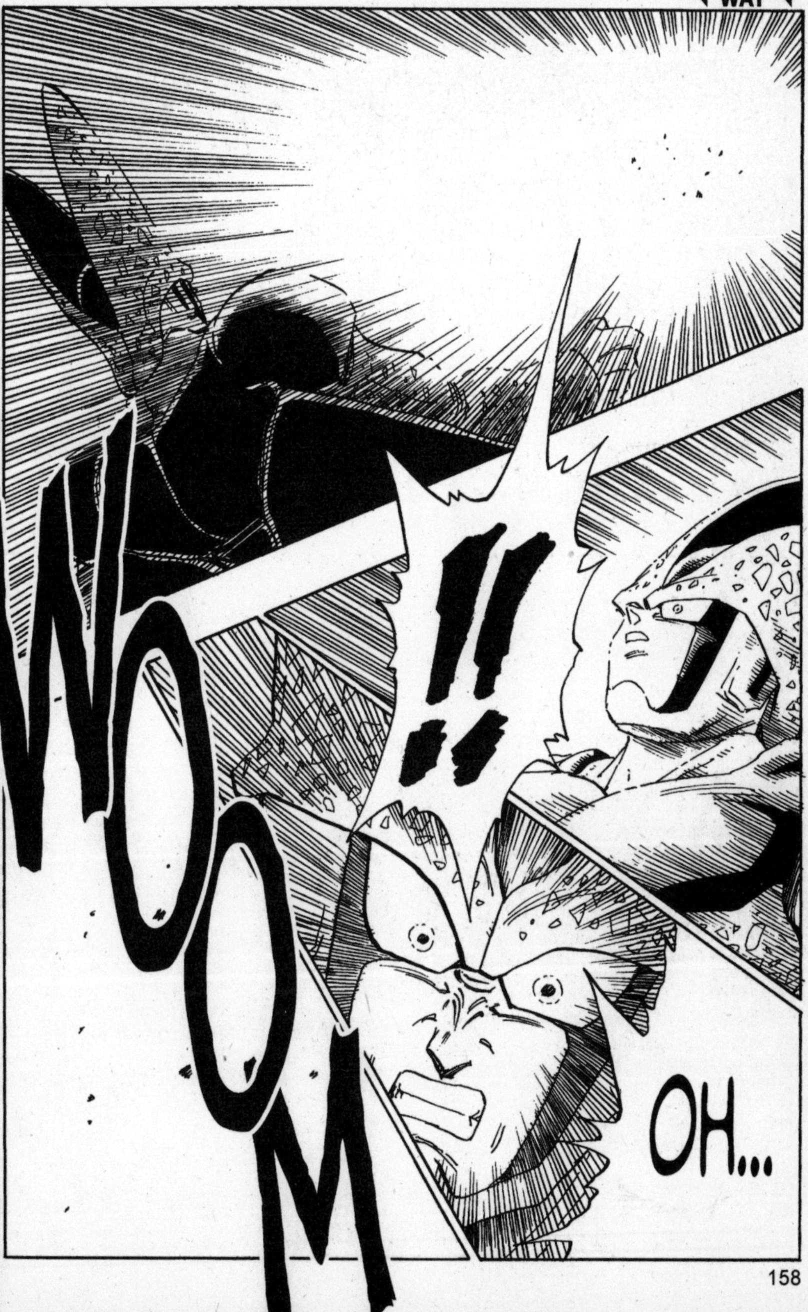
!!
OH...
WOOM

READ THIS WAY

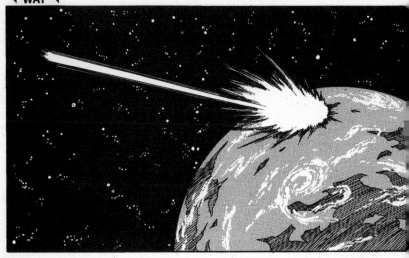

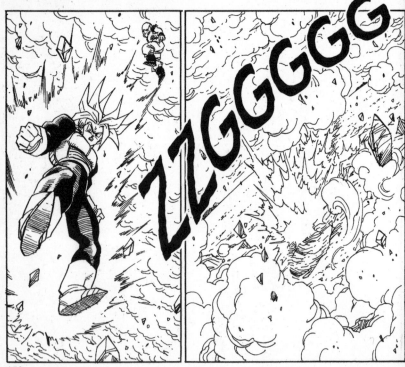

ZZGGGGGG

READ THIS WAY

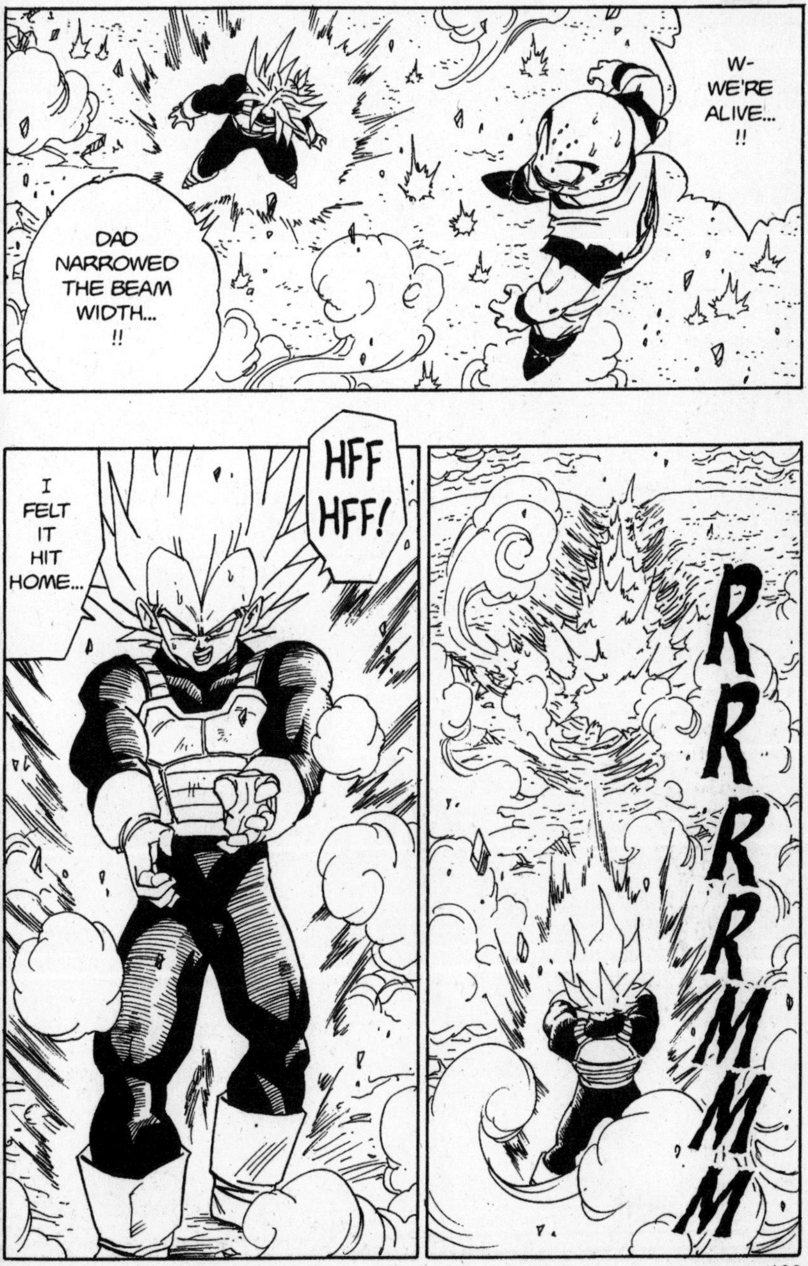
W- WE'RE ALIVE... !!
DAD NARROWED THE BEAM WIDTH... !!
RRRRMMM
HFF HFF!
I FELT IT HIT HOME...

READ THIS WAY

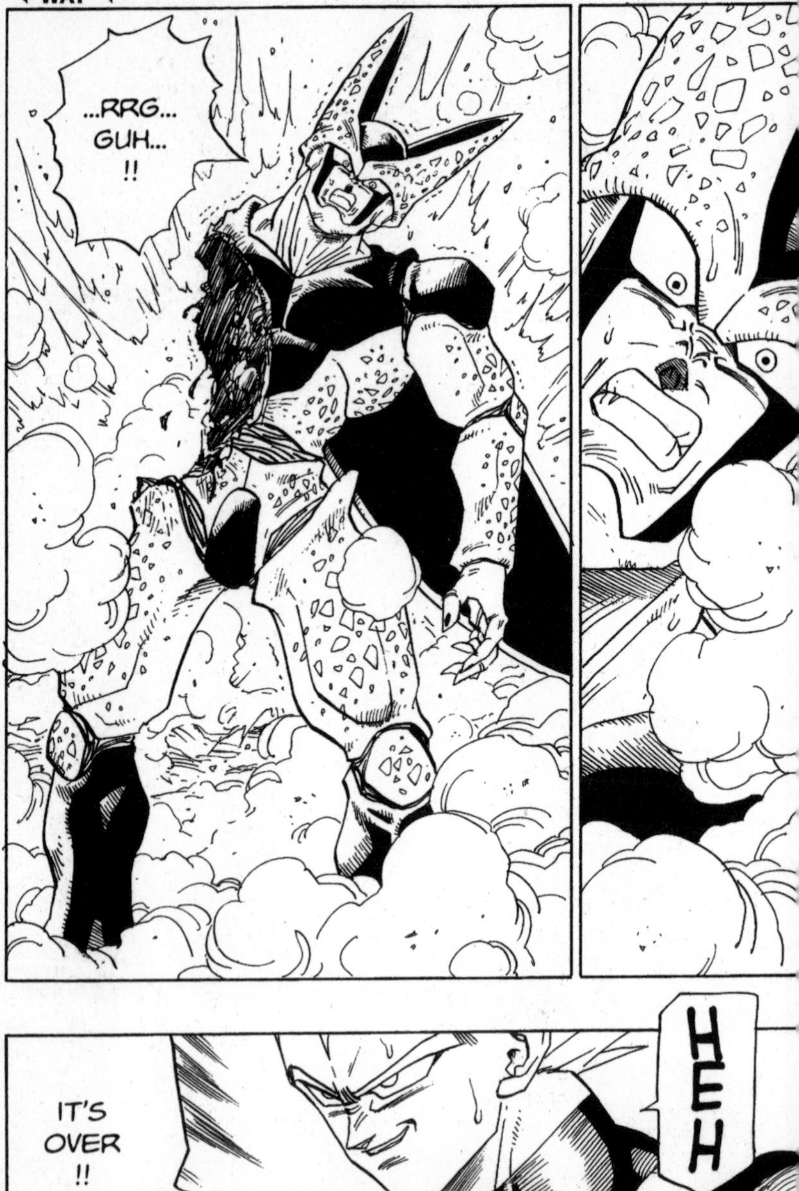
...RRG... GUH... !!
HEH
IT'S OVER !!

NEXT: Shock After Shock...!

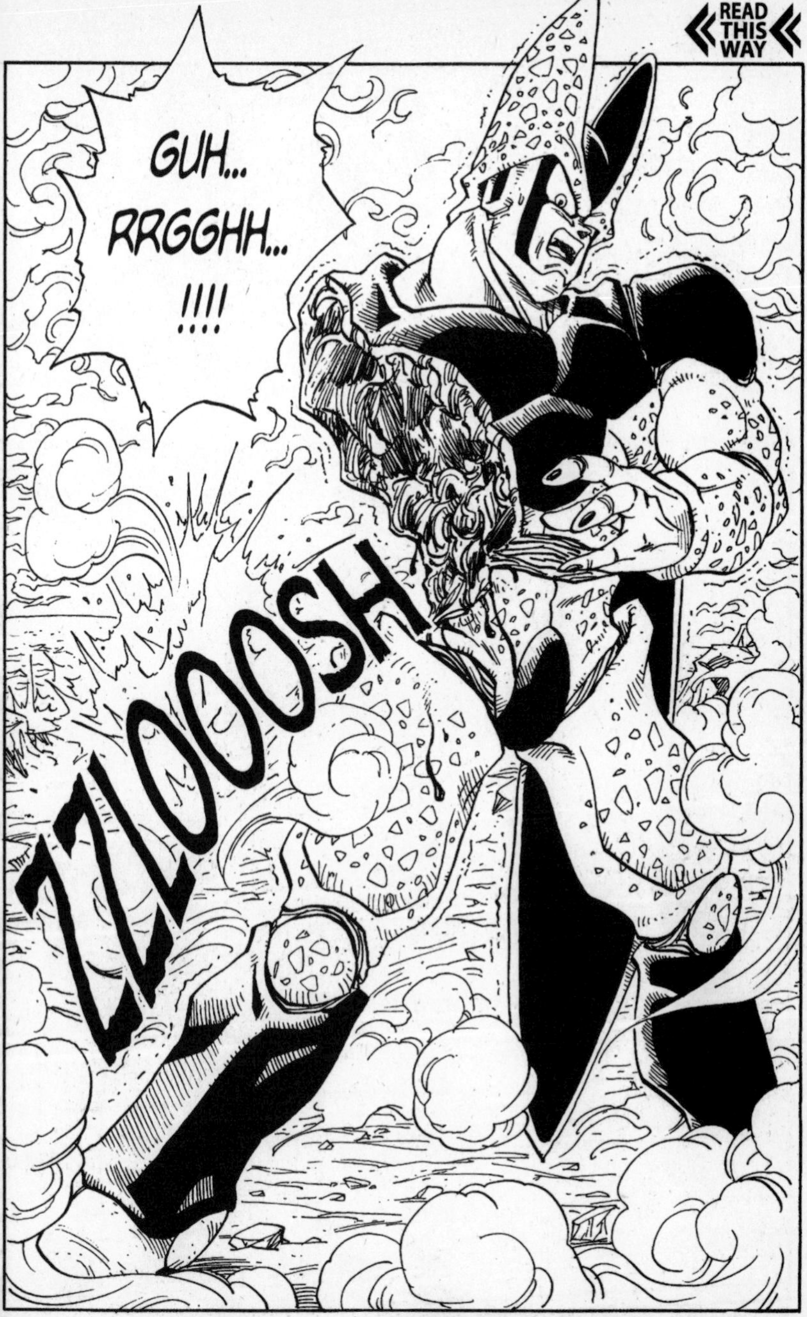
GUH... RRGGHH... !!!!
ZZOOOSH

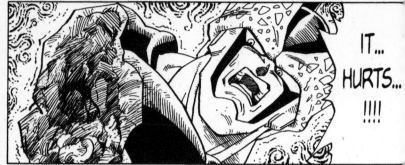

IT... HURTS... !!!!

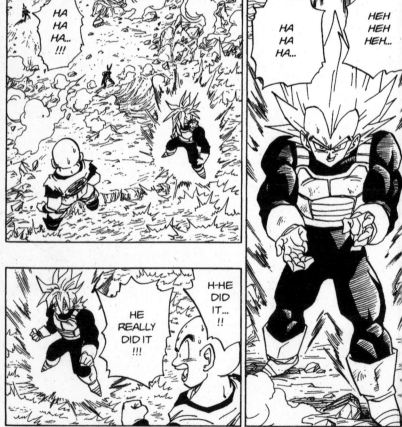

HA HA HA... !!!

HEH HEH HEH...

HA HA HA...

HE REALLY DID IT !!!

H-HE DID IT... !!

HE DID IT...

163

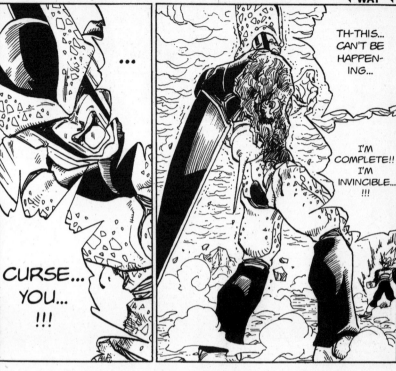

...

TH-THIS...
CAN'T BE
HAPPEN-
ING...

I'M
COMPLETE!!
I'M
INVINCIBLE...
!!!

CURSE...
YOU...
!!!

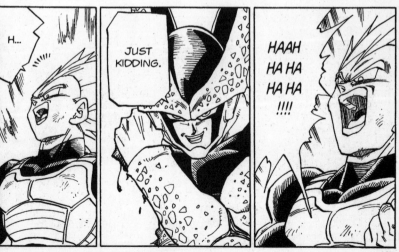

H...

JUST
KIDDING.

HAAH
HA HA
HA HA
!!!!

164

READ THIS WAY

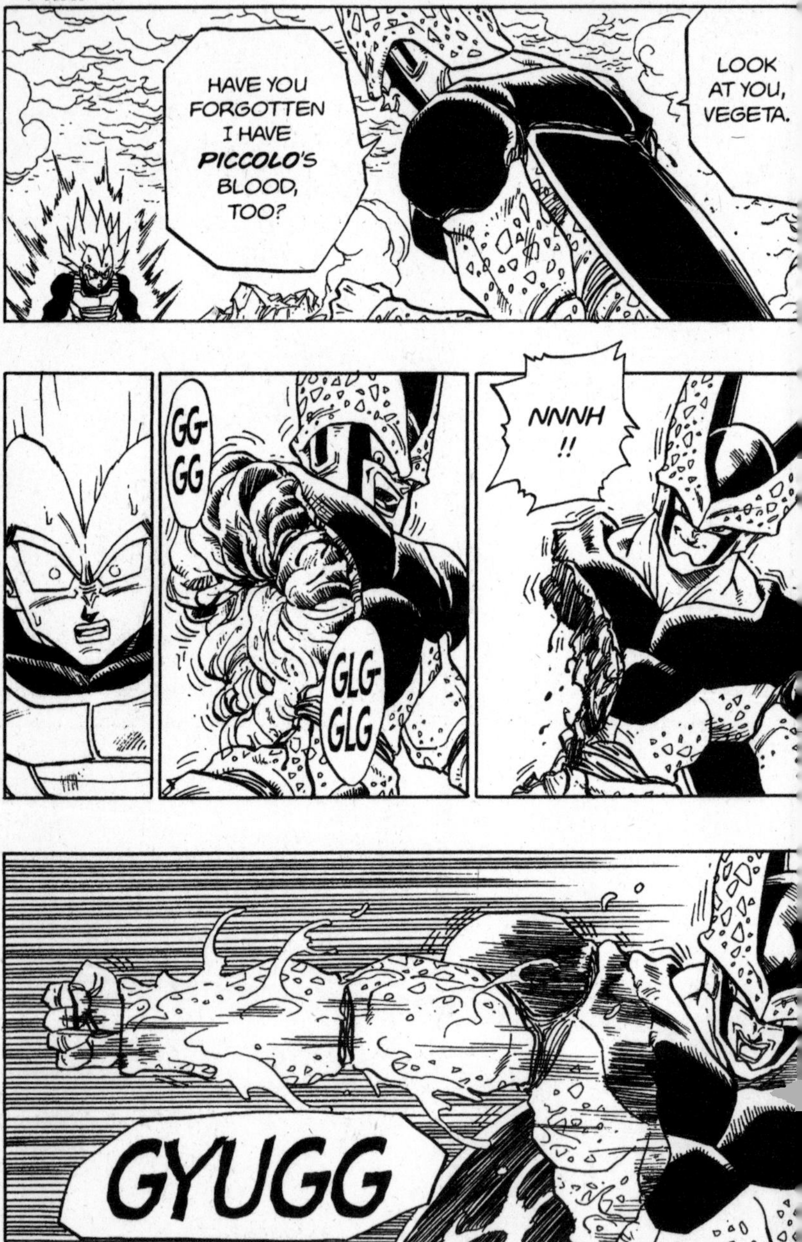
LOOK AT YOU, VEGETA.
HAVE YOU FORGOTTEN I HAVE **PICCOLO**'S BLOOD, TOO?
NNNH !!
GG-GG
GLG-GLG
GYUGG

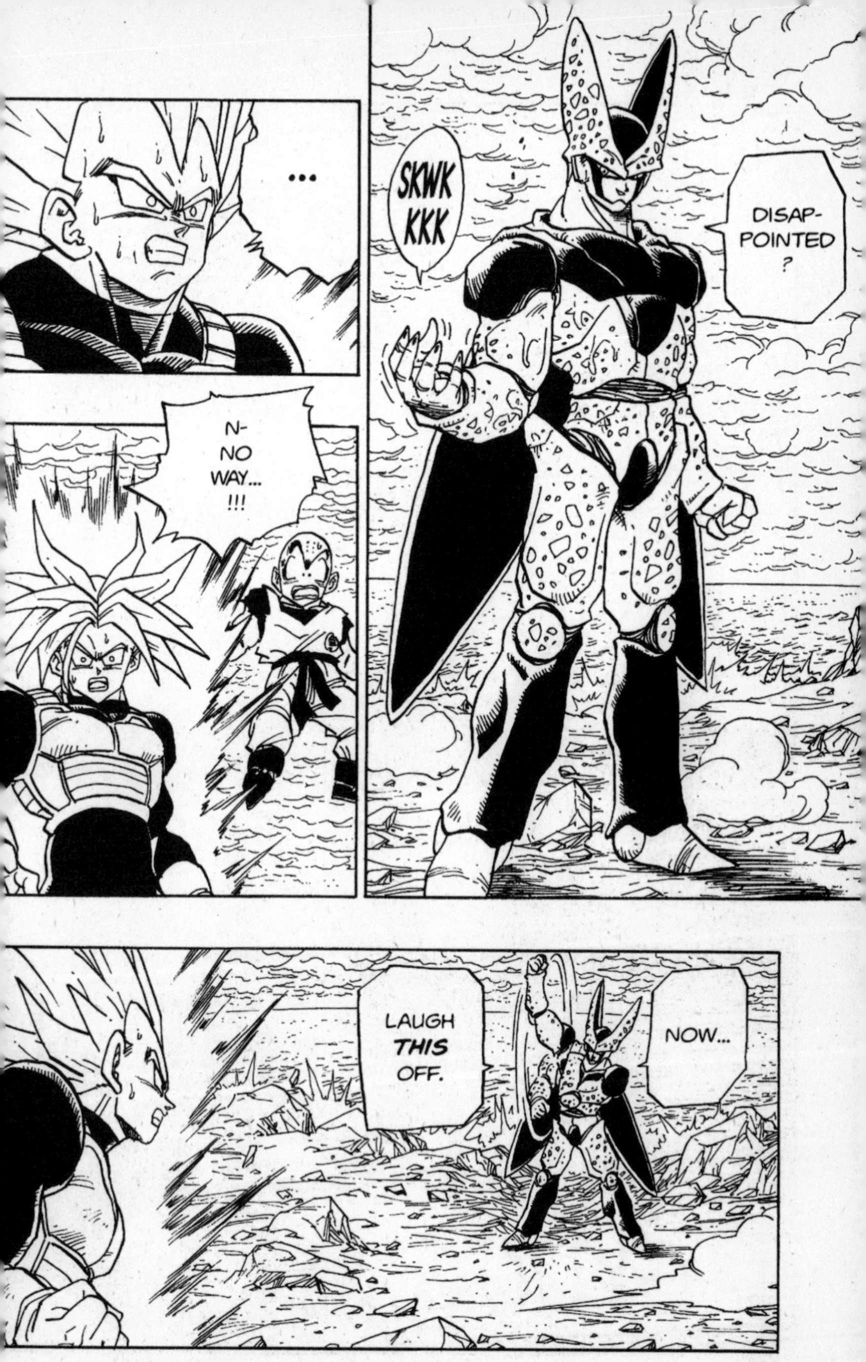
DISAP-POINTED?
SKWK KKK
...
N-NO WAY...!!!
NOW...
LAUGH THIS OFF.

READ THIS WAY

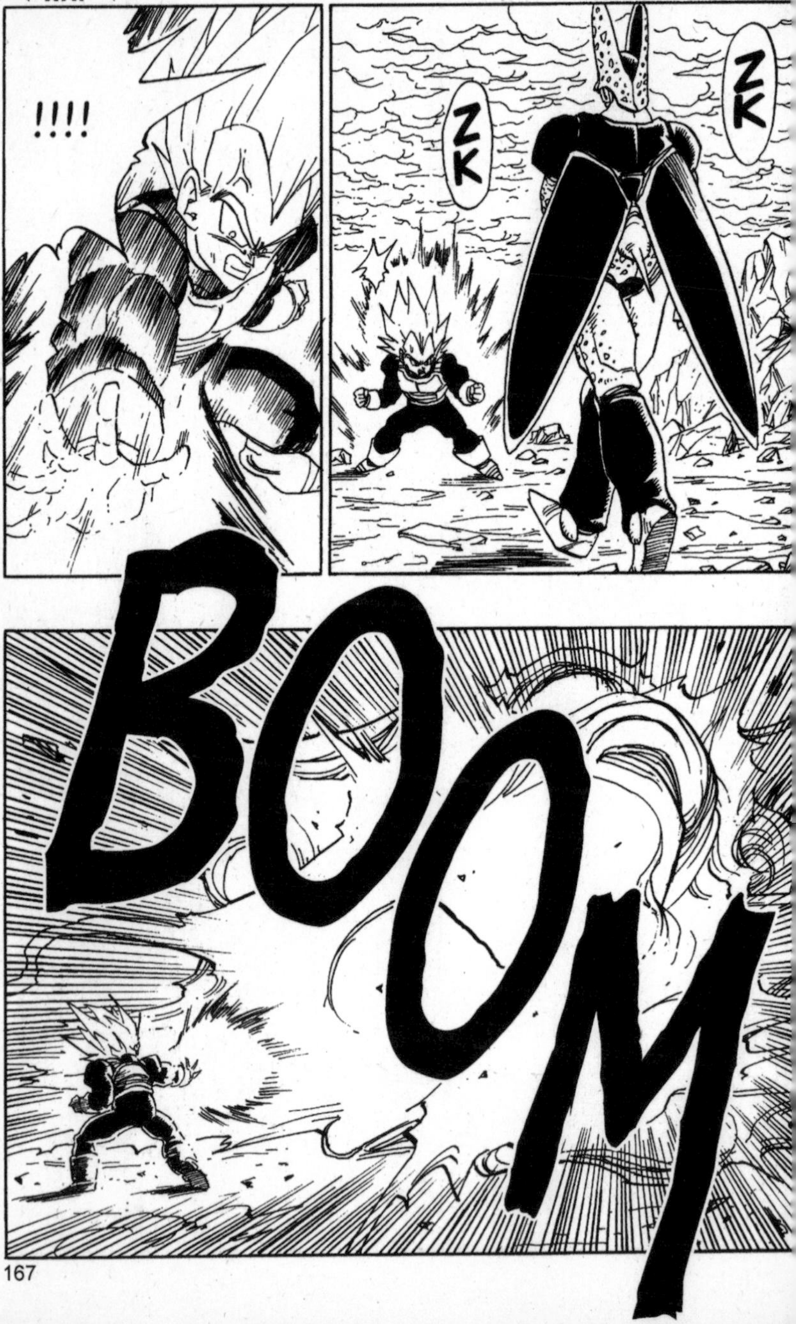

ZK
ZK
!!!!
BOOM

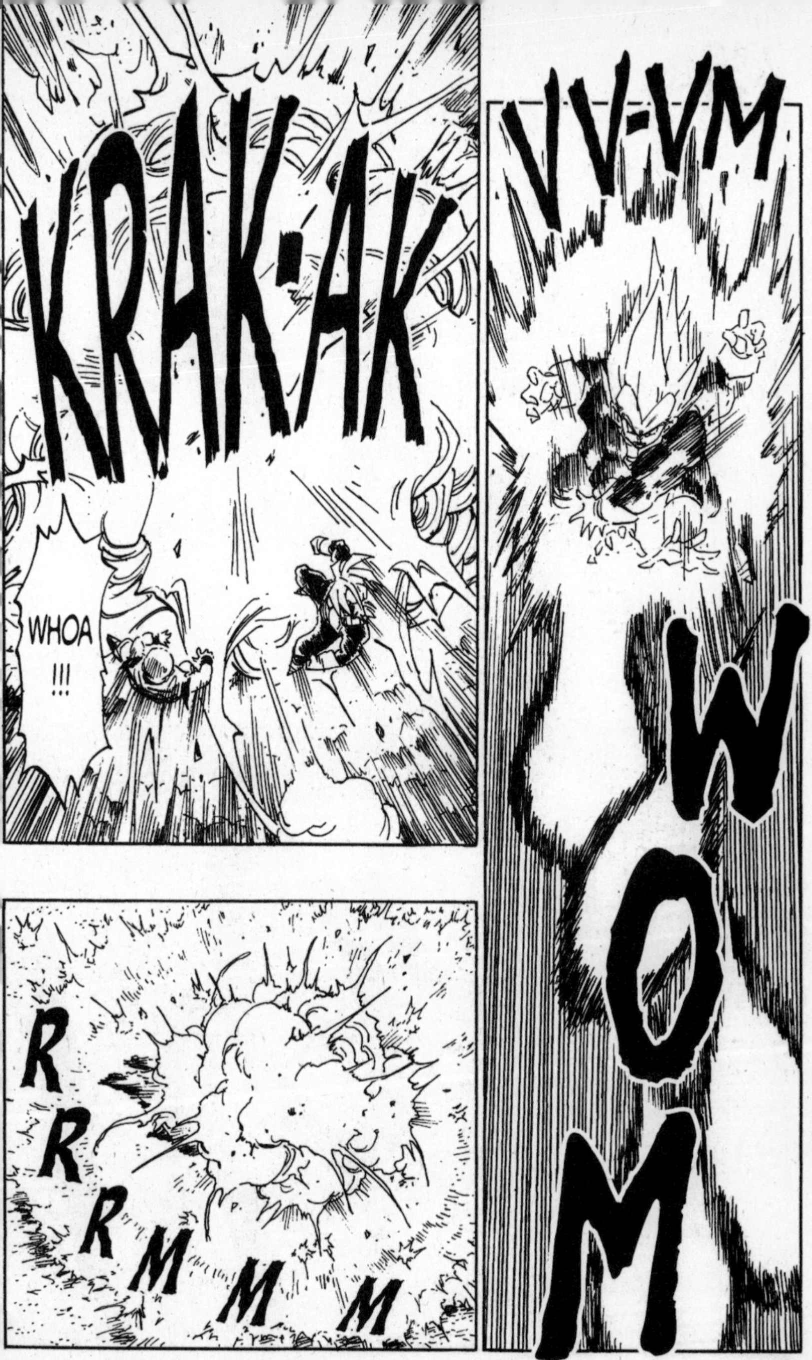
VV-VM
WOM
KRAK-AK
WHOA !!!
RRRMMM

READ THIS WAY

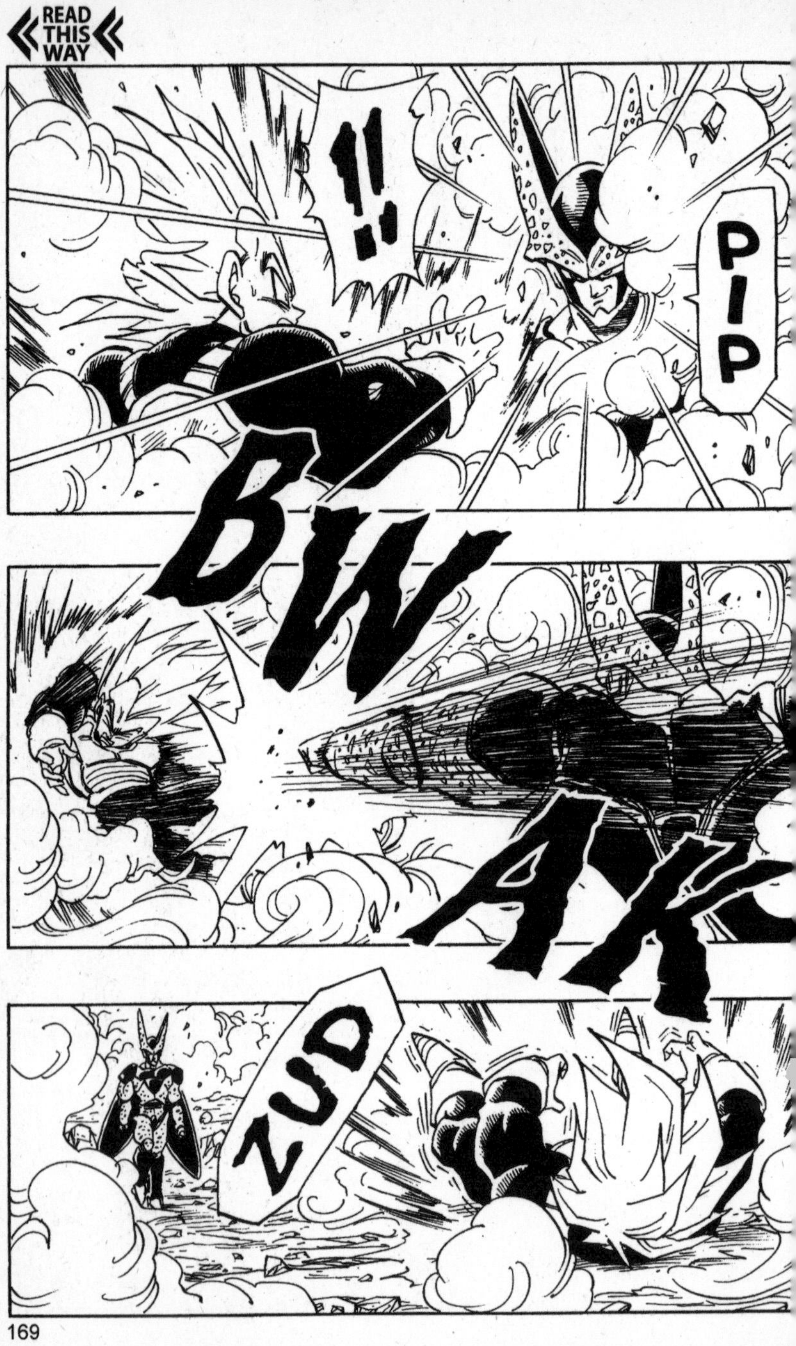
PIP
!!
BWAK
ZUD

READ THIS WAY

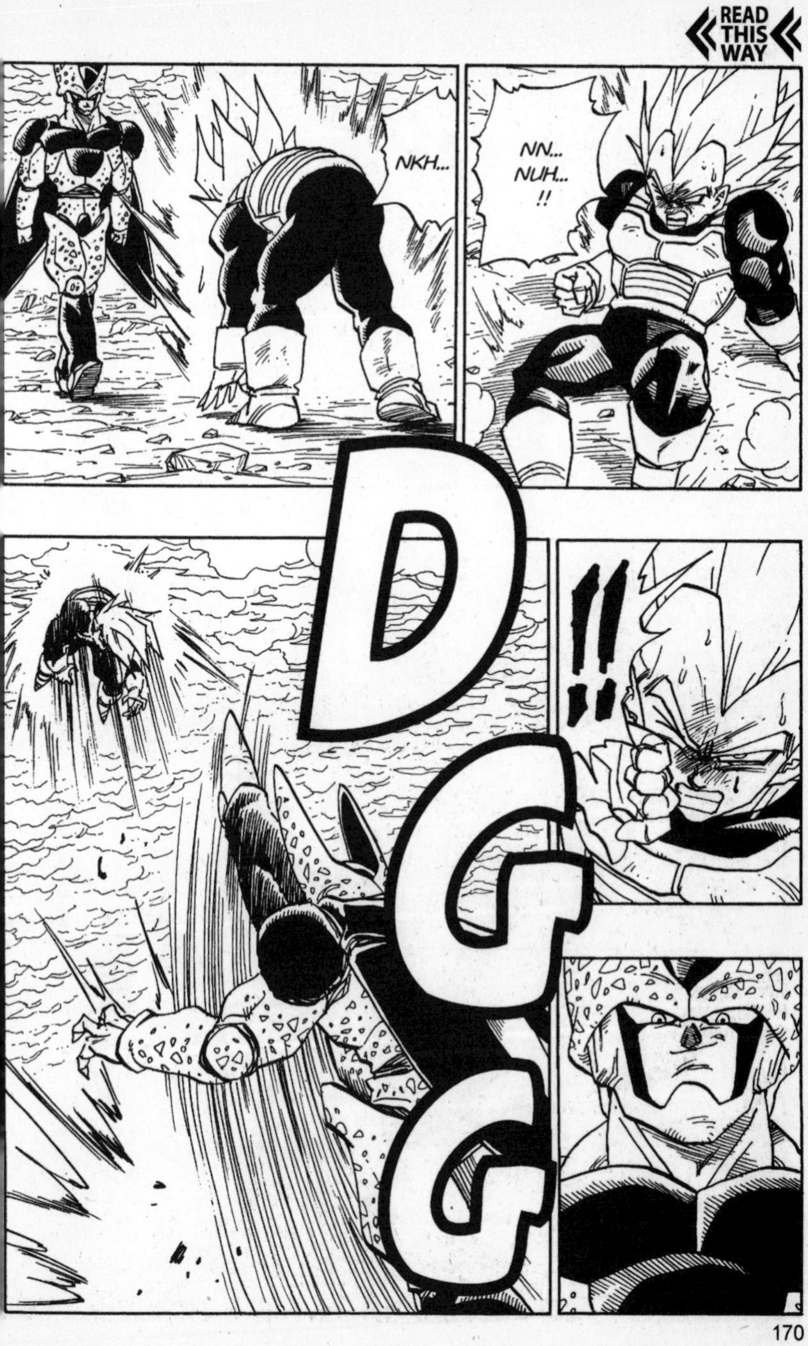

NN... NUH... !!
NKH...
!!
DGG

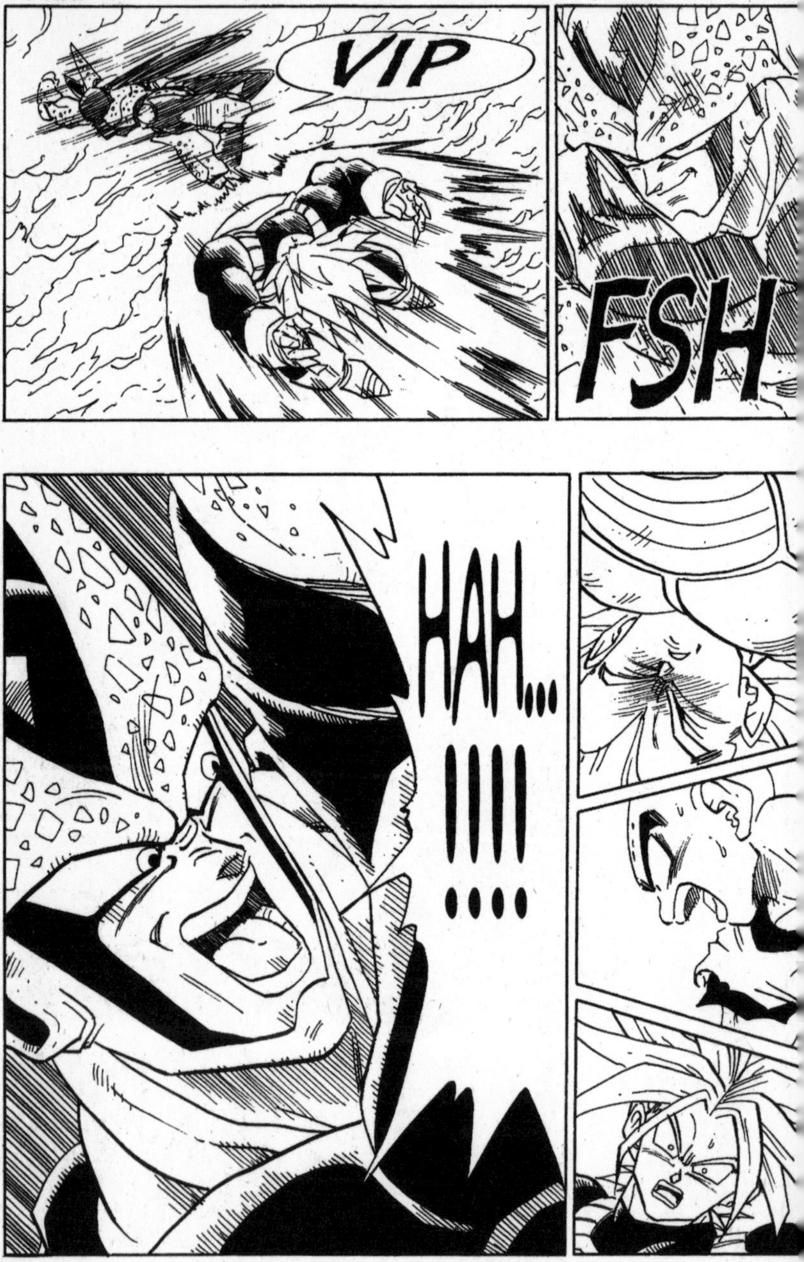
FSH
VIP
HAH...
!!!!
....

READ THIS WAY

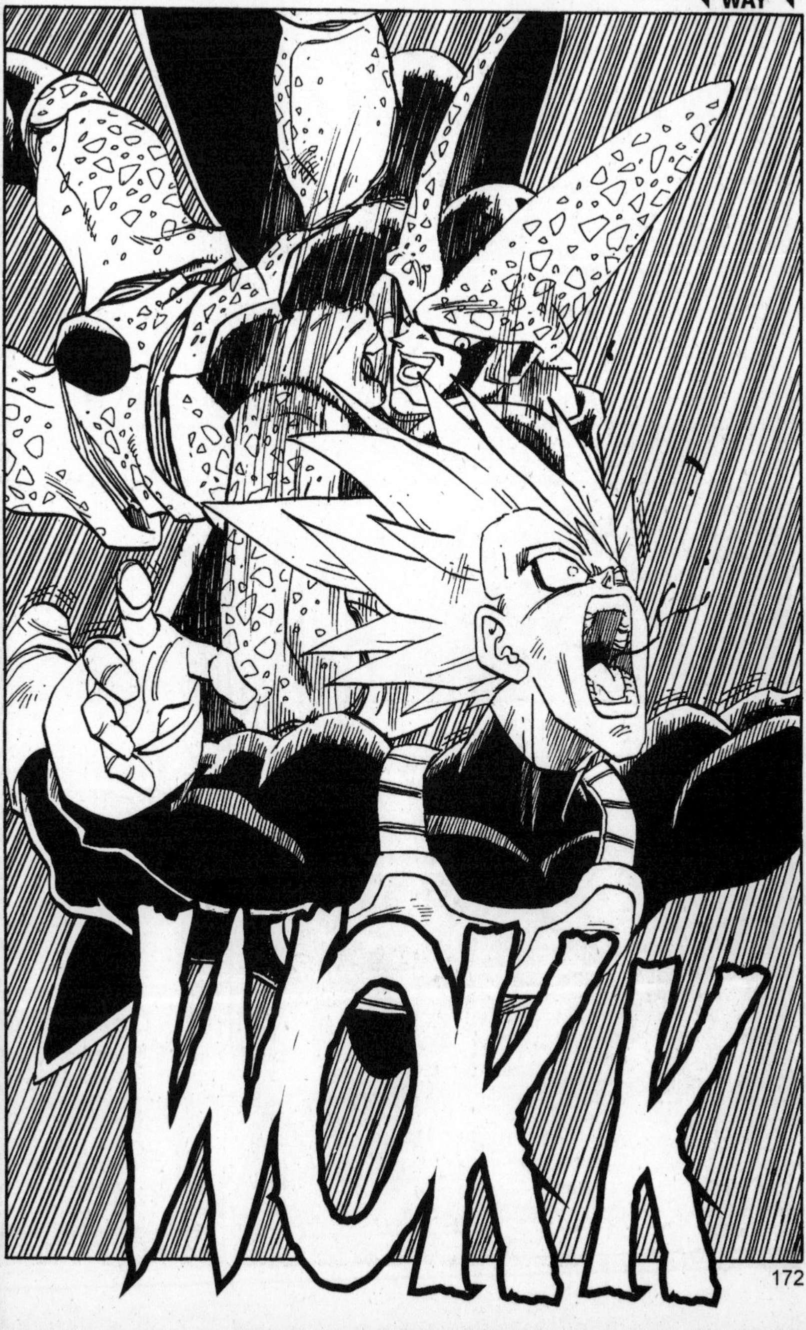
WOKK

READ THIS WAY

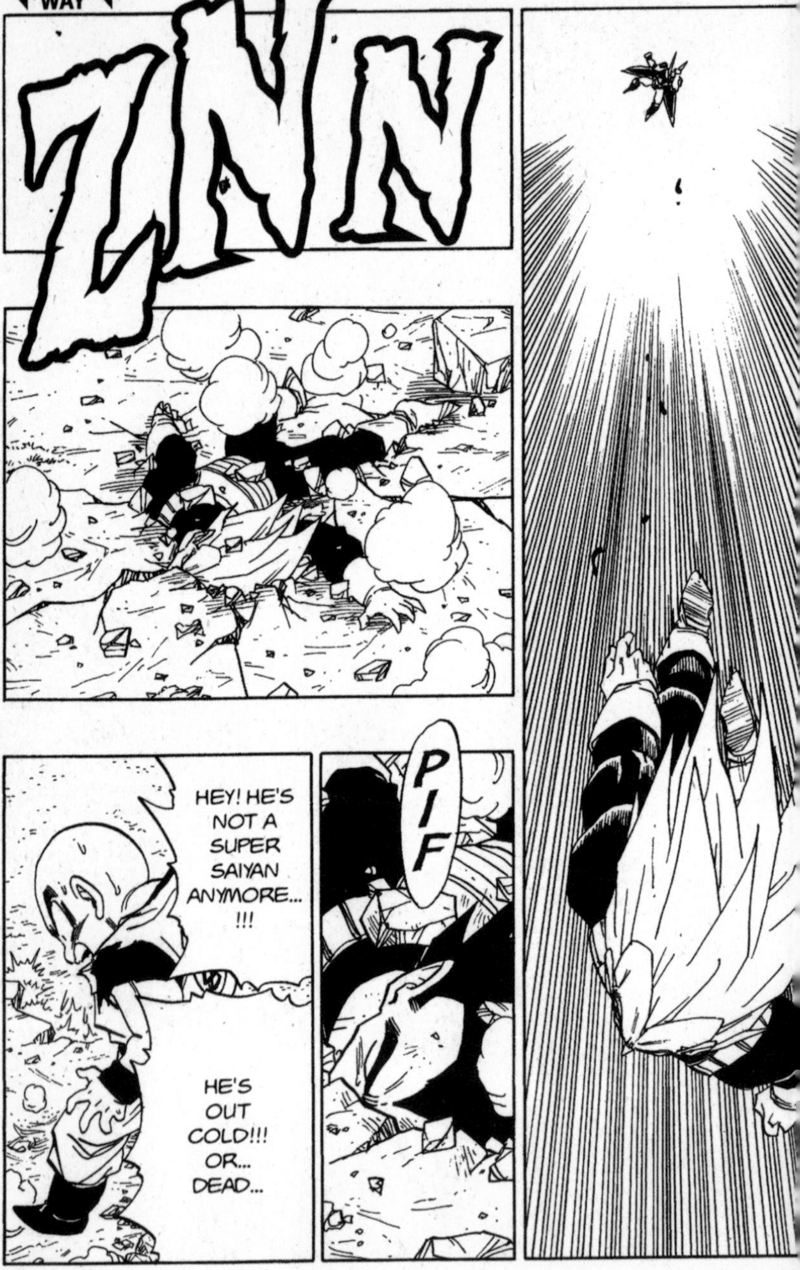
ZNN
PIF
HEY! HE'S NOT A SUPER SAIYAN ANYMORE... !!!
HE'S OUT COLD!!! OR... DEAD...

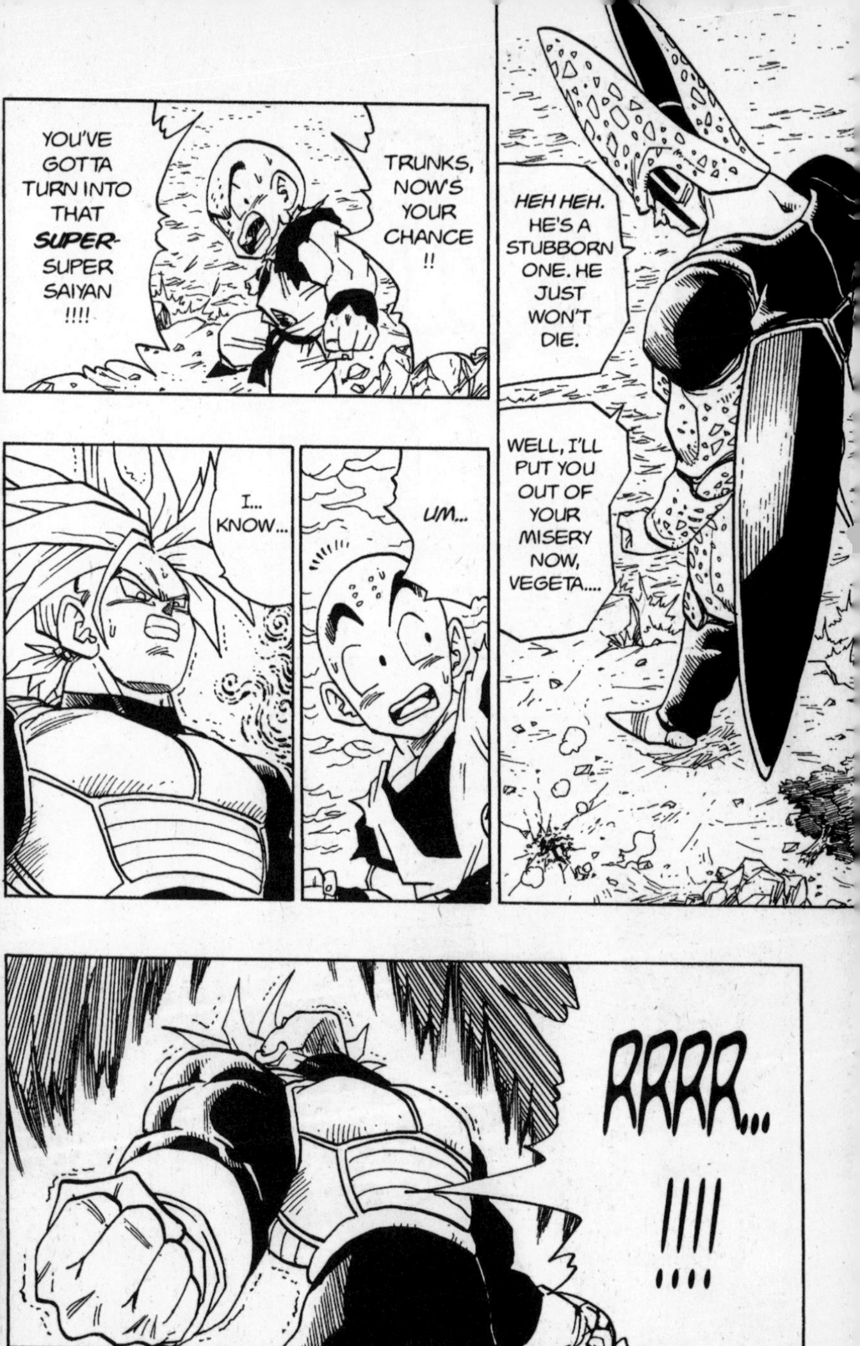
HEH HEH. HE'S A STUBBORN ONE. HE JUST WON'T DIE.
WELL, I'LL PUT YOU OUT OF YOUR MISERY NOW, VEGETA....
TRUNKS, NOW'S YOUR CHANCE !!
YOU'VE GOTTA TURN INTO THAT SUPER-SUPER SAIYAN !!!!
UM...
I... KNOW...
RRRR... !!!!! .....

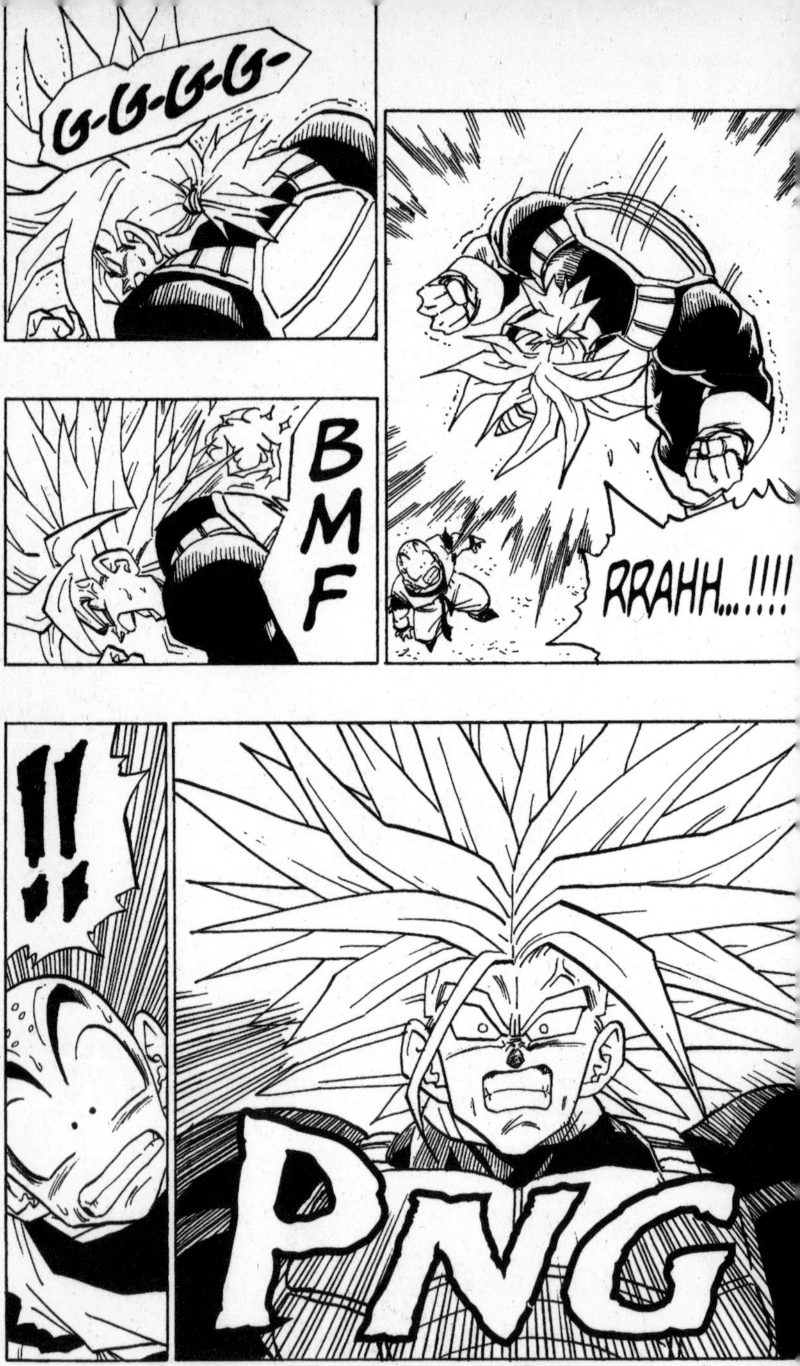
RRAHH...!!!!
G-G-G-G-
BMF
PNG
!!

NEXT: The Super Super Saiyan

TITLE PAGE GALLERY

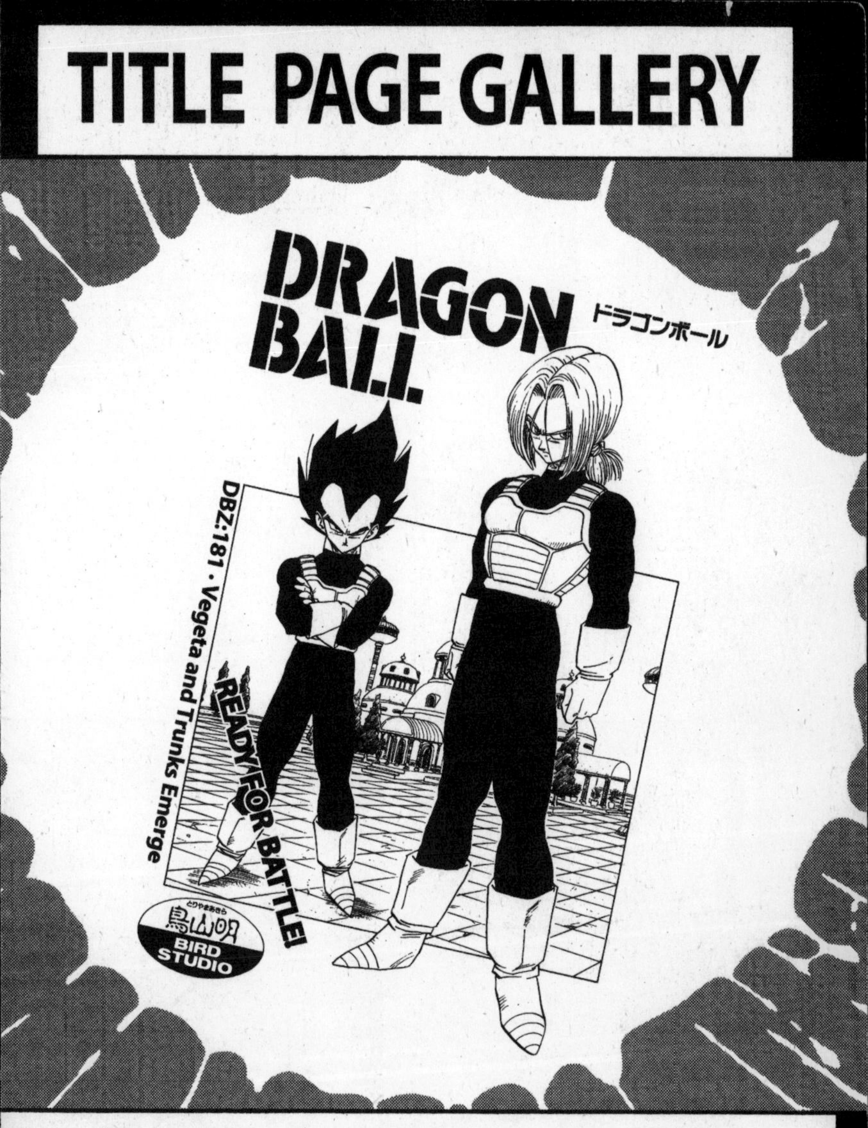
DRAGON BALL
ドラゴンボール
DBZ:181 · Vegeta and Trunks Emerge
READY FOR BATTLE!
鳥山明
BIRD STUDIO

These title pages were used when these chapters of **Dragon Ball Z** were originally published in Japan in 1992 in **Weekly Shonen Jump** magazine.

DRAGON BALL

ドラゴンボール

とりやまあきら
鳥山明
BIRD STUDIO

DBZ:182 • Vegeta's Confidence

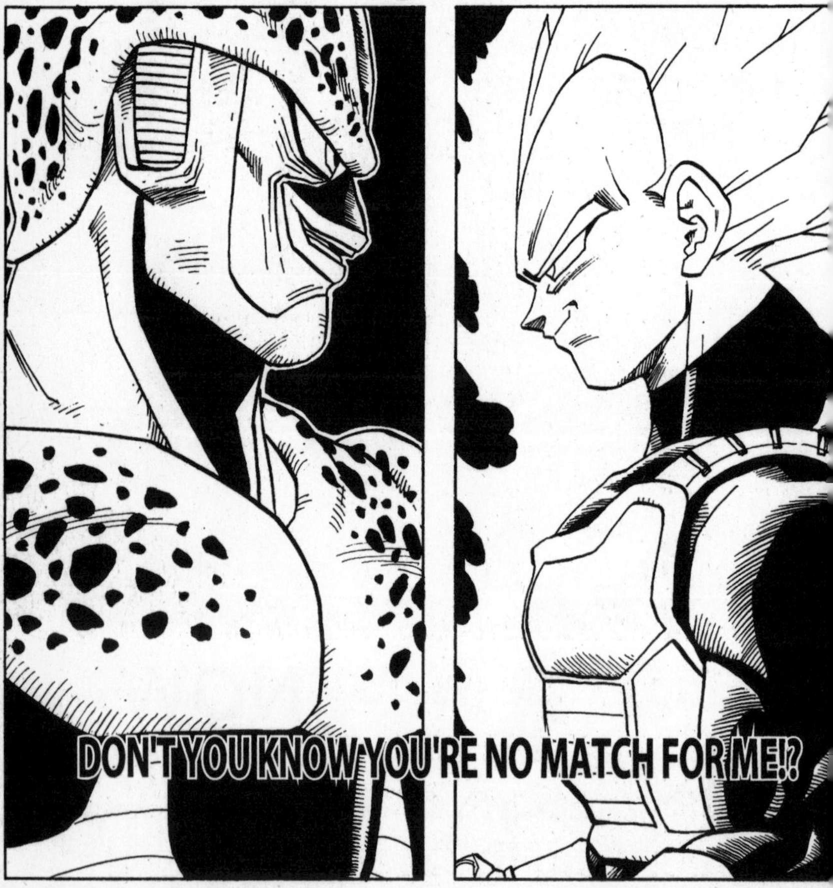
DON'T YOU KNOW YOU'RE NO MATCH FOR ME!?

DRAGON BALL

ドラゴンボール

DBZ:183
Beyond the Super Saiyan

とりやまあきら
鳥山明
BIRD STUDIO

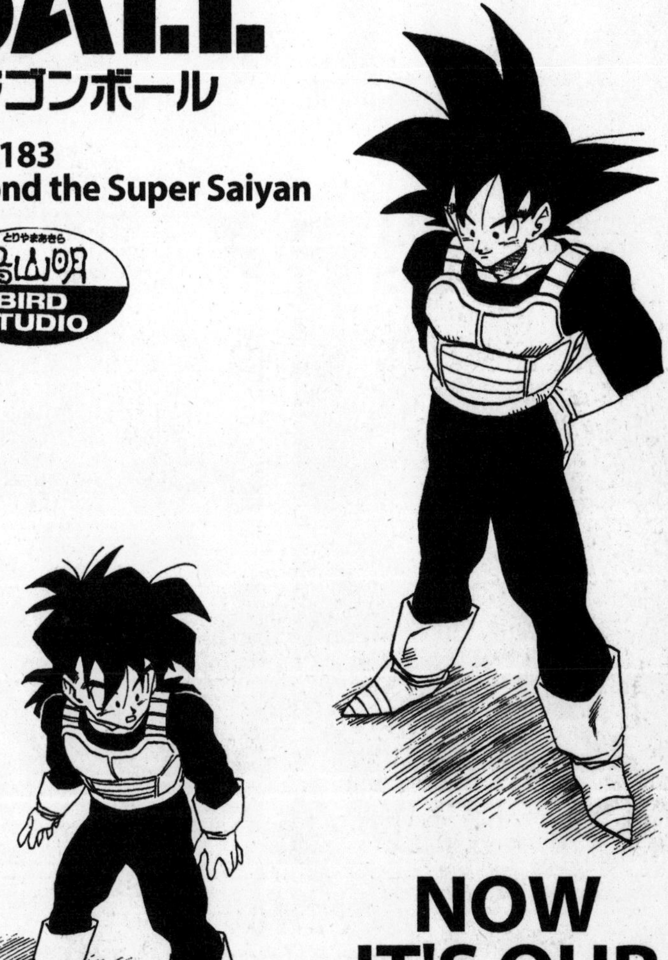

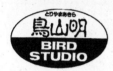

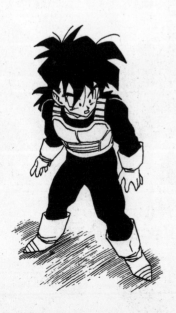

NOW IT'S OUR TURN TO TRAIN.

DRAGON BALL

ドラゴンボール

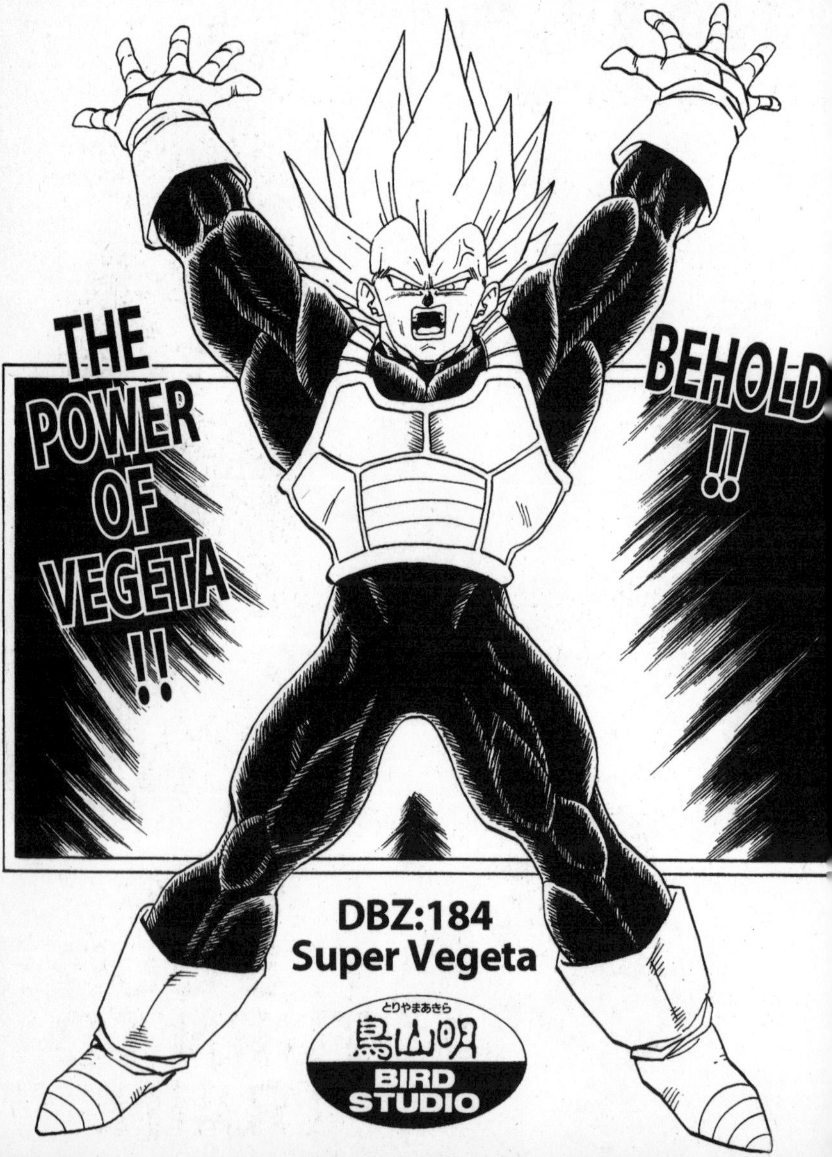
BEHOLD!!
THE POWER OF VEGETA!!
とりやまあきら
鳥山明
BIRD STUDIO

DBZ:184
Super Vegeta

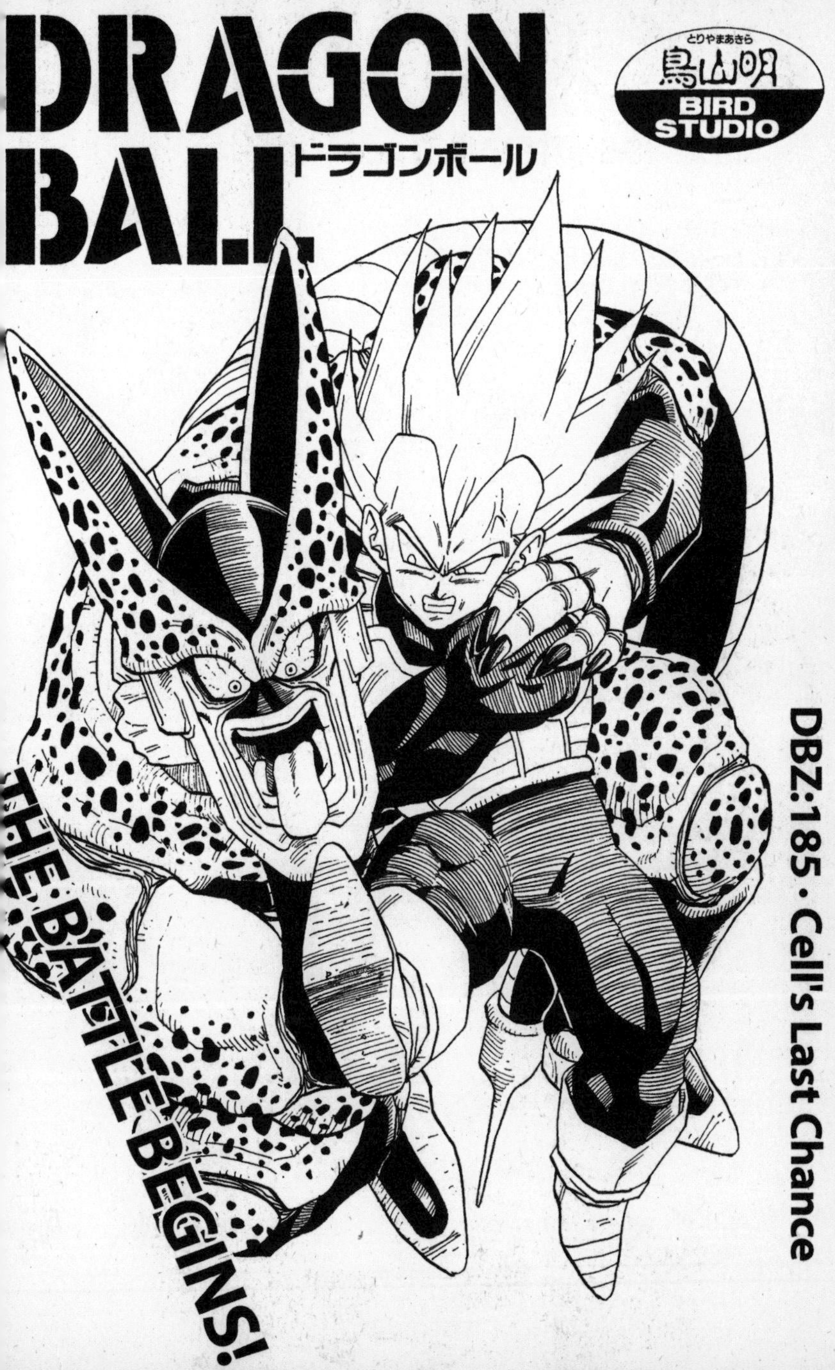

DRAGON BALL
ドラゴンボール
とりやまあきら
鳥山明
BIRD STUDIO
DBZ:185 • Cell's Last Chance
THE BATTLE BEGINS!

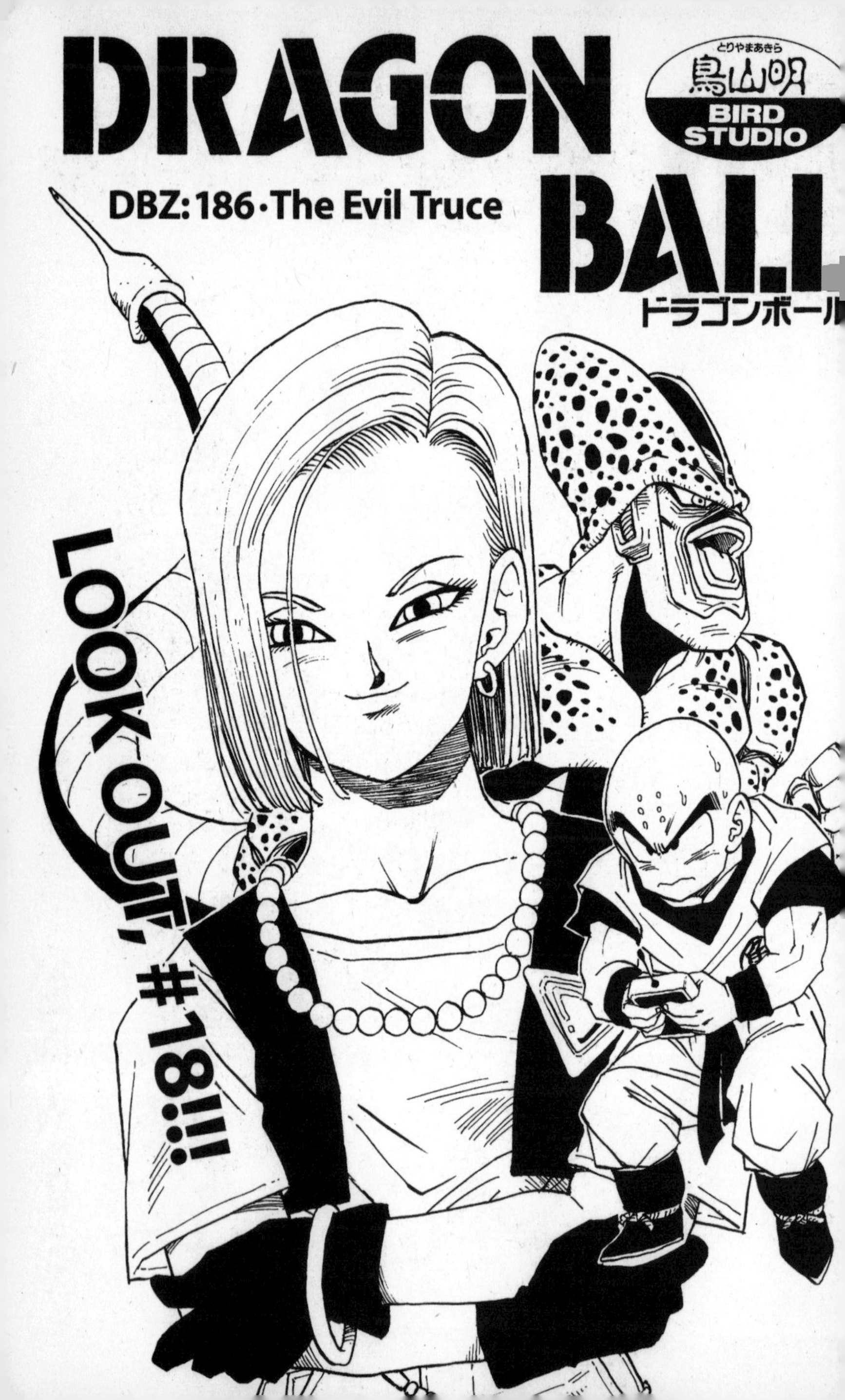

DRAGON BALL
ドラゴンボール
とりやまあきら
鳥山明
BIRD STUDIO
DBZ: 186 • The Evil Truce
LOOK OUT, #18!!!!

DRAGON BALL ドラゴンボール

DBZ: 187 · Vegeta vs. Trunks?

とりやまあきら
鳥山明
BIRD STUDIO

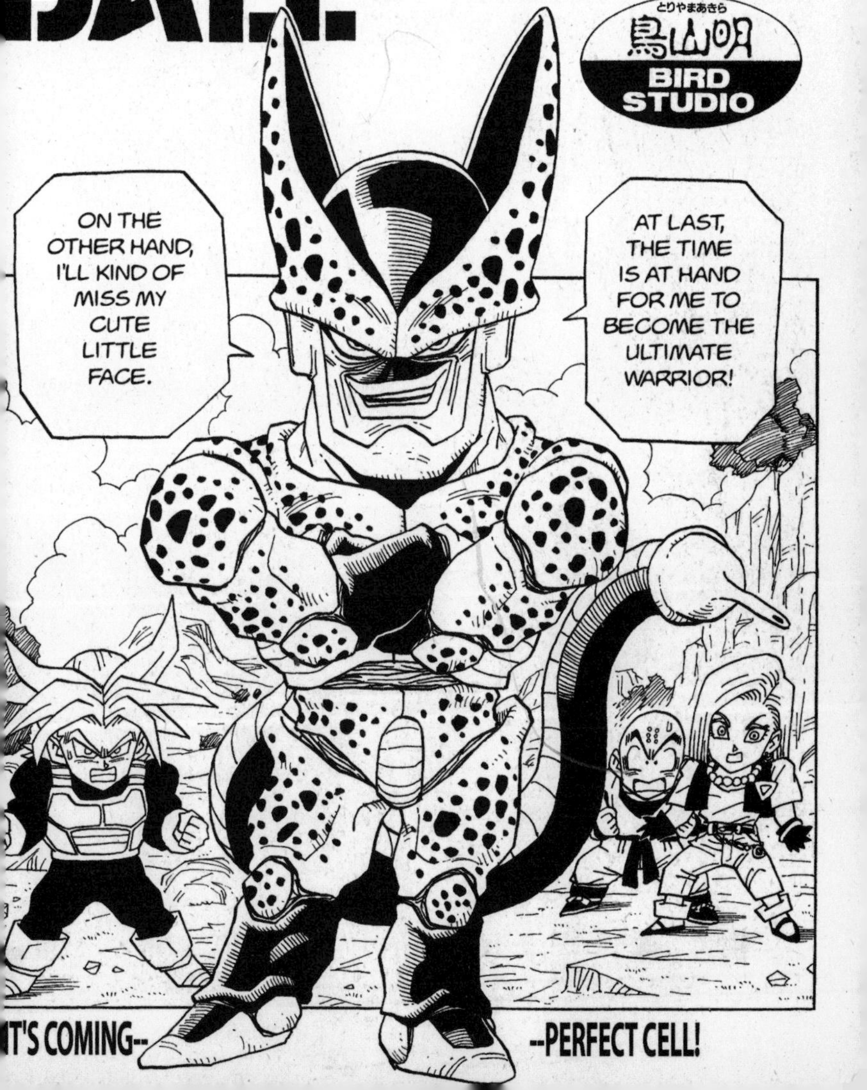
AT LAST, THE TIME IS AT HAND FOR ME TO BECOME THE ULTIMATE WARRIOR!
ON THE OTHER HAND, I'LL KIND OF MISS MY CUTE LITTLE FACE.
IT'S COMING--
--PERFECT CELL!

DRAGON BALL

ドラゴンボール

DBZ:188
The Complete Cell

とりやまあきら
鳥山明
BIRD STUDIO

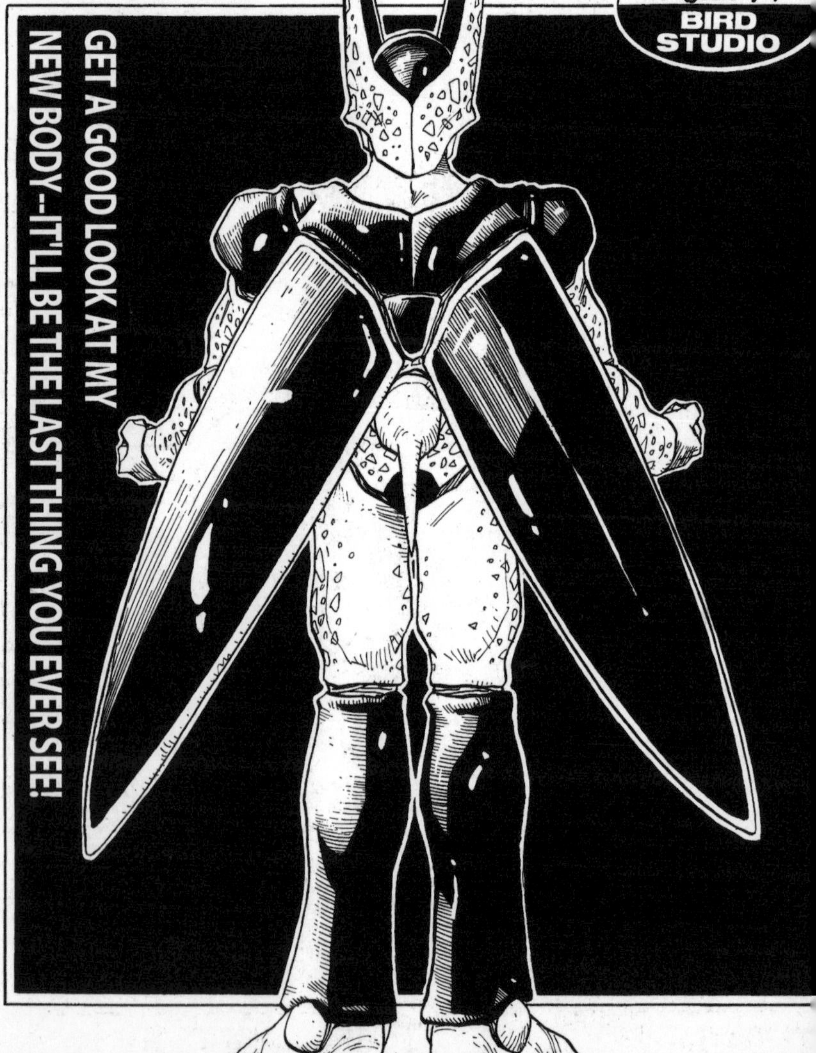
GET A GOOD LOOK AT MY
NEW BODY--IT'LL BE THE LAST THING YOU EVER SEE!

DRAGON BALL

とりやまあきら
鳥山明
BIRD STUDIO

ドラゴンボール

DBZ:189
Reversal

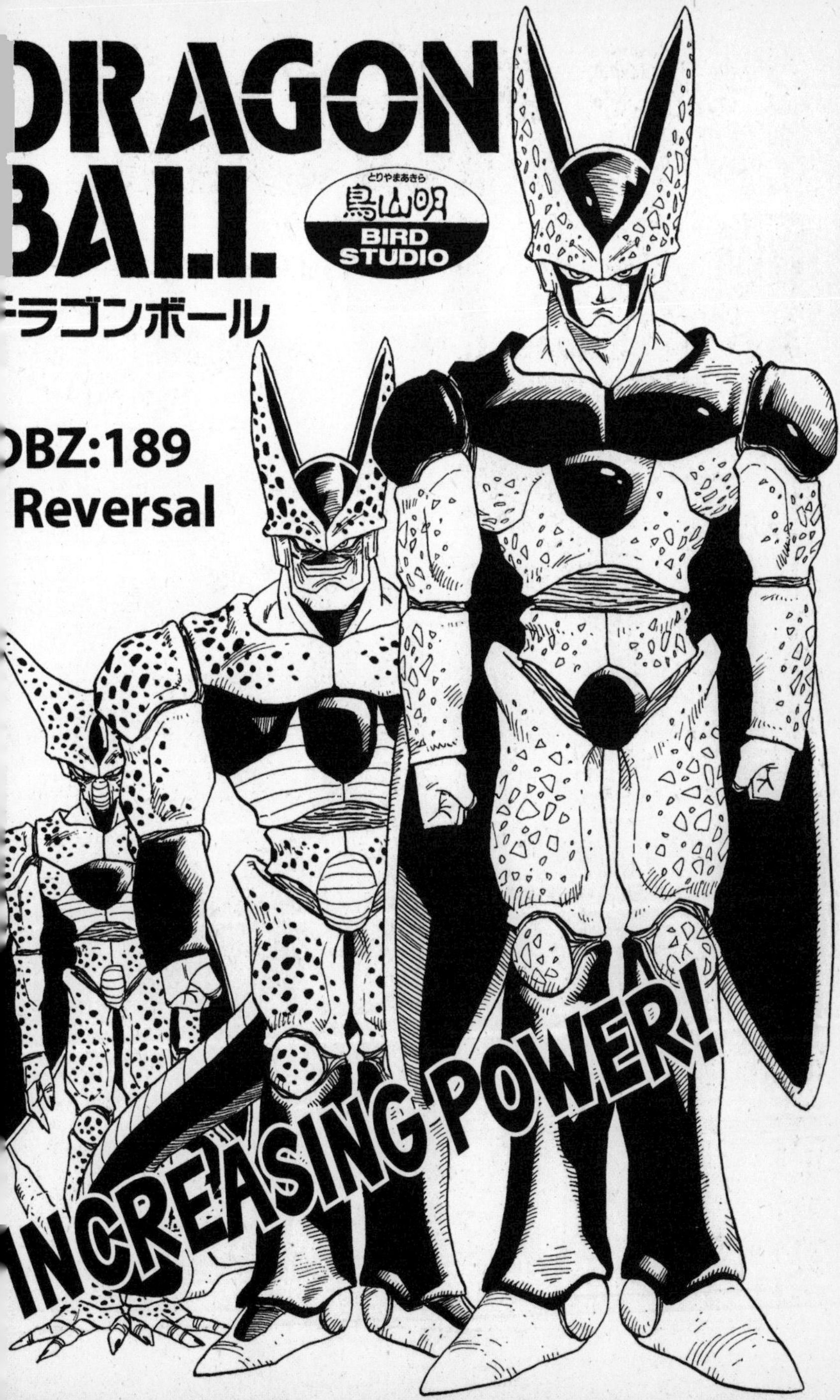
INCREASING POWER!

DRAGON BALL

ドラゴンボール

DBZ:190
The Final Flash

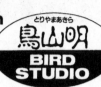

とりやまあきら
鳥山明
BIRD STUDIO

WHEN YOU TRAIN, YOU'VE GOTTA START WITH THE BASICS!

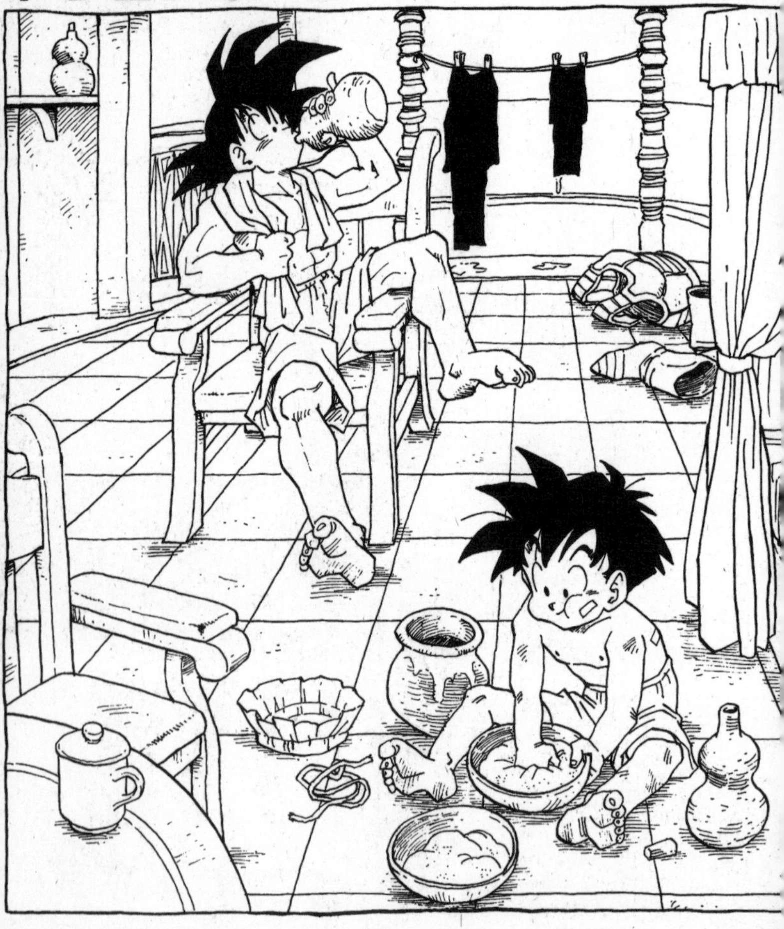

DRAGON BALL

とりやまあきら
鳥山明
BIRD STUDIO

DBZ:191 • Trunks Steps In

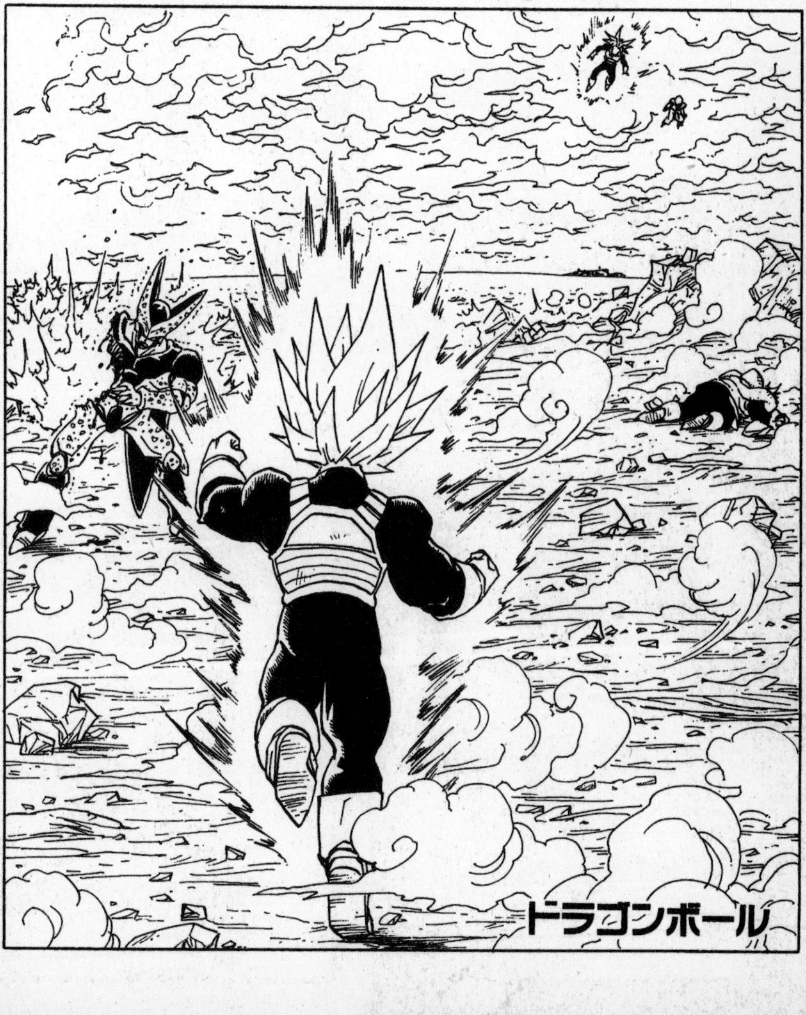
ドラゴンボール

IN THE NEXT VOLUME...

Now in his complete form, Cell is supposed to be stronger than any other being in the universe! Can Trunks' muscled-out new form defeat the deadly bioweapon? Or will the world have to wait for the results of Goku and Gohan's training? Finding no competition on Earth, Cell invades a TV studio and gives the world an ultimatum: produce a fighter who can beat him in one-on-one combat, or he will methodically slaughter every living thing!

AVAILABLE NOW!

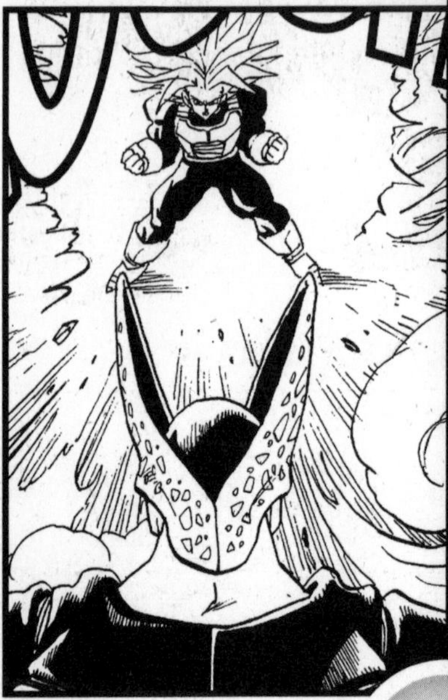

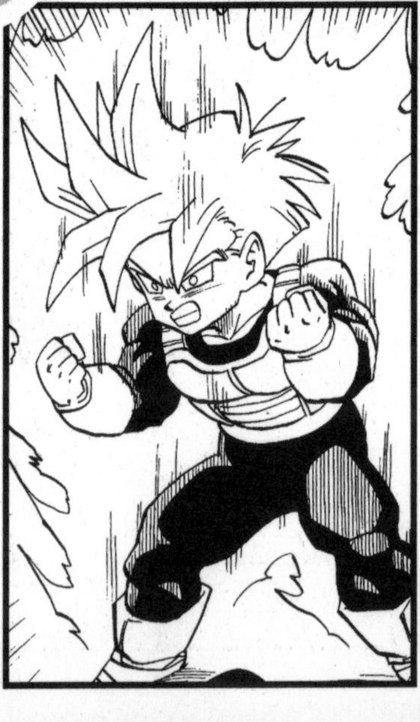

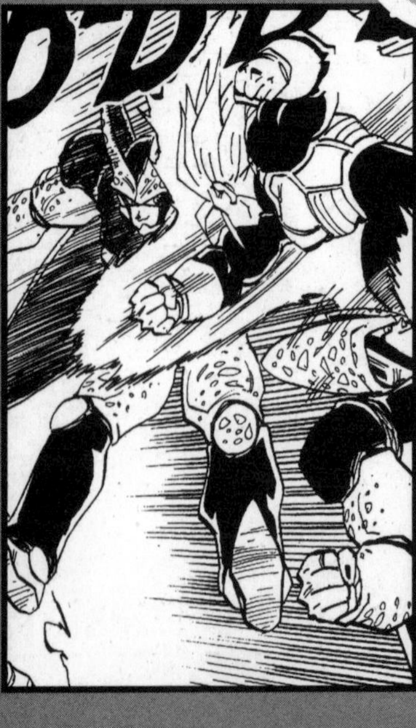

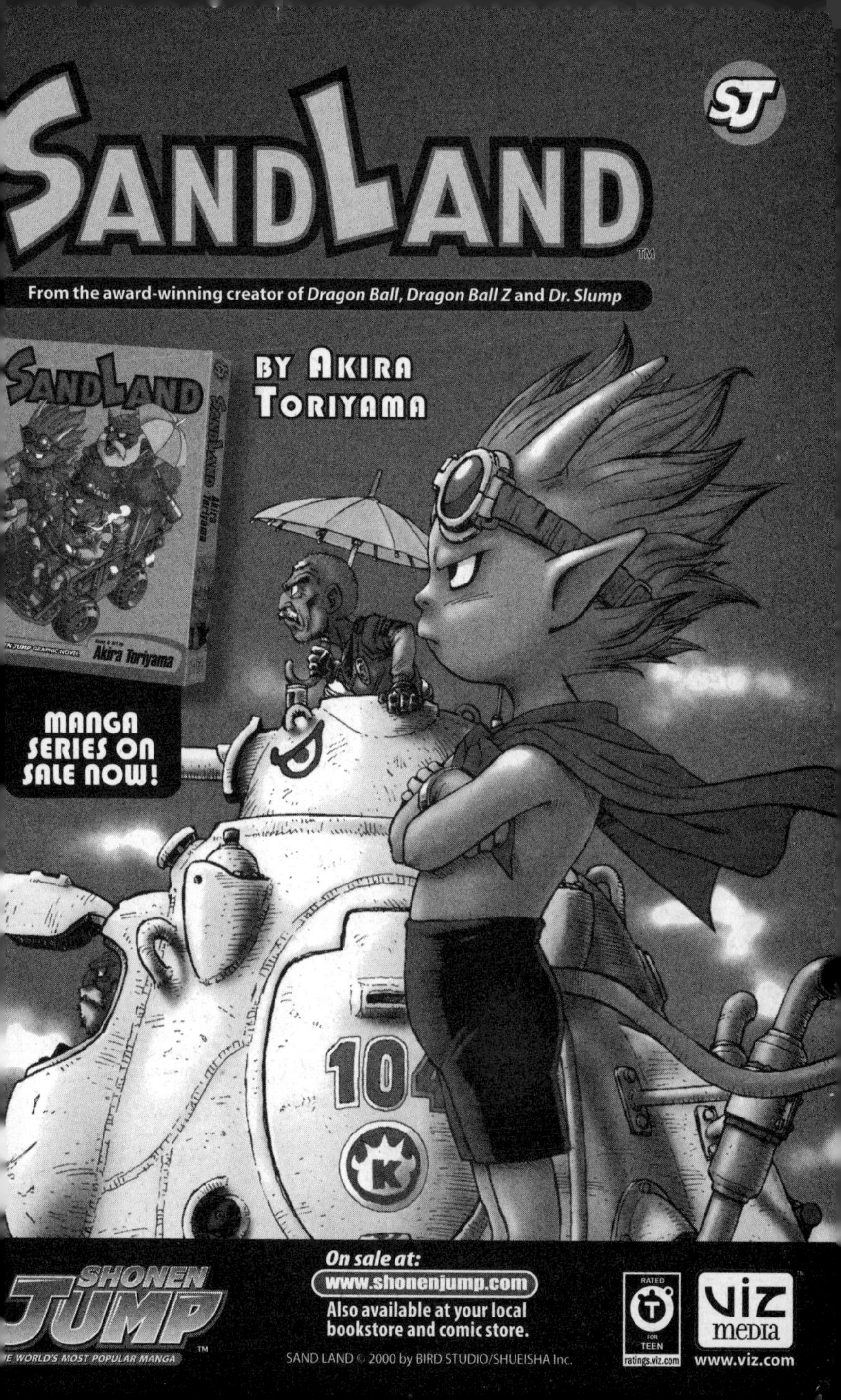
SJ
SANDLAND™
From the award-winning creator of Dragon Ball, Dragon Ball Z and Dr. Slump
BY AKIRA TORIYAMA
SANDLAND
Akira Toriyama
MANGA SERIES ON SALE NOW!
104
K
SHONEN JUMP™
THE WORLD'S MOST POPULAR MANGA
On sale at:
www.shonenjump.com
Also available at your local bookstore and comic store.
SAND LAND © 2000 by BIRD STUDIO/SHUEISHA Inc.
RATED T FOR TEEN
ratings.viz.com
viz media
www.viz.com

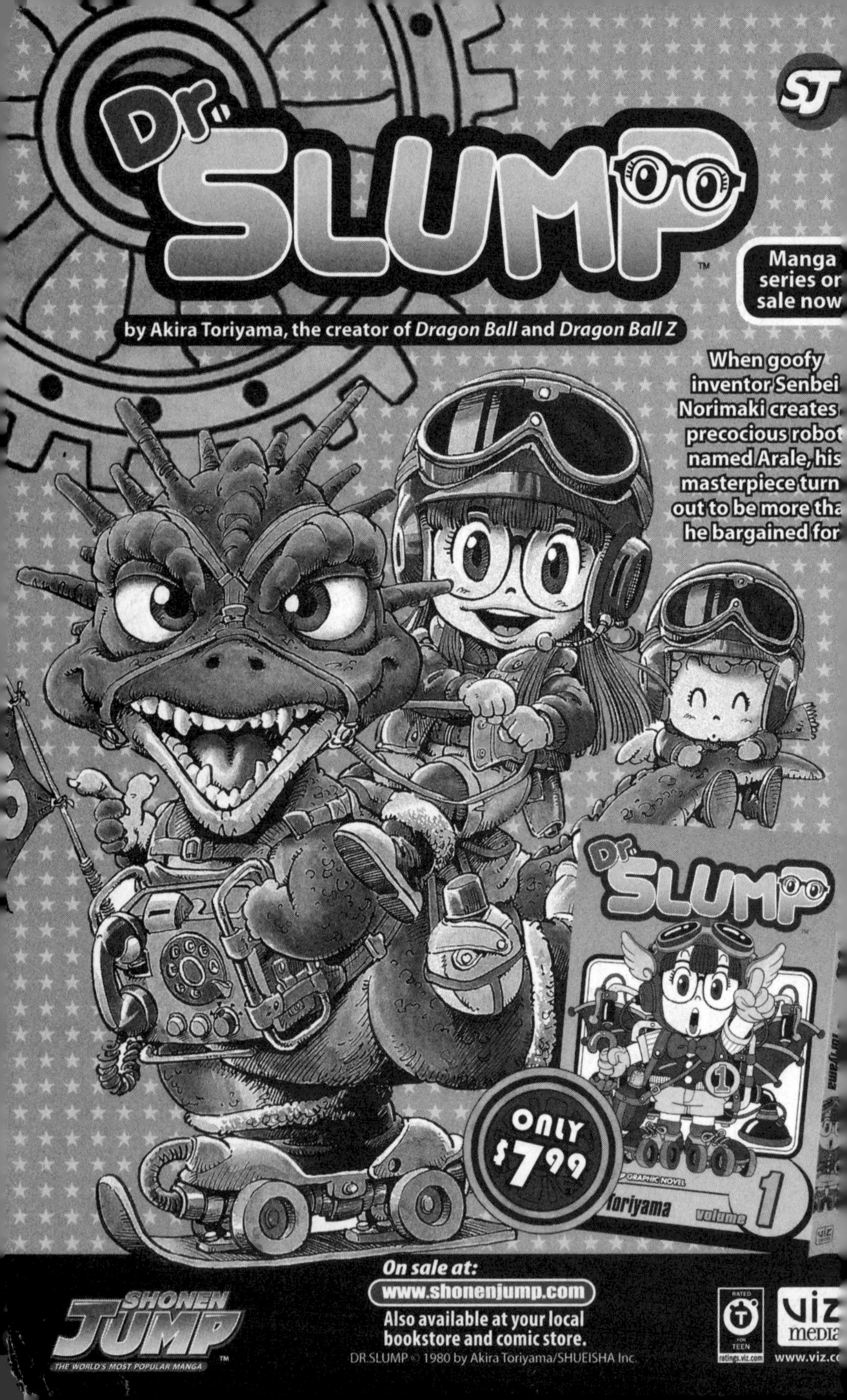
SJ
Dr. SLUMP™
Manga
series o
sale now
by Akira Toriyama, the creator of *Dragon Ball* and *Dragon Ball Z*
When goofy
inventor Senbei
Norimaki creates
precocious robot
named Arale, his
masterpiece turn
out to be more tha
he bargained for
Dr. SLUMP™
GRAPHIC NOVEL
toriyama
volume 1
ONLY $7.99
On sale at:
www.shonenjump.com
Also available at your local
bookstore and comic store.
DR.SLUMP © 1980 by Akira Toriyama/SHUEISHA Inc.
SHONEN JUMP™
THE WORLD'S MOST POPULAR MANGA
RATED T FOR TEEN
ratings.viz.com
viz media
www.viz.c

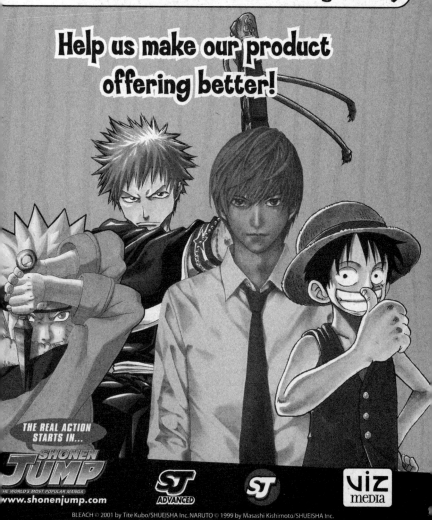

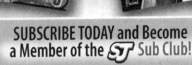

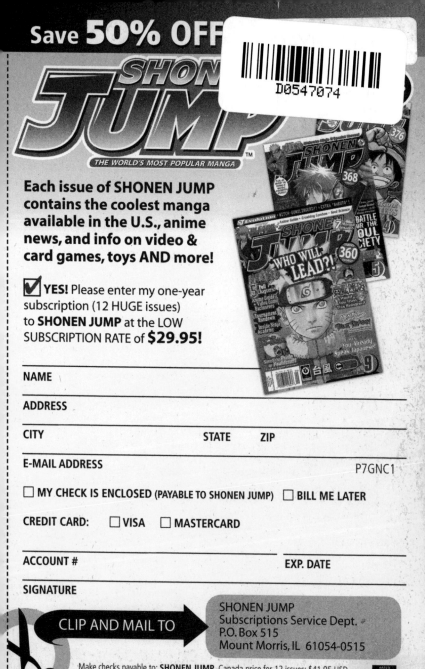

Save **50% OFF**

D0547074

SHONEN JUMP
THE WORLD'S MOST POPULAR MANGA

Each issue of SHONEN JUMP contains the coolest manga available in the U.S., anime news, and info on video & card games, toys AND more!

☑ **YES!** Please enter my one-year subscription (12 HUGE issues) to **SHONEN JUMP** at the LOW SUBSCRIPTION RATE of **$29.95!**

NAME

ADDRESS

CITY _____ STATE _____ ZIP

E-MAIL ADDRESS _____ P7GNC1

☐ **MY CHECK IS ENCLOSED** (PAYABLE TO SHONEN JUMP)   ☐ **BILL ME LATER**

CREDIT CARD: ☐ **VISA**   ☐ **MASTERCARD**

ACCOUNT #

EXP. DATE

SIGNATURE

CLIP AND MAIL TO ➤

SHONEN JUMP
Subscriptions Service Dept.
P.O. Box 515
Mount Morris, IL 61054-0515

Make checks payable to: **SHONEN JUMP**. Canada price for 12 issues: $41.95 USD, including GST, HST and QST. US/CAN orders only. Allow 6-8 weeks for delivery.

RATED **T** TEEN
ratings.viz.com